# Readings in
# Christian
# Theology

# Readings in Christian Theology

## Volume 2

# Man's Need and God's Gift

## Millard J. Erickson, Editor

**BAKER BOOK HOUSE**
Grand Rapids, Michigan 49506

TO MY DAUGHTER
SANDY

# Preface

Three years ago I edited an anthology entitled *The Living God.* It was a tool for the teaching of systematic theology, possibly to be followed by one or two additional volumes. The reception accorded *The Living God* has encouraged me to bring forth this sequel, treating the doctrines of man, sin, and the person and work of Jesus Christ.

I wish to express appreciation to all who helped make this work possible. My students in systematic theology classes at Bethel Theological Seminary during the winter quarters of 1971 and 1973 evaluated materials from which these selections were drawn. Colleagues in systematic theology in other institutions encouraged me to continue the work already begun. My former teaching assistant, Mr. L. Arnold Hustad, helped to compile early drafts, and my current assistant, Mrs. Mary Forsberg, gave editorial assistance on the final draft and proofread galley proofs. Typing was done by Mrs. Cheri Zaderaka and Mrs. Aletta Whittaker. Once again the editorial staff of Baker Book House was most helpful.

I also wish to acknowledge the cooperation of those who have granted permission to reprint copyrighted material: Macmillan Publishing Co., Inc.—*The Modern Use of the Bible* and *The New Theology;* Charles Scribner's Sons—*The Nature and Destiny of Man* and *God Was in Christ;* Zondervan Publishing House—*A Systematic Theology of the Christian Religion;* Fleming H. Revell Company—*Systematic Theology;* The Westminster Press—*Jesus—God and Man* and *The Christian Doctrine of Creation and Redemption;* Harper and Row Publishers, Inc.—*A Theology of the Living Church* and *Christ and the Christian;* Nazarene Publishing House—*Christian Theology;* William B. Eerdmans Publishing Co.—*Systematic Theology, The Lord from Heaven, Man in Community,* and *Somewhat Less than God; Christianity Today*—"Man's Difficulty—Ignorance or Evil?" "Have We Outmoded Chalcedon?" "The Deity of Christ," "Our Lord's Virgin Birth," and "The Virgin Birth of Christ"; T. and T. Clark Limited, Publishers—*The Christian Doctrine of Man;* and the Rev. Canon D. R. G. Owen—*Body and Soul.*

MILLARD J. ERICKSON

*Arden Hills, Minnesota*
*December, 1975*

# The Authors

**Anselm** was archbishop of Canterbury in the late eleventh and early twelfth centuries.

**Thomas Aquinas**'s writings cast the shape of Roman Catholic theology for many centuries. His teaching career was spent at the University of Paris. He worked on the *Summa Theologica* from 1265 until his death in 1274.

**Donald Baillie** was professor of systematic theology at St. Andrews University, Scotland. *God Was in Christ* first appeared in 1948.

**Louis Berkhof** was professor of dogmatic theology and president of Calvin Theological Seminary. He authored *Systematic Theology* in 1938.

**F. F. Bruce** is head of the department of New Testament language and literature in the University of Manchester.

**Emil Brunner,** together with Karl Barth one of the founders of neo-orthodoxy, spent most of his academic career at the University of Zurich. *The Christian Doctrine of Creation and Redemption* appeared in English in 1952.

**Horace Bushnell** was pastor of the North Church, Hartford, Connecticut, from 1833 to 1859, when forced to resign because of ill health. He continued writing theology until his death in 1876.

**J. Oliver Buswell, Jr.,** served as president of Wheaton (Illinois) and Shelton colleges, and dean of Covenant Seminary. *A Systematic Theology of the Christian Religion* appeared in 1962.

**Reginald J. Campbell** was minister of the City Temple, London, when he wrote *The New Theology* in 1907.

**Edward J. Carnell** served as professor of apologetics at Fuller Theological Seminary, and when he wrote "The Virgin Birth of Christ" in 1959 was its president.

**L. Harold De Wolf**, after many years at Boston University School of Theology, became professor of systematic theology and dean of Wesley Theological Seminary, Washington, D. C. He published *A Theology of the Living Church* in 1953.

**Jonathan Edwards** was a Congregational pastor in Northampton, Massachusetts, in the first half of the eighteenth century, during which time the "Great Awakening" began in his parish. He died in 1758, just five weeks after his inauguration as president of the College of New Jersey (now Princeton University).

**Nels F. S. Ferre** spent the major portion of his teaching career at Andover Newton Theological School. *Christ and the Christian* was published in 1958.

**Charles G. Finney** was an eighteenth-century Congregationalist evangelist and theologian, and served as president of Oberlin College. His *Lectures on Systematic Theology* was first published in 1846.

**Harry Emerson Fosdick** was for many years professor of practical theology at Union Theological Seminary, New York, and minister of Riverside Church of New York. *The Modern Use of the Bible* was published in 1924.

**Hugo Grotius** was a Dutch statesman, lawyer, and theologian, active in the first half of the seventeenth century.

**Carl F. H. Henry**, after several years as editor-in-chief of *Christianity Today,* is visiting professor of theology at Trinity Evangelical Divinity School. His editorial in the December 7, 1959, issue of *Christianity Today* is reprinted here.

**Charles Hodge** was professor of didactic theology and New Testament exegesis at Princeton Theological Seminary from 1822 until his death in 1878. The selection reprinted here is from his magnum opus, *Systematic Theology* (1871-1873).

**Calvin Linton** is dean and professor of English literature at Columbian College, George Washington University. His article appeared in *Christianity Today* in 1965.

**Hugh R. Mackintosh** taught systematic theology at the University of Edinburgh, publishing *The Doctrine of the Person of Jesus Christ* in 1912.

**William J. Martin** is head of the department of Old Testament languages in the University of Liverpool.

**Leon Morris** is vice-principal, Ridley College, Melbourne, Australia. *The Lord from Heaven* was published in 1958.

**J. Theodore Mueller** served for many years as professor of systematic theology and exegesis at Concordia Seminary, St. Louis. "Have We Outmoded Chalcedon?" dates from 1959.

**Reinhold Niebuhr**, for many years professor of applied Christianity at Union Theological Seminary, New York, produced his magnum opus, *The Nature and Destiny of Man,* from his Gifford Lectures of 1939-40. Volume 1 was published in 1941.

**James Orr** served as professor of apologetics and theology in Glasgow College of the United Free Church of Scotland. *Sin as a Problem of Today* was first published in 1910.

**D. R. G. Owen** is professor of religious studies at Trinity College, University of Toronto. *Body and Soul* first appeared in 1956.

**Wolfhart Pannenberg** is professor of systematic theology in the University of Munich, Germany. *Jesus–God and Man* dates from 1968.

The **Racovian Catechism** was drawn up by a group of Socinians in Rakow, Poland, in 1605.

**H. Wheeler Robinson** was professor of philosophy of religion in Rawdon College, Leeds, and principal of Regent's Park College, London and Oxford, as well as lecturer in Biblical studies in the University of Oxford. *The Christian Doctrine of Man* (1911) was his first book.

**Russell Shedd** has served in several posts, including one at the Baptist Seminary in Leiria, Portugal. *Man in Community* was published in 1964.

**Augustus H. Strong** was for many years president and professor of Biblical theology in Rochester (New York) Theological Seminary. He first published his *Systematic Theology* in 1907.

**F. R. Tennant**, for many years lecturer in theology and fellow of Trinity College, Cambridge University, published *The Origin and Propagation of Sin* in 1902.

**Leonard Verduin**, for many years pastor of the Campus Chapel of the Christian Reformed Church at the University of Michigan, wrote *Somewhat Less Than God* in 1970.

**Gustave F. Wiggers** was professor of theology in the University of Rostock, Germany. The selection here included first appeared in German in 1821 and deals with the thought of Pelagius, who lived and wrote in the later fourth and early fifth centuries.

**H. Orton Wiley** was president of Pasadena College and editor of the *Herald of Holiness.* He wrote *Christian Theology* in 1940.

# Contents

## PART ONE: MAN

Editor's Introduction . . . . . . . . . . . . . . . . . . . . . . . . . . . . . . . . . . .13

### Man's Origin

1  J. Oliver Buswell, Jr., *The Origin of Man* . . . . . . . . . . . . . . . . . . .17
2  Augustus H. Strong, *Man a Creation and Child of God* . . . . . . . . .21

### Man as God's Image

3  Thomas Aquinas, *Made to the Image of God* . . . . . . . . . . . . . . . .37
4  Emil Brunner, *Man and Creation* . . . . . . . . . . . . . . . . . . . . . . . . .45
5  Leonard Verduin, *A Dominion-Haver* . . . . . . . . . . . . . . . . . . . . .55

### Man's Make-up

6  Charles Hodge, *Nature of Man* . . . . . . . . . . . . . . . . . . . . . . . . . . .75
7  D. R. G. Owen, *"Body" and "Soul" in the New Testament* . . . . . . .85

## PART TWO: SIN

Editor's Introduction . . . . . . . . . . . . . . . . . . . . . . . . . . . . . . . . . . .99

### The Nature of Sin

8  H. Wheeler Robinson, *Old Testament Terminology for Sin* . . . . . .103

### The Source of Sin

9  F. R. Tennant, *Evolutionary Theory of the Empirical Origin
   of Sin* . . . . . . . . . . . . . . . . . . . . . . . . . . . . . . . . . . . . . . . . . . . . .107
10  Calvin Linton, *Man's Difficulty—Ignorance or Evil?* . . . . . . . . . . .125

### The Result of Sin: Corruption

11  Jonathan Edwards, *Some Evidences of Original Sin from
    Facts and Events* . . . . . . . . . . . . . . . . . . . . . . . . . . . . . . . . . . . .131
12  Gustave F. Wiggers, *The Pelagian View of Original Sin* . . . . . . . . .153
13  Reinhold Niebuhr, *Sin and Man's Responsibility* . . . . . . . . . . . . . .159

### The Result of Sin: Guilt

14  James Orr, *Sin as Guilt—The Divine Judgment* . . . . . . . . . . . . . . .169
15  Charles G. Finney, *Accounting for Moral Depravity* . . . . . . . . . . .183

### The Transmission of Sin

16  Louis Berkhof, *The Transmission of Sin* . . . . . . . . . . . . . . . . . . . .195
17  Russell Shedd, *Paul's Conception of Human Solidarity* . . . . . . . . .203

## PART THREE: THE PERSON OF CHRIST

Editor's Introduction . . . . . . . . . . . . . . . . . . . . . . . . . . . . . . . . . . . .235

### The Incarnation

18  J. Theodore Mueller, *Have We Outmoded Chalcedon?* . . . . . . . . . .239
19  Leon Morris, *Jesus the Man* . . . . . . . . . . . . . . . . . . . . . . . . . . . . .243
20  F. F. Bruce and William J. Martin, *The Deity of Christ* . . . . . . . .251
21  Harry Emerson Fosdick, *Jesus, the Messiah* . . . . . . . . . . . . . . . . .265
22  Donald Baillie, *The Paradox of the Incarnation* . . . . . . . . . . . . . . .275
23  Wolfhart Pannenberg, *The Significance of Jesus' Resurrection* . . . .291

### The Sinlessness of Christ

24  Louis Berkhof, *Scripture Proof for the Sinless Humanity
      of Christ* . . . . . . . . . . . . . . . . . . . . . . . . . . . . . . . . . . . . . . . . . . .301
25  Nels F. S. Ferre, *Very God, Very Man* . . . . . . . . . . . . . . . . . . . . .303
26  Hugh R. Mackintosh, *The Sinlessness of Jesus* . . . . . . . . . . . . . . .307

### The Virgin Birth

27  Carl F. H. Henry, *Our Lord's Virgin Birth* . . . . . . . . . . . . . . . . . .311
28  Edward J. Carnell, *The Virgin Birth of Christ* . . . . . . . . . . . . . . . .315
29  L. Harold De Wolf, *The Doctrine of the Virgin Birth* . . . . . . . . . . .319
30  Reginald J. Campbell, *The Incarnation of the Son of God* . . . . . . .323

## PART FOUR: THE WORK OF CHRIST

Editor's Introduction . . . . . . . . . . . . . . . . . . . . . . . . . . . . . . . . . . . .333

### The Three Offices of Christ

31  H. Orton Wiley, *The Offices and Titles of Christ* . . . . . . . . . . . . . .337

### The Atonement

32  Horace Bushnell, *The Protestant Views of the Atonement* . . . . . . .343
33  Hugo Grotius, *The Catholic View of the Satisfaction
      of Christ* . . . . . . . . . . . . . . . . . . . . . . . . . . . . . . . . . . . . . . . . . . . .351
34  *The Racovian Catechism: The Person and Death of Christ* . . . . . .359
35  Anselm, *Cur Deus Homo* . . . . . . . . . . . . . . . . . . . . . . . . . . . . . . . .367

# Man

## Editor's Introduction

The several areas of theology have differing degrees of pertinence, and the significance comes in varying forms. Some of the doctrines seem to the non-Christian to be far removed from his concerns. He may have little interest in some far-off god or what such a god may will. Similarly, the existence of a divinely revealed book is of no significance to him. A story of God coming from another world to become a man; of His dying, being raised from the dead, and ascending to heaven; and of His coming again at some future time may strike him as bizarre, to say the least.

The doctrine of man is different, however. Rather than speaking of what is unknown or dubious, the object of this doctrine is rather familiar: man himself. In our age, interest centers less upon physical nature, and even less upon the supernatural or the metaphysical, than upon man, his personality and needs, and his interaction with others. A doctrine that at least purports to relate to such subjects seems to have some meaningful reference for even the unbeliever. While the perspective of the discussion is different, the referents are the same as those of his more mundane concern, or at least they overlap.

The question of man's origin is generally the first one considered in theology. Christian faith affirms that a first significant fact about man is that he is not merely the product of blind forces. "Identity crisis" is a very real factor in contemporary man's experience, especially for young people. "Who am I?" is a question not easily ignored or answered. In a technologically oriented society one tends to answer the question in terms of what one does. This has ultimately a rather unsatisfying and unsatisfactory effect. In a day when historical concerns have been largely ignored and the future is unknown, there naturally is confusion over the question.

Christianity, however, affirms that the key to understanding man is that he is a creature of God. He owes his existence to the originating will and action of the eternal God.

This affirmation carries two implications. On the one hand, it implies that man is dependent. He is not self-sufficient. His life derives from and hence is owed to God. He is not the most inclusive or most significant frame of reference for understanding himself. He will find the meaning of his life in discerning the intention of his Creator for him and in attempting to fulfill that intention. It also implies that he and his present life are not merely the product of blind forces. An intelligent, powerful, and benevolent being has produced him.

Theologians vary in their understanding of the degree of directness in this creative act of God. Some argue that the Bible teaches a totally *de novo* creation of man in his entirety, both his physical and psychical make-up. One representative of this position is **J. Oliver Buswell, Jr.** Others, such as **Augustus H. Strong**, maintain that man's physical or material nature has been derived from an animal being, and that God therefore employed a previously existing form of life for this creative act. The issue rests upon exegesis of the Biblical materials (particularly of the opening chapters of Genesis), the understanding of the scientific data, and the relative weight given to each of these.

The concept of man as creature emphasizes the affinity of man to the rest of creation. He does not stand over against plants and animals as distinguished from them. He shares with them the same origin. He is to find his place in the creation in harmony with the rest of nature, not in conflict with it. This has far-reaching ecological implications.

If this concept stresses the oneness of man with the rest of creation, the Biblical text and the Christian tradition also emphasize the uniqueness of man as contrasted with the other creatures. Each of these creatures is said to be made "after his kind." Man, however, is described as created in the "image and likeness" of God. Precisely what this Godlikeness consists of is not delineated in the Bible. Its nature has been the subject of considerable discussion by theologians striving to do justice to the full richness of human nature.

At times men have even seen this likeness to God in man's physical nature, but this is not a widely held view because most theologians consider God a spiritual being. Perhaps the only extant group of any size that holds this view is the Mormons. **Thomas Aquinas** does suggest that the upright stance of man, adapting him to look upward to heaven, may be an indication of his unique status. For the most part, however, theologians have located the image in other aspects of man's nature.

One favorite candidate for the image of God in man is man's reason. This is what seems to distinguish man most clearly from the rest of the creatures. Consequently, it makes it possible to conceive of, and so believe in, God. Partly because of the influence of neo-Platonic philosophy, this view developed extensively in Christian theology. Athanasius, Clement, Augustine, Aquinas, and others expounded this view. The selection from Thomas is representative of this position.

**Emil Brunner** sees the image not in this capacity of reason, but rather in man's ability to relate to God. The image of God, as found in all creation, is the reflection by any creature of the likeness to God. In the case of man, this reflecting is not merely passive. It is an active, spontaneous freedom to respond. He is responsible, able to respond. This free self, capable of self-determination, belongs to the nature of man as he came from the hand of God in creation. It is present whether in sinner or saint. This is the formal aspect of the image of God, this sheer capability for response.

There is also a material aspect of the image of God, as Brunner sees it. This is the actual giving of the answer that God intends, the response in which God is honored. This material obedience and response man no longer possesses or makes. He is appropriately spoken of as having lost the image in this sense, not partially but wholly. It is necessary for this image to be restored, recreated. This is indeed being done. It is nothing other than the gift of God in Jesus Christ, received by faith.

For Thomas, the image of God in man is substantive. It is part of the make-up of man's nature, a power resident within him. It is part of the very structure of his being. According to Brunner's understanding, however, the image is dynamic and relational. It is not somehow permanently present in man. It is present only when man is in relationship to God.

If Thomas's view is substantive and Brunner's is relational, then **Leonard Verduin**'s must be termed *functional*. Verduin observes that, in the Bible, the statement that man was made in the image and likeness of God is followed immediately by the command to have dominion. Since God is the Lord, the master, of all creation, it is reasonable to expect that man, who is in God's image, also will exercise this rule over nature. Man can be said to be in the image of God as he performs this function. Verduin applies this concept to several areas of practical concern, and his way of doing this makes a rather unique contribution to this collection. His reminder that all men are in the image of God and thus should participate in this dominion-having is also a check upon certain excessive and distorted forms of the doctrine.

A further issue that has concerned the church is the make-up of man. Of how many elements is man's nature composed? What is the role or function of each (however many there may be), and what is the inter-relationship among them? The conclusions we reach here have significant implications for the way we treat man, the way we regard the source and basis of sin, and the way we understand the future life (particularly the period between death and resurrection) of individual men.

Earlier discussions assumed a composite or complex nature of man, generally focusing on either the dichotomous view (that man is made up of two elements, body and soul) or the trichotomous view (that man is made up of body, soul, *and spirit*). The debate generally centered upon the significance and denotation of certain Biblical terms. **Charles Hodge's** article represents the dichotomist position. Working with a substance philosophy, he discusses the pertinent Biblical passages. He also considers and rebuts the arguments generally advanced by trichotomists. He does not particularly discuss the view that man is a unitary being, a more recent emphasis. In terms of the present discussion, therefore, the value of his piece lies in the positive presentation of his own views.

**D. R. G. Owen** represents the unitary view of man. He makes a sharp contrast between the Hebrew and Greek ways of thinking, an antithesis that has been questioned by some scholars in this area. According to Owen the Hebrew view of man tended to be unitary, the Greek dualistic. Owen considers the Greek ideas in the New Testament to be minor and alien intrusions into the mainstream of thought.

When Owen examines the Biblical texts bearing on the question of man's make-up, he therefore disregards these Greek elements. Man is basically a unity. There is no immortal "soul" that survives the death of the body. While the status of the individual between his death and the "last day" seems to pose a problem for this view, it is merely a pseudo-problem, resulting from incorrectly reading eschatological language in temporal terms. There is no interval, for the "last day" is not an event in time at all. Thus, Owen can simply affirm that man as a unitary being is incapable of any sort of disembodied existence.

1

## J. Oliver Buswell, Jr.

## The Origin of Man

*Fiat Creationism*

In the preceding chapters we have studied the nature of man as created in the image of God and as fallen in sin. It has been with deliberate purpose that I have postponed until now the question of the origin and the antiquity of man except insofar as the question of human origin has been involved in other subjects.

Whereas the origin of any object of our investigation throws light upon its nature, conversely the nature of any object of study necessarily gives implications as to its origin. If man is what he has been observed to be, a spiritual being capable of receiving the Word of God, yet a being bearing the marks of his fall, we should expect to discover that man has had an origin consistent with and accounting for his nature. Man being what he is, we are pursuing reasonable inference from effect to cause if we accept the view that man's origin was a creative act of God.

### Contemporary Opposition

In our day and age, however, there is an increasing tendency among our contemporaries to think of man, and everything else in the universe, as

From *A Systematic Theology of the Christian Religion* (Grand Rapids: Zondervan Publishing House, 1962), 1:321-25. Used by permission.

coming from naturalistic, that is non-supernaturalistic origins. In this respect our day differs from some periods of the past.

In the first century A.D. Paul could appeal to Stoics and Epicureans in the Areopagus on the basis of their own literature, and could find common intellectual ground with them in the assumption of the supernatural origin of the human race. Paul said, "Certain also of your own poets have said 'We also are His offspring' " (Acts 17:28). The quotation is from Aratus (d. c. 245 B.C.) from his poem entitled *Phaenomena.* Cleanthes who died about the middle of the third century B.C. is quoted as using a similar expression.

In ancient paganism, even in Lucretius' *De Rerum Natura,* Christianity did not have to meet any systematic anti-theistic view of human origins comparable with current naturalism. When genuine biblical Christianity revived in the sixteenth century, though faced with overwhelming obstacles of ignorance, corruption, and superstition, there was no sheer denial of the supernatural. Humanism of the day was sometimes indifferent, but never was Christianity confronted with an elaborated anti-supernaturalism such as is found in the writings of Fred Hoyle[1] or in *Naturalism and the Human Spirit.* [2]

In our day the idea of "the stability of the solar system" as advanced by Laplace (1749-1827) is no longer philosophically acceptable because of far more extensive physical data. Laplace's reply to Napoleon, however, is more popular than in Laplace's day. When Napoleon asked whether it was true that in his *Mecanique celeste* Laplace had not mentioned the Creator, he replied, *"Je n'avais pas besoin de cette hypothese-la"* (I have not had need of that hypothesis).[3] This is an attitude which one frequently finds developed and firmly entrenched in contemporary thought.

For us the crux of the matter is well stated by Warfield,[4] "The fundamental assertion of the biblical doctrine of the origin of man is that he owes his being to a creative act of God." The article from which this statement is quoted was originally published in 1911. A half century later the central point of importance has not shifted, but the question has been greatly intensified.

## Biblical Doctrine

The biblical doctrine of the special creation of man has been discussed on pp. 231ff., in connection with the doctrines of theism, and above in this section in the discussion of the doctrine of the image of God in man. It will not be necessary to repeat much of what has been said, but only to summarize it for purposes of the present discussion.

In Genesis 1:26, 27, the simple fact of divine creation is stated. God created man male and female, created him in His own image, and gave him dominion over the rest of the creation. It is in Genesis 2:7, 21, 22, in the more detailed account of creation, that we have the statement, "And the Lord God formed man of the dust of the ground, and breathed into his nostrils the breath of life; and man became a living soul. . . . and the Lord God caused a deep sleep to fall upon Adam, and he slept; and He took one of his ribs and closed up the flesh instead thereof; and the rib, which the Lord God had taken from man, made He a woman, and brought her unto the man."

It seems *prima facie* evident that the Genesis record of the creation of man is intended to convey the impression of a special act of creation not from previously existing biological forms. Certainly nothing else than special creation can be made of the record of the creation of Eve.

### "Theistic Evolution"

There are devout Christians who hold that the process by which man was created was biological and genetic, in other words that man's physical being was produced by evolution. A form of this theory, I well remember, appealed to me many years ago in my undergraduate days in the university. I devoutly believed in the inerrancy of the Bible, but I thought the Bible record could be harmonized with the idea that Adam was produced by a mutation, and that he was constituted as man in the image of God by a special supernatural act. I did not question the special creation of Eve. I argued that the mutation by which Adam's physical nature might have been produced would have been so great that he could not have mated with any of the stock from which his body was derived. I even went so far as to note that a gorilla's skeleton which hung in our biology lecture room at Minnesota had thirteen ribs whereas man ordinarily has only twelve!

However, I became thoroughly convinced many years ago that this hypothesis is untenable. First, the data of Mendelism, the science of genetics, seem to corroborate the Genesis phrase, "after their kind," which recurs frequently in the creation record.

Further, evolution does not solve any difficulties. It is more complicated than the simple special creation view. The natural processes, except where personal intelligence intervenes, tend toward the simple and homogenous rather than toward what we call higher forms of life.

As for the Darwinian theory of the survival of the fittest, it has often been said that Darwinism does not explain the *arrival* of the fit. There is nothing in naturalistic processes to account for man as we now observe him.

Moreover, in the study of philosophy I have not infrequently found the opinion among non-Christian philosophers that biological evolution explains nothing, in view of the vastness of the cosmic process. It throws no light upon the enormous philosophical problem of the cosmic reaches of the physics of astronomy.

Again, the statement of Genesis 2:7, to the effect that "The Lord God formed man of the dust of the ground," seems to indicate rather strongly that man's body was formed, not from some previously existing animal, but rather from inorganic material.

There is observable a gap which some anthropologists have called a bio-cultural gap between man and the other animals. That is to say, both the biology and the culture of man as a tool-making creature, differ widely from the non-human; and I am told by students of this field that, as human archaeology progresses, the bio-cultural gap is not diminishing but is becoming even more sharply defined.

Finally, I am impressed that the theory of the derivation of the human physical body from merely animal ancestry is extremely difficult to harmonize with the doctrine of man created in the image of God, man as a fallen creature, man as redeemable in Christ. It is particularly difficult to harmonize the evolutionary view with the doctrine of the incarnation, Christ as *Deus-homo*, God manifest in the flesh.

For the reasons enumerated, and for other general considerations, I am compelled to conclude that man, as observed, can only be explained as the result of a special act of creation such as is recorded in the early chapters of Genesis.

## The Origin of Life

Bible-believers sometimes take refuge behind defensive positions not supported by the Bible itself. The Bible does not teach that the world is flat, or that it was created in the year 4004 B.C., or that the earth, or the solar system, or our galaxy is the center of the material universe. Adhering to non-Biblical positions in a dogmatic "religious" spirit has created unnecessary problems for biblical faith.

The Bible nowhere teaches that man cannot by physical and chemical processes make living, self-propagating organisms out of inorganic material. I am no bio-chemist. I doubt that man will, as they say, "create life." But I have nothing at stake so far as my Christian faith is concerned. W. H. Thorpe, a Cambridge biologist,[5] says of certain achievement in bio-chemistry, "But as a result of these and other considerations I believe that modern developments in bio-chemistry and biophysics are in a fair way to providing far more striking evidence for the doctrine of emergence than was open to the philosophers and scientists of an earlier generation."

Well, if living, self-propagating tissue can be made from inorganic material, let the *facts* be known. But the *"doctrine* of emergence," if this means the denial of special creation, is an entirely different matter. Man can fly, non-stop, across the ocean, but this does not prove anything as to the source of American aborigines. There are devout Bible-believing Christians who believe that bio-chemists will "create life." Culturally we are interested. Theologically we have nothing at stake.

## Notes

[1] See J. Oliver Buswell, *A Systematic Theology of the Christian Religion,* vol. 1, part 2, chapter 2.

[2] Krikorian, ed., Columbia University Press, 1944.

[3] *Newton's Principia,* Florian Cajori, ed., University of California Press, 1946, Appendix, p. 677.

[4] Benjamin B. Warfield, *Studies in Theology,* Oxford Press, article entitled, "On the Antiquity and the Unity of the Human Race," p. 235.

[5] *Biology, Psychology and Belief,* Cambridge University Press, 1961, pp. 41f.

**Augustus H. Strong**

*Theistic Evolution*

# Man a Creation and Child of God

The fact of man's creation is declared in Gen. 1:27—"And God created man in his own image, in the image of God created he him"; 2:7—"And Jehovah God formed man of the dust of the ground, and breathed into his nostrils the breath of life; and man became a living soul."

(*a*) The Scriptures, on the one hand, negative the idea that man is the mere product of unreasoning natural forces. They refer his existence to a cause different from mere nature, namely, the creative act of God.

Compare Hebrews 12:9—"the Father of spirits"; Num. 16:22—"the God of the spirits of all flesh"; 27:16—"Jehovah, the God of the spirits of all flesh"; Rev. 22:6—"the God of the spirits of the prophets." Bruce, The Providential Order, 25—"Faith in God may remain intact, though we concede that man in all his characteristics, physical and psychical, is no exception to the universal law of growth, no breach in the continuity of the evolutionary process." By *"mere* nature" we mean nature apart from God. Our previous treatment of the doctrine of creation in general has shown that the laws of nature are only the regular methods of God, and that the

From *Systematic Theology* (Westwood, N.J.: Fleming H. Revell, 1907), pp. 465-76. Used by permission.

conception of a nature apart from God is an irrational one. If the evolution of the lower creation cannot be explained without taking into account the originating agency of God, much less can the coming into being of man, the crown of all created things. Hudson, Divine Pedigree of Man: "Spirit in man is linked with, because derived from, God, who is spirit."

(b) But, on the other hand, the Scriptures do not disclose the method of man's creation. Whether man's physical system is or is not derived, by natural descent, from the lower animals, the record of creation does not inform us. As the command "Let the earth bring forth living creatures" (Gen. 1:24) does not exclude the idea of mediate creation, through natural generation, so the forming of man "of the dust of the ground" (Gen. 2:7) does not in itself determine whether the creation of man's body was mediate or immediate.

We may believe that man sustained to the highest preceding brute the same relation which the multiplied bread and fish sustained to the five loaves and two fishes (Matt. 14:19), or which the wine sustained to the water which was transformed at Cana (John 2:7-10), or which the multiplied oil sustained to the original oil in the O.T. miracle (II Kings 4:1-7). The "dust," before the breathing of the spirit into it, may have been animated dust. Natural means may have been used, so far as they would go. Sterrett, Reason and Authority in Religion, 39—"Our heredity is from God, even though it be from lower forms of life, and our goal is also God, even though it be through imperfect manhood."

Evolution does not make the idea of a Creator superfluous, because evolution is only the method of God. It is perfectly consistent with a Scriptural doctrine of Creation that man should emerge at the proper time, governed by different laws from the brute creation yet growing out of the brute, just as the foundation of a house built of stone is perfectly consistent with the wooden structure built upon it. All depends upon the plan. An atheistic and undesigning evolution cannot include man without excluding what Christianity regards as essential to man; see Griffith-Jones, Ascent through Christ, 43-73. But a theistic evolution can recognize the whole process of man's creation as equally the work of nature and the work of God.

Schurman, Agnosticism and Religion, 42—"You are not what you have come from, but what you have become." Huxley said of the brutes: "Whether *from* them or not, man is assuredly not *of* them." Pfleiderer, Philos. Religion, 1:289—"The religious dignity of man rests after all upon what he *is,* not upon the mode and manner in which he has *become* what he is." Because he came *from* a beast, it does not follow that he *is* a beast. Nor does the fact that man's existence can be traced back to a brute ancestry furnish any proper reason why the brute should become man. Here is a teleology which requires a divine Creatorship.

J. M. Bronson: "The theist must accept evolution if he would keep his argument for the existence of God from the unity of design in nature. Unless man is an *end,* he is an *anomaly.* The greatest argument for God is the fact that all animate nature is one vast and connected unity. Man has developed not *from* the ape, but *away from* the ape. He was never anything but potential man. He did not, as man, come into being until he became a conscious moral agent." This conscious moral nature, which we call personality, requires a divine Author, because it surpasses all the powers which can be found in the animal creation. Romanes, Mental Evolution in Animals, tells us that: 1. Mollusca learn by experience; 2. Insects and spiders recognize offspring; 3. Fishes make mental association of objects by their similarity; 4. Reptiles recognize persons; 5. Hymenoptera, as bees and ants, communicate ideas; 6. Birds recognize pictorial representations and understand words; 7. Rodents, as rats and foxes, understand mechanisms; 8. Monkeys and elephants learn to use tools; 9. Anthropoid apes and dogs have indefinite morality.

But it is definite and not indefinite morality which differences man from the brute. Drummond, in his Ascent of Man, concedes that man passed through a period when he resembled the ape more than any known animal, but at the same time declares that no anthropoid ape could develop into a man. The brute can be defined in terms of man, but man cannot be defined in terms of the brute. It is significant that in insanity the higher endowments of man disappear in an order precisely the reverse of that in which, according to the development theory, they have been acquired. The highest part of man totters first. The last added is first to suffer. Man moreover can transmit his own acquisitions to his posterity, as the brute cannot. Weismann, Heredity, 2:69—"The evolution of music does not depend upon any increase of the musical faculty or any alteration in the inherent physical nature of man, but solely upon the power of transmitting the intellectual achievements of each generation to those which follow. This, more than anything, is the cause of the superiority of men over animals—this, and not merely human faculty, although it may be admitted that this latter is much higher than in animals." To this utterance of Weismann we would add that human progress depends quite as much upon man's power of reception as upon man's power of transmission. Interpretation must equal expression; and, in this interpretation of the past, man has a guarantee of the future which the brute does not possess.

(*c*) Psychology, however, comes in to help our interpretation of Scripture. The radical differences between man's soul and the principle of intelligence in the lower animals, especially man's possession of self-consciousness, general ideas, the moral sense, and the power of self-determination, show that that which chiefly constitutes him man could not have been derived, by any natural process of development, from the inferior creatures. We are compelled, then, to believe that God's "breathing into man's nostrils the breath of life" (Gen. 2:7), though it was a mediate creation as presupposing existing material in the shape of animal forms, was yet an immediate creation in the sense that only a divine reinforcement of the process of life turned the animal into man. In other words, man came not *from* the brute, but *through* the brute, and the same immanent God who had previously created the brute created also the man.

Tennyson, In Memoriam, XLV—"The baby new to earth and sky, What time his tender palm is pressed Against the circle of the breast, Has never thought that 'this is I': But as he grows he gathers much, And learns the use of 'I' and 'me,' And finds 'I am not what I see, And other than the things I touch.' So rounds he to a separate mind From whence clear memory may begin, As thro' the frame that binds him in His isolation grows defined." Fichte called that the birthday of his child, when the child awoke to self-consciousness and said "I." Memory goes back no further than language. Knowledge of the ego is objective, before it is subjective. The child at first speaks of himself in the third person: "Henry did so and so." Hence most men do not remember what happened before their third year, though Samuel Miles Hopkins, Memoir, 20, remembered what must have happened when he was only 23 months old. Only a conscious person remembers, and he remembers only as his will exerts itself in attention.

Jean Paul Richter, quoted in Ladd, Philosophy of Mind, 110—"Never shall I forget the phenomenon in myself, never till now recited, when I stood by the birth of my own self-consciousness, the place and time of which are distinct in my memory. On a certain forenoon, I stood, a very young child, within the house-door, and was looking out toward the wood-pile, as in an instant the inner revelation 'I am I,' like lightning from heaven, flashed and stood brightly before me; in that moment I had seen myself as I, for the first time and forever."

Höffding, Outlines of Psychology, 3—"The beginning of conscious life is to be placed probably before birth. . . . Sensations only faintly and dimly distinguished from the general feeling of vegetative comfort and discomfort. Still the experiences undergone before birth perhaps suffice to form the foundation of the consciousness of an external world." Hill, Genetic Philosophy, 282, suggests that this early state, in which the child speaks of self in the third person and is devoid of *self*-consciousness, corresponds to the brute condition of the race, before it had reached self-consciousness, attained language, and become man. In the race, however, there was no heredity to predetermine self-consciousness—it was a new acquisition, marking transition to a superior order of being.

Connecting these remarks with our present subject, we assert that no brute ever yet said, or thought, "I." With this, then, we may begin a series of simple distinctions between man and the brute, so far as the immaterial principle in each is concerned. These are mainly compiled from writers hereafter mentioned.

(1.) The brute is conscious, but man is self-conscious. The brute does not objectify self. "If the pig could once say, 'I am a pig,' it would at once and thereby cease to be a pig." The brute does not distinguish itself from its sensations. The brute has perception, but only the man has apperception, *i. e.*, perception accompanied by reference of it to the self to which it belongs.

(2.) The brute has only percepts; man has also concepts. The brute knows white things, but not whiteness. It remembers things, but not thoughts. Man alone has the power of abstraction, *i. e.,* the power of deriving abstract ideas from particular things or experiences.

(3.) Hence the brute has no language. "Language is the expression of general notions by symbols" (Harris). Words are the symbols of concepts. Where there are no concepts there can be no words. The parrot utters cries; but "no parrot ever yet spoke a true word." Since language is a sign, it presupposes the existence of an intellect capable of understanding the sign,—in short, language is the effect of mind, not the cause of mind. See Mivart, in Brit. Quar., Oct. 1881:154-172. "The ape's tongue is eloquent in his own dispraise." James, Psychology, 2:356—"The notion of a sign as such, and the general purpose to apply it to everything, is the distinctive characteristic of man." Why do not animals speak? Because they have nothing to say, *i. e.*, have no general ideas which words might express.

4. The brute forms no judgments, *e. g.*, that *this* is like *that*, accompanied with belief. Hence there is no sense of the ridiculous, and no laughter. James, Psychology, 2:360—"The brute does not associate ideas by similarity. . . . Genius in man is the possession of this power of association in an extreme degree."

5. The brute has no reasoning—no sense that *this* follows from *that*, accompanied by a feeling that the sequence is necessary. Association of ideas without judgment is the typical process of the brute mind, though not that of the mind of man. See Mind 5:402-409, 575-581. Man's dream-life is the best analogue to the mental life of the brute.

6. The brute has no general ideas or intuitions, as of space, time, substance, cause, right. Hence there is no generalizing, and no proper experience or progress. There is no capacity for improvement in animals. The brute cannot be trained, except in certain inferior matters of association, where independent judgment is not required. No animal makes tools, uses clothes, cooks food, breeds other animals for food. No hunter's dog, however long its observation of its master, ever learned to put wood on a fire to keep itself from freezing. Even the rudest stone implements show a break in continuity and mark the introduction of man; see J. P. Cook, Credentials of Science, 14. "The dog can see the printed page as well as a man can, but no dog was ever taught to read a book. The animal cannot create in its own mind the thoughts of the writer. The physical in man, on the contrary, is only an aid to the spiritual. Education is a trained capacity to discern the inner meaning and deeper relations of things. So the universe is but a symbol and expression of spirit, a garment in which an invisible Power has robed his majesty and glory"; see S. S. Times, April 7, 1900. In man, mind first became supreme.

7. The brute has determination, but not self-determination. There is no freedom of choice, no conscious forming of a purpose, and no self-movement toward a predetermined end. The donkey is determined, but not self-determined; he is the victim of heredity and environment; he acts only as he is acted upon. Harris, Philos. Basis of Theism, 537-554—"Man, though implicated in nature through his bodily organization, is in his personality supernatural; the brute is wholly submerged in nature. . . . Man is like a ship in the sea—in it, yet above it—guiding his course, by observing the heavens, even against wind and current. A brute has no such power; it is in nature like a balloon, wholly immersed in air, and driven about by its currents, with no power of steering." Calderwood, Philosophy of Evolution, chapter on Right and Wrong: "The grand distinction of human life is self-control in the field of action—control over all the animal impulses, so that these do not spontaneously and of themselves determine activity" [as they do in the brute]. By what Mivart calls a process of "inverse anthropomorphism," we clothe the brute with the attributes of freedom; but it does not really possess them. Just as we do not transfer to God all our human imperfections, so we ought not to transfer all our human perfections to the brute, "reading our full selves in life of lower forms." The brute has no power to choose between motives; it simply obeys motive. The necessitarian philosophy, therefore, is a correct and excellent philosophy for the brute. But man's power of initiative—in short, man's free

will—renders it impossible to explain his higher nature as a mere natural development from the inferior creatures. Even Huxley has said that, taking mind into the account, there is between man and the highest beasts an "enormous gulf," a "divergence immeasurable" and "practically infinite."

(8.) The brute has no conscience and no religious nature. No dog ever brought back to the butcher the meat it had stolen. "The aspen trembles without fear, and dogs skulk without guilt." The dog mentioned by Darwin, whose behavior in presence of a newspaper moved by the wind seemed to testify to "a sense of the supernatural," was merely exhibiting the irritation due to the sense of an unknown future; see James, Will to Believe, 79. The bearing of flogged curs does not throw light upon the nature of conscience. If ethics is not hedonism, if moral obligation is not a refined utilitarianism, if the right is something distinct from the good we get out of it, then there must be a flaw in the theory that man's conscience is simply a development of brute instincts; and a reinforcement of brute life from the divine source of life must be postulated in order to account for the appearance of man. Upton, Hibbert Lectures, 165-167—"Is the spirit of man derived from the soul of the animal? No, for neither one of these has self-existence. Both are self-differentiations of God. The latter is simply God's preparation for the former." Calderwood, Evolution and Man's Place in Nature, 337, speaks of "the impossibility of tracing the origin of man's rational life to evolution from a lower life. . . . There are no physical forces discoverable in nature sufficient to account for the appearance of this life." Shaler, Interpretation of Nature, 186—"Man's place has been won by an entire change in the limitations of his psychic development. . . . The old bondage of the mind to the body is swept away. . . . In this new freedom we find the one dominant characteristic of man, the feature which entitles us to class him as an entirely new class of animal."

John Burroughs, Ways of Nature: "Animal life parallels human life at many points, but it is in another plane. Something guides the lower animals, but it is not thought; something restrains them, but it is not judgment; they are provident without prudence; they are active without industry; they are skilful without practice; they are wise without knowledge; they are rational without reason; they are deceptive without guile. . . . When they are joyful, they sing or they play; when they are distressed, they moan or they cry; . . . and yet I do not suppose they experience the emotion of joy or sorrow, or anger or love, as we do, because these feelings in them do not involve reflection, memory, and what we call the higher nature, as with us. Their instinct is intelligence directed outward, never inward, as in man. They share with man the emotions of his animal nature, but not of his moral or aesthetic nature; they know no altruism, no moral code." Mr. Burroughs maintains that we have no proof that animals in a state of nature can reflect, form abstract ideas, associate cause and effect. Animals, for instance, that store up food for the winter simply follow a provident instinct but do not take thought for the future, any more than does the tree that forms new buds for the coming season. He sums up his position as follows: "To attribute human motives and faculties to the animals is to caricature them; but to put us in such relation to them that we feel their kinship, that we see their lives embosomed in the same iron necessity as our own, that we see in their minds a humbler manifestation of the same psychic power and intelligence that culminates and is conscious of itself in man—that, I take it, is the true humanization." We assent to all this except the ascription to human life of the same iron necessity that rules the animal creation. Man is man, because his free will transcends the limitations of the brute.

While we grant, then, that man is the last stage in the development of life and that he has a brute ancestry, we regard him also as the offspring of God. The same God who was the author of the brute became in due time the creator of man. Though man came *through* the brute, he did not come *from* the brute, but from God, the Father of spirits and the author of all life. Oedipus' terrific oracle: "Mayst thou ne'er know the truth of what thou art!" might well be uttered to those who believe only in the brute origin of man. Pascal says it is dangerous to let man see too clearly that he is on a level with the animals unless at the same time we show him his greatness. The doctrine that the brute is imperfect man is logically connected with the doctrine that man is a perfect brute. Thomas Carlyle: "If this brute philosophy is true, then man should go on all fours, and not lay claim to the dignity of being moral." G. F. Wright, Ant. and Origin of Human Race, lecture IX—"One or other of the lower animals may exhibit all the faculties used by a child of fifteen months. The difference may seem very little, but what there is is very important. It is like the difference in direction in the early stages of two separating curves, which go on forever diverging. . . . The probability is that both in his bodily and in his mental development man appeared as a *sport* in nature, and leaped at once in some single pair from the plane of irrational being to the possession of the higher powers that have ever since characterized him and dominated both his development and his history."

Scripture seems to teach the doctrine that man's nature is the creation of God. Gen. 2:7—"Jehovah God formed man of the dust of the ground, and breathed into his nostrils the breath of life; and man became a living soul"—appears, says Hovey (State of the Impen. Dead, 14), "to distinguish the vital informing principle of human nature from its material part, pronouncing the former to be more directly from God, and more akin to him, than the latter." So in Zech. 12:1—"Jehovah, who stretcheth forth the heavens, and layeth the foundation of the earth, and formeth the spirit of man within him"—the soul is recognized as distinct in nature from the body, and of a dignity and value far beyond those of any material organism. Job 32:8—"there is a spirit in man, and the breath of the Almighty giveth them understanding"; Eccles. 12:7—"the dust returneth to the earth as it was, and the spirit returneth unto God who gave it." A sober view of the similarities and differences between man and the lower animals may be found in Lloyd Morgan, Animal Life and Intelligence. See also Martineau, Types, 2:65, 140, and Study, 1:180; 2:9, 13, 184, 350; Hopkins, Outline Study of Man, 8:23; Chadbourne, Instinct, 187-211; Porter, Hum. Intellect, 384, 386, 397; Bascom, Science of Mind, 295-305; Mansel, Metaphysics, 49, 50; Princeton Rev., Jan. 1881:104-128; Henslow, in Nature, May 1, 1879:21, 22; Ferrier, Remains, 2:39; Argyll, Unity of Nature, 117-119; Bib. Sac., 29:275-282; Max Müller, Lectures on Philos. of Language, no. 1, 2, 3; F. W. Robertson, Lectures on Genesis, 21; LeConte, in Princeton Rev., May, 1884: 236-261; Lindsay, Mind in Lower Animals; Romanes, Mental Evolution in Animals; Fiske, The Destiny of Man.

(*d*) Comparative physiology, moreover, has, up to the present time, done nothing to forbid the extension of this doctrine to man's body. No single instance has yet been adduced of the transformation of one animal species into another, either by natural or artificial selection; much less has it been demonstrated that the body of the brute has ever been developed into that of man. All evolution implies progress and reinforcement of life, and is unintelligible except as the immanent God gives new impulses to the process. Apart from the direct agency of God, the view that man's physical system is descended by natural generation from some ancestral simian form can be regarded only as an irrational hypothesis. Since the soul, then, is an immediate creation of God, and the forming of man's body is mentioned by the Scripture writer in direct connection with this creation of the spirit, man's body was in this sense an immediate creation also.

For the theory of natural selection, see Darwin, Origin of Species, 398-424, and Descent of Man, 2:368-387; Huxley, Critiques and Addresses, 241-269, Man's Place in Nature, 71-138, Lay Sermons, 323, and art.: Biology, in Encyc. Britannica, 9th ed.; Romanes, Scientific Evidences of Organic Evolution. The theory holds that, in the struggle for existence, the varieties best adapted to their surroundings succeed in maintaining and reproducing themselves, while the rest die out. Thus, by gradual change and improvement of lower into higher forms of life, man has been evolved. We grant that Darwin has disclosed one of the important features of God's method. We concede the partial truth of his theory. We find it supported by the vertebrate structure and nervous organization which man has in common with the lower animals; by the facts of embryonic development; of rudimentary organs; of common diseases and remedies; and of reversion to former types. But we refuse to regard natural selection as a complete explanation of the history of life, and that for the following reasons:
1. It gives no account of the origin of substance, nor of the origin of variations. Darwinism simply says that "round stones will roll down hill further than flat ones" (Gray, Natural Science and Religion). It accounts for the selection, not for the creation, of forms. "Natural selection originates nothing. It is a destructive, not a creative, principle. If we must idealize it as a positive force, we must think of it, not as the preserver of the fittest, but as the destroyer, that follows ever in the wake of creation and devours the failures; the scavenger of creation, that takes out of the way forms which are not fit to live and reproduce themselves" (Johnson, on Theistic Evolution, in Andover Review, April, 1884:363-381). Natural selection is only unintelligent repression. Darwin's Origin of Species is in fact "not the Genesis, but the Exodus, of living forms." Schurman: "The *survival* of the fittest does nothing to explain the *arrival* of the fittest"; see also DeVries, Species and Varieties, *ad finem.* Darwin himself acknowledged that "Our ignorance of the laws of variation is profound. . . . The cause of each slight variation and of each monstrosity lies much more in the nature or constitution of the organism than in the nature of the surrounding conditions" (quoted by Mivart, Lessons from Nature, 280-301). Weismann has therefore modified the Darwinian theory by asserting that there would be no development unless there were a spontaneous, innate tendency to variation. In this innate tendency we see, not mere nature, but the work of an originating and superintending God. E. M.

Caillard, in Contemp. Rev., Dec. 1893:873-881—"Spirit was the moulding power, from the beginning, of those lower forms which would ultimately become man. Instead of the physical derivation of the soul, we propose the spiritual derivation of the body."

2. Some of the most important forms appear suddenly in the geological record, without connecting links to unite them with the past. The first fishes are the Ganoid, large in size and advanced in type. There are no intermediate gradations between the ape and man. Huxley, in Man's Place in Nature, 94, tells us that the lowest gorilla has a skull capacity of 24 cubic inches, whereas the highest gorilla has 34½. Over against this, the lowest man has a skull capacity of 62; though men with less than 65 are invariably idiotic; the highest man has 114. Professor Burt G. Wilder of Cornell University: "The largest ape-brain is only half as large as the smallest normal human." Wallace, Darwinism, 458—"The average human brain weighs 48 or 49 ounces; the average ape's brain is only 18 ounces." The brain of Daniel Webster weighed 53 ounces; but Dr. Bastian tells of an imbecile whose intellectual deficiency was congenital, yet whose brain weighed 55 ounces. Large heads do not always indicate great intellect. Professor Virchow points out that the Greeks, one of the most intellectual of nations, are also one of the smallest-headed of all. Bain: "While the size of the brain increases in arithmetical proportion, intellectual range increases in geometrical proportion."

Respecting the Enghis and Neanderthal crania, Huxley says: "The fossil remains of man hitherto discovered do not seem to me to take us appreciably nearer to that lower pithecoid form by the modification of which he has probably become what he is. . . . In vain have the links which should bind man to the monkey been sought: not a single one is there to show. The so-called *Protanthropos* who should exhibit this link has not been found. . . . None have been found that stood nearer the monkey than the men of to-day." Huxley argues that the difference between man and the gorilla is smaller than that between the gorilla and some apes; if the gorilla and the apes constitute one family and have a common origin, may not man and the gorilla have a common ancestry also? We reply that the space between the lowest ape and the highest gorilla is filled in with numberless intermediate gradations. The space between the lowest man and the highest man is also filled in with many types that shade off one into the other. But the space between the highest gorilla and the lowest man is absolutely vacant; there are no intermediate types; no connecting links between the ape and man have yet been found.

Professor Virchow has also very recently expressed his belief that no relics of any predecessor of man have yet been discovered. He said: "In my judgment, no skull hitherto discovered can be regarded as that of a predecessor of man. In the course of the last fifteen years we have had opportunities of examining skulls of all the various races of mankind—even of the most savage tribes; and among them all no group has been observed differing in its essential characters from the general human type. . . . Out of all the skulls found in the lake-dwellings there is not one that lies outside the boundaries of our present population." Dr. Eugene Dubois has discovered in the Post-pliocene deposits of the island of Java the remains of a preeminently hominine anthropoid which he calls *Pithecanthropus erectus*. Its cranial capacity approaches the physiological minimum in man, and is double that of the gorilla. The thigh bone is in form and dimensions

the absolute analogue of that of man, and gives evidence of having supported a habitually erect body. Dr. Dubois unhesitatingly places this extinct Javan ape as the intermediate form between man and the true anthropoid apes. Haeckel (in The Nation, Sept. 15, 1898) and Keane (in Man
Past and Present, 3), regard the *Pithecanthropus* as a "missing link." But
"Nature" regards it as the remains of a human microcephalous idiot. In
addition to all this, it deserves to be noticed that man does not degenerate
as we travel back in time. "The Enghis skull, the contemporary of the
mammoth and the cave-bear, is as large as the average of to-day, and might
have belonged to a philosopher." The monkey nearest to man in physical
form is no more intelligent than the elephant or the bee.

3. There are certain facts which mere heredity cannot explain, such for
example as the origin of the working-bee from the queen and the drone,
neither of which produces honey. The working-bee, moreover, does not
transmit the honey-making instinct to its posterity; for it is sterile and
childless. If man had descended from the conscienceless brute, we should
expect him, when degraded, to revert to his primitive type. On the contrary, he does not revert to the brute, but dies out instead. The theory can
give no explanation of beauty in the lowest forms of life, such as molluscs
and diatoms. Darwin grants that this beauty must be of use to its pos-
sessor, in order to be consistent with its origination through natural selection. But no such use has yet been shown; for the creatures which possess
the beauty often live in the dark, or have no eyes to see. So, too, the large
brain of the savage is beyond his needs, and is inconsistent with the principle of natural selection which teaches that no organ can permanently
attain a size unrequired by its needs and its environment. See Wallace,
Natural Selection, 338-360. G. F. Wright, Man and the Glacial Epoch,
242-301—"That man's bodily organization is in some way a development
from some extinct member of the animal kingdom allied to the anthropoid
apes is scarcely any longer susceptible of doubt. . . . But he is certainly not
descended from any *existing* species of anthropoid apes. . . . When once
*mind* became supreme, the bodily adjustment must have been rapid, if
indeed it is not necessary to suppose that the bodily preparation for the
highest mental faculties was instantaneous, or by what is called in nature a
*sport.*" With this statement of Dr. Wright we substantially agree, and therefore differ from Shedd when he says that there is just as much reason for
supposing that monkeys are degenerate men, as that men are improved
monkeys. Shakespeare, Timon of Athens, 1:1:249, seems to have hinted
the view of Dr. Shedd: "The strain of man's bred out into baboon and
monkey." Bishop Wilberforce asked Huxley whether he was related to an
ape on his grandfather's or grandmother's side. Huxley replied that he
should prefer such a relationship to having for an ancestor a man who used
his position as a minister of religion to ridicule truth which he did not
comprehend. "Mamma, am I descended from a monkey?" "I do not know,
William, I never met any of your father's people."

4. No species is yet known to have been produced either by artificial or
by natural selection. Huxley, Lay Sermons, 323—"It is not absolutely
proven that a group of animals having all the characters exhibited by
species in nature has ever been originated by selection, whether artificial or
natural"; Man's Place in Nature, 107—"Our acceptance of the Darwinian
hypothesis must be provisional, so long as one link in the chain of evidence
is wanting; and so long as all the animals and plants certainly produced by

selective breeding from a common stock are fertile with one another, that link will be wanting." Huxley has more recently declared that the missing proof has been found in the descent of the modern horse with one toe, from Hipparion with two toes, Anchitherium with three, and Orohippus with four. Even if this were demonstrated, we should still maintain that the only proper analogue was to be found in that artificial selection by which man produces new varieties, and that natural selection can bring about no useful results and show no progress, unless it be the method and revelation of a wise and designing mind. In other words, selection implies intelligence and will, and therefore cannot be exclusively natural. Mivart, *Man and Apes*, 192—"If it is inconceivable and impossible for man's body to be developed or to exist without his informing soul, we conclude that, as no natural process accounts for the different kind of soul—one capable of articulately expressing general conceptions,—so no merely natural process can account for the origin of the body informed by it—a body to which such an intellectual faculty was so essentially and intimately related." Thus Mivart, who once considered that evolution could account for man's body, now holds instead that it can account neither for man's body nor for his soul, and calls natural selection "a puerile hypothesis" (Lessons from Nature, 300; Essays and Criticisms, 2:289-314).

(*e*) While we concede, then, that man has a brute ancestry, we make two claims by way of qualification and explanation: first, that the laws of organic development which have been followed in man's origin are only the methods of God and proofs of his creatorship; secondly, that man, when he appears upon the scene, is no longer brute, but a self-conscious and self-determining being, made in the image of his Creator and capable of free moral decision between good and evil.

Both man's original creation and his new creation in regeneration are creations from within, rather than from without. In both cases, God builds the new upon the basis of the old. Man is not a product of blind forces, but is rather an emanation from that same divine life of which the brute was a lower manifestation. The fact that God used preëxisting material does not prevent his authorship of the result. The wine in the miracle was not water because water had been used in the making of it, nor is man a brute because the brute has made some contributions to his creation. Professor John H. Strong: "Some who freely allow the presence and power of God in the age-long process seem nevertheless not clearly to see that, in the final result of finished man, God successfully revealed himself. God's work was never really or fully done; man was a compound of brute and man; and a compound of two such elements could not be said to possess the qualities of either. God did not really succeed in bringing moral personality to birth. The evolution was incomplete; man is still on all fours; he cannot sin, because he was begotten of the brute; no fall, and no regeneration, is conceivable. We assert, on the contrary, that, though man came *through* the brute, he did not come *from* the brute. He came from God, whose immanent life he reveals, whose image he reflects in a finished moral personality. Because God succeeded, a fall was possible. We can believe in the age-long creation of evolution, provided only that this evolu-

tion completed itself. With that proviso, sin remains and the fall." See also
A. H. Strong, Christ in Creation, 163-180.

An atheistic and unteleological evolution is a reversion to the savage
view of animals as brethren, and to the heathen idea of a sphynx-man
growing out of the brute. Darwin himself did not deny God's authorship.
He closes his first great book with the declaration that life, with all its
potencies, was originally breathed "by the Creator" into the first forms of
organic being. And in his letters he refers with evident satisfaction to
Charles Kingsley's finding nothing in the theory which was inconsistent
with an earnest Christian faith. It was not Darwin, but disciples like
Haeckel, who put forward the theory as making the hypothesis of a
Creator superfluous. We grant the principle of evolution, but we regard it
as only the method of the divine intelligence, and must moreover consider
it as preceded by an original creative act, introducing vegetable and animal
life, and as supplemented by other creative acts at the introduction of man
and at the incarnation of Christ. Chadwick, Old and New Unitarianism,
33—"What seemed to wreck our faith in human nature [its origin from the
brute] has been its grandest confirmation. For nothing argues the essential
dignity of man more clearly than his triumph over the limitations of his
brute inheritance, while the long way that he has come is prophecy of the
moral heights undreamed of that await his tireless feet." All this is true if
we regard human nature, not as an undesigned result of atheistic evolution,
but as the efflux and reflection of the divine personality. R. E. Thompson,
in S. S. Times, Dec. 29, 1906—"The greatest fact in heredity is our descent
from God, and the greatest fact in environment is his presence in human
life at every point."

The atheistic conception of evolution is well satirized in the verse:
"There was an ape in days that were earlier; Centuries passed and his hair
became curlier; Centuries more and his thumb gave a twist, And he was a
man and a Positivist." That this conception is not a necessary conclusion
of modern science, is clear from the statements of Wallace, the author with
Darwin of the theory of natural selection. Wallace believes that man's
body was developed from the brute, but he thinks there have been three
breaks in continuity: 1. the appearance of life; 2. the appearance of sensation and consciousness; and 3. the appearance of spirit. These seem to
correspond to 1. vegetable; 2. animal; and 3. human life. He thinks natural
selection may account for man's place *in* nature, but not for man's place
*above* nature, as a spiritual being. See Wallace, Darwinism, 445-478—"I
fully accept Mr. Darwin's conclusion as to the essential identity of man's
bodily structure with that of the higher mammalia, and his descent from
some ancestral form common to man and the anthropoid apes." But the
conclusion that man's higher faculties have also been derived from the
lower animals "appears to me not to be supported by adequate evidence,
and to be directly opposed to many well-ascertained facts" (461). . . . The
mathematical, the artistic and musical faculties, are results, not causes, of
advancement,—they do not help in the struggle for existence and could not
have been developed by natural selection. The introduction of life (vegetable), of consciousness (animal), of higher faculty (human), point clearly
to a world of spirit, to which the world of matter is subordinate
(474-476). . . . Man's intellectual and moral faculties could not have been
developed from the animal, but must have had another origin; and for this
origin we can find an adequate cause only in the world of spirit."

Wallace, Natural Selection, 338—"The average cranial capacity of the lowest savage is probably not less than five-sixths of that of the highest civilized races, while the brain of the anthropoid apes scarcely amounts to one-third of that of man, in both cases taking the average; or the proportions may be represented by the following figures: anthropoid apes, 10; savages, 26; civilized man, 32." *Ibid.*, 360—"The inference I would draw from this class of phenomena is, that a superior intelligence has guided the development of man in a definite direction and for a special purpose, just as man guides the development of many animal and vegetable forms. . . . The controlling action of a higher intelligence is a necessary part of the laws of nature, just as the action of all surrounding organisms is one of the agencies in organic development,—else the laws which govern the material universe are insufficient for the production of man." Sir Wm. Thompson: "That man could be evolved out of inferior animals is the wildest dream of materialism, a pure assumption which offends me alike by its folly and by its arrogance." Hartmann, in his Anthropoid Apes, 302-306, while not despairing of "the possibility of discovering the true link between the world of man and mammals," declares that "that purely hypothetical being, the common ancestor of man and apes, is still to be found," and that "man cannot have descended from any of the fossil species which have hitherto come to our notice, nor yet from any of the species of apes now extant." See Dana, Amer. Journ. Science and Arts, 1876:251, and Geology, 603, 604; Letze, Mikrokosmos, vol. I, bk. 3, chap. 1; Mivart, Genesis of Species, 202-222, 259-307, Man and Apes, 88, 149-192, Lessons from Nature, 128-242, 280-301, The Cat, and Encyclop. Britannica, art.: Apes; Quatrefages, Natural History of Man, 64-87; Bp. Temple, Bampton Lect., 1884:161-189; Dawson, Story of the Earth and Man, 321-329, Duke of Argyll, Primeval Man, 38-75; Asa Gray, Natural Science and Religion; Schmid, Theories of Darwin, 115-140; Carpenter, Mental Physiology, 59; McIlvaine, Wisdom of Holy Scripture, 55-86; Bible Commentary, 1:43; Martensen, Dogmatics, 136; Le Conte, in Princeton Rev., Nov. 1878:776-803; Zöckler Urgeschichte, 81-105; Shedd, Dogm. Theol., 1:499-515.

cp. Jn 1'.12

(*f*) The truth that man is the offspring of God implies the correlative truth of a common divine Fatherhood. God is Father of all men, in that he originates and sustains them as personal beings like in nature to himself. Even toward sinners God holds this natural relation of Father. It is his fatherly love, indeed, which provides the atonement. Thus the demands of holiness are met and the prodigal is restored to the privileges of sonship which have been forfeited by transgression. This natural Fatherhood, therefore, does not exclude, but prepares the way for, God's special Fatherhood toward those who have been regenerated by his Spirit and who have believed on his Son; indeed, since all God's creations take place in and through Christ, there is a natural and physical sonship of all men, by virtue of their relation to Christ, the eternal Son, which antedates and prepares the way for the spiritual sonship of those who join themselves to him by faith. Man's natural sonship underlies the history of the fall, and qualifies the doctrine of Sin.

Texts referring to God's natural and common Fatherhood are: Mal. 2:10—"Have we not all one father [Abraham]? hath not one God created us?" Luke 3:38—"Adam, the son of God"; 15:11-32—the parable of the prodigal son, In which the father is father even before the prodigal returns; John 3:16—"God so loved the world, that he gave his only begotten Son"; John 15:6—"If a man abide not in me, he is cast forth as a branch, and is withered; and they gather them, and cast them into the fire, and they are burned";—these words imply a natural union of all men with Christ,— otherwise they would teach that those who are spiritually united to him can perish everlastingly. Acts 17:28—"For we are also his offspring"— words addressed by Paul to a heathen audience; Col. 1:16, 17—"in him were all things created . . . and in him all things consist"; Heb. 12:9—"the Father of spirits." Fatherhood, in this larger sense, implies: 1. Origination; 2. Impartation of life; 3. Sustentation; 4. Likeness in faculties and powers; 5. Government; 6. Care; 7. Love. In all these respects God is the Father of all men, and his fatherly love is both preserving and atoning. God's natural fatherhood is mediated by Christ, through whom all things were made, and in whom all things, even humanity, consist. We are naturally children of God, as we were *created* in Christ; we are spiritually sons of God, as we have been *created anew* in Christ Jesus. G. W. Northrop: "God never *becomes* Father to any men or class of men; he only becomes a *reconciled* and *complacent* Father to those who become ethically like him. Men are not sons in the full ideal sense until they comport themselves as sons of God." Chapman, Jesus Christ and the Present Age, 39—"While God is the Father of all men, all men are not the children of God; in other words, God always realizes completely the idea of Father to every man; but the majority of men realize only partially the idea of sonship."

Texts referring to the special Fatherhood of grace are: John 1:12, 13—"as many as received him, to them gave he the right to become children of God, even to them that believe on his name; who were born, not of blood, nor of the will of the flesh, nor of the will of man, but of God"; Rom. 8:14—"for as many as are led by the Spirit of God, these are sons of God"; 15—"ye received the spirit of adoption, whereby we cry, Abba, Father"; II Cor. 6:17—"Come ye out from among them, and be ye separate, saith the Lord, and touch no unclean thing, and I will receive you, and will be to you a Father, and ye shall be to me sons and daughters, saith the Lord Almighty"; Eph. 1:5, 6—"having foreordained us unto adoption as sons through Jesus Christ unto himself"; 3:14, 15—"the Father, from whom every family [marg. 'fatherhood'] in heaven and on earth is named" (= every race among angels or men—so Meyer, Romans, 158, 159); Gal. 3:26—"for ye are all sons of God, through faith, in Christ Jesus"; 4:6—"And because ye are sons, God sent forth the Spirit of his Son into our hearts, crying, Abba, Father"; I John 3:1, 2—"Behold what manner of love the Father hath bestowed upon us, that we should be called children of God: and such we are. . . . Beloved, now are we children of God." The sonship of the race is only rudimentary. The actual realization of sonship is possible only through Christ. Gal. 4:1-7 intimates a universal sonship, but a sonship in which the child "differeth nothing from a bondservant though he is lord of all," and needs still to "receive the adoption of sons." Simon, Reconciliation, 81—"It is one thing to be a father; another to discharge all the fatherly functions. Human fathers sometimes fail to behave like fathers for reasons lying solely in themselves;

sometimes because of hindrances in the conduct or character of their children. No father can normally discharge his fatherly functions toward children who are unchildlike. So even the rebellious son is a son, but he does not act like a son." Because all men are naturally sons of God, it does not follow that all men will be saved. Many who are naturally sons of God are not spiritually sons of God; they are only "servants" who "abide not in the house forever" (John 8:35). God is their Father, but they have yet to "become" his children (Matt. 5:45).

The controversy between those who maintain and those who deny that God is the Father of all men is a mere logomachy. God is physically and naturally the Father of all men; he is morally and spiritually the Father only of those who have been renewed by his Spirit. All men are sons of God in a lower sense by virtue of their natural union with Christ; only those are sons of God in the higher sense who have joined themselves by faith to Christ in a spiritual union. We can therefore assent to much that is said by those who deny the universal divine fatherhood, as, for example, C. M. Mead, in Am. Jour. Theology, July, 1897:577-600, who maintains that sonship consists in spiritual kinship with God, and who quotes, in support of this view, John 8:41-44—"If God were your Father, ye would love me. . . . Ye are of your father, the devil" = the Fatherhood of God is not universal; Matt. 5:44, 45—"Love your enemies . . . in order that ye may become sons of your Father who is in heaven"; John 1:12—"as many as received him, to them gave he the right to become children of God, even to them that believe on his name." Gordon, Ministry of the Spirit, 103—"That God has created all men does not constitute them his sons in the evangelical sense of the word. The sonship on which the N.T. dwells so constantly is based solely on the experience of the new birth, while the doctrine of universal sonship rests either on a daring denial or a daring assumption—the denial of the universal fall of man through sin, or the assumption of the universal regeneration of man through the Spirit. In either case the teaching belongs to 'another gospel' (Gal. 1:7), the recompense of whose preaching is not a beatitude, but an 'anathema' (Gal. 1:8)."

But we can also agree with much that is urged by the opposite party, as for example, Wendt, Teaching of Jesus, 1:193—"God does not *become* the Father, but *is* the heavenly Father, even of those who become his sons. . . . This Fatherhood of God, instead of the kingship which was the dominant idea of the Jews, Jesus made the primary doctrine. The relation is ethical, not the Fatherhood of mere origination, and therefore only those who live aright are true sons of God. . . . 209—Mere kingship, or exaltation above the world, led to Pharisaic legal servitude and external ceremony and to Alexandrian philosophical speculation. The Fatherhood apprehended and announced by Jesus was essentially a relation of love and holiness." A. H. Bradford, Age of Faith, 116-120—"There is something sacred in humanity. But systems of theology once began with the essential and natural worthlessness of man. . . . If there is no Fatherhood, then selfishness is logical. But Fatherhood carries with it identity of nature between the parent and the child. Therefore every laborer is of the nature of God, and he who has the nature of God cannot be treated like the products of factory and field. . . . All the children of God are by nature partakers of the life of God. They are called 'children of wrath' (Eph. 2:3), or 'of perdition' (John 17:12), only to indicate that their proper relations and duties have been violated. . . . Love for man is dependent on something worthy of love, and that is found in man's essential divinity." We object to this last statement, as attributing to man at the beginning what can come to him only through grace. Man was indeed created in Christ (Col. 1:16) and was a son of God by virtue of his union with Christ (Luke 3:38; John 15:6). But since man has sinned and has renounced his sonship, it can be restored and realized, in a moral and spiritual sense, only through the atoning work of Christ and the regenerating work of the Holy Spirit (Eph. 2:10—"created in Christ Jesus for good works"; II Peter 1:4—"his precious and exceeding great promises; that through these ye may become partakers of the divine nature").

Many who deny the universal Fatherhood of God refuse to carry their doctrine to its logical extreme. To be consistent they should forbid the unconverted to offer the Lord's Prayer or even to pray at all. A mother who did not believe God to be the Father of all actually said: "My children are not converted, and if I were to teach them the Lord's Prayer, I must teach them to say: 'Our father who art in hell'; for they are only children of the devil." Papers on the question: Is God the Father of all Men? are to be found in the Proceedings of the Baptist Congress, 1896:106-136. Among these the essay of F. H. Rowley asserts God's universal Fatherhood upon the grounds: 1. Man is created in the image of God; 2. God's fatherly treatment of man, especially in the life of Christ among men; 3. God's universal claim on man for his filial love and trust; 4. Only God's Fatherhood makes incarnation possible, for this implies oneness of nature between God and man. To these we may add: 5. The atoning death of Christ could be efficacious only upon the ground of a common nature in Christ and in humanity; and 6. The regenerating work of the Holy Spirit is intelligible only as the restoration of a filial relation which was native to man, but which his sin had put into abeyance. For denial that God is Father to any but the regenerate, see Candlish, Fatherhood of God; Wright, Fatherhood of God. For advocacy of the universal Fatherhood, see Crawford, Fatherhood of God; Lidgett, Fatherhood of God.

# Man as God's Image

3

## Thomas Aquinas

*Scholastic*

## Made to the Image of God

*We proceed thus to the Sixth Article:* Whether the image of God is in man as regards the mind only?

*Objection* 1. It would seem that the image of God is not only in man's mind. For the Apostle says (I Cor. 11:7) that *the man is the image . . . of God.* But man is not only mind. Therefore the image of God is to be observed not only in his mind.

*Obj.* 2. Further, it is written (Gen. 1:27): *God created man to His own image; to the image of God He created him; male and female He created them.* But the distinction of male and female is in the body. Therefore the image of God is also in the body, and not only in the mind.

*Obj.* 3. Further, an image seems to apply principally to the shape of a thing. But shape belongs to the body. Therefore the image of God is to be seen in man's body also, and not in his mind.

*Obj.* 4. Further, according to Augustine (*Gen. ad lit.* xii.7, 24) there is a threefold vision in us, *corporeal, spiritual,* or imaginary, and *intellectual.* Therefore, if in the intellectual vision that belongs to the mind there exists in us a trinity by reason of which we are made to the image of God, for the like reason there must be another trinity in the others.

*On the contrary,* The Apostle says (Eph. 4:23, 24): *Be renewed in the spirit of your mind, and put on the new man.* Whence we are given to

From *Summa Theologica*, part 1, question 93, articles 6-8.

understand that our renewal which consists in putting on the new man, belongs to the mind. Now, he says (Col. 3:10): *Putting on the new* man; *him who is renewed unto knowledge* of God, *according to the image of Him that created him,* where the renewal which consists in putting on the new man is ascribed to the image of God. Therefore to be to the image of God belongs to the mind only.

*I answer that,* While in all creatures there is some kind of likeness to God, in the rational creature alone we find a likeness of *image* as we have explained above (AA. 1, 2); whereas in other creatures we find a likeness by way of a *trace.* Now the intellect or mind is that whereby the rational creature excels other creatures; wherefore this image of God is not found even in the rational creature except in the mind; while in the other parts, which the rational creature may happen to possess, we find the likeness of a˙ *trace,* as in other creatures to which, in reference to such parts, the rational creature can be likened. We may easily understand the reason of this if we consider the way in which a *trace,* and the way in which an *image,* represents anything. An *image* represents something by likeness in species, as we have said; while a *trace* represents something by way of an effect, which represents the cause in such a way as not to attain to the likeness of species. For imprints which are left by the movements of animals are called *traces:* so also ashes are a trace of fire, and desolation of the land a trace of a hostile army.

Therefore we may observe this difference between rational creatures and others, both as to the representation of the likeness of the Divine Nature in creatures, and as to the representation in them of the uncreated Trinity. For as to the likeness of the Divine Nature, rational creatures seem to attain, after a fashion, to the representation of the species, inasmuch as they imitate God, not only in being and life, but also in intelligence, as above explained (A. 2); whereas other creatures do not understand, although we observe in them a certain trace of the Intellect that created them, if we consider their disposition. Likewise, as the uncreated Trinity is distinguished by the procession of the Word from the Speaker, and of Love from both of these, as we have seen (Q. 28, A. 3); so we may say that in rational creatures wherein we find a procession of the word in the intellect, and a procession of the love in the will, there exists an image of the uncreated Trinity, by a certain representation of the species. In other creatures, however, we do not find the principle of the word, and the word and love; but we do see in them a certain trace of the existence of these in the Cause that produced them. For the fact that a creature has a modified and finite nature, proves that it proceeds from a principle; while its species points to the (mental) word of the maker, just as the shape of a house points to the idea of the architect; and order points to the maker's love by reason of which he directs the effect to a good end; as also the use of the house points to the will of the architect. So we find in man a likeness to God by way of an *image* in his mind; but in the other parts of his being by way of a *trace.*

*Reply Obj.* 1. Man is called the image of God; not that he is essentially an image; but that the image of God is impressed on his mind; as a coin is an image of the king, as having the image of the king. Wherefore there is no need to consider the image of God as existing in every part of man.

*Reply Obj.* 2. As Augustine says (*De Trin.* xii. 5), some have thought that the image of God was not in man individually, but severally. They held that *the man represents the Person of the Father; those born of man denote the person of the Son; and that the woman is a third person in likeness to the Holy Ghost, since she so proceeded from man as not to be his son or daughter.* All of this is manifestly absurd; first, because it would follow that the Holy Ghost is the principle of the Son, as the woman is the principle of the man's offspring; secondly, because one man would be only the image of one Person; thirdly, because in that case Scripture should not have mentioned the image of God in man until after the birth of the offspring. Therefore we must understand that when Scripture had said, *to the image of God He created him,* it added, *male and female He created them,* not to imply that the image of God came through the distinction of sex, but that the image of God belongs to both sexes, since it is in the mind, wherein there is no sexual distinction. Wherefore the Apostle (Col. 3:10) [Gal. 3:28], after saying, *According to the image of Him that created him,* added, *Where there is neither male nor female* (Vulg., *neither Gentile nor Jew*).

*Reply Obj.* 3. Although the image of God in man is not to be found in his bodily shape, yet because *the body of man alone among terrestrial animals is not inclined prone to the ground, but is adapted to look upward to heaven, for this reason we may rightly say that it is made to God's image and likeness, rather than the bodies of other animals,* as Augustine remarks (QQ. 83; qu. 51). But this is not to be understood as though the image of God were in man's body; but in the sense that the very shape of the human body represents the image of God in the soul by way of a trace.

*Reply Obj.* 4. Both in the corporeal and in the imaginary vision we may find a trinity, as Augustine says (*De Trin.* xi. 2). For in corporeal vision there is first the species of the exterior body; secondly, the act of vision, which occurs by the impression on the sight of a certain likeness of the said species; thirdly, the intention of the will applying the sight to see, and to rest on what is seen.

Likewise, in the imaginary vision we find first the species kept in the memory; secondly, the vision itself, which is caused by the penetrative power of the soul, that is, the faculty of imagination, informed by the species; and thirdly, we find the intention of the will joining both together. But each of these trinities falls short of the Divine image. For the species of the external body is extrinsic to the essence of the soul; while the species in the memory, though not extrinsic to the soul, is adventitious to it; and thus in both cases the species falls short of representing the con-naturality and co-eternity of the Divine Persons. The corporeal vision, too, does not proceed only from the species of the external body, but from this, and at the same time from the sense of the seer; in like manner imaginary vision is not from the species only which is preserved in the memory, but also from the imagination. For these reasons the procession of the Son from the Father alone is not suitably represented. Lastly the intention of the will joining the two together, does not proceed from them either in corporeal or spiritual vision. Wherefore the procession of the Holy Ghost from the Father and the Son is not thus properly represented.

*We proceed thus to the Seventh Article:* Whether the image of God is to be found in the acts of the soul?

*Objection* 1. It would seem that the image of God is not found in the acts of the soul. For Augustine says (*De Civ. Dei* xi. 26), that *man was made to God's image, inasmuch as we exist and know that we exist, and love this existence and knowledge.* But to exist does not signify an act. Therefore the image of God is not to be found in the soul's acts.

*Obj.* 2. Further, Augustine (*De Trin.* ix. 4) assigns God's image in the soul to these three things—mind, knowledge, and love. But mind does not signify an act, but rather the power or the essence of the intellectual soul. Therefore the image of God does not extend to the acts of the soul.

*Obj.* 3. Further, Augustine (*De Trin.* x. 11) assigns the image of the Trinity in the soul to *memory, understanding, and will.* But these three are *natural powers of the soul,* as the Master of the Sentences says (1 *Sent., D.* iii). Therefore the image of God is in the powers, and does not extend to the acts of the soul.

*Obj.* 4. Further, the image of the Trinity always remains in the soul. But an act does not always remain. Therefore the image of God does not extend to the acts.

**On the contrary,** Augustine (*De Trin.* xi. 2 *seqq.*) assigns the trinity in the lower part of the soul, in relation to the actual vision, whether sensible or imaginative. Therefore, also, the trinity in the mind, by reason of which man is like to God's image, must be referred to actual vision.

*I answer that,* As above explained (A. 2), a certain representation of the species belongs to the nature of an image. Hence, if the image of the Divine Trinity is to be found in the soul, we must look for it where the soul approaches the nearest to a representation of the species of the Divine Persons. Now the Divine Persons are distinct from each other by reason of the procession of the Word from the Speaker, and the procession of Love connecting Both. But in our soul word *cannot exist without actual thought,* as Augustine says (*De Trin.* xiv. 7). Therefore, first and chiefly, the image of the Trinity is to be found in the acts of the soul, that is, inasmuch as from the knowledge which we possess, by actual thought we form an internal word; and thence break forth into love. But, since the principles of acts are the habits and powers, and everything exists virtually in its principle, therefore, secondarily and consequently, the image of the Trinity may be considered as existing in the powers, and still more in the habits, forasmuch as the acts virtually exist therein.

*Reply Obj.* 1. Our being bears the image of God so far as it is proper to us, and excels that of the other animals, that is to say, in so far as we are endowed with a mind. Therefore, this trinity is the same as that which

Augustine mentions (*De Trin.* ix. 4), and which consists in mind, knowledge, and love.

*Reply Obj.* 2. Augustine observed this trinity, first, as existing in the mind. But because the mind, though it knows itself entirely in a certain degree, yet also in a way does not know itself—namely, as being distinct from others (and thus also it searches itself, as Augustine subsequently proves—*De Trin.* x. 3, 4); therefore, as though knowledge were not in equal proportion to mind, he takes three things in the soul which are proper to the mind, namely, memory, understanding, and will; which everyone is conscious of possessing; and assigns the image of the Trinity preeminently to these three, as though the first assignation were in part deficient.

*Reply Obj.* 3. As Augustine proves (*De Trin.* xiv. 7), we may be said to understand, will, and to love certain things, both when we actually consider them, and when we do not think of them. When they are not under our actual consideration, they are objects of our memory only, which, in his opinion, is nothing else than habitual retention of knowledge and love [cf. Q. 79, A. 7, *ad* 1]. *But since,* as he says, *a word cannot be there without actual thought (for we think everything that we say, even if we speak with that interior word belonging to no nation's tongue), this image chiefly consists in these three things, memory, understanding, and will. And by understanding I mean here that whereby we understand with actual thought; and by will, love, or dilection I mean that which unites this child with its parent.* From which it is clear that he places the image of the Divine Trinity more in actual understanding and will, than in these as existing in the habitual retention of the memory; although even thus the image of the Trinity exists in the soul in a certain degree, as he says in the same place. Thus it is clear that memory, understanding, and will are not three powers as stated in the *Sentences.*

*Reply Obj.* 4. Someone might answer by referring to Augustine's statement (*De Trin.* xiv. 6), that *the mind ever remembers itself, ever understands itself, ever loves itself;* which some take to mean that the soul ever actually understands, and loves itself. But he excludes this interpretation by adding that *it does not always think of itself as actually distinct from other things.* Thus it is clear that the soul always understands and loves itself, not actually but habitually; though we might say that by perceiving its own act, it understands itself whenever it understands anything. But since it is not always actually understanding, as in the case of sleep, we must say that these acts, although not always actually existing, yet ever exist in their principles, the habits and powers. Wherefore, Augustine says (*De Trin.* xiv. 4): *If the rational soul is made to the image of God in the sense that it can make use of reason and intellect to understand and consider God, then the image of God was in the soul from the beginning of its existence.*

*We proceed thus to the Eighth Article:* Whether the image of the divine Trinity is in the soul only by comparison with God as its object?

*Objection* 1. It would seem that the image of the Divine Trinity is in the soul not only by comparison with God as its object. For the image of the Divine Trinity is to be found in the soul, as shown above (A. 7), according as the word in us proceeds from the speaker; and love from both. But this is to be found in us as regards any object. Therefore the image of the Divine Trinity is in our mind as regards any object.

*Obj.* 2. Further, Augustine says (*De Trin.* xii. 4) that *when we seek trinity in the soul, we seek it in the whole of the soul, without separating the process of reasoning in temporal matters from the consideration of things eternal.* Therefore the image of the Trinity is to be found in the soul, even as regards temporal objects.

*Obj.* 3. Further, it is by grace that we can know and love God. If, therefore, the image of the Trinity is found in the soul by reason of the memory, understanding, and will or love of God, this image is not in man by nature but by grace, and thus is not common to all.

*Obj.* 4. Further, the saints in heaven are most perfectly conformed to the image of God by the beatific vision; wherefore it is written (II Cor. 3:18): *We . . . are transformed into the same image from glory to glory.* But temporal things are known by the beatific vision. Therefore the image of God exists in us even according to temporal things.

**On the contrary,** Augustine says (*De Trin.* xiv. 12): *The image of God exists in the mind, not because it has a remembrance of itself, loves itself, and understands itself; but because it can also remember, understand, and love God by Whom it was made.* Much less, therefore, is the image of God in the soul, in respect of other objects.

*I answer that,* As above explained (AA. 2, 7), image means a likeness which in some degree, however small, attains to a representation of the species. Wherefore we need to seek in the image of the Divine Trinity in the soul some kind of representation of species of the Divine Persons, so far as this is possible to a creature. Now the Divine Persons, as above stated (AA. 6, 7), are distinguished from each other according to the procession of the word from the speaker, and the procession of love from both. Moreover the Word of God is born of God by the knowledge of Himself; and Love proceeds from God according as He loves Himself. But it is clear that diversity of objects diversifies the species of word and love; for in the human mind the species of a stone is specifically different from that of a horse, while also the love regarding each of them is specifically different. Hence we refer the Divine image in man to the verbal concept born of the knowledge of God, and to the love derived therefrom. Thus the image of God is found in the soul according as the soul turns to God, or possesses a nature that enables it to turn to God. Now the mind may turn towards an object in two ways: directly and immediately, or indirectly and mediately; as, for instance, when anyone sees a man reflected in a looking-glass he may be said to be turned towards that man. So Augustine says (*De Trin.* xiv. 8), that *the mind remembers itself, understands itself, and loves itself. If we perceive this, we perceive a trinity, not, indeed, God, but, nevertheless, rightly called the image of God.* But this is due to the fact, not that the mind reflects on itself absolutely, but that thereby it can furthermore turn to God, as appears from the authority quoted above (Arg. *On the contrary*).

*Reply Obj.* 1. For the notion of an image it is not enough that something proceed from another, but it is also necessary to observe what proceeds and whence it proceeds; namely, that what is Word of God proceeds from knowledge of God.

*Reply Obj.* 2. In all the soul we may see a kind of trinity, not, however, as though besides the action of temporal things and the contemplation of eternal things, *any third thing should be required to make up the trinity,* as he adds in the same passage. But in that part of the reason which is concerned with temporal things, *although a trinity may be found; yet the image of God is not to be seen there,* as he says farther on; forasmuch as this knowledge of temporal things is adventitious to the soul. Moreover even the habits whereby temporal things are known are not always present; but sometimes they are actually present, and sometimes present only in memory even after they begin to exist in the soul. Such is clearly the case with faith, which comes to us temporally for this present life; while in the future life faith will no longer exist, but only the remembrance of faith.

*Reply Obj.* 3. The meritorious knowledge and love of God can be in us only by grace. Yet there is a certain natural knowledge and love as seen above (Q. 12, A. 12; Q. 56, A. 3; Q. 60, A. 5). This, too, is natural that the mind, in order to understand God, can make use of reason, in which sense we have already said that the image of God abides ever in the soul; *whether this image of God be so obsolete,* as it were clouded, *as almost to amount to nothing,* as in those who have not the use of reason; *or obscured and disfigured,* as in sinners; or *clear and beautiful,* as in the just; as Augustine says (*De Trin.* xiv. 6).

*Reply Obj.* 4. By the vision of glory temporal things will be seen in God Himself; and such a vision of things temporal will belong to the image of God. This is what Augustine means (*ibid.*), when he says that *in that nature to which the mind will blissfully adhere, whatever it sees it will see as unchangeable;* for in the Uncreated Word are the types of all creatures.

4

## Emil Brunner

## Man and Creation   *Relational*

### The Starting-Point

As we shall see, we shall do justice to this postulate by holding firmly
to our theological canon, namely: that in all theological statements about
the divine revelation we must begin with Jesus Christ, as the Word of God
Incarnate, and that we are not bound by any Biblical passages taken in
isolation, and certainly not by isolated sections of the Old Testament.
Here too the method which has already proved fruitful in the doctrine of
Creation will show us the way out of a difficulty which has only arisen out
of a mistaken view of the Bible, and for the same reason is constantly
repeated.

As, in the doctrine of Creation, we gave up any idea of starting from
the Old Testament account of Creation, and decided to begin with the
New Testament witness to Creation in the Prologue to the Gospel of John,
so we must do the same here with the doctrine of Man. When we do this,
we shall see that the difficulties caused by the idea of the Creation of the
world in Six Days, the idea of a Primitive State, and of an "Adam in
Paradise," vanish into thin air. Thus we see that fidelity to this theological

From *The Christian Doctrine of Creation and Redemption,* trans. Olive
Wyon (Philadelphia: Westminster Press, 1952), pp. 53-63. Used by permission.

principle, which we believe to be sound, sets us free from problems caused by the fact that we had been, theologically, on the wrong line. This conclusion is confirmed by the fact that this view lessens the tension between the modern and the ancient view of the world; in fact, it is now seen that the change of outlook does not really affect the fundamental Biblical truth, and it certainly does not need a prominent place in our discussion. In so doing it is, of course, understood . . . that we shall gain a great deal of truth from the testimony of the Old Testament in spite of its mythical form. Thus we shall not gather up all the anthropological statements of the Bible and set them out, in order, as is usually done, so as to construct Christian anthropology as a doctrinal whole, but we shall start from the centre, from the revelation of God in Jesus Christ; we shall then ask ourselves what this teaches us about man; then we shall introduce particular statements about man from the Old and the New Testaments, interpreted in the light of this central truth, in order to complete and confirm it.[1]

Our Christo-centric method would be misunderstood, however, if we were to deduce from it that the first thing we have to do is to establish a doctrine of the Humanity of Christ. To look at man *in the light* of Jesus Christ is not the same thing as knowing Jesus Christ. Here our concern is with anthropology, not with Christology, even if this anthropology, like every other doctrine within Christian dogma as a whole, must have a Christological foundation. Jesus Christ as the Word of God Incarnate is here not the object, but the source and norm of truth.[2]

### Man as Creature

To meet God the Lord means that we acknowledge that we are creatures. It may seem tautological to say: To know God the Creator means to know ourselves as creatures. But this tautology expresses the truth: that the knowledge of God as Creator, and the knowledge of ourselves as creatures, are correlative truths. We cannot know the one without the other. Since God the Lord meets me in Jesus Christ I know that He is Creator, and that I am His creature. And conversely: I only know that I am a creature in this encounter. There may be a *general* sense of religious "creatureliness,"[3] it is true, a sense of weakness, of transience, of nothingness. But to the extent in which this "divine" is not the real Creator I do not know myself truly as a creature. Not every feeling of impotence and nothingness means knowledge of one's nature as a creature. I know that I am a creature because I know of the Creator, and I know of the Creator because I know and recognize the fact that I am a creature.

This knowledge of, and this recognition of, our "creatureliness" is not something we can take for granted. The more that man is able to distinguish himself from the rest of creation, the more he becomes conscious of himself as subject, as an "I," to whom the whole world is Object, the more does he tend to confuse himself with God, to confuse his spirit with the Spirit of God, and to regard his reason as divine reason. The "I" philosophy of India, the Greek doctrine of the divine νοῦς, and modern

Idealism, all confirm this statement. It is only the man who has not yet become aware of his nature as a spiritual being, who still regards himself as one object among many others, who thinks it is easy to reject the temptation to become like God. The man who has no spiritual view thinks it is ridiculous that man could possibly confuse himself with God. But the more fully developed man becomes in mind and spirit, the more clearly he makes a distinction between persons and things, the more is he inclined to identify the human and the divine Subject. Indeed, from Heraclitus onwards, Western philosophy—when untouched by materialism—has made repeated attempts to achieve this identification, while Indian philosophy has not hesitated to go all lengths—in its pantheism. Further, where man *thinks* God by his own efforts, and does not meet the God who reveals Himself, in the last resort he cannot help achieving this identification, although he may qualify his theory in many directions. It is only the encounter with the Living God which eliminates this error.

It is not—at least not primarily—the fact that the human Self is connected with a material body, like that of the lower animals, which makes clear the absurdity of the illusion of divinity. The desire to deify the Self has always made short work of this fact of the connexion with the body. The body, the animal nature with the senses, does not belong—so they say—really to "me" at all. It is a prison into which I have somehow or other fallen, a tomb, a shadow, a "double," a relic, an illusion; in short it is not the "true Self" which is the spirit. Thus it is not the perception of the connexion with the body which impels man to recognize that he is a creature, and not the Creator, but conversely, it is because he admits his "creatureliness," that he knows, in faith, that the body is really part of him, and is not an alien addition. He becomes aware of his creatureliness not through the perception of his corporeality, but through the fact that God, when He confronts him as Lord, claims him wholly for Himself. As a creature "I" belong wholly to God; I am not independent and free, but I am a being who is derived from, and made for, God. This perception of what it means to be a "creature" does not deny our freedom, but it springs from the fact that our freedom is founded in God, and is limited by that. The belief in Creation does not deny that man is different from the world; rather it acknowledges this when it says that man has been created in the Image of God; this means, however, that we cannot speak of our "creatureliness" without dealing at the same time with the truth that man has been created in the Image of God.

## The Image of God and Creation

This truth also must be understood from the point of view of the New Testament, and not primarily from that of the Old Testament; that is, we must start from the Centre. In Jesus Christ God meets me as the One who imparts Himself to me in freedom, since as Holy Love He claims me wholly for Himself. It is as such that He reveals Himself to me. But the fact that He so reveals Himself to me means that He also at the same time reveals myself to me: that is, He shows me my relation to Himself. He is the One who wills to have from me a free response to His love, a response which gives back love for love, a living echo, a living reflection of His glory. I cannot meet the holy loving God in Christ without knowing this about myself. Once more, both are correlated and connected; to be aware of the holy Loving God, and to be aware of the fact that my nature is created by God, comes to the same thing. It is thus, and not otherwise, that I am intended to be by the Creator. This generous will which claims me, of the God who wills to glorify Himself, and to impart Himself, is the cause of my being, and the fundamental reason for my being what I am, and as I am. Now we must go into some particular points in greater detail.

(*a*) God, who wills to glorify Himself and to impart Himself, wills man to be a creature who responds to His call of love with a grateful, responsive love. God wills to possess man as a free being. God wills a creature which is not only, like other creatures, a mere object of His will, as if it were a reflector of His glory as Creator. He desires from us an active and spontaneous response in our "reflecting"; He who creates through the Word, who as Spirit creates in freedom, wills to have a "reflex" which is more than a "reflex," which is an answer to His Word, a free spiritual act, a correspondence to His speaking. Only thus can His love really impart itself as love. For love can only impart itself where it is received in love. Hence the heart of the creaturely existence of man is freedom, selfhood, to be an "I," a person. Only an "I" can answer a "Thou," only a Self which is self-determining can freely answer God. An automaton does not respond; an animal, in contradistinction from an automaton, may indeed *re*-act, but it cannot *re*-spond. It is not capable of speech, of free self-determination, it cannot stand at a distance from itself, and is therefore not *re*-sponsible.

The free Self, capable of self-determination, belongs to the original constitution of man as created by God. But from the very outset this freedom is limited. It is not primary but secondary. Indeed, it does not posit itself—like the Self of Idealism—but it is posited; it is not *a se* but *a Deo*. Hence although man's answer is free, it is also limited. God wills my freedom, it is true, because He wills to glorify Himself, and to give Himself. He wills my freedom in order to make this answer possible; my freedom is therefore, from the outset, a responsible one. Responsibility is *restricted* freedom, which distinguishes human from divine freedom; and it is a restriction which is also *free*—and this distinguishes our human limited freedom from that of the rest of creation. The animals, and God, have no responsibility—the animals because they are below the level of responsibility, and God, because He is above it; the animals because they have no freedom, and God because He has absolute freedom. Man, however, has a limited freedom. This is the heart of his being as man, and it is the "condition" on which he possesses freedom. In other words, this limited human freedom is the very purpose for which man has been created: he possesses *this* "freedom" in order that he may respond to God, in such a way that through this response God may glorify Himself, and give Himself to His creature.

(*b*) Now, however, it is of the essence of this responsible freedom that its purpose may or may not be fulfilled. This open question is the consequence of freedom. Thus it is part of the divinely created nature of man that it should have both a formal and a material aspect. The fact that man must respond, that he is responsible, is fixed; no amount of human freedom, nor of the sinful misuse of freedom, can alter this fact. Man is, and remains, responsible, whatever his personal attitude to his Creator may be. He may deny his responsibility, and he may misuse his freedom, but he cannot get rid of his responsibility. Responsibility is part of the unchangeable structure of man's being. That is: the actual existence of man—of every man, not only the man who believes in Christ—consists in the positive fact that he has been *made* to respond—to God.

Whatever kind of response man may make to the call of the Creator—in any case he does respond, even if his reply is: "I do not know any Creator, and I will not obey any God." Even this answer *is* an answer, and it comes under the inherent law of responsibility. This formal essential structure cannot be lost. It is identical with human existence as such, and indeed with the quality of being which all human beings possess equally; it only ceases where true human living ceases—on the borderline of imbecility or madness.

In the Old Testament, the Bible describes this formal aspect of human nature by the concept of "being made in the image of God." In the thought of the Old Testament the fact that man has been "made in the Image of God" means something which man can never lose; even when he sins he cannot lose it.[4] This conception is therefore unaffected by the contrast between sin and grace, or sin and obedience, precisely because it describes the "formal" or "structural," and not the "material" aspect of human nature. Then how is it possible to perceive reflected similarity in this formal likeness to God? The similarity consists in being "subject," being "person," freedom. Certainly, man has only a limited freedom, because he is responsible, but he *has* freedom; only so *can* he be responsible. Thus the formal aspect of man's nature, as a being "made in the image of God," denotes his being as Subject, or his freedom; it is this which differentiates man from the lower creation; this constitutes his specifically *human* quality; it is this which is given to him—and to him alone—and under all circumstances—by Divine appointment.

The New Testament simply presupposes this fact that man—in his very nature—has been "made in the image of God"; it does not develop this any further. To the Apostles what matters most is the "material" realization of this God-given quality; that is, that man should really give *the* answer which the Creator intends, the response in which God is honoured, and in which He fully imparts Himself, the response of reverent, grateful love, given not only in words, but in his whole life. The New Testament, in *its* doctrine of the *Imago Dei,* tells us that this right answer has not been given; that a quite different one has been given instead, in which the glory is not given to God, but to men and to creatures, in which man does not live in the love of God, but seeks himself. Secondly, the New Testament is the proclamation of what God has done in order that He may turn this false answer into the true one.

Here, therefore, the fact that man has been "made in the image of God" is spoken of as having been lost, and indeed as wholly, and not partially lost. Man no longer possesses this *Imago Dei;* but it is restored through Him, through whom God glorifies and gives Himself: through Jesus Christ. The restoration of the *Imago Dei,* the new creation of the original image of God in man, is identical with the gift of God in Jesus Christ received by faith.[5]

The *Imago Dei* in the New Testament, "material" sense of the word, is identical with "being-in-the-Word" of God. This means that man does not possess his true being in himself, but in God. Thus it is not a fact which can be discovered in man, something which can be found through intro- spection. It is not the "Thou" of Idealistic philosophy, but it is the "I" derived from the "Thou." Hence it cannot be understood by looking at man, but only by looking at God, or, more exactly, by looking at the Word of God. To be true man, man must not be "himself," and in order to understand his true being he must not look at himself. Our true being is *"extra nos et alienum nobis"* (Luther); it is "eccentric" and "ecstatic"; man is only truly human when he is in God. Then, and then only, is he truly "himself."

From the standpoint of sinful man the *Imago Dei* is existence in Jesus Christ, the Word made flesh. Jesus Christ is the true *Imago Dei,* which man regains when through faith he is "in Jesus Christ." Faith in Jesus Christ is therefore the *restauratio imaginis,* because He restores to us that existence in the Word of God which we had lost through sin. When man enters into the love of God revealed in Christ he becomes truly human. True human existence is existence in the love of God. Thus also the true freedom of man is complete dependence upon God. *Deo servire libertas* (Augustine). The words "Whose service is perfect freedom" express the essence of Christian faith. True humanity is not genius but love, that love which man does not possess from or in himself but which he receives from God, who is love. True humanity does not spring from the full development of human potentialities, but it arises through the reception, the perception, and the acceptance of the love of God, and it develops and is preserved by "abiding" in communion with the God who reveals Himself as Love. Hence separation from God, sin, is the loss of the true human quality, and the destruction of the quality of "being made in the Image of God." When the heart of man no longer reflects the love of God, but himself and the world, he no longer bears the "Image of God," which simply consists in the fact that God's love is reflected in the human heart.

Since through faith in Jesus Christ man once more receives God's Primal Word of love, once more the divine Image (*Urbild*) is reflected in him,[6] the lost *Imago Dei* is restored. The *Imago Dei,* in the sense of true humanity—not in the sense of formal or structural humanity—is thus iden- tical with the true attitude of man in relation to God, in accordance with God's purpose in Creation. Your attitude to God determines what you are.

If your attitude towards God is "right," in harmony with the purpose of Creation, that is, if in faith you receive the love of God, then you *are* right; if your attitude to God is wrong, then *you* are wrong, as a whole.

It is evident that our thought will become terribly muddled if the two ideas of the *Imago Dei*—the "formal" and "structural" one of the Old Testament, and the "material" one of the New Testament—are either confused with one another, or treated as identical. The result will be: either that we must deny that the sinner possesses the quality of humanity at all; or, that which makes him a human being must be severed from the *Imago Dei;* or, the loss of the *Imago* in the material sense must be regarded merely as an obscuring, or a partial corruption of the *Imago,* which lessens the heinousness of sin. All these three false solutions disappear once the distinction is rightly made.

(*c*) The process of making this distinction aright, however, is made more difficult by the fact that in both instances the fact that man has been made in the Image of God is conceived not as a self-existing substance but as a relation. And this is the most important point to grasp. Responsibility is a relation; it is not a substance. If, on the contrary, as in the Catholic tradition, the *Imago Dei* is conceived in the formal structural sense as the endowment with reason, as creative freedom, then Man possesses the Image of God *in himself. This* view of the *Imago Dei* is the gate by which a pantheistic or an idealistic deification of man can enter. Man then possesses the divine reason in himself; his spirit is then a "spark" from the Divine Spirit. He has "divinity within himself"; *"est Deus in Nobis."* Then the Divine element in man, and the destiny of man, will consist in this participation in the divine reason; then man will only need to become aware of this divine reason within himself, by making a clear distinction between it and that other lower part of his nature, which is non-divine, the body. The result of this erroneous conception of the *Imago Dei*—as substance and not as relation—is a mistakenly "spiritualized" view of man and his destiny.

It is, however, difficult for us to combine the ideas of "structure" and "relation." And yet it is the distinctive quality of human existence that its "structure" is a "relation": responsible existence, responsive actuality. The Biblical testimony on this point is ruthlessly logical; man is the being who stands "before God," even if he is godless. The fact that man, misusing his freedom and denying his responsibility, turns his back on God, does not mean that he no longer stands "before God." On the contrary, he stands "before God" as a sinner; he stands before God in a wrong attitude, hence he is "under the wrath of God." We shall be dealing with this point later on; here all I want to do is this: to make it clear that the loss of the *Imago,* in the material sense, does not remove responsibility from man; he still stands "before God," and he is still a human being. Only human beings can be sinners; to be a sinner it is necessary to possess that quality which distinguishes man from the animals. The loss of the *Imago,* in the material sense, presupposes the *Imago* in the formal sense. To be a sinner is the negative way of being responsible.

(*d*) We must note, however, that necessary as it is for us to think of the *Imago Dei* with this distinction between the formal and material aspect, from the point of view of the divine Creation it does not exist. God calls man into existence in order that he may respond to Him aright—not in order that he may respond wrongly or rightly. Man is not destined to choose between faith and unbelief, obedience and disobedience; God has made man in such a way that he can respond as God wills Him to do. A certain freedom of choice, which makes this response possible, only becomes visible when the wrong response has been made. Formal freedom, severed from material freedom, from existence in the love of God, is already a result of sin. Man ought to know nothing of this freedom save in the form of the generous love of God. The fact that he is aware of this freedom of choice is already the effect of sin, and of separation from his connexion with God.[7] We shall be seeing later that this is the origin of the contrast between the Law and the Gospel. Responsibility, severed from the generous grace of the Creator, can only be understood as legal responsibility. Legal responsibility is therefore already a result of the false autonomy of man, and has a correlative relation to it.

From the side of God, therefore, this distinction between the "formal" and the "material" does not exist; it is not legally valid. But it does exist—wrongly. This means that when we look at the *Imago Dei* from our angle, that is, the angle of sinful man, it necessarily appears under this twofold aspect of the "formal," that is, the responsibility which cannot be lost, and the "material," lost destiny, lost "existence in the love of God." This is why, when man meets God in Jesus Christ, he must hear both the Law and the Gospel—the Law which makes him responsible for sin, without, however, making him able to fulfil it, and the Gospel, which gives him existence in the love of God, without law, through faith.

### Man as Embodied Spirit

It is a well-known fact, at least within the Christian Church, and among readers of the Bible, that the Bible understands man as a whole, as an entity consisting of "soul" or "spirit" and "body." The Biblical view leaves no room for the dualistic notion that though the "spirit" (or "soul") is of divine origin and divine in character, the body on the other hand is something lower and inferior. But it is less well-known *why* the Bible takes this view. Whence comes this dignity given to the body as something created by, and therefore willed by God? We have already suggested the answer to this important question, when we said how difficult it is for man to understand himself as a "creature." The man who does not know the Creator is always trying either to deny God, or to regard his physical nature as something which does not really belong to him, in order to be able to maintain the divinity of his "real" spiritual nature.

The natural man is always either an Idealist or a Materialist; an Idealist who regards his spirit as part of the divine Spirit; a Materialist, who, owing to his corporeal nature, regards himself merely as a "more highly developed animal," and denies his higher eternal destiny. It seems to him impossible that body and spirit[8] can come equally from God.

In point of fact—how can he possibly understand this? Of himself, he cannot know the Creator. The Creator only permits Himself to be known through revelation as the Lord who meets man. As the Lord who meets man, however, He is One who claims me in the totality of my existence, who claims me as I am, body and soul. If He is the Creator of the *World*, He is also the Creator of the *body*. The God whom man invents for himself has no relation to the material world and to human corporeality. From the point of view of faith in the Creator, the material body, and matter as such, are the distinctive marks of the created, as opposed to the uncreated existence of the Creator. The physical nature of man is therefore the sign, the concrete expression of the creaturely nature of man, of the fact that he is not God. But the fact that man is not God does not mean that he is without God. Man as soul-and-body has therefore been created to glorify God; hence, conversely, the highest self-communication of God is the Incarnation of the Word in a man of flesh and blood. For one who meets the Incarnate Word of God, it is no longer possible to despise the body, and to regard his spiritual nature as divine, but his physical nature as something foreign to God. For him, the body is "the temple of the Holy Spirit."[9]

The relation of body and soul is determined by the divine revelation in the Incarnate Word. Indeed, the fact that man has been made in the image of God implies that the body is equally the means of expression, and the instrument, of the spirit and the will. The body, this definite body, has been given to man by the Creator, in order that in it he may express his higher calling and make its realization concrete.[10] The body which God has created for man is full of the symbolism of his divine-human destiny, and is admirably suited for its realization.

The spirit, on the other hand, is that aspect of human nature by means of which man can perceive his divine destiny and, knowing and recognizing this, can receive it, and transmit it to the body, as the instrument through which it is accomplished. The spirit receives the Word of God, as it is the Spirit[11] of God which speaks to it within the human spirit. The Spirit of God "beareth witness with our spirit that we are children of God." It is significant that this passage suggests that the actual "place" where God reveals Himself to man, and the place where man realizes his responsibility for sin, is not the "spirit," apart from the body, but the "place" where "spirit" and "body" are one, that is, the "heart." This is in harmony with the fact that God's Word never comes to us as a purely spiritual word, but is always mediated to us through physical means as a spiritual message, as a word that is spoken with the lips, and that the perfect revelation of God took place through the Incarnation of the Word. It is not in an abstract spirituality, but in a spirituality of faith, connected with the body, that man receives the divine self-revelation. As He is the God who wills to reveal Himself *through* the world, and in the world, so He creates a creature in His likeness, which by nature is a unity of body and soul. The divine love in its self-revelation can only be received by "the heart," by the heart which is destined to love. This throws a light also upon the fact of sexual polarity.

## Notes

[1] Excellent material for this procedure is provided by (*a*) Eichrodt, *Das Menschenverständnis des Alten Testaments,* and (*b*) Kümmel, *Das Bild des Menschen im Neuen Testament.*

[2] This second way, here rejected, is taken by Karl Barth, *K.D.*, III, 2, but it does not lead to any result which contradicts my main argument.

[3] Cf. Otto, *The Idea of the Holy.*

[4] Cf. the article on εἰκών (by V. Rad) in Kittel's *Th. Wb. z. N.T.*, II, pp. 387ff., and also K. Barth, *K.D.*, III, I, pp. 224ff.

[5] II Cor. 3:18; Rom. 8:29; Eph. 4:24; Col. 3:10.

[6] This is precisely what is said in II Cor. 3:18.

[7] This is the theological meaning of the prohibition of the knowledge of good and evil—addressed to Adam in Paradise.

[8] Here, and in other places in this chapter, "spirit" (*Geist*) = "personal being" (*Tr.*).

[9] I Cor. 6:19.

[10] I Cor. 6:20.

[11] Rom. 8:16.

# 5

**Leonard Verduin**

*Functional View* (handwritten)

# A Dominion-Haver

In the Christian view of things man is a creature in possession of the prerogative of dominion-having. Dominion-having is definitive of man as he is portrayed in the Christian Scriptures.

This is apparent already in the divine soliloquy concerning the creature man. We read, in Genesis 1:26, of a plan taking shape in the mind of the Creator: "Let us make man in our image, after our likeness, and let them have dominion over the fish of the sea, and over the birds of the air, and over every creeping thing that creeps upon the earth."

Here we have the blueprint according to which man was to be constructed. Here is the conception of the Great Artificer when man was as yet nothing more than a twinkle in the eyes of God. Central in it is the idea of dominion-having.

When the Creator has acted upon this impulse to make a creature "in His own likeness, having dominion," we find Him, in verse 28, addressing the creature He has just made, in His first word to it, as follows: "Be fruitful and multiply and fill the earth and have dominion over the fish of

From *Somewhat Less Than God* (Grand Rapids: William B. Eerdmans, 1970), pp. 27-48. Used by permission.

the sea, the birds of the air, and over every living thing that moves upon the earth." Again the idea of dominion-having stands out as the central feature. That man is a creature meant for dominion-having and that as such he is in the image of his Maker—this is the burden of the creation account given in the book of Genesis, the Book of Origins. It is the central point the writer of this account wanted to make.

And we have evidence that he made it. Men have realized from the beginning that this was the heart of the matter. The writer of Psalm 8, for instance, was certainly a person who knew the Genesis account; he not only knew it but also knew what was central in it. He wrote, as he contemplated the creature known as man: "What is man that thou art mindful of him, and the son of man that thou dost care for him? Yet thou hast made him little less than God, and dost crown him with glory and honor. Thou hast given him dominion over the works of thy hands; thou hast put all things under his feet, all sheep and oxen, and also the beasts of the field, the birds of the air, and the fish of the sea, and whatsoever passes through the paths of the sea." As he contemplates man thus clothed with the prerogative of dominion-having he cries out in admiration of the One who made things thus: "O Lord, our Lord, how majestic is thy name in all the earth!" For this ancient poet the majesty of the "name" of God (by the "name" of God is meant, as John Calvin saw so very correctly, that which is known of God by virtue of His self-disclosure) becomes apparent in the fact that the Great Dominion-haver (for that is the meaning of "Lord, our Lord") has made a creature "a little less than God," a creature sharing in the divine attribute of dominion-having, a creature that reflects in a creaturely way one of the definitive attributes of the Maker Himself, the attribute of dominion-having. . . .

The word *dominion* is related to the Latin word *dominus;* and a *dominus* is one who has achieved mastery, who has overcome; he is one who has gained the upper hand; he has come out on top. To exercise dominion in the given situation is to fasten one's will upon that situation; to exercise dominion is to subordinate, render subject, make subservient.

Man is therefore by definition a subordinator; and he is this because he was made in the image and after the likeness of the Great Subordinator. In the Christian perspective man is the subduer of the rest of creaturedom, and as such he is the creaturely version of the Great Subduer. God is the archetype in the matter of dominion-having and man is the ectype.

This, as we have already said, is the big news in the Story of Origins. It may even be said that all the rest of the story has *this* as its purpose and objective. The story of the coming-into-being of the rest of creaturedom, of plants, of plying things, of land animals, is told because they are to constitute the domain of the dominion-haver; they are the subjects, and their coming-into-being is related because the writer of the account has on his mind the story of the coming-into-being of the creature intended to be their conqueror.

As we have had occasion to say, the Genesis account is not so much a cosmogony (a recital of the coming-into-being of the cosmos) as an anthropogeny (a recital of the coming-into-being of man). And the author of the account given in Genesis 1 brings in man, as the dominion-haver, at the very end of his story, where it would seem to belong logically. However, the author of the account given in Genesis 2 (whether the two accounts are from one and the same hand or not is a question that does not need to detain us here) throws the matter of chronology to the winds; he *begins* the account with the creation of man. He writes: "In the day that the Lord God made the earth and the heavens, when no plant of the field was as yet in the earth and no herb of the field had as yet sprung up (for the Lord God had not caused it to rain upon the earth and there was no man to till the ground, but a mist went up from the earth and watered the whole face of the ground), then the Lord God formed man of the dust of the ground, and breathed into his nostrils the breath of life; and man became a living soul. And the Lord God planted a garden . . . and there he put the man whom he had formed. And out of the ground the Lord God made to grow every tree that is pleasant to the sight and good for food. . . ."

Here we have the dominion-haver introduced *before* mention is made of the domain over which he was set to rule. Why the author of the second account saw fit thus to invert the order we are not told, but we may surmise that he departed from what was probably the true historic order (departed, that is, from the order of the earlier account) because he wanted to throw the full light, at once and at the outset, upon the central actor in the world of created things, upon man, the dominion-haver. For that reason, it seems, he saw fit to begin his story with the account of the coming-into-being of man. In order to give to man his rightful place in the creatural order the author of this ancient account allows himself something akin to literary license.

Now that we have this example of literary license before us, we may perhaps be pardoned for bringing up a second example of it. Although the account of Genesis 1 has man existing as male and female from the very beginning—so that there is even a directive concerning the bisexual reproductive process—the writer of the second account allows himself to depart from this representation. He has a human being of the male sex existing *in solo* for some time. We read of a garden planted—bounded by four watercourses that were identifiable to his readers; the so-called Trial Command is given; God forms beast and bird and causes these to parade before the man "to see what he would name them," each kind filing past in its male and its female version. This makes the man's aloneness to stand out, an aloneness which the divine Onlooker judges to be "not good." Acting on this appraisal of the man's aloneness, God causes him to fall into a "deep sleep," a sleep during which (whether the reference is to a rest-sleep or to a vision-sleep is open to discussion; the verb used suggests the latter alternative) the defect in the man's mode of existence is bettered, in that a second exemplar of man (this time in female version) comes to stand over against the man. He awakes and calls her *ishshah,* man-ess. The story ends with the remark that this precedent sets the pattern for the cohabitation of a man and a woman. What are we to make of this sequence? Is this literal history? Or is this another attempt on the part of the ancient scribe to get an idea across to his reader, the idea that man is a creature intended for interpersonal relationships, of which marriage is the classic example and epitome? If so, then the whole tale of the sleep and of the rib is an embroidery on the theme that "it is not good for the man to be alone." And then it speaks volumes that the help-meet-for-him was derived from the man's costal region; not from his head as if to be his ruler, nor from his feet as if to be his slave, but from his side so as to be his companion and partner. If this is the point of the story, then it would be an error to make too much of sequence and procedure. Just so would it be an error to make too much of the sequence and procedure of the second account's recording of the coming-into-being of man, the crown and capstone of God's creative enterprise.

As we have already intimated, the idea that man is by definition a dominion-haver is a potent one. It has had a mighty and incalculably great influence upon any and all who have lived in its presence. Wherever this idea became a part of a given people's life and world view it led to tremendous change.

This idea has caused man to approach the entire created reality as something that is not as it ought to be. This idea has led men to look upon all the rest of creation as an order that is to be subdued, brought under the scepter of that creature who was made in the image of God and who therefore was intended for dominion-having. This idea was for all who incorporated it into their system like a shot of adrenalin for the heart.

The insight that man is meant for dominion-having braced man for a hard, long fight. It made him ready for the encountering of resistance; it steeled him for the inevitable contest and conflict. It made man look upon opposition, wherever he encountered it, as a matter of course.

We must hasten to say, and to say with considerable emphasis, that in the authentic Christian view of things the opposition man experiences is *normal*, so intended. Too often has "work" in the life and experience of man been described as an *abnormal* thing. Too often men have, in theological parlance, made work in man's life one of the bitter fruits of the "Fall." This is certainly an error, an error far from innocent. No, the command to subdue the earth, that is, the command to gain the mastery, the order to have dominion, antedates the "Fall." To subdue the earth was an assignment in an as-yet-"unfallen" order. When man meets resistance to his efforts to subdue the earth he experiences things as they were intended to be. The Garden of Eden was not intended to be a place where man's life was one long siesta. We do not know whether "unfallen" man's week was a forty-hour week—what we do know is that it was a six-day week. And we feel the urge to say, in the light of these things, that when men think that the shorter the week becomes the better it is, they give evidence of harboring less-than-Christian views as to the place of honest toil in the life of man.

All this is not to say that the "Fall" did not, according to authentic

Christianity, bring with it a dimension of bitterness touching the toil of man. It did, and we shall return to this matter a little later.

One of the first things listed as proper grist for the dominion-haver's mill was the achievement of mastery over the lower creatures. In line with this it is but natural that man's first exploits as a dominion-haver were the domestication of hitherto undomesticated creatures. It could perhaps be argued that man does occur without the domestication of lesser creatures, but it must be granted by all that civilizations (if indeed they can be called civilizations) without domestication are regularly extremely primitive. We have, to cite an example, the North American Indian prior to the coming of the white man. He (generally speaking) had no domesticated things and his existence was correspondingly primitive. (We say "generally speaking," for the tribes of the Southwest are an exception, in that they did have domesticated creatures, notably turkeys. But their civilization was also decidedly less primitive than was that of the rest of the North American aborigines.)

As man advanced in civilization, he managed to domesticate more and more of the creatures below him, until he had tamed successfully virtually every species. The writer of the Epistle of James, reflecting on this early variety of dominion-having, could therefore speak of "putting bits into horses' mouths" (that is, make them subservient to the dominion-haver), "and they obey us, and we guide their whole bodies"; and then this writer adds, not without a quite apparent sense of triumph, that "every kind of beast and bird, of reptile and sea creature, can be tamed and has been tamed by humankind."

Men have indeed tamed wolves, calling them "dogs" in their domesticated form—and what varieties of services dogs have rendered to the dominion-haver! Men have tamed the wild ox and ass—and what loads these patient brutes have borne for their masters! Men have gained dominion over the lowly camel—and what long and tiring cargoes has this ship of the desert hauled for the dominion-haver! Man has put chains on the massive hulk of the elephant—and what burdens this patient beast has moved for the subduer-by-nature! Think, too, of the domestication of sheep and goats and of larger cattle, and the boon of milk and butter derived from these!

It is not too much to say that man as we know him is hardly thinkable apart from such domestications. Strip man of these fruits of his successful forays into the area of dominion-having and you return him to his most primitive mode of existence.

Man's God-given urge to achieve dominion goes beyond the domestication of the lower animals; it leads at once to the assumption that inanimate things must also be taken in hand, to make them serve man in a larger way than they do when left to themselves. The assumption is ready to hand that the earth as it lies does not lie as it should. Fields must be cleared of stones; rivers must be hemmed in by dikes; their waters must be diverted to moisten otherwise dry and arid soil.

Trees and other native vegetation must be cleared away; the plowshare must be made to bite into primeval sod so as to make room for plants that will serve man in a larger way than does the unkept and unkempt jungle. There is such a thing as the domestication of plants, and man has from very early times tried his hand at it. (There is reason to believe that when the prophet Amos said of himself that he was originally a "dresser of sycamore trees" [Amos 7:14], he was referring to the kind of husbandry we have called the domestication of plant varieties.) Wild varieties had to be made more useful to man—a thing very early achieved by selection and later also by artificial pollenization. Varieties that seemed useless to man (these he called "weeds") had to be made to give place to more serviceable varieties.

Societies that do not know man as dominion-haver and have for that reason not attained to the domestication program of which we have been speaking, these we call "gathering societies." They get along on such things as come up of themselves and bear their fruit without the benefit of human intervention. Such societies are rightly called "primitive." The North American Indians were, we are told, such "gathering" societies, by and large, and they were quite primitive. (We say "by and large" because the tribes of the Southwest had graduated beyond this stage; they represented "farmer societies," in that they planted, tended, irrigated, and harvested crops, sometimes in considerable abundance. By this token they were less primitive than were the rest.)

There are "gathering" societies in existence in our own times. One could point to the bushmen society of the Kalahari desert in southern Africa by way of example. The Bushmen are by all standards primitive, and they are this because made-in-His-image-having-dominion is unknown to them, and because unknown therefore also unpracticed.

As man becomes more sophisticated, his dominion-having becomes progressively more sophisticated likewise. His urge to come out on top begins to express itself in increasingly intricate ways. If the anopheles injects the malaria parasite into his bloodstream so that his body is consequently racked by fever, then he works out controls whereby the pest is restrained and put back into its proper place, that is, *under* the dominion-haver. And so on, without end or letup. Each newly achieved mastery beckons the dominion-haver on to more and greater subjugation of created reality. The dominion-haver never reaches the end of the road; while the earth stands he will, if he continues to see himself as such, continue the job that was his first assignment.

The Christian view of man, the idea that man is "made in God's likeness, having dominion," has changed the face of the earth. In a large way the Christian heritage is the world's only religious heritage that has sent man to his work. Most other religions tend to make men satisfied with the *status quo* and impel them to fight off work. Nothing, for example, has tended to retard the tribes of "dark Africa" as much and as effectively as the religion-inspired notion that things must stay as they have always been, seeing that to change them is to affront the spirits of the ancestors, which they fear with a religious dread. So also in the case of the Hindu faith; it makes "striving" the essence of bad behavior, the one thing for which atonement must be made, if not in this life then in a subsequent incarnation. This ingrained averseness to the battle for dominion has contributed more than a little to the backwardness of present-day India and the frightful problems connected therewith. Mohammedanism seems to have a similar effect. In the Moslem system the essence of piety is submission to that which comes one's way, bowing to it as the bulrushes bow to the flood. This, too, lays the foundation for passivity and so contrasts sharply with the Christian life and world view with its emphasis on activity. It is not by chance that Moslem lands, the Arab world for instance, are lethargic save for the abrasive effect of contact with an other culture. Yes, the Christian vision of "made in His image, having dominion" has changed the face of the earth and is destined to change it even more.

When a student who works his way through college by working hard at a part-time job is called a "capitalist" for it (as the present writer witnessed it not long ago), then one may be sure that post-Christian forces are on the loose. In the present case it was incarnate in a dreary-eyed creature that for smell and looks could have been garbed in the pelt of a billy goat. With such an attitude we are back in pre-Christian society where, as in pre-Christian Greece, hard work is the one thing that must be avoided. The New World was settled by peoples that had the idea that the earth is to be subdued, and this had a great deal to do with the development, both as to its extent and its rapidity, that took place. Peoples all over the world would like to duplicate what took place here. To do so will have as a prerequisite the adoption of the Christian view of man. It can indeed be taken on by groups not now in possession of it. And it can be lost by peoples who have had it for a long time and have harvested the benefits it provides.

When we say that Western man has gone far in the work of subduing, we do not wish to leave the impression that mere technological skill is the standard of man's humanness. Man has been called *anthropos,* the creature that looks up, and he finds himself looking down while he is engaged in subduing the earth. It can therefore be his undoing as man. If he looks down so intently and so constantly that he has no time left to look up, he is embarking on a dangerous path. It is not for nothing that the writer of Psalm 8 says as he celebrates the fact that man is the great dominion-haver that he is nevertheless *under* God. The dominion-haver is also under dominion—to the archetypal Dominion-haver. This means that he is accountable, accountable also in his dominion-having. If this is ignored or denied, then his very dominion-having may result in his doom. It is possible for the Dominion-haver to put an end—right now—to the dominion-haver as such. Dominion-having must be responsible dominion-having; the subduer must know that he, too, has a Master. If he erases this out of his mind he is none the better for his dominion-having—and much the worse. Then it would have been better if he had been content to stay on the level of the gatherer; he would then have been unable to be so massively inhuman.

The command to subdue the earth was given to man in the state of rectitude; he began to work out the assignment in his "fallen" condition. This means that the "sin problem" insinuates itself into the business of dominion-having; this means that "sin" as well as "grace" comes to expression in the subduing. Man can subdue as a "sinner"; he can also subdue as a "saint." In fact, he will have to be the one or the other; mere subduing, subduing without an adjectival or adverbial modifier, is no longer an option.

We must therefore be prepared for evidences of "fallenness" in the story of man's dominion-having, man's subduing odyssey. There will be evidence enough that he often went to his work secularly, that is, without looking up. There will be evidence enough that often his desire to subdue was driven by the desire to fill his animal needs rather than his human needs—as though it *is* possible for man to live by "bread alone."

The record has more blots on it than this one. Men, even men who thought they were being Christian men, have often, too often, lost sight of the fact that the command to subdue the earth was given to "Adam" (a noun that must sometimes be taken to stand for the race of men as such); that this is an assignment in which all men were supposed to take part. The command which was given in an as yet unfragmented situation went into its execution in the climate of that fracturization that came with the "Fall." The fracturization of the human race led to a fractured or piece-meal subjugation.

The fractional or piecemeal approach to dominion-having has led to many evils, evils from which we shall not soon escape. One of these evils is the evil of stark individualism in the matter of dominion-having. In this individualistic view of the cultural mandate it is assumed that the individual man is the unit by which the subjugation is to take place. In this atomized view each individual man considers it his God-given business to subdue a tract (as large a tract as he can force his neighbors to abide by) and put a fence around it, whereby he thinks to isolate himself, and his tract, from the rest of humanity and the rest of the to-be-subdued earth  little realizing, it seems, that by so doing he thereby does something to every other human being, by denying that piece of earth to all others.

It is a horrible thought—although not a surprising one—that if the whole story were told it would appear that such "ownership" took its origin in an act of *violence*. The first entry in the abstract of almost any Deed is a deed whereby the weaker was forced to abide by boundaries imposed by the stronger. It is a solemn fact that virtually every abstract begins with a piece that goes: "The United States of America, party of the first part . . . ," although such entry is in actuality the *second* entry—the first being the record of property lines imposed on earlier tenants.

Although this starkly individualistic program of subjugation is still heralded by some (mostly those who stand to lose if it should be challenged) as the very epitome of the Christian view of men and of things, it is probably significant and certainly heartening to discover that in moments when the Christian community is "on white bread" (to borrow a

Dutch idiom for "being on honeymoon"), it intuitively feels that such atomism in regard to mine and thine falls tragically short. It is surely no mere coincidence that in the halcyon days in which "with great power the apostles gave their testimony to the resurrection of the Lord Jesus and great grace was upon them all," it happened that "no one said that any of the things he possessed was his own but they had everything in common. . . . there was not a needy person among them, for as many as were possessors of lands or houses sold them, and brought the proceeds of what they had sold and laid it at the apostles' feet, and distribution was made to each as he had need" (Acts 4:32ff.).

There have been other moments in history when a new awareness of the power of the resurrection made men feel the incongruity of stark mine and thine and felt less than happy with the fences and the keep-off signs. One such moment came in the days of the great renewal that historians have called the Reformation. The fact that the rest of the supposedly Christian world talked at best of "detesting" such people (cf. Article 36 of the Belgic Confession) and at worst of putting them to death, only goes to show how far behind authentic Christianity historic Christianity may lag.

It is reason for thanking God and taking courage to discover that men in the midst of such fragmentized dominion-having have sometimes given evidence of being unable to look themselves in the face. At a time when in the New World each "homesteader" was "proving-up" his quarter section, and putting a fence around it, a movement gained momentum to set aside large tracts of land by definition not open to such individualism. The result is the National Parks and the National Forests. The carving out of these public domains is in itself the proof that man has a conscience. . . . Perhaps these areas of non-private exploitation are likewise the outcome of the mighty insight that man requires something besides tilled fields. The command to subdue the earth means to make the earth and its resources serve man in a maximal way, an objective not necessarily attained to by plowing it all up.

A second evil, resulting likewise from the fragmentation of human society and the bearing which that fragmentation has on the business of dominion-having, was that tribal units, peoples, language groups made it their business to subdue not only the tracts on which they lived but also the tracts on which certain other tribes lived. This came to be called the colonial system. It was very much like the starkly individualistic system of which we spoke a moment ago, in that it, too, carved out a zone of influence as big as it could force upon the less well-situated group. Colonialism also had as the first chapter in its account an act of violence; colonialisms regularly began with a show of force; and they were kept going by subsequent show of force.

It is humbling to recall that the colonialisms of which we speak were all of them launched by societies that wished to be known as *Christian*. It must be said that the Christianity of the "mother" country was a thing geared to the hereafter; it had little awareness of what the Christian faith means for the here and now. By and large it had long since ceased to hear any Christian overtones as it went about subduing the earth; this was the realm of "business" where, so it was thought, other rules apply than those contained in the Christian vision.

It is also true, and hardly less humbling, that the colonialists came hand in hand with missionaries, missionaries whom the governments of the colonial powers were quite ready to subsidize. Was this perhaps a sort of pacifier, to quiet down the disquieting voice of conscience? In any event, the religion these missionaries brought was primarily a medicine for the *soul;* even if taken according to the prescription, it was not likely to provide health for the *body*—the aspect of human existence for which the colonizing power was present. As a result it came about that even after centuries of such missionary activity the subduing of the earth for the benefit of those who dwelt on it was virtually where it had been before the exploiter (and his clergyman) had come.

This colonialism has had its day. In most parts where it was known it has already breathed its last; even in those parts of the world where it is still fighting for breath (as, for example, in Angola, Rhodesia, South Africa) the handwriting is on the wall. It has left in its wake a large swell of resentment on the part of the "natives," who should have been given their just and proper part in the work and the reward of subduing the earth but were denied it. The "Foreign Aid" programs of postcolonial times may perhaps be looked upon as a sort of (belated) penance for falling short of authentic Christianity's idea touching dominion-having, falling short by thinking of such dominion-having as a thing intended *for some,* for segments of humanity, rather than for humanity in its entirety.

This brings us face to face with still another abuse in the matter of dominion-having, one not unrelated to the abuses of which we spoke in the foregoing paragraphs. We refer to the institution of human slavery. Slaveholding is an unwarranted extension of dominion-having. By this unwarranted extension the to-be-subdued was thought to extend also so as to include humans (such humans as can be made by a show of force to submit to it). Slavery happens if and when, and only if and when, men lengthen the Biblical catalog of the to-be-subdued so that now it includes also human beings. If and when men make slaves of their fellow men, they must, however, first expel them out of the company of the dominion-haver. To make a slave of a fellow image-bearer is a contradiction in terms. Men have felt this, intuitively. For that reason those who supported slaveholding have always, without exception, taught that the genuine humanness of their victims is at least open to debate. To make a slave you must first reduce him to an animal, so that you may be able to live with yourself as you then proceed to domesticate him, and so make him bear your burdens. Since in the Christian vision all men were made in the image of God (with none who are half-men), therefore all men are potential dominion-havers, which leaves none to be the object of this dominion-having. Authentic Christianity therefore leaves no room for the institution of slavery.

It is of course true that from very early times men have made slaves of their fellow men, sometimes of whole tribes. The enslavement of the Hebrew people in the Egypt of the Pharaohs is a classic example. It must also be granted that even among people who had the benefit of the Bible slaveholding was by no means unknown. The "hewers of wood and the drawers of water" of Joshua 9 are a case in point. But it is also a part of the record that some of the Jehovah prophets, for example the prophet Amos, castigated in no uncertain terms those who were guilty of "carrying a whole people into exile to deliver them to Edom" (the slave traders of antiquity). From this rebuke at the hand of an eighth-century prophet we may perhaps conclude that their scoring of slavery represents one of those evolutions toward a higher position that is characteristic of the divine revelation, an advance upon things that were tolerated in earlier times.

It is quite true, sad to say, that moral philosophers in medieval Christendom justified the enslavement of non-Christians, mentioning by name the Saracens. By so pontificating, these medieval moralists gave evidence of having slipped into pre-Christian ways of thinking. Did not the followers of Mohammed likewise approve of slave traffic—if the victims of their inhumanity were *kaffirs* (the word is of Arabic origin and signifies *infidel* or *unbeliever,* one who is not a Moslem)?

It must also be granted that in these United States the enslavement of man by his fellow man was sustained, with specious argument drawn from the Christian Scriptures, right up to modern times and even into them. It is instructive to note that these arguments were largely drawn from Old Testament precedent. It was desirable for the sake of this argument to keep the preliminary character of the Old Testament from showing.

It is also true that under cover of the Christian name slaveholding was justified in South Africa (where it was known as *baasskap*) right into our own times, again with an argument drawn primarily from the Old Testament. The word *kaffir* (which has the flavor of our *nigger*), as well as the word *baasskap,* is in disrepute in present-day South Africa; but the idea survives, replaced by the word *voogdyskap* (a word that designates a situation of warden and ward). The concept of "separate development" is a still less offensive name for a situation of boss and bossed.

All these developments on supposedly Christian soil are an anomaly. In the Christian vision all men are in the image of God and are, for that reason, intended for dominion-having; every man is the subject of the transaction and no man is the object of it. It is in line with this to say that "all men are created free and equal, endowed by their Creator with certain inalienable rights."

(This cuts wide and deep. It has its repercussions in the state and the power vested in it. If, as authentic Christianity teaches, man is a creature to whom all the rest of creaturality is to be subject, he himself being subject only to the One who is higher than the sum total of creaturality, then every dominion over man is by definition non-final and subject to all sorts of checks and balances. In this view the power vested in the state derives its dignity from the fact that it is God's authority, mediated through imperfect human beings, and for that reason always subject to recall by those over whom it holds sway. Any view of the state that does not begin with God must see the state as a "power structure," wherein man is subjected to man. On the other hand, any simple identification of the voice of the state and the voice of God is bound to give to that which is itself creatural, i.e., the state, a dignity too great for the frail shoulders of man, a creature whose breath is in his nostrils. What we have said has repercussions also in family relationships. Ethnic civilizations have put women in bondage to their men—in a way quite of a piece with the bondage of a domesticated animal. Although men have lived in this way even after the light of Christian truth had shone on them, such man-wife relationships are an anomaly. In the Christian view man is indeed the head of the wife—but as such under the constant scrutiny of the God who is the only final Head, of both him and her. In the relationship of parents and children things are in the Christian vision structured along these same lines.)

We must return to the place from which this parenthesis drew us away, to the uninhibited assertion that in the business of dominion-having we have made a sorry mess of things. And after that we must apply ourselves to the question as to what can and should be done to make the bad situation somewhat less bad. What can we do for and with those people and groups for whom dominion-having is a virtually unknown experience, whether because the idea of "in His image, having dominion" was unknown in their past or because the Christian message had reached them but without it having led to their participation in the business of subduing? Christians are people who do not give up easily; they do not grant readily that a cause is hopeless; for they have been taught that even death can be overcome, by life. What is to be done?

To the present writer it seems that we must stop apologizing for the fact that to an unprecedented extent we have succeeded in subduing the earth, have found ways and means to make the earth serve man in ways heretofore undreamed of. We must stop apologizing for the fact that we are no longer a society of gatherers, that we have become first a farming civilization, and then an industrial one. We say that we must stop apologizing, because there are those, in hippy colonies if nowhere else, who try to tell us that the subduing man is an evil man. There are those who seem to think that if we were to return to the "gathering" stage we would be moving in the right direction, with everybody stripping edibles from a supposedly ever-abundant vine! No, we must continue to *produce;* and continue not only, but produce as never before, produce "like mad."

Let no one forget that what the rest of the world wants is the good things that factories as developed in the "Western" world can pour out in fantastic volume. This is what the "undeveloped" countries hanker after. This is what they want. If they sometimes evince a dislike for countries that are better off in these things, then this dislike turns about the fact that they do not have the means of production that give these other countries their abundance. It is this that the international tensions turn upon, and it serves no good purpose to picture it otherwise.

Another question that will have to be faced is the question whether the *fruits* of the Christian view of man (for that is what it is all about) can be coaxed forth without the root system on which they have historically grown and ripened. Can a "backward" country be put in possession of the fantastic achievements resulting from dominion-having unless and until it adopts that view of man which goes with it? Can that which took literally millenniums to bring about, and under the inspiration of a specific life and world view, be conjured out of the ground in a fortnight, come up and mature between sunset and sunrise—like some Jonah's gourd?

Let us assume that the centuries can indeed be compressed. Let us take for granted that to do it a second time need not take as long as it did the first time. Let us proceed upon the assumption that as with the charging of a battery there is such a thing as a "quicky charge." After all, it should make a difference that what was once learned by trial and error can now be learned without such wasteful procedure. Let us act as though it is possible. Let us put the theory to the test.

And as we do so, let us remember that the problem we are facing and which we are trying to solve has in a large way been created by the (earlier) fragmented approach to the business of dominion-having. If we remember this, we will perhaps be in a mood to subsidize the venture to make good, the venture to bring abreast those whom we should never have allowed to fall so far behind.

And let those who are being helped remember that they, too, have homework to do. The experiment cannot succeed unless the Christian attitude toward toil is taken over by them—for Christianity does have a peculiar attitude toward toil; its heritage of "made in His image, having dominion" gives it this attitude. The kind of abundant life the "undeveloped" countries covet did not come easy. In fact, it came hard, unbelievably hard. It was wrought in blood and sweat and tears. Hard work is part of the heritage and the "undeveloped" countries must not for one moment think they or anyone else can slide easily into the abundant life.

In some instances it will require a very conscious effort to begin to assume the Christian stance toward toil—and we must sympathize with every man who is faced with this challenge. In many cases he has what is virtually a "slave past," a mode of existence that automatically breeds a less-than-Christian attitude toward toil. The laboratory out of which he came was certain to produce a creature with a built-in aversion to toil, for it was toil that was unaccompanied by its God-intended reward. The joys that come from achievement, the fun of achieving mastery, did not come his way. He must be given a maximum opportunity to catch up; he too must have opportunity to know himself as "made in His image, having dominion."

In the nature of the thing this joy cannot be bequeathed to him; it cannot be bequeathed as chattels are bequeathed. It can only be earned. For just as it is impossible to *give* another person an education (the best we can do is give him an opportunity to *get* one) just so is it impossible to impart to a man the joy of achievement by any other route than the route of actively participating in the common human assignment of subduing the earth.

We have asserted above that in the Christian vision man is a creature intended for mastery-achieved-with-much-toil; and we have said that this implies that such toil is *normal,* that its presence in a human life is not the result of any "Fall." Because this fact is so often denied (for example in Bruce Barton's *The Man Nobody Knows*), we address ourselves to this mistaken notion.

Although the Bible teaches that work is *normal,* it also teaches that somewhere along the line human toil has picked up a heretofore unknown dimension of bitterness. We find this set forth in that part of the "curse" that overtook man because of his disobedience, a "curse" that contains the announcement of the earth "bringing forth thorns and thistles" so that "in the sweat of thy brow thou shalt eat bread" (Genesis 3:17-19). With these words the new dimension of bitterness is ushered in.

Perhaps we may picture the two situations by comparing a man busy with a hobby and a man toiling at the assignment whereby he keeps the wolf from the door. As everyone knows, hobby-work can be quite strenuous—as much so as daily toil; but hobby-work is never irksome; it never galls. Hobby-work is devoid of that dimension of bitterness that now regularly attends ordinary toil.

What makes hobby-work appealing is the fact that in it a challenge is successfully met. Whether it be the carving out of a walking stick or (as in the case of Winston Churchill) the building of a stone wall, that which brings a man to such activity is the thrill he gets out of meeting challenge successfully. This kind of work is the normal thing for man. It is a gift of God's grace that something of the same exhilaration can still attend man's daily toil. Happy is the man who with *The Village Blacksmith* can rejoice in it that "each morning sees some task begun, each evening sees its close; something attempted, something done, has earned the night's repose." This is the frame of mind in which man's daily toil should take place.

In any event, primitive man at the mercy of creaturedom around him, cowering in his cave for fear of wild beasts, his body racked with hunger and pain—this, in the language of the Bible, is what the "Fall" has done to man; it is a case of the dominion-haver being at the mercy of that which he was commissioned to rule!

Some of the miracles attributed to Christ take on a new meaning in this context; they demonstrate what "grace" can do to "fallenness." We see the Master's disciples huddled fearfully in a fishing vessel at the mercy of creatural powers, the should-be-ruler at the mercy of the to-be-ruled. In this situation Jesus appears as the Dominion-haver *par excellence* with His "Peace, be still!" In this exercise of dominion the Savior of mankind shows Himself to be precisely that: by putting the dominion-haver back on top and the to-be-ruled back in a subordinate position, He "saves." What the "curse" had ruined, the Curse-remover again sets right.

It is therefore not surprising at all that whenever the Gospel of this Christ finds its way, a yearning for mastery, for the exercise of controls calculated to enrich human life, follows in its wake. If the Gospel does not do this then something has "dropped out" of it.

A people that has had the Gospel for a long time but still is in the category of the "undeveloped nations" is laboratory proof of such "dropping out." It is not too harsh to say that the Gospel that came to such a land was a truncated Gospel—truncated in that it manifestly failed to convey a sizeable piece of the Christian message, the piece that set forth man as a creature "made in His image, having dominion." Nor is it too much to say that it was this truncated Gospel that set the stage for the rise of communism. (It is a humbling fact that communism was hatched out on supposedly "Christian" soil.) The grievously bad situation that communism promises to correct would never have developed if the version of Christianity that preceded it had not allowed the idea to go into eclipse that man is a creature whose first assignment was to have dominion.

In the climate of this truncated Gospel dominion-having was not encouraged. One of its fatal faults was that it concentrated so heavily on life-after-death that it could be quite nonchalant as to the here and now. It whispered something in the ear of enslaved peasants about "pie in the sky by and by." Because of its one-sided emphasis on the hereafter it failed to develop that unique view of man and man's relationship to the rest of creaturedom that is given in the Christian Scriptures. And because it failed to convey the theory it failed quite as sadly in practice. The implications of "made in His image, having dominion" were, as a consequence, a *terra incognita* for medieval man.

The truncated Gospel of which we speak committed even greater sins. It actually discouraged and rebuked the urge for the acquisition of controls. Its adherents acted as if it had never been said, "Be fruitful and multiply and then subdue the earth"! In so doing they led the world back to pre-Christian attitudes and policies in the matter of controls.

For it is part of the pre-Christian way of thinking to frown on the acquisition of controls. A good example of this pre-Christian heritage came to our attention as we lectured to Bantu seminary students in South Africa. We were saying that the Christian vision as to controls doesn't know the idea that achievable controls are by definition forbidden to man. We gave by way of example the much-discussed idea of controlling the clouds and so the rainfall. We found the minds of these students quite closed to this teaching. Even though they had embraced Christianity and had attained to some degree of sophistication (they were, after all, men preparing for the Christian ministry), they were unable to go along with the idea that if man *can* control the weather he then also *may*. Such a hold did pre-Christian limitations-of-control have on them.

One finds such essentially pre-Christian limitations set for the exercise of controls lingering on in areas that were evangelized long ago. We recall how that the introduction of lightning rods was for a time opposed on (mistaken) religious grounds. So also in regard to newly discovered control techniques in the form of vaccines; poorly instructed Christians have at times raised such a furor against smallpox vaccines (which they in derogation called "medicine made of pus") that governments were obliged to make provision for persons with qualms of conscience anent the matter, even though non-immunization posed a threat to public health.

In these and other examples that might be cited it is the *new* control that (poorly taught) men have opposed. By a queer quirk of conscience men who had learned to live with *older* control techniques resisted the invasion of *new* ones. This too was the outcome of a less-than-Christian appraisal of things. This attitude gets dangerously close to the essentially pagan notion that human controls are all right up to a certain point, the point where the domain of divine control begins. In this (pagan) version of things religion comes into play at the point where human controls end and divine controls begin. This (pagan) way of looking at the matter of controls finds its classic expression in the exclamation of the Egyptian sorcerers of Exodus 8:19. As long as they were able to copy the controls of Moses and Aaron they saw no reason to say anything religious; but when they saw a control technique that went beyond them they cried out in astonishment: "This is the finger of God!" But it is a mongrel version of the Christian faith to see a religious dimension only after the boundaries of human control have been crossed.

Resistance to the exercise of controls has been especially prevalent and extraordinarily acute in connection with that form of control known as birth control. Because of its perennial interest and in view of the fact that the matter is very much in the air in our times (not the least because of the Pope's recent encyclical touching the matter), we shall give the remaining space in this chapter on man as a dominion-haver to a discussion of this particular instance of control and of men's reactions to the idea of controls exercised in this area.

It can hardly be said that the resistance to birth control is to be ascribed to the newness thereof—for it is quite apparent that some kind of birth control has been practiced since early times. No, it is not the novelty of birth control that inspires the opposition it encounters. Rather, the opposition is born of a less-than-Christian view of sex—more precisely put, a less-than-Christian view of the *raison d'être* (the reason for being) of the sexual differentiation in the human species. Unless and until we have a genuinely Christian view as to the *raison d'être* of sex in man, it is impossible for us to have a genuinely Christian view of birth control, including the matter of its legitimacy. We must therefore ask the reader's time as we seek to recover the Biblical delineation of the *raison d'être* of sex.

As has been intimated already, the Genesis account as to origins is composite in that it weaves together two distinct accounts. (Whether the two are from one and the same hand or not is of no consequence for our present purpose.) Each of these two accounts supplies its own answer to the question of the why of sexual differentiation in man.

In the former account the sexual differentiation, the occurrence of male and female, is introduced as a device for the propagation of the species. Do we not read: "So God created man in his own image, in the image of God created he him, male and female created he them; and God said unto them, 'Be fruitful and multiply and fill the earth and subdue it and have dominion.' . . ."? Here sex is described as a device serving the cause of reproduction. Small wonder that in *this* account mankind is pictured as male and female right from the start.

If now we turn to the latter account, we find the *raison d'être* of the sexual differentiation set in a different, let us say, a complementary, light. Here sex is relational, for fellowship, for the ultimate in human companionship—with not a word said about any procreation. This time the divine soliloquy is: "It is not good for the man to be alone; I will make him a helper fit for him." Then follows the story of the "sleep" or trance, in which out of a rib of the man is fashioned the contemplated companion. Here the *raison d'être* of sex is relational, a device for companionship, companionship expressing itself as the man and his life-partner (we say *life*-partner because the writer of this account plainly has in mind the founding of a new home, similar to the one a man leaves by the espousal of such a partner) coalesce, become "one flesh." Small wonder that in this account mankind is first a solitary male and only after that male and female.

The former account says nothing about companionship; the latter says nothing about procreation. Not that the former excludes companionship and the latter the begetting of children. The two are complementary to each other. The fact that the Revealing Spirit saw fit to convey the God-pleasing view of the *raison d'être* of sex in *two* installments (He could have done it in *one*) certainly warrants the assertion that the really Biblical idea of sex is that it is like a tapestry—consisting of warp and woof. The two accounts when combined give us the Biblical *raison d'être* of sex. Manifestly both sex-as-a-device-for-procreation and sex-as-a-device-for-companionship are good in their own right. Both are God-willed. Both result from the Creator's kind concern for man. That the two are broached separately shows that they are indeed differentiable; that they are broached in each other's context shows that they are normally found complementing each other.

The nub of the question as to the propriety of birth control resides in the question whether in the mind of the Creator sex-for-procreation (hereafter designated "P") and sex-for-companionship (hereafter designated "C") are indissolubly tied together. That the two are twins is apparent. We may be prepared to say that they are identical twins. But are they Siamese twins, inseparable ones at that? This is the heart of the question.

As we seek light on this question we may once more point to the fact that Genesis 1 as it speaks of P says nothing about C and that Genesis 2 as it speaks of C says nothing about P. This literary procedure (assuming, as we do in the authentic Christian version, that one and the same Revealing Spirit was responsible for both) would seem to imply that P and C are in the mind of God not necessarily inseparable.

If now we turn to the testimony of the "Book of Nature" (to borrow the language of the Belgic Confession in its Article II) as to the matter in hand, we find that its testimony points strongly in the direction of separableness. The "Book of Nature" reveals that although sexual activity in the life of the lower animals occurs only in the context of procreation, such is not the case with man. Among the lower animals the initiation of pregnancy implies the cessation of sexual interest; but such is not the case with man. If for man sex was intended simply to serve P then it would, as in the lower animals, automatically cancel out and become quiescent once *that* purpose had been served; such is not the case, however, for sex as a device for companionship carries over beyond the inception of pregnancy. The "Book of Nature" seems therefore to favor the idea of separableness of P and C in man.

To continue our reading of the "Book of Nature," we find further endorsement for the idea of separableness. If sex in humans were indissolubly associated with P, then we would expect the so-called menopause in the human female to be accompanied by the quiescence of sexual interest, sex having become meaningless with the cessation of ovulation; yet such is not the case. In the human species the sex life of the female extends beyond the menopause, the point at which sex loses its procreational significance. . . .

The pattern of human sexuality differs also and quite markedly from that of the lower creatures in that with the latter sexuality is dormant save during a specific season, the season known as the mating season—which is associated with ovulation in the female. There is no such seasonality in the human species. It would seem that the arrangement of a mating season tends to regulate the birth rate in field and forest, hold it down to manageable dimensions. Does the human deviation from this pattern of the mating season point to *other* techniques calculated to attain to the same end but by a different route?

It would seem that the meaning of man's other and different sex-life pattern lies in with the fact that man is a creature intended for controls. Man is intended for *living* rather than for *being lived;* his assignment is *not* to let things take their course but to steer the ship of his life. His being by nature a dominion-haver is reflected in his sex-life pattern.

We must hasten to point out that all this does not yet mean that man is permitted to separate P and C according to his every whim and fancy. Even though P and C are differentiable and even though it be granted that they are not in all situations inseparably bound together, the fact remains that in the over-all picture they do belong together. In normal situations sex-for-companionship must not be allowed to be involved in an Eighty Years War with sex-for-procreation.

A final point or two need to be made in the matter of birth control. It is that the Genesis account makes the out-populating of the race a means to an end. Do we not read: "Be fruitful and multiply and fill the earth and subdue it"? The out-populating of the race is a means to the subduing of the earth. The idea is that since the subduing is a big assignment, one that requires a sizeable task force, therefore man must "be fruitful and multiply." It would follow that just as soon as the earth is "filled," filled full enough to make possible maximal dominion-having, then the command to multiply loses its erstwhile urgency. Surely we may conclude that if and when the very numerousness of the human family becomes an impediment to the subduing—as is the case, for example, in present-day India where the procedures necessary to getting the earth to serve men in a maximal way are precluded by the very existence of so many mouths to feed—then population control becomes not only permissible but even obligatory. This means for subduing must not be allowed to get in the way of the subduing itself; the means must not be allowed to usurp the end. And that implies that in the given situation population control is in order, and imperative.

Much of the traditional opposition to birth control derives from a less-than-Christian view of sexuality as such. The notion is current in some Christian circles that those functions of the human organism that have their seat below the diaphragm are a moral liability. This idea is certainly of pagan origin and as such is at variance with the tenets of authentic Christianity. The Apostle Paul seems to have known of this essentially pagan assessment of the below-the-navel functions and he seems to have anticipated its invasion into the thinking of the Christian Church, for he warns against the encroachment with these words: "Now the Spirit expressly says that in later times some will depart from the faith by giving heed to deceitful spirits and doctrines of demons . . . forbidding marriage and enjoining abstinence from foods, which God created to be received with thanksgiving . . . for everything created by God is good and nothing is to be rejected . . ." (I Timothy 4:1-5).

To say no to the alimentary tract and to the sexual apparatus is not Christian; it is a pagan encroachment, specifically a neo-platonic one.

Nor is the resulting doctrine at all Christian—the doctrine that sexual congress between husband and wife puts the participants in the red morally so that they must shoulder the burdens of parenthood as a sort of atonement for evil done. In the train of this pagan encroachment Psalm 51:5 ("Behold, I was brought forth in iniquity, and in sin did my mother conceive me") has been (mistakenly) taken to mean that pregnancy and subsequent motherhood are the outcome of sinful traffic between a man and a woman. This pagan encroachment has brought oceans of anguish into human lives. Its prevalence is attested to by the question, put recently to a clergyman in charge of a radio Gospel hour, as to how "be fruitful and multiply" can be harmonized with "conceived and born in sin."

No, the sex act does not of and by itself put a person in debt, debt for which the burden of parenthood is required expiation. It does not as such incur guilt; and, for that reason, requires no atonement.

It is the lingering conviction that it does incur guilt and that therefore it has to be matched with the distasteful chores that are wont to be associated with parenthood that is causing the ruckus we are witnessing currently in some areas of Christendom anent the use of birth-regulating techniques. This lingering conviction is carried by a piece of pagan thinking that has been incorporated in the Christian tradition. Unless such pagan encroachment is recognized for what it is—and repudiated—the ruckus will continue.

Such repudiation will no doubt be painful to some, especially to those for whom tradition means a great deal. It will require the repudiation of voices that have carried great authority for a long time, voices such as that of St. Augustine (a man otherwise dear to both Protestants and Catholics alike). Augustine has taught that all that which makes sex non-prosaic is the fruit of the "Fall," that "if man were still in the state of rectitude the sex act would be as nonchalantly performed as is the expulsion of the catamenial flux!" This and the whole complex of ideas of which it is a part will have to be shed if we are to have a truly Biblical view of sex and all that pertains to it. And that is prerequisite for a truly Biblical view of the kind of dominion-having that comes to expression in the thing called birth control.

# Man's Make-up

6

## Charles Hodge

## Nature of Man

### Scripture Doctrine

The Scriptures teach that God formed the body of man out of the dust of the earth, and breathed into him the breath of life and he became *nepeš hayyâ, a living soul.* According to this account, man consists of two distinct principles, a body and a soul: the one material, the other immaterial; the one corporeal, the other spiritual. It is involved in this statement, first, that the soul of man is a substance; and, secondly, that it is a substance distinct from the body. So that in the constitution of man two distinct substances are included.

The idea of substance, as has been before remarked, is one of the primary truths of the reason. It is given in the consciousness of every man, and is therefore a part of the universal faith of men. We are conscious of our thoughts, feelings, and volitions. We know that these exercises or phenomena are constantly changing, but that there is something of which they are the exercises and manifestation. That something is the self which remains unchanged, which is the same identical something, yesterday, to-day, and to-morrow. The soul is, therefore, not a mere series of acts; nor is

From *Systematic Theology* (Grand Rapids: William B. Eerdmans, 1952), 2:42-51.

it a form of the life of God, nor is it a mere unsubstantial force, but a real subsistence. Whatever acts *is,* and what *is* is an entity. A nonentity is nothing, and nothing can neither have power nor produce effects. The soul of man, therefore, is an essence or entity or substance, the abiding subject of its varying states and exercises. The second point just mentioned is no less plain. As we can know nothing of substance but from its phenomena, and as we are forced by a law of our nature to believe in the existence of a substance of which the phenomena are the manifestation, so by an equally stringent necessity we are forced to believe that where the phenomena are not only different, but incompatible, there the substances are also different. As, therefore, the phenomena or properties of matter are essentially different from those of mind, we are forced to conclude that matter and mind are two distinct substances; that the soul is not material nor the body spiritual. "To identify matter with mind," says Cousin, in a passage before quoted, "or mind with matter; it is necessary to pretend that sensation, thought, volition, are reducible, in the last analysis, to solidity, extension, figure, divisibility, etc.; or that solidity, extension, figure, etc., are reducible to sensation, thought, will."[1] It may be said, therefore, despite of materialists and idealists, that it is intuitively certain that matter and mind are two distinct substances; and such has been the faith of the great body of mankind. This view of the nature of man which is presented in the original account of his creation, is sustained by the constant representations of the Bible.

### Truths on this Subject Assumed in Scripture

The Scriptures do not formally teach any system of psychology, but there are certain truths relating both to our physical and mental constitution, which they constantly assume. They assume, as we have seen, that the soul is a substance; that it is a substance distinct from the body; and that there are two, and not more than two, essential elements in the constitution of man. This is evident, (1.) From the distinction everywhere made between soul and body. Thus, in the original account of the creation a clear distinction is made between the body as formed from the dust of the earth, and the soul or principle of life which was breathed into it from God. And in Gen. 3:19, it is said, "Dust thou art, and unto dust shalt thou return." As it was only the body that was formed out of the dust, it is only the body that is to return to dust. In Eccles. 12:7, it is said, "Then shall the dust return to the earth as it was, and the spirit shall return unto God who gave it." Isa. 10:18, "Shall consume . . . both soul and body." Daniel says (7:15), "I Daniel was grieved in my spirit in the midst of my body." Our Lord (Matt. 6:25) commands his disciples to take no thought for the body; and, again (Matt. 10:28), "Fear not them which kill the body, but are not able to kill the soul: but rather fear him which is able to destroy both soul and body in hell." Such is the constant representation of the Scriptures. The body and soul are set forth as distinct substances, and the two together as constituting the whole man. (2.) There is a second class of passages equally decisive as to this point. It consists of those in which the body is represented as a garment which is to be laid aside; a tabernacle or house in which the soul dwells, which it may leave and return to. Paul, on a certain occasion, did not know whether he was in the body or out of the body. Peter says he thought it meet as long as he was in this tabernacle to put his brethren in remembrance of the truth, "knowing," as he adds, "that shortly I must put off this my tabernacle." Paul, in II Cor. 5:1, says, "If our earthly house of this tabernacle were dissolved we have a building of God." In the same connection, he speaks of being unclothed and clothed upon with our house which is from heaven; and of being absent from the body and present with the Lord, knowing that while we are at home in the body we are absent from the Lord. To the Philippians (1:23, 24) he says, "I am in a strait betwixt two, having a desire to depart, and to be with Christ; which is far better: nevertheless, to abide in the flesh is more needful for you." (3.) It is the common belief of mankind, the clearly revealed doctrine of the Bible, and part of the faith of the Church universal, that the soul can and does exist and act after death. If this be so, then the body and soul are two distinct substances. The former may be disorganized, reduced to dust, dispersed, or even annihilated, and the latter retain its conscious life and activity. This doctrine was taught in the Old Testament, where the dead are represented as dwelling in Sheol, whence they occasionally reappeared, as Samuel did to Saul. Our Lord says that as God is not the God of the dead but of the living, his declaring himself to be the God of Abraham, Isaac, and Jacob, proves that Abraham, Isaac, and Jacob are now alive. Moses and Elijah conversed with Christ on the Mount. To the dying thief our Lord said, "To-day shalt *thou*" (that in which his personality resided) "be with me in Paradise." Paul, as we have just seen, desired to be absent from the body and present with the Lord. He knew that his conscious personal existence was to be continued after the dissolution of his body. It is unnecessary to dwell on this point, as the continued existence of the soul in full consciousness and activity out of the body and in the interval between death and the resurrection, is not denied by any Christian Church. But if this be so it clearly proves that the soul and body are two distinct substances, so that the former can exist independently of the latter.

### Relation of the Soul and Body

Man, then, according to the Scriptures, is a created spirit in vital union with a material organized body. The relation between these two constituents of our nature is admitted to be mysterious. That is, it is incomprehensible. We do not know how the body acts on the mind, or how the mind acts on the body. These facts, however, are plain, (1.) That the relation between the two is a vital union, in such a sense as that the soul is the source of life to the body. When the soul leaves the body the latter ceases to live. It loses its sensibility and activity, and becomes at once subject to the chemical laws which govern unorganized matter, and by their operation is soon reduced to dust, undistinguishable from the earth whence it was originally taken. (2.) It is a fact of consciousness that certain states of the body produce certain corresponding states of the mind. The mind takes cognizance of, or is conscious of, the impressions made by external objects on the organs of sense belonging to the body. The mind sees, the mind hears, and the mind feels, not directly or immediately (at least in our present and normal state), but through or by means of the appropriate organs of the body. It is also a matter of daily experience that a healthful condition of the body is necessary to a healthful state of the mind; that certain diseases or disorders of the one produce derangement in the operations of the other. Emotions of the mind affect the body; shame suffuses the cheek; joy causes the heart to beat and the eyes to shine. A blow on the head renders the mind unconscious, *i. e.,* it renders the brain unfit to be the organ of its activity; and a diseased condition of the brain may cause irregular action in the mind, as in lunacy. All this is incomprehensible, but it is undeniable. (3.) It is also a fact of consciousness that, while certain operations of the body are independent of the conscious voluntary action of the mind, as the processes of respiration, digestion, secretion, assimilation, etc., there are certain actions dependent on the will. We can will to move; and we can exert a greater or less degree of muscular force. It is better to admit these simple facts of consciousness and of experience, and to confess that, while they prove an intimate and vital union between the mind and body, they do not enable us to comprehend the nature of that union, than to have recourse to arbitrary and fanciful theories which deny these facts, because we cannot explain them. This is done by the advocates of the doctrine of occasional causes, which denies any action of the mind on the body or of the body on the mind, but refers all to the immediate agency of God. A certain state of the mind is the occasion on which God produces a certain act of the body; and a certain impression made on the body is the occasion on which God produces a certain impression on the mind. Leibnitz's doctrine of a preestablished harmony is equally unsatisfactory. He denied that one substance could act on another of a different kind; that matter could act on mind or mind on matter. He proposed to account for the admitted correspondence between the varying states of the one and those of the other on the assumption of a prearrangement. God had foreordained that the mind should have the perception of a tree whenever the tree was presented to the eye, and that the arm should move whenever the mind had a volition to move. But he denied any causal relation between these two series of events.

### Realistic Dualism

The Scriptural doctrine of the nature of man as a created spirit in vital union with an organized body, consisting, therefore, of two, and only two, distinct elements or substances, matter and mind, is one of great importance. It is intimately connected with some of the most important doctrines of the Bible; with the constitution of the person of Christ, and consequently with the nature of his redeeming work and of his relation to the children of men; with the doctrine of the fall, original sin, and of regeneration; and with the doctrines of a future state and of the resurrection. It is because of this connection, and not because of its interest as a question in psychology, that the true idea of man demands the careful investigation of the theologian.

The doctrine above stated, as the doctrine of the Scriptures and of the Church, is properly designated as realistic dualism. That is, it asserts the existence of two distinct *res,* entities, or substances; the one extended, tangible, and divisible, the object of the senses; the other unextended and indivisible, the thinking, feeling, and willing subject in man. This doctrine stands opposed to materialism and idealism, which although antagonistic systems in other respects, agree in denying any dualism of substance. The one makes the mind a function of the body; the other makes the body a form of the mind. But, according to the Scriptures and all sound philosophy, neither is the body, as Delitzsch[2] says, a precipitate of the mind, nor is the mind a sublimate of matter.

The Scriptural doctrine of man is of course opposed to the old heathen doctrine which represents him as the form in which nature, der Naturgeist, the *anima mundi,* comes to self-consciousness; and also to the wider pantheistic doctrine according to which men are the highest manifestations of the one universal principle of being and life; and to the doctrine which represents man as the union of the impersonal, universal reason or λόγος, with a living corporeal organization. According to this last mentioned view, man consists of the body (σῶμα), soul (ψυχή), and λόγος, or the impersonal reason. This is very nearly the Apollinarian doctrine as to the constitution of Christ's person, applied to all mankind.

## Trichotomy

It is of more consequence to remark that the Scriptural doctrine is opposed to Trichotomy, or the doctrine that man consists of three distinct substances, body, soul, and spirit; σῶμα, ψυχή, and πνεῦμα; *corpus, anima,* and *animus.* This view of the nature of man is of the more importance to the theologian because it has not only been held to a greater or less extent in the Church, but also because it has greatly influenced the form in which other doctrines have been presented; and because it has some semblance of support from the Scripture themselves. The doctrine has been held in different forms. The simplest, the most intelligible, and the one most commonly adopted is, that the body is the material part of our constitution; the soul, or ψυχή, is the principle of animal life; and the mind, or πνεῦμα, the principle of our rational and immortal life. When a plant dies its material organization is dissolved and the principle of vegetable life which it contained disappears. When a brute dies its body returns to dust, and the ψυχή, or principle of animal life by which it was animated, passes away. When a man dies his body returns to the earth, his ψυχή ceases to exist, his πνεῦμα alone remains until reunited with the body at the resurrection. To the πνεῦμα which is peculiar to man, belong reason, will, and conscience. To the ψυχή which we have in common with the brutes, belong understanding, feeling, and sensibility, or, the power of sense-perceptions. To the σῶμα belongs what is purely material.[3] According to another view of the subject, the soul is neither the body nor the mind; nor is it a distinct subsistence, but it is the resultant of the union of the πνεῦμα and σῶμα.[4] Or according to Delitzsch,[5] there is a dualism of being in man, but a trichotomy of substance. He distinguishes between being and substance, and maintains, (1.) that spirit and soul (πνεῦμα and ψυχή) are not verschiedene Wesen, but that they are verschiedene Substanzen. He says that the nepeš ḥayyâ, mentioned in the history of the creation, is not the compositum resulting from the union of the spirit and body, so that the two constituted man; but it is a tertium quid, a third substance which belongs to the constitution of his nature. (2.) But secondly, this third principle does not pertain to the body; it is not the higher attributes or functions of the body, but it pertains to the spirit and is produced by it. It sustains the same relation to it that breath does to the body, or effulgence does to light. He says that the ψυχή (soul) is the ἀπαύγασμα of the πνεῦμα and the bond of its union with the body.

## Trichotomy Anti-Scriptural

In opposition to all the forms of trichotomy, or the doctrine of a threefold substance in the constitution of man, it may be remarked, (1.) That it is opposed to the account of the creation of man as given in Gen. 2:7. According to that account God formed man out of the dust of the earth and breathed into him the breath of life, and he became nepeš ḥayyâ, i. e., a being (ăšer-bô nepeš ḥayyâ) in whom is a living soul. There is in this account no intimation of anything more than the material body formed of the earth and the living principle derived from God. (2.) This doctrine (trichotomy) is opposed to the uniform usage of Scripture. So far from the nepeš, ψυχή, anima, or soul, being distinguished from the rûaḥ, πνεῦμα, animus, or mind as either originally different or as derived from it, these words all designate one and the same thing. They are constantly interchanged. The one is substituted for the other, and all that is, or can be predicated of the one, is predicated of the other. The Hebrew nepeš, and the Greek ψυχή, mean breath, life, the living principle; that in which life and the whole life of the subject spoken of resides. The same is true of rûaḥ and πνεῦμα, they also mean breath, life, and living principle. The Scriptures therefore speak of the nepeš or ψυχή not only as that which lives or is the principle of life to the body, but as that which thinks and feels, which may be saved or lost, which survives the body and is immortal. The soul is the man himself, that in which his identity and personality reside. It is the Ego. Higher than the soul there is nothing in man. Therefore it is so often used as a synonym for self. Every soul is every man; my soul is I; his soul is he. What shall a man give in exchange for his soul. It is the soul that sins (Lev. 4:2); it is the soul that loves God. We are commanded to love God, ἐν ὅλῃ τῇ ψυχῇ. Hope is said to be the anchor of the soul, and the word of God is able to save the soul. The end of our faith is said to be (I Peter 1:9), the salvation of our souls; and John (Rev. 6:9; 20:4), saw in heaven the souls of them that were slain for the word of

God. From all this it is evident that the word ψυχή, or soul, does not designate the mere animal part of our nature, and is not a substance different from the πνεῦμα, or spirit. (3.) A third remark on this subject is that all the words above mentioned, *nepeš, rûaḥ,* and *nᵉšāmāh* in Hebrew, ψυχή and πνεῦμα in Greek, and soul and spirit in English, are used in the Scriptures indiscriminately of men and of irrational animals. If the Bible ascribed only a ψυχή to brutes, and both ψυχή and πνεῦμα to man, there would be some ground for assuming that the two are essentially distinct. But such is not the case. The living principle in the brute is called both *nepeš* and *rûaḥ,* ψυχή and πνεῦμα. That principle in the brute creation is irrational and mortal; in man it is rational and immortal. "Who knoweth the spirit of man that goeth upward, and the spirit of the beast that goeth downward to the earth?" Eccles. 3:21. The soul of the brute is the immaterial principle which constitutes its life, and which is endowed with sensibility, and that measure of intelligence which experience shows the lower animals to possess. The soul in man is a created spirit of a higher order, which has not only the attributes of sensibility, memory, and instinct, but also the higher powers which pertain to our intellectual, moral, and religious life. As in the brutes it is not one substance that feels and another that remembers; so it is not one substance in man that is the subject of sensations, and another substance which has intuitions of necessary truths, and which is endowed with conscience and with the knowledge of God. Philosophers speak of world-consciousness, or the immediate cognizance which we have of what is without us; of self-consciousness, or the knowledge of what is within us; and of God-consciousness, or our knowledge and sense of God. These all belong to one and the same immaterial, rational substance. (4.) It is fair to appeal to the testimony of consciousness on this subject. We are conscious of our bodies and we are conscious of our souls, *i. e.,* of the exercises and states of each; but no man is conscious of the ψυχή as distinct from the πνεῦμα, of the soul as different from the spirit. In other words consciousness reveals the existence of two substances in the constitution of our nature; but it does not reveal the existence of three substances, and therefore the existence of more than two cannot rationally be assumed.

## Doubtful Passages Explained

(5.) The passages of Scriptures which are cited as favouring the opposite doctrine may all be explained in consistency with the current representations of Scripture on the subject. When Paul says to the Thessalonians, "I pray God your whole spirit, and soul, and body, be preserved blameless unto the coming of our Lord Jesus Christ" (I Thessalonians 5:23), he only uses a periphrasis for the whole man. As when in Luke 1:46, 47, the virgin says, "My soul doth magnify the Lord, and my spirit hath rejoiced in God my Saviour," soul and spirit in this passage do not mean different things. And when we are commanded "Thou shalt love the Lord thy God with all thy heart, and with all thy soul, with all thy strength, and with all thy mind" (Luke 10:27), we have not an enumeration of so many distinct substances. Nor do we distinguish between the mind and heart as separate entities when we pray that both may be enlightened and sanctified; we mean simply the soul in all its aspects or faculties. Again, when in Heb. 4:12, the Apostle says that the word of God pierces so as to penetrate soul and spirit, and the joints and marrow, he does not assume that soul and spirit are different substances. The joints and marrow are not different substances. They are both material; they are different forms of the same substance; and so soul and spirit are one and the same substance under different aspects or relations. We can say that the word of God reaches not only to the feelings, but also to the conscience, without assuming that the heart and conscience are distinct entities. Much less is any such distinction implied in Phil. 1:27, "Stand fast in one spirit (ἐν ἐνὶ πνεύματι), with one mind (μιᾷ ψυχῇ)." There is more difficulty in explaining I Cor. 15:44. The Apostle there distinguishes between the σῶμα ψυχικόν and the σῶμα πνευματικόν; the former is that in which the ψυχή is the animating principle; and the latter that in which the πνεῦμα is the principle of life. The one we have here, the other we are to have hereafter. This seems to imply that the ψυχή exists in this life, but is not to exist hereafter, and therefore that the two are separable and distinct. In this explanation we might acquiesce if it did not contradict the general representations of the Scriptures. We are constrained, therefore, to seek another explanation which will harmonize with other portions of the word of God. The general meaning of the Apostle is plain. We have now gross, perishable, and dis-honorable, or unsightly bodies. Hereafter we are to have glorious bodies, adapted to a higher state of existence. The only question is, why does he call the one psychical, and the other pneumatic? Because the word ψυχή, although often used for the soul as rational and immortal, is also used for the lower form of life which belongs to irrational animals. Our future bodies are not to be adapted to those principles of our nature which we have in common with the brutes, but to those which are peculiar to us as men, created in the image of God. The same individual human soul has certain susceptibilities and powers which adapt it to the present state of existence, and to the earthly house in which it now dwells. It has animal appetites and necessities. It can hunger and thirst. It needs sleep and rest. But the same soul has higher powers. The earthly body is suited to its earthly state; the heavenly body to its heavenly state. There are not two substances ψυχή and πνεῦμα, there is but one and the same substance with different susceptibilities and powers. In this same connection Paul says, Flesh and blood cannot inherit the kingdom of heaven. Yet our bodies are to inherit that kingdom, and our bodies are flesh and blood. The same material substance now constituted as flesh and blood is to be so changed as to be like Christ's glorious body. As this representation does not prove a substantial difference between the body which now is and that which is to be hereafter, so neither does what the Apostle says of the σῶμα ψυχικόν and the σῶμα πνευματικόν prove that the ψυχή and πνεῦμα are distinct substances.

This doctrine of a threefold constitution of man being adopted by

Plato, was introduced partially into the early Church, but soon came to be regarded as dangerous, if not heretical. It being held by the Gnostics that the πνεῦμα in man was a part of the divine essence, and incapable of sin; and by the Apollinarians that Christ had only a human σῶμα and ψυχή, but not a human πνεῦμα, the Church rejected the doctrine that the ψυχή and πνεῦμα were distinct substances, since upon it those heresies were founded. In later times the Semi-Pelagians taught that the soul and body, but not the spirit in man were the subjects of original sin. All Protestants, Lutheran and Reformed, were, therefore, the more zealous in maintaining that the soul and spirit, ψυχή and πνεῦμα, are one and the same substance and essence. And this, as before remarked, has been the common doctrine of the Church.[6]

## Notes

[1] *Elements of Psychology*, Henry's translation, N.Y. 1856, p. 370.

[2] *Biblische Psychologie*, p. 64.

[3] August Hahn, *Lehrbuch des christlichen Glaubens*, p. 324.

[4] Göschel in Herzog's *Encyklopädie*, Article "Seele."

[5] *Biblische Psychologie*, §4, p. 128.

[6] See G. L. Hahn, *Theologie des N. T.* Olshausen, *De Trichotomia Naturae Humanae, a Novi Testamenti Scriptoribus recepta.* Ackermann, *Studien und Kritiken*, 1839, p. 882. J. T. Beck, *Umriss d. biblischen Seelenlehre*, 1843.

**7**

**D. R. G. Owen**

# "Body" and "Soul"
# in the New Testament

It would be very unlikely that a library of books, such as the Bible is, written by many different people varying in gifts and living in widely separated periods of time, would be perfectly consistent and uniform in all its views. It is certainly the case that in the Bible we find traces of several different traditions and thought-systems. The remarkable fact, about which Biblical scholars are in increasing agreement, is that there is a very high degree of unity in the principal ideas that are developed throughout the books of the Bible.

In trying to ascertain the Biblical teaching on any particular subject, we should concentrate on the main direction and momentum in the development of the relevant ideas, disregarding the minor deviations and departures from the norm. This is what we have done in tracing the Old Testament understanding of man. We have recognized that there are some traces of the "religious" anthropology in the wisdom literature and especially in the Apocrypha, but we have maintained that these were unimportant accretions of Greek thought and that they did not represent the main Biblical tradition on this subject.

From *Body and Soul* (Philadelphia: Westminster Press, 1956), pp. 180-97. Used by permission.

In the inter-Testamental period, these Greek ideas flourished more vigorously in certain Jewish circles, notably in the Hellenistic Judaism of Alexandria. This was the background of Philo's well-known attempt to work out a synthesis of Greek and Hebrew ideas. This kind of influence was undoubtedly strong at the time when the New Testament books were written. Not only were these books written in the Greek language, but their authors were also exposed to the Greek way of thinking, and a writer like the author of the Fourth Gospel may well have been a follower of Philo before he became a follower of Christ.

It would not be surprising, then, if some traces of the dualism and asceticism of the "religious" anthropology were to turn up in the Gospels and Epistles. It seems beyond question that they do. The following questions then arise. Are these Greek ideas in the New Testament, like their predecessors in the wisdom literature and the Apocrypha, to be considered as minor and alien intrusions in the main stream of thought? If so, then we have to reconstruct the normal New Testament view of man, disregarding these unimportant remainders of a quite different and inconsistent anthropology. Or are we forced to come to the conclusion that already in the New Testament itself, and even earlier, there existed a synthesis of Greek and Hebrew ideas and that this synthesis is the appropriate human vehicle for the communication of the gospel? If this is the case, then the patristic and medieval anthropologies, where they incorporate Greek ideas, do not represent a departure from the Biblical teaching but are simply a development of it.

It should be apparent by now that we shall adopt the former alternative. It will be our contention that the main line of thought in the New Testament view of man, as in the Old Testament, is radically different from, and irreconcilable with, the "religious" anthropology. It is the Hebrew, and not the Greek, conception that the New Testament, for the most part, assumes.

## The First Three Gospels

In order to establish this contention, we shall turn first of all to the Synoptic Gospels and the sayings ascribed there to our Lord himself. Here we must guard against the tendency to assume that the Greek words in which these sayings are expressed must be interpreted in a Greek way. Our Lord spoke Aramaic and not Greek, and the meaning of his words and phrases must be sought, not in the Greek, but in the Hebrew background out of which, humanly speaking, he sprang.

This observation is relevant, first of all, to the use of the words "soul" and "body and soul" in the dominical sayings. In Hebrew thought, as we have seen, the word translated "soul" regularly stands simply for the personal pronoun and means the self. And the phrase "body and soul," though its occurrence is rare in both Testaments, stands for the Hebrew idea that man is an "animated body" and not for the Greek view that he is an "incarnated soul."

It is in this way that we must understand the verse: "And fear not them which kill the body, but are not able to kill the soul: but rather fear him which is able to destroy both soul and body in hell" (Matt. 10:28). This saying is always cited by those who believe that the New Testament, and indeed Jesus himself, asserts the essential immortality and incorruptibility of the soul, with all the dualistic implications of this belief. Thus Dr. Eugene Fairweather, in drawing attention to this passage, writes that here "the doctrine of the immortality of the soul, subject only to divine omnipotence, is plainly indicated."[1] But it is only "plainly indicated" if the verse is interpreted in terms of Greek presuppositions. And there is no reason for supposing that Jesus thought in such terms. The Judaism in which he was brought up was Palestinian and not Hellenistic. If we interpret this passage in the light of its Hebrew background, the plain meaning seems to be this: "Fear not man who can only bring your present existence to an end but cannot annihilate the essential self; but fear God who is able to destroy the whole man eternally."[2]

There are only a few other passages in the Synoptic Gospels that might be taken to imply a Greeklike depreciation of the bodily and earthy, on the one hand, and an exaltation of the "spiritual" and heavenly, on the other, along with the body-soul dualism that such a contrast implies. We may cite the following:

> Lay not up for yourselves treasures upon earth, where moth and rust doth corrupt, and where thieves break through and steal: But lay up for yourselves treasures in heaven, where neither moth nor rust doth corrupt, and where thieves do not break through nor steal. (Matt. 6:19, 20)

> Take no thought for your life, what ye shall eat, or what ye shall drink; nor yet for your body, what ye shall put on. Is not the life more than meat, and the body than raiment? . . . Therefore, take no thought, saying, What shall we eat? or, What shall we drink? or, Wherewithal shall we be clothed? . . . for your heavenly Father knoweth that ye have need of all these things. But seek ye first the kingdom of God, and his righteousness; and all these things shall be added unto you. (Matt. 6:25ff.)

We should notice, first of all, that the importance of the body and of physical needs in general is by no means denied here. The body and its needs are far from being depreciated. "Is not the life more than meat, and the body than raiment?" Man's physical existence is *more* than a question of food and clothes; it has a higher significance and destiny. Moreover, "your heavenly Father knoweth that ye have need of all these things" and "all these things shall be added unto you." There is not the slightest suggestion here of any "puritanical" suppression of the physical demands; it is simply a question, as everyone except the most extreme advocates of free self-expression would agree, of subordinating the physical requirements and putting them in their proper place. It is a question of putting first things first. But this does not mean that second things are denied any place at all. Far from it; in their proper place they receive their proper satisfaction. "Seek ye first the kingdom of God . . . and all these things shall be added unto you."

"The kingdom of God" in the one passage and the "treasures in heaven" in the other stand for the true end of life; they symbolize God's ultimate purpose for man. This end and purpose should be our primary aim, the final good in accordance with which we should make our decisions. Food, drink, clothing, "treasures on earth" have their place and value, but only in relation to this highest value. And this ultimate end is the Kingdom of Heaven established on earth. It is the transfiguration (not the annihilation) of the whole physical order and of everything in it.

### The Johannine Literature

We turn next to the Gospel and Epistles ascribed traditionally to Saint John. In this body of writing we seem, at first sight, to come upon a definite strain of hostility to the world and the flesh, very similar to the attitude of the "religious" anthropology. The following are representative passages:

> That which is born of the flesh is flesh; and that which is born of the Spirit is spirit. (John 3:6)

> It is the Spirit that quickeneth; the flesh profiteth nothing. (John 6:63)

> He that hateth his life in this world shall keep it unto life eternal. (John 12:25)

> In the world ye shall have tribulation: but be of good cheer; I have overcome the world. (John 16:33)

> Love not the world, neither the things that are in the world. If any man love the world, the love of the Father is not in him. For all that is in the world, the lust of the flesh, and the lust of the eyes, and the pride of life, is not of the Father, but is of the world. And the world passeth away, and the lust thereof: but he that doeth the will of God abideth for ever. (I John 2:15-17)

All this sounds very like that Greek and Eastern denigration of this world that condemns it as ephemeral and bad in contrast to the purity and eternity of the "spiritual" realm. Indeed, the Greek doctrine of immortality, always part of such a view, seems clearly indicated in the last sentence quoted, as well as in the words, "Whosoever liveth and believeth in me shall never die" (John 11:26; cf. ch. 6:50-58).

In considering such passages, we must remember, first of all, that in the Johannine literature and, for that matter, in the Bible generally, there is an ambivalent attitude to the world and the flesh. On the one hand, as created by God, they are evaluated as inherently good. Indeed, it is in The Gospel According to St. John itself that we read that "God so loved the world, that he gave his only begotten Son" and that "God sent not his Son into the world to condemn the world; but that the world through him might be saved" (John 3:16-17). The world, as made by God, is good, and he loves it with an everlasting and unfailing love. On the other hand, according to the Bible, this world has fallen away from its Creator. It is a "fallen" world and is in rebellion against God. It is in its "fallen" and rebellious condition that the world is opposed by God and should be resisted by man. The fact that it is "fallen" does not mean, however, that God will destroy it. The New Testament teaching is that he has taken decisive steps to re-create and save it.

Similarly, the flesh as made by God is good—so much so that it is possible, as Saint John again tells us, for the Word of God to *be made flesh*. But the flesh too is "fallen" and has become bad. However, it will not for that reason be annihilated by God. On the contrary, the Word was made flesh in order to remake and to redeem our flesh. Thus, Christians are called, not to leave the flesh and the world and depart to some other realm, but rather to remain in the flesh and in the world. "I pray not that thou shouldst take them out of the world" (John 17:15). "Now I am no more in the world, but these are in the world" (John 17:11). "As thou hast sent me into the world, even so have I also sent them into the world" (John 17:18). Christians must remain in the world; it is in itself good and it is their abode. On the other hand, "they are not of the world, even as I am not of the world" (John 17:16). They are not "worldly," in the sense of acquiescing in the world's "fallen" condition. Because of the ambivalent status of the world, as both created by God and "fallen," Christians are in an ambivalent relation to the world: they are in, but not of, the world. What exactly it means to be "of the world," to be worldly and fleshly-minded, and what is meant by the contrast between "the world" and "the flesh," on the one hand, and "the Spirit," on the other, are questions that we shall leave until we come to the Pauline material that deals at length with this subject.

We have still to deal with the Johannine passages that state, in the English version, that whoever believes in Christ will abide forever or "never die." If such a person never dies, then it follows, since the body is certainly doomed to dissolution, that there is a part of man that is at any rate capable of immortality. And if this is the case we have arrived again at dualism. Once more, however, a quite different interpretation is possible, especially if we look at the Greek original. First of all, in the Greek, the adjective in phrases such as "everlasting life" and "eternal life" is *aiōnios.* Now the noun *aiōn* in the New Testament very often means "the age to come"; and therefore the adjective *aiōnios* may very well mean, not "everlasting," in the sense of continuous, unbroken survival, but rather "having to do with the age to come." If this is the case, then "eternal" life means the kind of life that belongs to the age to come; and "everlasting" is a mistranslation.

In the same way, if we look at the Greek of the verses translated, "Whosoever liveth and believeth in me shall never die" (John 11:26), and,

"He that doeth the will of God abideth for ever" (I John 2:17), we shall find that in both cases the relevant verses might be translated literally, "Will not be dead," or, "Will abide in the age to come." This interpretation seems to be confirmed by two other passages in which the believer is promised eternal or *aiōnios* life:

> And this is the will of him that sent me, that every one which seeth the Son, and believeth on him, may have everlasting [*aiōnios*] life: and I will raise him up at the last day. (John 6:40)

> Whoso eateth my flesh, and drinketh my blood, hath eternal [*aiōnios*] life; and I will raise him up at the last day. (John 6:54)

The meaning here seems unmistakable: The believer has *aiōnios* life, that is to say, "I will raise him up at the last day." Similarly, it should be noted that the saying translated, "Whosoever liveth and believeth in me shall never die," is given in the context of the raising of Lazarus from the dead, and immediately follows the great declaration, "I am the resurrection, and the life: he that believeth in me, though he were dead, yet shall he live" (John 11:25). In other words, in every case, *aiōnios* life is related, not to the immortality of the soul, but to the resurrection of the body at "the last day." It is an eschatological concept, developed from the Hebrew tradition, and not a metaphysical concept, borrowed from the Greek.[3]

There is one more point to be made in this connection. The Johannine teaching usually refers to eternal or *aiōnios* life as a present possession. The believer *has* eternal life here and now. How can this be so, if eternal life is the life proper to the age *to come?* The answer is that eschatological concepts like "the age to come" and "the last day" do not refer to the historical future; they are not temporal concepts at all; it is only the poverty of our language and thought-forms that makes it necessary for us to express them in this misleading way. The New Testament teaching is that in Jesus Christ the "last things" have broken into time and space and that the believer, in so far as he is "in Christ," has within himself a pledge and earnest of the final consummation.

Perhaps we have here too a clue to the persistent question: If the Christian view of the "future life" is entirely eschatological and has nothing to do with any "immortality of the soul," then what happens to the individual between the time of his death and the "time" of the general resurrection at the "last day"? The answer is that the question is asked in the wrong way; phrases like the "future life" and the "time" of the general resurrection indicate that the problem is a pseudo problem, based on a misreading of eschatological language in temporal terms. There is no interval between the death of the individual and the "last day" that has to be accounted for by postulating an intermediate state and a ghostly, disembodied survival. The "last day" is not a future event; it is not an event in time at all. There is therefore no "time" of the general resurrection, no "interval" between the individual's death and the "last day," nor is it proper to speak of eternal or *aiōnios* life as a "future" life.

This is a negative answer to a very pressing question. But the truth is that the Bible tells us very little about what happens "after" death or about the nature of the final consummation of God's purposes for man. It may be that we are told as much as we are capable of understanding. And that is certainly not very much. Where we do not know the answers, it is best to say so, and to remain frankly agnostic.

## The Pauline Epistles

In Saint Paul we find a further doctrinal development of the implications of the gospel. It seems probable that, as far as his Jewish background was concerned, he was influenced by both the Hellenistic and the Palestinian types of Judaism. He certainly had some familiarity with Greek thought, and there are undoubtedly traces, here and there, of the "religious" anthropology in his writings. We shall argue, however, that this influence is not nearly so strong as is often supposed and that the main line of his thought is a development of Hebrew ideas.

J. A. T. Robinson, in a most careful and thorough study of the Pauline literature, asserts without hesitation that Paul's view of man is derived from Hebrew rather than from Greek sources.[4] For Greek thought, man is a soul incarcerated in a physical frame, from which he hopes to escape. For the Hebrews and for Paul, on the contrary, man is, in Wheeler Robinson's phrase, "an animated body." In the words of Pedersen, "the body is the soul in its outward form."[5] According to J. A. T. Robinson, Paul follows the Hebrew tradition as formulated in the dictum: "Man does not have a body; he is a body." "He is flesh-animated-by-soul, the whole conceived as a psychophysical unity."[6] In fact, in Paul's usage, as we shall see, the Greek word *sōma* (body) is very nearly what we mean by personality: it stands for the whole man. We remember again Wheeler Robinson's remark that for the Hebrews "the body was the man."[7] All this, of course, is almost the exact opposite of the Greek view.

If these were Paul's presuppositions, it follows that he could not possibly have adopted any form of body-soul dualism. The doctrine of the immortality of a disembodied soul would be just inconceivable. And it would be equally out of the question to identify the "body" and its appetites as the source of evil.

What are we to say, then, of the well-known Pauline contrast between the "flesh" and the "Spirit"? Let us look at two typical passages:

> For they that are after the flesh do mind the things of the flesh; but they that are after the Spirit, the things of the Spirit. For to be carnally minded is death; but to be spiritually minded is life and peace. Because the carnal mind is enmity against God: . . . So then they that are in the flesh cannot please God. But ye are not in the flesh, but in the Spirit. . . . And if Christ be in you, the body is dead because of sin; but the Spirit is life because of righteousness. . . . Therefore, brethren, we are debtors, not to the flesh, to live after the flesh. For if ye live after the

flesh, ye shall die: but if ye through the Spirit do mortify the
deeds of the body, ye shall live. (Rom. 8:5ff.)

This I say then, Walk in the Spirit, and ye shall not fulfil the
lust of the flesh. For the flesh lusteth against the Spirit, and the
Spirit against the flesh: and these are contrary the one to the
other. . . . And they that are Christ's have crucified the flesh with
the affections and lusts. If we live in the Spirit, let us also walk in
the Spirit. (Gal. 5:16ff.)

These two passages are always cited to support the charge that Christianity, especially in the Pauline version, was responsible for spreading the
doctrines of dualism, antiphysical asceticism, and "spiritual" otherworldliness in the Western world.[8]

The first thing to point out, in showing that such an interpretation of
the Pauline teaching is entirely mistaken, is that Paul in these and similar
passages never uses the Greek words for "body" and "soul" (*sōma* and
*psychē*). He always employs a different pair of terms, namely, *sarx* and
*pneuma* (translated "flesh" and "spirit"). If he had intended to take over
the typical Greek body-soul dualism, he would certainly have used the
Greek words *sōma* and *psychē* that were standard in that doctrine. But his
antithesis is, in fact, an entirely different one, and he therefore uses a quite
different set of words in which to express it.

What really clinches the argument against the dualistic and "puritanical" interpretation of the Pauline contrast is the list of "lusts" or "works
of the flesh" that he gives in one of the very passages cited (Gal., ch. 5).
There are seventeen "works of the flesh" listed there, and only six of them
have any connection with the "body," as usually understood: "adultery,
fornication, uncleanness, lasciviousness, drunkenness, revellings, and such
like." And, of course, it is obvious that what is referred to here is the
abuse of physical appetites and not the appetites themselves. But what is
far more telling is that the remaining eleven "lusts" have nothing whatever
to do with physical impulses and desires. The other "works of the flesh"
are "idolatry, witchcraft, hatred, variance, emulations, wrath, strife, sedi-
tions, heresies, envyings, murders." In another place, Paul writes, "Ye are
yet carnal: for . . . there is among you envying, and strife, and divisions"
(I Cor. 3:3). This is what it means to be "carnal" and "fleshly-minded";
this is what it means to be "worldly," and to "live after the flesh." These
are "the affections and lusts" of the flesh.

This seems to prove conclusively that in Paul the phrase "the flesh"
does not stand for one part of man, such as his "body," nor the phrase
"the Spirit" for another part, such as his "soul," the former being thought
of as by nature bad and the latter good.

At the same time, Paul is certainly making a very sharp antithesis between "the flesh" and "the Spirit." What do these terms stand for, and
what is the nature of the contrast that he has in mind? There can be no
doubt that "the flesh" and "the Spirit" stand, not for two separate and
opposing parts of human nature, but rather for two different kinds of
man.

The word *sarx* (flesh) in the Pauline epistles frequently means just the whole man, regarded from one point of view.[9] In this, Paul is following a fairly common Biblical usage. We recall sayings like "all flesh is grass," "all flesh shall see the salvation of God," and "the Word was made flesh." So in Paul, *sarx* is often[10] interchangeable with the personal pronoun. And the point of view from which the whole man is here regarded is the point of view of his creatureliness, his oneness with nature, and "his difference and distance from God";[11] here *sarx* stands for the "natural man." In some cases, *sarx* means no more than this, and therefore has no sinful connotations at all.

More frequently, however, and especially in the passages where "the flesh" is contrasted with "the Spirit," *sarx* stands for the whole man, not only in his natural status, but in his "fallen" and unregenerate nature, in the same way that the "natural man" in Christian theology usually means sinful man. In this usage, *sarx* means the whole man regarded from the point of view of his sinfulness. But this sinfulness does not reside in the physical aspects of his nature in contrast to the alleged purity of his "spiritual" dimension. Man's sinfulness, according to the Pauline (and indeed the whole Biblical) teaching, consists precisely in his refusal to admit his creaturely status and in his unwillingness to recognize his "difference from God." Instead of recognizing that he is a creature of God, he wants to "set up on his own"; he claims absolute autonomy and complete self-sufficiency.

This is how J. A. T. Robinson, giving a long list of references, summarizes the Pauline position on this question:

> Living "after the flesh" is sinful not because the flesh is evil or impure but because such an attitude is a denial of the human situation over against God . . . a distortion of the fundamental relation of the creature to God. One could describe the situation by saying that *sarx* as neutral [the first meaning quoted above] is man living in the world, *sarx* as sinful [second meaning] is man living for the world; he becomes "a man of the world" by allowing his being-in-the-world, itself God-given, to govern his whole life and conduct. . . . Consequently, as Bultmann rightly stresses, "the mind of the flesh" stands primarily for a denial of man's dependence on God and for a trust in what is of human effort and origin.[12]

Thus, as Robinson goes on to point out, the passage beginning, "Having begun in the Spirit, are ye now made perfect by the flesh?" (Gal. 3:3) refers "not to a lapse into sensuality but to a return to reliance upon the law and represents human self-sufficiency." Similarly "fleshly wisdom" (II Cor. 1:12) is "a man's trust in his own knowledge and experience" rather than in God. Thus Paul "recapitulates the message of the Old Testament: 'Cursed be the man that trusteth in man, and maketh flesh his arm, and whose heart departeth from the Lord' " (Jer. 17:5). *Sarx,* in this usage, is man with his whole nature corrupted by the sin of titanic pride; it is the condition of man who, being an adjective, claims to be a noun.

Thus, the meaning of "the flesh," like the meaning of "the world," is ambivalent in Paul, as in the Bible generally. The flesh and the world, as created by God, are man's intended lot and, as such, are the objects of God's love. But when the world and the flesh deny their creaturely status, rebel against God and claim independence and sufficiency, they become bad; and in this sense worldliness and carnal- or fleshly-mindedness are synonymous with sinfulness. But this view of sin has nothing in common with the antiphysical bias.

It is also obvious that the antithesis between "the flesh" and "the Spirit" has nothing in common with body-soul dualism. "The flesh" does not stand for one part of man, his "body," which is bad. "The flesh" stands, rather, for a certain kind of man. It stands for the kind of man in whom the whole person (the spiritual and psychical aspects, just as much as the physical, to revert to our earlier usage) is misdirected, because turned in upon himself in self-centeredness and self-satisfaction. In traditional theological language, "the flesh" stands for "fallen," sinful, unregenerate man.

If this is the case, the meaning of "the Spirit" in Paul is clear. "The Spirit" represents, not another part of man, his "soul," which is pure, but rather another kind of man. It represents the kind of man in whom the whole person (the physical and psychical, just as much as the spiritual aspects) is directed outward in love toward God and his neighbor; it is the man in whom we see "the fruit of the Spirit"—"love, joy, peace, long-suffering, gentleness, goodness, faith, meekness, temperance" (Gal. 5:22, 23). In short, it is redeemed man, the man who is "in Christ."

There is no actual man, of course, except Jesus Christ himself, who fully exemplifies what Paul means by "the Spirit" or the "spiritually-minded," in contrast to "the flesh" and the "fleshly-minded." In all men, even the best of them, a conflict continues: "For the good that I would, I do not: but the evil that I would not, that I do. . . . So then with the mind I myself serve the law of God; but with the flesh the law of sin" (Rom. 7:19-25). But this is not a conflict between the bad body and the pure mind. The conflict consists in the fact that in me, "the flesh," the old, self-centered man, is not wholly "crucified with Christ" but keeps rearing up to misdirect, not just my "body" and its appetites, but my whole being, in opposition to "the Spirit," the new man "in Christ," who is struggling to be born, "to rise with him." The Christian life involves a real and terrible conflict, but this conflict has no dualistic or "puritanical" implications.

So much for the meaning of *sarx* and *pneuma* in Paul. What, then, is the meaning of *sōma* and *psychē* in his writings? We have already mentioned Robinson's view that in Paul *sōma* ("body") is used much the same way as we use "personality": "*sōma,* again like *sarx,* does not mean simply something external to a man himself, something he *has.* It *is* what he is. Indeed, *sōma* is the nearest equivalent to our word 'personality.' "[13] Now, in the Hebrew, it is *nephesh* that stands for the personal pronoun, and Paul usually translates this word as *psychē.* Thus we arrive at the conclusion that in Paul *sōma* and *psychē*, as well as *sarx* and *pneuma*, are all used to stand for the whole man, but for the whole man regarded from different points of view.[14]

Robinson distinguishes many different usages of the word *sōma* in the Pauline writings. In all of them the term stands for the whole, and not a detachable part of, man. Two of these usages are relevant to our purpose. In the first meaning of *sōma*, it is virtually equivalent to *sarx* and stands, like *sarx*, for the whole man as seen in both his weakness and sinfulness, over against the power and holiness of God.[15] Thus, in one passage, "the deeds of the body," which must be "mortified," are none other than the results of living "after the flesh" (Rom. 8:13). In fact, as Robinson observes, in some manuscripts they have become "the deeds of the flesh."[16] "The identification of *sōma* with *sarx* seems complete. In fact, in Col. 2:11, it is closed in the phrase, 'the body of the flesh'—the whole personality organized for, and geared into, rebellion against God."[17] There is no question but that here *sōma* stands for the whole man in his "fallen," sinful condition. But it is equally obvious that *sōma* in this context has nothing in common with the *sōma* of the *sōma-sēma* doctrine in the "religious" anthropology.

As Robinson points out, "The very phrase ['the body of the flesh'] indicates the possibility of a *sōma* that is not *tēs sarkos* ['of the flesh'] ."[18] This brings us to the second Pauline usage of *sōma* that we must mention. In this usage, *sōma* means the whole man as destined for membership in God's Kingdom; it stands for man as God meant him to be. Thus *sōma*, while it may become identified with *sarx*, due to man's "fallen" condition, is by no means identical with *sarx*.[19] For *sarx* is destined for death and destruction, but *sōma* is the carrier of man's resurrection. While *sarx* stands for man "as wholly perishable," *sōma* stands for man "as wholly destined for God."[20] "While *sarx* stands for man, in the solidarity of creation, in his distance from God, *sōma* stands for man, in the solidarity of creation, as made for God."[21] The body is "for the Lord; and the Lord for the body. And God hath both raised up the Lord, and will also raise up us by his own power" (I Cor. 6:13, 14).

Man, as *sarx*, cannot inherit the Kingdom of God (I Cor. 15:50), but man, as *sōma* (and only as *sōma*), can. The fact that the *sōma* is to be raised indicates, of course, that it too must first die; for the resurrection is the "resurrection of the dead" (I Cor. 15:21). So also the *sōma* to be raised will be a radically changed *sōma*. The radical change is emphasized in the *locus classicus* on this subject and is described there as a change from a "natural [*psychikon*] body" to a "spiritual [*pneumatikon*] body" (I Cor. 15:35ff.), that is to say, a change from human personality in its weakness and sinfulness to human personality as God meant it to be. And yet, as we saw earlier, this change, however radical, does not involve a completely fresh start. The resurrection "body," or new man, is not new in the sense that it has no connection with the old. It is new in the sense that it is the old made new. As Robinson points out, it is "not a *nea* but a *kaine ktisis*"[22] (II Cor. 5:17); or, to put it into contemporary idiom, it is not a brand-new but a reconditioned model. In Paul's analogy, it is like the relationship between the seed and the full-grown plant (I Cor. 15:35ff.); there is a great change, but it is a change that perfects and brings to maturity. And this change happens, perhaps partly through growth and development in the Christian life, but only finally and completely, "in a moment, in the twinkling of an eye, at the last trump: for the trumpet shall sound, and the dead shall be raised incorruptible, and we shall be changed" (I Cor. 15:52).

It seems safe to say that this brief review of the New Testament writings has established our main contention. The New Testament anthropology, where it takes over earlier views, is in the Hebrew rather than the Greek tradition. There is little trace of body-soul dualism; instead, man is regarded as a unity. This personal unity that is man can be called, as a whole, either *sōma* (body) or *psychē* (soul) or *sarx* (flesh) or *pneuma* (Spirit), depending on the point of view from which man is being considered. But the point is that none of these terms refers to a part of man; they all refer to the whole. It follows that if man is an indivisible unity, there is no detachable part of him that can survive death. The New Testament, therefore, does not teach a doctrine of the immortality of the separated soul. Instead, it promises a resurrection of the whole man (the *sōma*). Finally, in this context of ideas, there can be no "puritanical" depreciation of, and hostility to, the physical aspects of human existence, with its accompanying exaltation of pure "spirituality."[23] The physical, both in the individual and in reality in general, has its essential and eternal role to play in human life. Man's ultimate destiny belongs, not to the ethereal regions but to "the world to come," "the world without end." And in this "world to come," the individual will be a "new body" and this earth will be a "new earth." But this newness will be a *kaine* and not a *nea* creation.

### Appendix: Antiphysical Asceticism and Otherworldliness in the New Testament

There are a few passages in the New Testament that suggest a hostile attitude to sex and even a tendency to regard the married state as a kind of concession to human frailty; e.g., Matt. 19:12: "There be eunuchs, which have made themselves eunuchs for the kingdom of heaven's sake. He that is able to receive it, let him receive it"; and a few notorious remarks of Saint Paul, especially I Cor., ch. 7, beginning, "It is good for a man not to touch a woman," and containing the assertion that "it is better to marry than to burn."

The remark attributed to our Lord in The Gospel According to St. Matthew is not repeated in any other Gospel. If it is taken as a disparagement of marriage, it is entirely out of keeping with our Lord's usual attitude to this state of life. If it is authentic, it may mean simply that some people are called to fulfill special roles in life that demand a sacrifice of some of the good things of life.

As for the various adverse comments on marriage that were made by

Saint Paul, there are a number of possible explanations. It may be that we have here some traces of the antiphysical bias of the "religious" anthropology that simply cannot be reconciled with the overall tenor of the normal Biblical view. Or these remarks may be "ad hoc recommendations to meet a specific local situation rather than general principles." Or they may be "due to the expectation that Christ would return at any moment" and that therefore no man should change his existing status. (See E. LaB. Cherbonnier, *Hardness of Heart* [Doubleday & Co., Inc., New York, 1955], pp. 83-84.)

There are also one or two passages in Saint Paul that suggest the possibility of escaping from the body in mystical vision, e.g., II Cor. 12:2, 3, and even the desire to escape from it altogether ultimately, e.g., ch. 5:6-8. These again may be due to the influence of "religious" otherworldliness and, in that case, would certainly be inconsistent with Saint Paul's normal attitude to the "body" as outlined in this chapter. The inconsistency is apparent in the latter passage itself; for just before he speaks of being "willing to be absent from the body and present with the Lord," he writes (v. 4), "We that are in this tabernacle do groan, being burdened: not for that we would be unclothed, but clothed upon, that mortality might be swallowed up of life." Here the doctrine of the resurrection of the body seems to be directly contrasted with the "religious" idea of the immortality of the "naked" soul (see v. 3).

In any case, as we have pointed out, and as Cherbonnier says, "The Bible contains within itself its own internal principles of self-criticism against which [such remarks] . . . can be tested." We have to bear in mind at all times "the spirit of the Bible as a whole" (*op. cit.,* p. 82). And "the spirit of the Bible as a whole" is definitely against the type of otherworldly mysticism that is suggested in the odd passage in Saint Paul.

## Notes

[1] E. R. Fairweather, "In Defense of Immortality," *Theology,* Vol. LVI, No. 396, pp. 219, 220.

[2] Cf. the version of this saying in Luke 12:4, 5 which seems to support our interpretation.

[3] My colleague Dr. F. W. Beare, who is a leading New Testament scholar, strongly disputes my exegesis of John 11:26. He points out that the construction here—"shall not die [or, as I put it, "be dead"] *eis ton aiōna"*—has an exact parallel in John 13:8: "Shall not wash my feet *eis ton aiōna."* The latter must be translated, "Shall *never* wash my feet." Therefore, he argues, the former must be translated, "Shall never die." I admit the force of this argument, of course. Nevertheless, it seems to me quite possible that the Greek word *aiōn,* where it is connected with the question of *death,* has its technical meaning, viz., "the age to come," while elsewhere it is combined with the negative in the ordinary way to mean "never." I attach a good deal of importance to the fact that phrases of this kind in Saint John are usually followed immediately by some such clause as, "And I will raise him up at the last day." Dr. Beare can only explain

this by saying that the author of the Fourth Gospel is simply combining two different ideas, namely, the resurrection of the body that was part of the new gospel he had received, and the immortality of the soul that was part of his earlier philosophy, and that he did not perceive that the two ideas were incompatible. This may be the proper explanation. If so, we should simply have to recognize that the "religious" doctrine of the immortality of the soul has crept in here, but is quite out of keeping with the main New Testament teaching. I myself, however, have more respect for the intellectual acumen of the author of this Gospel, and therefore prefer the exegesis I have given in the text. After all, the same linguistic construction may be used in different contexts with different meanings.

[4] *The Body*, p. 11. In what follows I am heavily indebted to this work.

[5] *Israel* 1-11, J. Pedersen, p. 171. Quoted in *The Body*, p. 14.

[6] *The Body, loc. cit.*

[7] "Hebrew Psychology," p. 366.

[8] See e.g., Professor White's essay "The Greek and Roman Contribution," in *The Heritage of Western Culture*, ed. R. C. Chalmers, pp. 19-21.

[9] *The Body*, pp. 17-19.

[10] See Eph. 5:28; II Cor. 7:5; Col. 1:24; II Cor. 4:11.

[11] *The Body*, p. 19. Cf. Job 10:4; Isa. 31:3.

[12] *Op. cit.*, pp. 25, 26. His references are to Rom. 16:18; Phil. 3:19; I Cor. 7:32; Gal. 5:16, 24; Rom. 13:14; Eph. 2:3; Col. 2:23; 3:2.

[13] *Op. cit.*, p. 28.

[14] *Op. cit.*, p. 13, footnote.

[15] *Op. cit.*, p. 26.

[16] Cf. Rom. 8:10; 7:22-25; Col. 3:5.

[17] *The Body*, pp. 30, 31.

[18] *Op. cit.*, p. 31.

[19] *Loc. cit.*

[20] *Op. cit.*, pp. 31, 32, footnote.

[21] *Op. cit.*, p. 31.

[22] *Op. cit.*, p. 82.

[23] See Appendix to this chapter.

# Sin

## Editor's Introduction

In part 1 we examined something of the ideal man, or man as he was intended to be when he came from the Creator's hand. Man, however, has a sickness, a serious sickness, and its name is sin. The selections in part 2 attempt to define sin and to describe its effects upon man.

A study of the nature of sin must begin with an examination of the Biblical terms for sin. This is done in the article by **H. Wheeler Robinson**. There are a number of such terms, reflecting the various nuances of meaning of sin. For the Hebrew terms there are, in most cases, corresponding Greek words in the New Testament. These give us insight into the fundamental principle of sin—deviation from God's will and character.

A further question, however, is, What is the source of sin? Or, to put it differently, Why does man sin? This in turn helps to define or at least to measure the seriousness of sin, for sin is less serious if it is in some way accidental than if it stems from a definite and deliberate voluntary decision of man, for which he is clearly and fully responsible.

A number of explanations of sin, proposing that it is of this accidental nature, have been advanced. One says that it is a product of man's animal origin, from which the evolutionary process has not fully freed him. His "sin" is simply a result of the survival instinct, necessary at the prerational stage and naturally manifesting itself in selfish tendencies. Another and rather contemporary variety explains sin as the result of cultural deprivation. Because of various conditioning factors, the actions termed *sin* are determined. Man is not really free in his actions, particularly here. **F. R. Tennant**'s selection falls into this category.

Another variety of this view sees sin stemming from ignorance. In the Platonic tradition, if man knew which course of action is the good and right one, he would will to do it and would be able to carry out that decision. Man's difficulty is his finitude. If his ability to discover and comprehend truth were not so limited, he would of course understand what he ought to do and do it. Because no man is responsible for his finitude, his sin is really not *evil.*

**Calvin Linton** opposes this view. Drawing more upon examples from general culture, he examines some of the statements of the view that man's imperfection results from ignorance rather than evil, and he systematically refutes these claims. His own view is that man sins because his nature has been radically corrupted. The once complete, perfect, ideal nature of man has been spoiled through the fall, which in turn resulted from man's freely chosen rebellion. Evil is not merely incidental to man, it is endemic to his nature as he is now found. Not only does the Christian doctrine of sin accurately describe man, but the Christian doctrine of salvation provides the only basis for optimism regarding the possibility of overcoming perpetual evil.

We must also ask about the consequences of sin, and especially of original sin. *Original sin* refers to the concept that man does not begin life with a good or even an innocent nature, but that he is already affected by the fall, or the sin, of Adam, the first man and the head of the human race. Conservatives have generally regarded the fall as an historical event, something that happened within time to a man and a woman, from whom all other humans are descended. Others regard the fall as a nonhistorical parable—describing human existence, as each of us finds it in ourselves and as it is at every point in time. It simply characterizes us as we are.

The traditional term for this debilitating effect of sin is *corruption.* Two selections here represent contrasting views on the topic. **Jonathan Edwards,** a New England preacher, presents the Calvinistic view of man as totally depraved or corrupted. He maintains that men received from Adam a nature that was, to say the least, "spoiled" by sin. This means that inevitably all men sin. Edwards sees a clear demonstration of this in the fact that men universally fall into sin. Certainly, if man is no worse than innocent, someone, somewhere, ought to live a perfect life. Thus human experience confirms what Scripture emphatically affirms. We do not begin life where Adam and Eve did, morally and spiritually, but with a propensity to sin.

The thought of Pelagius, presented by **Gustave F. Wiggers,** represents a very different position. Although living in the fourth century, the motivation behind his contentions sound, in some ways, strangely contemporary. Pelagius felt that the continual emphasis on man's depravity and wickedness caused him to sin. Expecting that he could not help but sin, he naturally sinned. Thus Pelagius and his followers developed the conception that all men, like Adam and Eve, begin life innocent, fully capable of fulfilling the requirements of God by their own efforts. Adam's sin did not directly disable his descendants, it only gave them a bad example to follow.

The selection from **Reinhold Niebuhr's** classic, *The Nature and Destiny of Man,* represents a different point of departure. Drawing heavily upon the existentialism of Sören Kierkegaard, Niebuhr's analysis is more psychological than theological. Man inevitably sins because his finiteness and the external obstacles and threats make him feel insecure. He seeks security in self-glorification and self-gratification. This combination of finitude, freedom, insecurity, and the attempt to obtain security by achieving infinity seem to be characteristic of all men. Thus, man sins inevitably yet is responsible for his actions. Niebuhr does not attempt to explain why man is the way he is, or in what way men are interconnected. He simply asserts that this is a universal phenomenon.

But another consequence of sin, whether the original sin of the race or the continued sinning of individuals, is guilt. This means not merely subjective feelings of guiltiness, which may be unjustified, but actual moral liability, deserving of punishment. **Charles G. Finney** and **James Orr** agree that the acts of each person bring him into a state of blameworthiness. In Finney's view, however, each man is guilty *only* for the acts he has personally performed. Orr, on the other hand, extends this guilt to the original sin, or the sin of the first pair, arguing that there are social and corporate dimensions to responsibility. He also maintains that the penalty for sin is not exhausted in this life, but rather carries over into the life beyond.

Finney, however, sees the consequences of sin as less serious. The original or primal sin only corrupts or depraves, it does not carry attendant guilt. This presupposes that guilt can properly be counted only where there is personal volitional action, with consequent responsibility. A person is not punished for the sinful nature which he inherits, only for the sins that he himself commits.

Among those who believe that guilt for sin is somehow "imputed" to the descendants of Adam, there are differences of opinion. **Louis Berkhof** represents what is sometimes referred to as the "federal headship" view. According to this view, Adam acted as our representative. He acted on our behalf, so that what he did was regarded as the action of the entire human race. Just as we are held responsible for the decisions and actions of the public servants whom we have chosen to represent us, so we are responsible for Adam's act. **Russell Shedd**, however, presents a view of the solidarity of the human race. In contrast to the individualism that has so strongly characterized Western man, the Hebrews thought of the nation of Israel as a unity, an organism. Paul extends this to include the idea that Adam was the human race, that in him all men sinned, and hence all became guilty.

# The Nature of Sin

## H. Wheeler Robinson

## Old Testament Terminology for Sin

The account already given of the development of individualism has itself involved the frequent recognition of a growing consciousness of sin amongst the religious thinkers of Israel. This fact is full of meaning for our subject; we shall find the most characteristic features of the doctrine of man at every period brought to light through the study of the doctrine of sin, just as the central and characteristic element in the doctrine of God will always be the doctrine of grace. Both sin and grace require a survey of the whole history of religion in any given period for their adequate doctrinal statement; in regard to religious experience they are complementary factors, so that in any detailed examination they would throw most light on each other by being studied together. It must be sufficient for the present purpose to glance at the chief successive phases of the conception of sin in the Old Testament. The most natural beginning is to attempt some classification of the terms for sin, in which the Hebrew vocabulary is so rich. But the value of such a classification is chiefly that it affords an

From *The Christian Doctrine of Man,* 3rd ed. (Edinburgh: T. and T. Clark, 1926), pp. 42-45. Used by permission.

introduction to the subject in its salient features; the revelation of the Old Testament is not philological, but historical; the mere term is a locked drawer until we have opened it with the key of history.

The principal terms employed in the Old Testament with reference to sin may be grouped in four classes, according as they denote (1) deviation from the right way; (2) the changed status (guilt) of the agent; (3) rebellion against a superior, or unfaithfulness to an agreement; (4) some characterization of the quality of the act itself.[1] In the first class, the most important term is the verb *ḥātā'* (with derivative nouns and adjectives), occurring 238 times, whilst the chief nominal form (*ḥaṭṭā'th*) is found 295 times. The original meaning of this root is that of *"missing"* some goal or path; thus, amongst the warriors of Benjamin, there were seven hundred men who were left-handed, "slinging with stones at a hair, and would not miss" (Judg. 20:16; cf. Prov. 19:2). The term tells us nothing that is definite about sin; it is the failure to do something or other, in relation (as the usage shows) either to man or God (I Sam. 2:25). The similar idea of *going astray* underlies the use of *āwōn,* usually rendered "iniquity," in regard to man (I Sam. 20:1) or God (Job 13:23), or of *shāgāh* (Ezek. 34:6; I Sam. 26:21; Lev. 4:13); and that of *turning aside* is equally capable of an ethical or religious (Exod. 32:8) as of a physical (I Sam. 6:12) connotation. The second class of terms includes one (*rāshā'*) of which the derivation is obscure, though the usage suggests that the verb was primarily employed in a forensic sense, *i.e.* to pronounce guilty (Exod. 22:8), whilst the corresponding adjective is used of the guilty as opposed to the innocent (Deut. 25:2). Another term specially used to imply guilt is *āshām* (Gen. 26:10; Prov. 14:9; Jer. 51:5; for the verb, Num. 5:7 and Ezek. 25:12, towards man; Lev. 5:19, towards God); the original suggestion may be that of the compensation paid for the wrong done (I Sam. 6:3, 4, 8, 17). But it should be noted that other terms (*e.g. āwōn,* Ps. 59:5, and *ḥātā',* Gen. 43:9) easily pass over to denote the guilt of sin. The third class is the most important, because it yields a positive idea of sin, that of *rebellion,* and because this idea conducts us along the line of the religious history of Israel to the specific sense of sin in relation to God. The most important term here (*pāshā'*) is illustrated in its primary meaning by the words, "Israel rebelled against the house of David" (I Kings 12:19; cf. II Kings 1:1; 3:5, 7; 8:20, 22), and in its religious application by Isa. 43:27: "Thy first father sinned, and thy ambassadors have rebelled against me"; the corresponding noun (inadequately rendered "trespass" or "transgression") is found in Gen. 31:36; 50:17 (against man), and Isa. 58:1 (against God). The intensity of meaning in this term is well illustrated by Job 34:37: "He addeth rebellion (*peshā'*) unto his sin (*ḥaṭṭā'th*)"; the forceful suggestiveness of the term, in the prophetic literature where it is first employed, is best seen in Isa. 1:2: "Sons I have brought up and reared, and *they* have rebelled against me," cries Yahweh, though the very ox and ass acknowledge their master. The word, as Davidson says (*Theology of the O.T.* p. 210), "describes sin as a personal, voluntary act. It also implies something rebelled against, something which is of the nature of a superior or an authority. . . . The word could not be used of the withdrawal of an equal from co-operation with another equal." The same idea of rebellion is implied in the terms *mārad* (II Kings 18:7, against a human king; Num. 14:9, against God), *mārāh* (Deut. 21:18, 20, against a father; Num. 20:10, against God), and *sārar* (Deut. 21:18, against a father; Isa. 65:2, against God). With these it is natural to group such terms as denote treachery or infidelity, such as *māʿal* (Num. 5:12, 27, of wife against husband; 5:6, against God) and *bāgad* (I Sam. 14:33). The fourth class is very wide in range, and hardly calls for detailed illustration; some salient aspect of sin or its consequences is brought to view, namely, its badness, violence, destructiveness, trouble, worthlessness, vanity, folly, senselessness; the most general of these terms (*rāʿāh*) covers all kinds of evil (I Sam. 12:17).

## Notes

[1] The terms are discussed in greater detail by Schultz, *Old Test. Theology* (E.T.), ii. pp. 281-291.

# The Source of Sin

## 9

**F. R. Tennant**

# Evolutionary Theory of the Empirical Origin of Sin

*I had not known sin but by the law. . . . for without the law sin was dead. (Rom. 7:7, 8)*

Our previous study of the history of the problem of human sin, its origin and propagation, would perhaps at least serve to show that the problem had not yielded to the attempts at its solution made either from the side of Theology or from that of Philosophy. Two main reasons may be assigned for this intractability.

In the first place it must largely be attributed to the tendency in the past to regard sin, in its essence and in its initial stages, too much as what it really comes to be only in the extremest forms of its development, viz., the conscious rebellion of the creature against God. This point of view, which the growth of the historical sense has rendered more and more unsatisfying, has been responsible for the far-fetched causes of catastrophic nature to which universal sinfulness has so generally been attributed in Theology, and sometimes in Philosophy.

From *The Origin and Propagation of Sin* (Cambridge: University Press, 1902), pp. 78-112.

In the second place, it is still more largely due to the difficulty of reconciling the two propositions that, on the one hand, evil is so universal as to suggest a common origin for the sinfulness of the whole race, independently of the self-determination of its individual members; whilst, on the other hand, our sense of guilt demands that each one is "the Adam of his own soul." It is with this latter source of difficulty that we have especially been concerned. The old antinomy which the Pelagian controversy first brought to light still stands, and mainly because it has hitherto been approached from the standpoint to which allusion has just been made. We have seen that the problem of the origin and universality of sin, even on its empirical side, and apart from deeper metaphysical questions to which it leads, has been acknowledged by theologians and philosophers alike to present an incomprehensible enigma. Dr. Julius Müller, who devoted to this subject the most thorough attention it has ever, perhaps, received, and who was resolute to do equal justice to both sides of the antinomy, was compelled, we saw, to postulate behind the fall of Adam an individual "turning away from the divine light to the darkness of self-absorbed selfishness in a life beyond the bounds of time."

We can scarcely hope, then, for a reconciliation of universal sin with individual guilt, in terms of knowledge pertaining to our present life alone, so long as the antinomy which has been repeatedly affirmed to be the *crux* of the problem is maintained in the form in which it has hitherto been stated. Now the Augustinian doctrine practically attempted to dispense with the one of the opposed propositions supplied by moral experience: that, namely, which makes guilt entirely a matter of personal responsibility. In so far as it did so, however, it failed to satisfy the developed Christian consciousness. It is the other side of the antinomy, then, which must be either abandoned or restated if the problem is to be attacked afresh. And what logic thus suggests, science has begun to demand. There are insuperable difficulties involved, as we have shown, in such conceptions as those of original righteousness, corrupted nature, hereditary transmission of acquired depravity. The influences of social environment, on which Schleiermacher and Ritschl have rightly insisted as an important factor in the explanation of the propagation of sin, are insufficient in themselves to account for its ubiquitous diffusion. They presuppose a real, physical, organic race-solidarity in respect of the non-moral conditions and material which our nature furnishes, to form a basis for the individual's receptivity and response. It remains, therefore, to inquire whether that side of the old antinomy which has hitherto been expressed in the form of an assertion of inborn sinfulness, or an inherited disturbance of our nature, cannot be modified and reinterpreted so as to be free from such notions as we have found good reason to reject; and further, whether this can be done without at the same time renouncing either the truth of our physical and organic unity, or that of our responsibility for sin. Instead of resorting to a hypothetical previous existence or extra-temporal self-decision, can we find the ground of the possibility and occasion for sin in our natural constitution regarded as the perfectly normal result of a process of development through which the race has passed previously to the acquisition of full moral personality; and can we assign the rise of evil itself simply to the difficulty of the task which has to be encountered by every individual person alike, the task of enforcing his inherited organic nature to obey a moral law which he has only gradually been enabled to discern?

This is the view which I would now endeavour to support. The effort is somewhat tentative, inasmuch as the construction of such a theory from first principles has not yet been undertaken by Theology, where alone the adverse influence of tradition raises prejudice against it. Some of its outlines, however, have been already drawn by a living German theologian: one of its fundamental ideas has been pregnantly expressed by a recent Hulsean Lecturer: and there are signs that popular thought has begun to feel after a reconstruction upon some such lines.

Archdeacon Wilson, in an address to the Church Congress of 1896, spoke very concisely of the relation of evolutionary theory to various Christian doctrines, and, amongst them, to the doctrine of sin. His reference was so brief that I may quote it in full:

"What is the bearing of the theory of evolution on the Christian doctrine of sin? Here we approach less familiar ground. . . . I think the popular view of sin as connected with a definite fall of the head of the race is considerably affected.

"Man fell, according to science, when he first became conscious of the conflict of freedom and conscience. To the evolutionist sin is not an innovation, but is the survival or misuse of habits and tendencies that were incidental to an earlier stage in development, whether of the individual or the race, and were not originally sinful, but were actually useful. Their sinfulness lies in their anachronism: in their resistance to the evolutionary and Divine force that makes for moral development and righteousness. Sin is the violation of a man's higher nature which he finds within, parallel to a lower nature. Under the law of evolution God has given men conscience which condemns certain actions, and under this law such actions pass through the stages, first of disapproval by the finer souls, then of condemnation by the ordinary conscience, and at last of punishment by the action of society. . . .

"Now, this conflict of freedom and conscience is precisely what is related as 'The Fall' *sub specie historiae*. It tells of the fall of a creature from unconscious innocence to conscious guilt, expressing itself in hiding from the presence of God. But this fall from innocence was in another sense a rise to a higher grade of being. It is in this sense that the theory of evolution teaches us to interpret the story of the fall. It gives a deeper meaning to the truth that sin is lawlessness."[1]

Such, in few words, is the suggestion offered by the Evolution theory as to the historical beginnings of sin in the human race.

A short sketch of the lines upon which a corresponding account of the origin of sin in the individual awaits to be developed, will be found in Professor Otto Pfleiderer's *Philosophy of Religion*. This writer seeks the determining cause of evil not in the inaccessible region of a beyond of thought, but in the course of development, traceable by Psychology, of the finite will, from its enchainment in nature to its freedom. "The psychological genesis of evil," he says, "is not difficult to understand, if we set out from the fact that the tendency towards the satisfaction of his natural impulses is as necessary to man as it is to every other living being." This tendency is not evil because the moral law with its "Thou shalt not" is as yet unknown. And when some knowledge of such law has begun to be acquired, the natural and necessary self-will of the individual by no means dies away before its increasing authority and sternness.

It is with difficulty that our natural, non-moral, tendencies are moralised or brought under the dominion of the higher nature; and every failure in the attempt, or every conscious desistance from the struggle, is sin. Our natural self-willing cannot strictly be called evil; that which *is* evil, again, cannot be called natural, because it belongs to the stage of acquired morality. And the transition from animal innocence to rational evil is gradual; it is not a sudden and inexplicable change, either here or in a previous life.[2]

Here we have an indication of the main lines on which an evolutionary account of the historical or empirical origin of sin in the individual must be constructed, as contrasted with the theories which trace the source of universal sinfulness to a definite fall and its inherited consequences. It corresponds to the briefer sketch, from a similar point of view, of the beginning of sin in the race as a whole, given by Archdeacon Wilson. So far as my knowledge of the literature of the subject goes, Dr. Pfleiderer is the only theologian who has appealed to the elementary facts of the empirical Psychology underlying the science of Ethics for light on the ancient paradox of original sin. His is therefore the only support that I find myself able to quote in favour of the view to which my own studies have led.[3]

Before proceeding to develop this view more fully, it will be well, perhaps, to remind my hearers once again that in discussing the initial stages of sin one must necessarily use language which would seem terribly inadequate to describe sin as it is present to the mind of the Christian penitent. Our present investigation, both in the case of the race and that of the individual, deals with transgressions of sanctions which only become identified with the will of an all-Holy God in the process of their gradual formation.

Bearing this thought in mind, we may first consider the beginning of sin in the race, in the light of the conception of development. It must be acknowledged at the outset that for the present we have to move largely in the sphere of theory and speculation. I cannot indeed accept the assertion, sometimes made,[4] that there is no positive science of prehistoric man; still less the implied belief that there never will be such a science. But that the beginnings of human life, of mind, of morals, and consequently of evil, are matters of inference from somewhat scanty facts rather than of full and direct knowledge, must be allowed.

I shall venture to assume as overwhelmingly probable that there is continuity between the physical constitution of man and that of the lower animals. Continuity of mental development is an infinitely more difficult question to dogmatise upon in the present state of our knowledge of animal Psychology. It would be unsafe, for instance, to define how far the germs of "conduct," or such sentiments as we call moral in ourselves, exist in the animal world lower than man. It would be unwise to commit oneself to more than the statement that there is sufficient evidence of continuity here and there to generate a strong presumption in favour of evolution all along the line. At present, however, this is far from actual demonstration. The question whether the moral has been developed out of the non-moral would seem to be largely a matter of words, and to depend on the definition we assign to the term "moral."[5] If we draw the line of separation between the moral and the non-moral at the emergence of such complex ideas as those of responsibility and obligation, it is more difficult to maintain that there is no bridge from the non-moral to the moral than if we make the sentiments of approval and disapproval in general the starting-point for the truly ethical. The break in the chain of continuity from the lowest to the highest forms of psychical life will then have to be put back at the point where memory and anticipation appear, faculties which cannot as yet be traced in the crudest forms of animal mind.

These, however, are considerations of little moment to our inquiry. Sufficient of Evolution is undoubted fact, whatever may become of the theory's wider claims, to show that Kant's self-imposed moral law, for instance, or the intuitionist's conscience, has a long, long, history. Morality at any rate is a social creation, not a ready-made endowment of the individual. As in the case of other things even more fundamental and elementary in our mental furniture, our conceptions of space and time and the external world, its synthesis was only possible through the prolonged intercourse of individuals. And though Anthropology cannot furnish anything like a complete account of man's moral growth, it can yet prove that there has been development from extremely rudimentary beginnings; and that this development has taken place along certain general lines is nowadays common knowledge.

It is generally recognised that in the earliest human society the tribe was all-important and the individual relatively insignificant. Of such society we have, of course, no *direct* knowledge; there is no such thing as prehistoric history. But if little is thus known of man's state before he reached the stage at which we begin to have historical evidence of his life and thought, there seems to be no reason to attribute to him, in his earlier condition, a course different from that of gradual development such as he certainly followed afterwards; and numerous sciences point to the overwhelming probability of such continuous evolution. We are justified then in using the method which the physicist calls "extrapolation" in arriving at an estimate of man's prehistoric mental life: the method which consists in producing backwards the curve of progress which history, when it once emerges, positively presents to us. And further, the critical study of savage life, as it now exists, is a useful auxiliary source of knowledge. For though the savage man, as we know him, is by no means identical with the primi-

tive man, whom we do not know but desire to reproduce, we are nevertheless enabled largely to eliminate from savagery those characteristics which
have been acquired in course of time, and so to form at least a probable
conjecture as to the essential marks of the primitive state. Now "among
savages moral consciousness is largely still in germ."[6] Action is to a great
extent impulsive, and "conduct," or the crude, unreflective morality
which they exhibit, is moulded in the main by tribal opinion expressed in
tribal custom. The further back we trace man, the less we find him the
person, or even the individual; the greater his dependence on the tribe and
family, and the more complete the solidarity of his moral consciousness. It
appears that man did not at first think of himself so much as an independent individual as part of a system. The "tribal self" preceded the
"personal self." The importance of this fact alone is great in its bearing on
our investigation, for it enables us to see that the idea of moral personality, in terms of which Theology has been wont exclusively to formulate its
doctrine of the origin of sin, emerged extremely late in human thought.[7]
May we not almost say indeed that it appeared with Christianity, to be lost
again, to a large extent, for centuries?

"The ethical sentiments and the judgments which express them" are,
then, "in their most primitive form . . . impersonal."[8] And morality, as the
words $\mathring{\eta}\theta o \varsigma$, mores, Sitten all testify, arises out of custom.

Custom inevitably hardens into formulated law. And inasmuch as rules
sometimes conflict with one another, and in any case are found too rigid
for the guidance of conduct in all circumstances, the application of
inelastic laws leads to reflection and discovery of their underlying principles.[9] Out of what was purely arbitrary or merely ceremonial in external
sanctions there emerged moral obligation carrying its own sanction, much
in the same way that the disciple becomes able, in time, to dispute the
pronouncements of his master. Thus appeared introspective morality, and
the formation of the general convictions as to one's obligations which we
collectively call conscience.[10] So much, at least, is matter of fact to be
read on the surface of Israel's history[11] and in the literature of other
ancient civilisations.

There is thus every reason to believe that the awakening of man's moral
sense or sentiment, his discovery of a law by which he came to know sin,
was an advance accomplished by a long series of stages. Consequently the
origin of sin, like other so-called origins, was also a gradual process rather
than an abrupt and inexplicable plunge. The appearance of sin, from this
point of view, would not consist in the performance of a deed such as man
had never done before, and of whose wickedness, should he commit it, he
was previously aware; it would rather be the continuance in certain prac-
tices, or the satisfying of natural impulses, after that they were first discovered to be contrary to a recognised sanction of rank as low as that of
tribal custom. The sinfulness of sin would gradually increase from a zero;
and the first sin, if the words have any meaning, instead of being the most
heinous, and the most momentous in the race's history, would rather be
the least significant of all.

This is of course only the extension, in terms of modern forms of thought, of the truth which S. Paul emphasised, that man did not know sin without the law. When the apostle goes on to speak of sin being "dead" without the law, it is probable that he had in mind the idea of sin as an objective and immanent power lying dormant in the soul from birth. Such language, implying a notion common in the Jewish schools of his time, is of course figurative: it involves a rhetorical concretion of an abstraction; and it would be absurd for us to translate it into technical terms and harden it into dogma. The evolutionary account of the origin of sin would substitute for it the assertion that sin does not, and cannot, exist at all without the law, and that the motions in man which the first recognised sanction condemned were natural and non-moral; not sinful, even in the sense of being abnormal or displeasing to God. For if man's physical nature is necessarily endowed with instincts, appetites and impulses,[12] with self-assertive tendencies inevitably accompanying the capacity to feel pleasure and pain, it contains abundance of raw material for the production of sin, as soon as these native propensities are brought into relation with any restraining or condemning influence. When we reflect that many of these propensities are inevitably strong because they are, or once were, useful or necessary to life, and were therefore through countless ages intensified by natural selection, there is no reason left for referring their clamorous importunity to an evil bias or a corrupted nature. They belong to man as God made him, and are to be controlled in proportion as the moral law becomes the more exacting because the more elaborately developed, and the more expressly associated with religion embracing the whole of life. There is indeed no need to marvel at the universality of sin throughout mankind when many of its most general forms, at least, are thus attributed to the self-assertion of powerful tendencies, with all their priority in time and fixity in instinct or habit, after the acquisition and superposition of a "higher nature" which demands their subordination to less immediate and tangible ends.

"To the evolutionist sin is not an innovation, but is the survival or misuse of habits and tendencies that were incidental to an earlier stage of development" and whose sinfulness "lies in their anachronism."

Such being the nature of the fall of the race to which Science and its theoretical generalisations point us, we have now to endeavour to trace the genesis of sin in the individual, which has hitherto been explained by the idea of the inheritance of a perverted nature.

The foundation from which we start is the fact already asserted of the race and now to be repeated of the individual, that we are natural before we are moral beings, and that the impulses of our nature are in full sway before the moral consciousness begins to dawn. And on passing from the race, as to the earliest state of which we have to rely much on inference and theory for guidance, to the case of the individual, we set foot upon more solid and certain ground. For here we enter the realm of empirical fact. And it is found that just as the embryo recapitulates within the womb the age-long history of the development of its species, so too, to some extent, does the infant's mind recapitulate the moral history of the race. The psychology of infancy is a branch of science which has recently been receiving much attention, and its investigations have led to the refutation of many *à priori* views. It is interesting to compare the estimates of child-nature attained from the starting-point of various kinds of prepossession with one another and with the results of actual experimental study. Some such estimates are collected in the works on childhood of Prof. Sully and M. Compayré.[13] Thus, Rousseau looked upon children as coming perfect from the Creator's hand. Wordsworth, too, attributed to infancy certain positive excellences, glimpses of a higher morality than ours, divine intuitions brought from a previous existence.[14] Others again, of whom the kindly Dupanloup, the children's bishop and catechist, may be taken as a type, have been led by the requirements of the doctrine of original sin to paint the child's nature in the blackest colours. And perhaps most people see in children's impatience of restraint, their wilfulness and passionate temper, their unconscious cruelty, their greed and envy and self-pleasing, so many confirmations of the doctrine that every child of man inherits a sadly vitiated nature.

Real knowledge of the mental and moral development of children, however, pronounces a judgment different from all of these, and one in which the investigators whose works I have been able to consult are unanimously agreed.[15] They find that the human infant is simply a nonmoral animal, and that its impulses and propensities are essential to its nature. The faculties, as we may still conveniently call them, of will and "moral sense," are made, not born. Even their germs are not apparent at the first. Experience commences in blank sensations, feelings of pleasure and pain; passes into the stage of apprehension of objects and response to suggestion and imitation; thence to imagination and volition, and finally becomes reflective, social and ethical.[16] The instincts which the human being brings with him into the world are extremely few, and even these mostly terminate with the rise of volition. No animal species, indeed, is so slenderly furnished at birth with ready-made endowments; but none shows so great receptivity and capacity for adaptation. Apart from the external educating environment, however, the child would remain on a level little superior in any respect to that of the brutes. Social, rather than physical, heredity[17] moulds the child. Hence the tendency to imitation, which seems to be one of the hereditary equipments of the infant, is of great importance for its mental and moral growth. Before the imitative period opens, however, the child is utterly organic. For some seven months the sway of the inborn tendencies, whose power is proportional to their fewness, is absolute. It need scarcely be repeated that nothing is found in these to lend colour to the view that their intensity results from a defection from original, ideal human nature. They are necessary, in their full power, to life or health or growth, or for the later realisation of the distinctively human mental attributes. And the same must be said of habits which soon begin to be formed under the stimulus of pleasant or painful feeling, the direction of the emerging and growing will, and the only known sanction of success. Of course such a pure little animal as the young child presents sometimes an appalling spectacle of self-centredness in the satisfaction of its impulses and appetites, and of passionate resentment to restraint on their indulgence. But if the upholder of the doctrine of a fallen nature sees in such an exhibition that false delight in freedom which is said to be one of the marks of inborn depravity, the naturalist reads there only a sign of future sanity and vigour. The young child is for him a sentient automaton admirably suited by nature for self-preservation and development under the conditions of its early nurture: an organism adapted for "parasitic assimilation of its environment" as it unconsciously follows the line of least effort. The apparent "faults" of infantile age are in fact organic necessities. There *must* be what looks to older eyes so much like unmitigated selfishness. There *must* be unmixed dislike of restraint until expanding intelligence discerns its reasonableness. Even the curious "contrariness" which often appears at a certain age, seeming like deliberate persistence in resisting every expressed wish or command, appears to be but an out-of-place example of an involuntary process of inhibition of response to suggestion which is essential to the learning of many complicated useful actions.

It has been proved, then, that the tendencies which casual observation or doctrinal preoccupation might plausibly construe as expressions, in the child, of divergence from the original or ideal type of human nature are necessarily incidental to the human organism. Man, as a sentient being endowed with instincts and impulses,[18] inevitably possesses propensities which belong to him not at all as a fallen and corrupted being, but as man, and which must of necessity involve him, from the time that his moral life begins, in a lasting series of struggles and efforts if he is to order himself as a rational being in accordance with the requirements of an ideal or a moral law. Fear and anger, envy and jealousy, self-centredness and self-pleasing are qualities which form part of the birthright of the human being in virtue of his animal ancestry. Whatever may be the degree of strength in which the elements of the "ape and tiger" in our nature are inherited,—they are of course liable to "variation"—they are natural and normal and necessary. It cannot be said of them, when we speak with reference to man in his yet unmoralised condition, that in any sense "they ought not to be." They are non-moral.[19]

And besides being non-moral, it must be added that these animal propensities are *neutral* in character. That is to say, they are not exclusively prophetic of evil in respect of the moral value of what may be shaped out of them. They are indifferent material waiting to be moralised. They may be turned to bad or they may be turned to good. Fear is the necessary basis both of cowardice and the highest courage. Anger is the source of righteous wrath as well as of vindictive passion. Our virtues and vices, in fact, have common roots. The crude material of natural disposition, of inherited propensities of emotion or of appetite, is neither good nor evil but the common ground of both.[20] We do not inherit separate collections of ready-made tendencies, some wholly good and some wholly bad, to war with one another. Our lowest appetites are the necessary basis of our finest moral sentiments: means of self-realisation in the highest sense, at the same time that they are the fateful rocks on which so many human lives make shipwreck. It is simply because the mastery of appetite and emotion by the moralised man has always proved so difficult that human thought has generally considered the animal side of our nature to be positively evil. S. Paul was no Hellenic dualist; he knew well that the propensities of our lower nature are servants to be controlled, not evils to be rooted out. Yet he allows himself to speak of the "sinful passions"; and in his description of the "sinful flesh," which of course has a practical rather than a scientific purpose, he accommodates himself to popular modes of speech. So also does the philosopher, at times, when off his guard. Even Prof. Pfleiderer, in the passage in which he states the outlines of a theory similar to that which I am endeavouring to elaborate, lapses into speaking of evil as "cleaving to all men from their very birth," and as present in us "as a power, the origin of which must accordingly be beyond the conscious exercise of our freedom."[21] Manichaean Dualism is perhaps the most perennial and ineradicable of all popular heresies; and it seems as if we must inevitably be committed to it if we allow ourselves to apply the ethical attributes of good and bad to anything except the activities of the will which knows a moral law. It is true we speak of motives as good and bad; not, however, because they are so in themselves, "but because they are the elements out of which is built up the good or bad character, which is identical with good or bad actions." It is true also that we speak of dispositions as good and bad: the various blendings of innate or nearly innate tendencies or qualities in their various degrees of intensity; but again, "disposition only comes up for strictly ethical judgment according to the volitions in which it issues."[22] In fact the occasion or the material of sin can only be termed sinful in a loose, rhetorical or metonymical sense.[23] The most clamorous passion which invites to sensual indulgence is just as little to be described as evil in itself as the sublime work of art which may goad a man to extravagance and debt. It is equally non-moral and indifferent. No natural impulse, then, is itself sinful, unless present through our volition, and therefore through our fault. It is the deliberate refusal to reject the impulse, the wilful surrender of the government of conduct to the non-moralised sensibility, in which evil takes its rise. Neither in the sense that they are foreign to human nature as it ought to be, nor in the sense that they are ethically classifiable under the categories of good and bad, can we call any of our inborn tendencies or earliest acquired habits "sinful." Neither deductive reasoning nor empirical observation will allow us to speak of a bias to evil or of moral contamination before the individual inheritor of our common nature has attained to moral consciousness and accountability. Indeed when the individual is passing through the natural or animal stage of his development, that which knows as yet no "law," his appetites are blind, more of the nature of mere wants than conscious desires; action is impulsive rather than purposive. And it is not until reason appears that these appetites are transmuted into desires directed towards an end. In the meantime life is a series "of simple reactions to ideational stimulation."

It is not necessary to present here what is known or supposed as to the origin and development of will. But it is the basal proposition of the theory of sin which is now being elaborated that until the will has emerged, and the life begins to be self-conducted, no germ of evil can be said to exist in the individual. The young child, in following the impulses and instincts which it is as yet unable to direct or control, is entirely fulfilling its life's purpose. With the dawn of will and reason morality first becomes a possibility. And until moral sentiment appears, the existence of sin is of course excluded.

The account of the actual genesis of sin in the individual which our theory has to offer will thus involve a description of the birth and growth of conscience which first makes sin a possibility: the "law" without which sin is "dead" or non-existent. It is comparatively lately that Psychology has supplied us with information on the subject that is of scientific value; and of a little of this information I must presently make use.

We have already seen that the infant, as shaped by heredity alone, is a non-volitional creature of impulse, only differing from the animal beneath him in the capacity of becoming, under certain conditions, what the other never could become. The status of a human person can only be realised through education. But, with all deference to Etymology, this education would seem to consist less in drawing out than putting in. The child's development is by no means the self-unfolding of what is immanently existent in him; it is much more the appropriation from without of what never could be his were it not for the human environment, with its long past history, in which he finds himself. Soon the moulding power of influences acquired by physical inheritance reaches, in most respects, the limit of its range. Then comes the turn of social heredity, in whose growing power practically all man's future progress, as a race, consists.[24] And the race's most important gift to the individual is the morality which itself has toilsomely and gradually won.

It is said that after three years or so from birth the child shows signs of the dawn of moral sentiment around the acts and attitudes of its will. The full story of the rise and growth of moral sensibility, however, need scarcely be repeated here. Only such broad outlines as are unquestionable can be safely given. It has long been recognised that obedience acquired by punishment plays a considerable part in evoking moral sentiment. But this, we are told by Prof. Baldwin, to whom I am chiefly indebted for information on the matter,[25] is by no means the only, or the most important, moral educator. The conflict of direction from without with desire that wells up from within is an experience which the child has already known. He has learned that he is now an assertive self that makes according to habit for what is pleasant, and now an accommodating self that yields and learns. But obedience calls forth yet a further self which denies its impulses in conforming to another's will; which obeys, in fact, unwillingly. Hence comes the idea of law. But the law to which he has learned to bow from various motives, the child can neither anticipate nor understand. In his attempts to do so he often blunders. He finds, however, that his parents and teachers also obey it: he sees them hesitating, doing what cannot be pleasant to them. He is thereby puzzled. But some of the law's content is learned through "suggestion" and imitation, through instruction and reflection. And so there grows up for him a moral ideal which is taken over into himself, an idea of goodness or right conduct which is perfectly concrete, embodied at first in a person, and afterwards in God. And it is continually revised and expanded throughout life.[26] Thus in temptations the child begins to get accustomed to the presence in him of something which represents his father or some other law-giving personality. Much experience is necessary to separate the abstract idea of good and bad from that of the will of his parents.[27] Good is, at first, what is permitted, and evil what is forbidden. But long before this separation of abstract from concrete has been effected, the new self that has thus arisen calls the child to account if he yields to his "self of habit." Here is conscience; and as it is being acquired one ceases to be innocent with the innocence of ignorance of good and evil.

The impulse toward the satisfaction of all desires, natural and inevitable from the first, and already strengthened by some years of use, now meets with the check of an internal law. And as the ethical ideal expands, and the widening world brings ever new occasions for failure in the steady realisation of the higher self, the experience of evil grows. Moreover the iron chains of habit have already begun to be forged before the expulsive power of new affection and reverence can be felt. The new-born moral agent, therefore, has much to unlearn and much to subdue, as he enters on the task of moralising his organic nature. He is indeed beset from the very first with those manifold temptations, "which death alone can cure," in that they belong of necessity to human nature as God ordained it to be constituted.

Thus "the way from nature to character is laborious and full of effort." Morality consists in the formation of the non-moral material of nature into character, in subjecting "the seething and tumultuous life of natural tendency, of appetite and passion, affection and desire," to the moulding influence of reflective purpose.[28] Here, and not in any universal and hereditarily transmitted disturbance of man's nature, is to be found the occasion or source of universal sinfulness. It is simply the general failure to effect on all occasions the moralisation of inevitable impulses and to choose the end of higher worth rather than that which, of lower value, appeals with the more clamorous intensity. And if goodness consists essentially in this steady moralisation of the raw material[29] of morality, its opposite, sin, cannot consist in the material awaiting moralisation, but in the will's failure to completely moralise it.

And in the growth of evil we have of course to emphasise the power of habit. Both Physiology and Psychology teach us that every action leaves behind it a tendency to repetition. Ends tend by repetition to coalesce with one another, as a psychologist expresses it. Selective effort gives way more and more to routine, and the voluntary life becomes more and more limited. Character is a habit of will and determines future action. Both virtue and vice become easier. "But the ascent reveals ever new heights of virtue yet unattained; and the effort of virtue is measured by the heights of the moral ideal, as well as by the heights of moral attainment. Thus, what at a lower level was character, becomes, at the higher, again mere nature, to be in turn transcended and overcome. 'We rise on stepping-stones of our dead selves to higher things.' There is no resting in the life of virtue,—it is a constant growth; to stereotype it, or to arrest it at any stage, however advanced, would be to kill it. There is always an 'old' man and a 'new': the very new becomes old, and has to die, and be surmounted." [30] The gate is ever strait, and the way ever narrow, in the life of virtue.

If the account of the genesis of sin which has now been given be substantially true, the universality of sinfulness will scarcely need another word of explanation. If we bear in mind the facts which Science and experience supply as to the origin, development, and organic constitution of man, the mode of appearance of his conscience, the nature of his social and physical environment, it will seem to savour of unreality to continue to demand some event of universal or of catastrophic nature to account once and for all for our present state. God forbid that one should seem to excuse sin at any stage of human development! But the absence of a solitary case of sinless life would seem, according to this doctrine of evil, to be no marvel that needs to be violently accounted for. Like the gospel in which lies man's only hope of salvation from its power sin requires no ascent on our part into the heavens, nor descent into the deep, to bring its actuality into the sphere of human life: its source is very nigh. But I would have it observed that in thus naturally accounting for the origin and universality of sin, we neither excuse evil nor explain it away. Let us once more remind ourselves that we have been considering sin only in its initial stages, not at all in its perfect development in relation to the law of Christ. If conscience is not immediately given in the infant mind of race or individual, but only came to be what it is—and who shall say what it shall be?—through many stages, its intuitions have for us, on that account, none the less validity.[31] If sin can be traced back, in race and single person, to its beginning in the transgression of a sanction not then recognised as that of God, it loses nothing of its exceeding sinfulness for us to whom it is none the less a deliberate grieving of the Holy Spirit. And further, if this account of sin sees in it something empirically inevitable for every man,— which of course accords with all experience,—it by no means implies that sin is theoretically, or on *à priori* grounds, an absolute necessity. If, finally, it avows fully and frankly that our nature, and the surroundings in which we are placed, are such as make the realisation of our better self a stupendously difficult task—as indeed the theory does—it thereby only emphasises, like the old doctrine of inherited depravity before it, man's crying need of grace and his capacity for a Gospel of Redemption. That the nature of redemption would need to be defined somewhat differently than in the terms to which we have long been used, is of course true; but that would not be a wholly new demand, nor perhaps an altogether idle one. But with regard to consequences, we have, as said before, to work and wait. Their possible gravity should make the student weigh his words, not seal his lips.

And, in conclusion, what has our theory done with the idea of human solidarity in evil which, as we have often seen, is a necessary and a permanent element in the problem of sin? It has re-emphasised as strongly as, and perhaps more pertinently than, the doctrine of Schleiermacher and Ritschl, the factor of social heredity which alone gives the moral law and makes sin possible, and the influences of social environment on moral life and the diffusion of sin in polluting the atmosphere in which the individual is reared.

But what of physical or organic solidarity? In relation to this question we have, of course, moved far away from the position of S. Augustine and the various Confessions of three or four hundred years ago. Yet not so far as to lose all contact with the great father's fundamental conception. The community which we have asserted with regard to the inborn contents of our present nature is not indeed a community in ready-made evil—a self-contradictory notion—nor in disorder, abnormality, deprivation, or corruption caused by the head of our race; but in instincts and propensities which are both neutral in value and non-moral in character, necessary and essential also to human nature as God purposed it to be. The Fall is exchanged for an animal origin and a subsequent superposition or acquisition of moral rationality. Taint of sin is replaced by normal self-directed tendencies, once very naturally, but nowadays very wrongly, called sinful. That man's performance lags behind his aspiration is attributed, not to a defection from a sinless yet moral state, but to the fact that he is rising in moral culture, which makes great demands upon his organic nature, whilst his inherited psychical and physical constitution is making no corresponding or adaptative change, no evolutionary progress.[32] The theory thus preserves the truth of solidarity of race, both in nature and in environment, along with that of individual responsibility and guilt. It transcends, in fact, the old antinomy which previously made our problems so intractable. But it yet remains for us to ascertain whether it satisfies further legitimate demands, both of reason and of Christian sentiment.

### Notes

[1] *The Guardian,* Oct. 7, 1896.

[2] *Philosophy of Religion,* E. Trans. of 2nd ed., vol. iv. pp. 34ff. For the passage from Pfleiderer see *The Origin and Propagation of Sin,* p. 211, note L.

[3] For a notice of other attempts in a similar direction which have since become known to me see *The Origin and Propagation of Sin,* p. 217, note M.

[4] e.g. by Dr. Newman Smyth in *Christian Ethics,* p. 146.

[5] To admit the difference between a natural or descriptive and a normative science, such as Ethics, the difference between *is* and *ought*, fact and worth, is not to admit that the moral and the factual judgment are different in such a sense that an absoluteness, an immediacy, and an origin are to be attributed to the moral which are denied to factual.

That the question indicated above is one of words and definitions may be seen by contrasting its treatment by Prof. J. Seth, e.g., with that by Mr. A. E. Taylor. The former writer (*Eth. Principles,* 5th ed. pp. 318ff.) argues that "morality cannot arise out of the non-moral"; the latter implies that if there is continuity of mental development from absence to presence of memory and anticipation, the moral must have originated from what is generally called the non-moral. Of course the last-named writer repudiates the view that unless such "primary" concepts as those of "obligation" and "free personality" are postulated as ultimate reality, there is no science of Ethics at all. This procedure he justifies at length; see *The Problem of Conduct,* pp. 119ff. His view that Ethics is to be based on Psychology and Sociology rather than on Metaphysics is followed in this lecture.

[6] Mackenzie, *Manual of Ethics,* 4th ed. p. 107.

[7] It is not only on its moral side that the primitive human consciousness evinces this solidarity; it holds with regard to savage psychology in general. The curious custom of the couvade, to mention but one example, testifies to the fact that the uncivilised mind possesses a very imperfect notion of separate individuality such as common sense regards as natural to all mankind. See Tylor, *Early History of Mankind,* 3rd ed. pp. 295ff.

[8] Taylor, *op. cit.* p. 124.

[9] I here almost quote Mackenzie, *op. cit.* p. 109.·

[10] For a full account of the origin of the higher moral concepts, obligation, conscience, responsibility, merit, etc., see the extremely able chapter on the Roots of Ethics in the *Problem of Conduct,* to which reference has several times been made. The discussion there of moral personality is most important.

[11] The student will recall portions of Robertson Smith's *Religion of the Semites.*

[12] I use these terms, of course, in the loose, vague mode of popular speech, which is here quite sufficient, and not as they are precisely defined in the psychological treatise. They are defined, however, further on.

[13] Sully, *Studies of Childhood;* Compayré, *L'Évolution intellectuelle et morale de l'enfant.*

[14] See the Ode "Intimations of Immortality from Recollections of Early Childhood."

[15] See, e.g., the works of Prof. Baldwin and Prof. Sully referred to in this lecture; Perez, *The First Three Years of Childhood;* Mezes, *Ethics* (where Royce is quoted as in agreement), and various papers in the American *Journal of Psychology.* M. Compayré (*op. cit.*) adduces also the authority of Renouvier, from whom he quotes the following words: "Nous

savons par l'observation de l'enfance, par l'expérience des effets de l'éducation, que l'hérédité ne fournit à l'homme naissant aucune détermination fixe des actes bons et mauvais."

[16] See Baldwin, *Mental Development in Child and Race*, p. 17.

[17] The term "social heredity," which has already been frequently used, is due, I believe, to Prof. Baldwin. It serves to express the "indebtedness of the individual to this social environment" or the truth "of social transmission by tradition," emphasised by writers such as Leslie Stephen, Lloyd Morgan, J. A. Thomson, Alexander, R. MacIntosh. Though widely different from physical heredity, Baldwin contends that it is a true "heredity" because the outcome of "a personal reaction" upon tradition. See this writer's *Social and Ethical Interpretations in Mental Development.*

[18] Instincts are defined by Prof. Baldwin (*Psychology*, p. 329) as "original tendencies of consciousness to express itself in motor terms in response to definite but generally complex stimulations of sense." Impulses are internally stimulated tendencies; instincts are stimulated by the environment. Of course the definition given above regards instinct on its psychological side; physiologically, an instinct is an innate tendency to a certain form of action when the appropriate external stimulus is presented.

[19] Hence it cannot be said that man inherits a "bias to evil." If an honest merchant takes over an unsuccessful business and, in his attempts to place it on a sound financial footing and to make it a prosperous concern, long needs to exercise the utmost diligence, and even to borrow money, in order to escape bankruptcy, it would be improper to speak of his evincing a bias to indebtedness. He might be the most independent person in the world. It is no less improper to speak of the individual member of the race who inherits the tendencies of the stock and consequently, from an early age, has to enter upon a laborious career of "self-conquest," as possessing a bias to evil. Bias can only be predicated of the will, which emerges after the "nature" is inherited.

[20] Cf. Bradley, *Ethical Studies*, on the origin of the good and bad self.

[21] If these words represent more than an unintentional lapse they repudiate the position for which the Professor would seem to be contending.

[22] Alexander, *Moral Order and Progress.*

[23] See *The Origin and Propagation of Sin*, p. 160, note B.

[24] We are told that evolution has exhausted its possibilities in perfecting man's body. Moreover man, when civilised, is not exposed to natural selection in the sense in which he once was. He is now a domesticated animal; his progress consists in the enrichment of his environment and in securing the transmission to the individual of its stored-up acquisitions.

[25] See especially *Mental Development in the Child and the Race*, chap. x. §3; *Social and Ethical Interpretations*, chap. i. §3.

[26] The content of the moral law is mainly learned by imitation till mature manhood. Without the "tone" and somewhat arbitrary sanctions of the public school, and without hero-worship in later youth, most of us

would have suffered in the building up of character. The unique power of Christianity, and the highest significance of the appearance of Jesus Christ, is connected with His embodiment of the ethical ideal and His appeal to the moral faculty in man.

[27] For striking examples see Perez, *op. cit.* E. T. p. 288.

[28] J. Seth, *Principles of Ethics.*

[29] In the account given here of the development of sin in the individual the "raw material of morality" has been spoken of as if it consisted merely of what is supplied by sensibility. This, however, has been only for simplicity and convenience' sake. Of course human instincts and impulses do not remain blind when rational life has become developed. Thought transmutes them and makes them but centres of "a complex of associated ramifications due to our richer life." "Hunger and love" may be the two root elements of human nature, the rockbed of morals. But reason gives greater scope for selfishness than mere instinct, and enormously extends the field which morality has to conquer. It too, no less than sensibility, has to be moralised, and yields the stuff from which sin is made.

[30] J. Seth, *op. cit.* pp. 52, 53.

[31] "Those who dispute the validity of moral or other intuitions on the ground of their derivation must be required to show, not merely that they are the effects of certain causes, but that these causes are of a kind that tend to produce invalid beliefs." H. Sidgwick, *Methods of Ethics,* 5th ed. p. 213. This error was made by Prof. T. H. Green, *Prolegomena,* p. 9. A similar confusion was made, curiously enough, by Chas. Darwin, with regard to man's rational faculties in general (*Life and Letters,* i. p. 313).

[32] Cf. Galton, *Hereditary Genius,* p. 349, where it is added: "We, men of the present centuries, are like animals suddenly transplanted among new conditions of climate and food: our instincts fail us under the altered circumstances." In short, our nature and our nurture are necessarily at cross-purposes, and sin arises, though not of necessity, from their necessary conflict.

# 10

**Calvin Linton**

# Man's Difficulty—
# Ignorance or Evil?

Among the more pathetically amusing traits man has exhibited over the period of his recorded history is his untiring effort to blame somebody or something else for his predicament. That he is in a predicament he never seems seriously to have doubted; but that the mess is not his fault he has vociferously insisted. "The woman whom thou gavest to be with me . . . ," said Adam, pointing accusingly in the earliest recorded version of a defensive ploy now equally automatic among children and adults. Many debates in the council chambers of the world, including the United Nations, are elaborations of this instinct to divert the blame—"*He* started it."

Speaking more broadly, it may be said that natural man's view of himself ranges from this of innocent bystander ("There came out this calf," said Aaron with well-simulated wonder when the wrath of Moses was unveiled) to that of lord of creation. When the going is rough, as it usually is, he adopts the former posture; when he feels perky and the sun is bright, he cries "Glory to man in the highest," with Swinburne. In sum, if it is bad, "*he*" did it; if it is good, hurray for me.

From *Christianity Today*, 12 March 1965, pp. 18-20. Used by permission.

The one view man cannot adopt without divine prodding and much assistance is that of the Bible: "All we like sheep have gone astray" (Isa. 53:6). "But they refused to hearken. . . . Yea, they made their hearts as an adamant stone, lest they should hear the law, and the words which the Lord of hosts hath sent in his spirit by the former prophets. . . ." (Zech. 7:11, 12). "Therefore thou art inexcusable, O man, whosoever thou art that judgest: for wherein thou judgest another, thou condemnest thyself; for thou that judgest doest the same things" (Rom. 2:1).

The most popular version of the "don't blame me" syndrome today may be found in two tightly clutched beliefs: first, man has not "fallen" from any higher previous condition; and second, man's problems are entirely due to ignorance (which is not his fault), not to evil.

The first of these views runs counter to the uniform conviction of every known ancient culture—that man has, owing to some primal disaster, fallen from high estate. The "Golden Age" was believed to have been in the past, not to be in the future. The alternative view came late. Indeed, as Harvard Professor Crane Brinton has reminded us in his preface to *The Portable Age of Reason,* "They [the men of the eighteenth century] had begun to believe in progress—a word that before 1700 meant in both French and English no more than a physical moving, as when a royal personage made a progress through the realm."

### Sin—an Error in the Sum?

The second of the two beliefs—that man's predicament is the consequence of innocent ignorance, not culpable evil—is one of the proudest achievements of that same Age of Reason and involves several corollary and necessary beliefs: that man is by nature good, and hence perfectible; that reason supplied with enough information is capable of reaching, and will always reach, the ultimate truth; that the truth, once known, will always be believed and acted on; and that (in the words of William Godwin) "vice is error." "Sin," in short, is the mistake in the sum at the bottom of a column of figures. Add the column correctly and the "sin" disappears.

One rather odd feature of these dogmas is that though they depend heavily on a philosophy of science now outmoded, they are uttered in our time as if they were quite up to date and compatible with "modern sensibility." Whatever nostalgia some of us may have for Newtonian physics, the consensus among scientists seems to be that it is no longer valid in the larger dimensions of reality; and yet the chief originators of the doctrines of progress through knowledge and of human perfectibility rested their faith on eighteenth- and nineteenth-century philosophies of science.

Over and over again in the writings of the prophets of perfectibility we read the assertion that total reality, once sufficient information about it is acquired, will be totally understandable by the average intelligence. "Every truth of this kind is comprehensible by all understandings," wrote Claude Adrien Helvetius in his *A Treatise on Man* in 1773.

And observe the Marquis of Condorcet staring into the crystal ball in

1794: "Since," he wrote, "as the number of known facts increases, the human mind learns how to classify them and to subsume them under more general facts . . . ; since, as more relations between various objects become known, man is able to present them in such a way that it is possible to grasp a greater number of them with the same degree of intellectual ability, . . ." so the day will arrive, he asserts, when all the most profound truths of the universe will be known and universally comprehended. Conduct, then based on perfect information, will be perfect, because men are always as good as they know how to be.

Today it is difficult to imagine a more stumbling prophecy. Instead of becoming more unified, more "rational," more understandable, more available to the average intellect, scientific knowledge has become more esoteric, more fragmented, and more impossible of comprehension save by the very few. And appallingly, somewhere along the line it has picked up the very unNewtonian burden of the irrational, the indeterminate, the unthinkable.

It was a beautiful dream. How encouraging to have believed that once the *Encyclopédie,* which was founded by Denis Diderot and contained every fact about everything, was published, man could "with almost complete assurance" predict everything and hence control everything.

True, even the encyclopedists had a few qualms about the nature of the ultimate victory over death. "It is reasonable to hope," wrote Condorcet, "that all . . . diseases may . . . disappear as their distant causes are discovered. . . . Certainly man will not become immortal; but will not the interval between the first breath that he draws and the time when . . . he expires increase indefinitely? . . . We are bound to believe that the average length of human life will forever increase." An oddly self-defeating prediction—at least to modern materialist existentialists, who assert that the inevitable extinction of every human life, no matter how long deferred, irrefutably demonstrates the Absurdity of human existence.

My chief aim, however, is not to rehearse this rather obvious portion of the history of ideas but to point out certain interesting irrationalities in the way the dogma of human perfectibility is preached by its contemporary adherents. As a matter of fact, the chief points I wish to make all appeared in a recent address by an eminent educator who said, as if the idea were not a rather quaint one based on outmoded science but a new one conceived at least partly by him: "Man's difficulties, it seems to me, are the consequence of his ignorance, not of something the theologians used to call 'evil.' "

## The Doubling and Redoubling

The first rational tangle in his talk came with the predictable assertion about the doubling and redoubling of man's "knowledge." In recorded human history, so that rubric runs, knowledge first doubled (from what? presumably zero?) in 1750. It doubled again in 1900, again in 1950, and again in 1960. It is expected to double again by 1965, and about every two hours on the hour after that.

The seeming sanctity lent by this pretense of statistical evidence is impressive to the unthinking listener. But a moment's thought will reveal the statement to be pure speculation. Note only two of many basic difficulties. First, no man knows *all* that the world has previously known. We are constantly amazed to learn that the ancients knew things that a generation ago it was not known they knew. Thus no man can measure the relative increase. When you don't know what you are talking about, you cannot say it doubled. Furthermore, there is no definition of the word "knowledge" as used in the dogma. "Information," presumably, would be a better word; for what seems to be meant is a body of quantified data, not knowledge, which is significantly qualitative, not quantitative. The distinction is vital, for we all realize that we "know" (comprehend) little about lots of things on which we have incalculable masses of information—electricity, gravity, the ultimate nature of the universe or of man; but we *know* a good deal about many things on which we have little information (quantified data)—the power of love, the appeal of beauty, the nature of happiness, the imperatives of the moral nature.

As the talk progressed, a second rational difficulty gaped: if man's only problem is ignorance; and if knowledge is the cure of ignorance; and if knowledge is doubling and redoubling at incredible rates—why is not man's demonstrable well-being now proportionately upgraded? Where is evidence of that vastly increased betterment in the human condition that should follow knowledge as the thermometer follows the temperature? (One finds himself as unimpressed as when he is told that "90 per cent of all scientists who ever lived are living today," which is almost analogous to saying that more people born in the twentieth century are alive today than all people born in previous centuries.)

There is a third difficulty, usually implicit, that normally appears in these utterances. We are told that with every discovery in science, more areas of our ignorance, previously unsuspected, are opened up than are illuminated by the new knowledge. The speaker to whom I have referred said, seemingly without awareness of the conflict with his main thesis, that scientists now believe there is no end to the quest for new knowledge. It would seem to follow, therefore, that man's cause of misery, ignorance, is forever incapable of solution. We are left moaning with Housman: "The troubles of our proud and angry dust are from eternity and shall not fail."

### Search for the Center of Meaning

A fourth built-in futility of the information-will-save-us view is the unusability of much of the incredible amount of information that has been stocked up. Most of it, according to Sir Julian Huxley, is "lying around unused," and much of it is unusable because it is so esoteric that few brains are capable of seeing basic relations. "If the situation is not to lead to chaos, despair, or escapism," writes Sir Julian in *The Humanist Frame* (quoted in the *Graduate Journal* for Fall, 1964), "man must reunify his life within the framework of a satisfactory idea-system." Agreed; but "satisfactory idea-systems" cannot emerge from the kind of computered mountains of quantified information referred to rejoicingly as man's "fantastic growth of knowledge." One does not even *begin* from there. "What seems lacking," runs an editorial in the same journal, "is something not altogether tangible—the critical values that give compelling meaning and a sense of direction to human life." No electronic retrieval system will ever be capable of giving the kind of knowledge needed to find the motionless center of meaning from which alone a purposeful direction of life can be charted.

Amid such illogicalities and internal contradictions, the dogma of salvation through knowledge is preached today to the faithful. Often the capping argument is added near the end: "We've tried Christianity for two thousand years. It has failed. Now let us try knowledge." It would appear that if anything about the past two thousand years is obvious, it is that the world has not been run in strict obedience to Christ's teachings. But when Christian principles *have* been tried, even with very imperfect obedience, the alleviation of human misery has been immediate and dramatic. In our present daily life, we are much more the beneficiary—in freedom, law, moral principles, justice, compassion, love—of Christianity than of modern technology. Indeed, "knowledge" (qualified data) has nothing really significant to say about any of these values; yet these values are what make life worth living.

Happily, when we weary of the tons of marvelous but irrelevant information that are the pride of our age, we can still turn to the Bible and there come to *know* the essential things. First, that the Lord, the Creator of all things, *is.* (Note that in the Book of Ezekiel alone there are over forty instances of the phrase, ". . . shall know that I am the Lord," or its equivalent.) No pile of statistics can ever reach this knowledge, any more than Babel could reach heaven.

Second, we come to know what we are—creatures of the Lord, made in his image for his glory and our happiness, but fallen, "a rebellious people, which walketh in a way that was not good, after their own thoughts" (Isa. 65:2). And, most transcendently, we come to know who the Saviour is, who came to seek and to save that which is lost. "Jesus said unto her, I am the resurrection, and the life: he that believeth in me, though he were dead, yet shall he live" (John 11:25).

Of these truths it might be said what T. S. Eliot once said about his own works: "I doubt whether what I am saying can convey very much to anyone for whom the doctrine of original sin is not a very real and tremendous thing." Clio, the muse of history, might say the same thing; for these truths, though unpalatable to natural man, are not offensive to human reason or to the student of human history. In fact, to try to understand history without allowing for the reality of evil is to make man's past a conundrum, a tissue of contradictions. The intellectual journey of a brilliantly endowed man like the late Dr. C. E. M. Joad illustrates this. As professor of philosophy and psychology at the University of London, he was characterized by *Time* magazine in 1948 as "an annoying, church-baiting agnostic" and in 1953 as "brilliantly voluble, . . . variously known as a socialist, pacifist, patriot, agnostic, and advocate of free love." No other man was so learnedly conversant with every modern theory of human moral no-responsibility. "Sin," he later wrote, "I dismissed as the incidental accompaniment of man's imperfect development."

But as the years went by, Joad grew less and less sure that such a dismissal was in accord with reason, history, and modern knowledge; and he later wrote: "I have come lately to disbelieve all this. I see now that evil is endemic in man, and that the Christian doctrine of original sin expresses a deep and essential insight into human nature." But he also found light in the darkness: "The more I knew of it, Christianity seemed to offer . . . consolation, strengthening, and assistance. . . . Once I had come as far as this, there was nothing to be lost and everything to be gained by going the whole way. What better hope was offered than by the Christian doctrine that God sent His Son into the world to save sinners?"

What, indeed?

# The Result of Sin: Corruption

11

## Jonathan Edwards

# Some Evidences of Original Sin from Facts and Events

### Section 1

By original sin, as the phrase has been most commonly used by divines, is meant the *innate sinful depravity of the heart*. But yet when the doctrine of original sin is spoken of, it is vulgarly understood in that latitude, as to include not only the depravity of nature, but the *imputation* of Adam's first sin; or in other words, the liableness or exposedness of Adam's posterity, in the divine judgment, to partake of the punishment of that sin. So far as I know, most of those who have held one of these, have maintained the other; and most of those who have opposed one, have opposed the other. Both are opposed by the author chiefly attended to in the following discourse, in his book against original sin. And it may perhaps appear in our future consideration of the subject, that they are closely connected, and that the arguments which prove the one establish the other, and that there are no more difficulties attending the allowing of one than the other.

From *Original Sin*, chapter 1 (sections 1-3). In *Works*, vol. 2 (New York: Robert Carter and Brothers, 1864), pp. 107-33.

I shall in the first place consider this doctrine more especially with regard to the corruption of nature; and as we treat of this, the other will naturally come into consideration in the prosecution of the discourse, as connected with it.

As all moral qualities, all principles, either of virtue or vice, lie in the disposition of the heart, I shall consider whether we have any evidence, that the heart of man is naturally of a corrupt and evil disposition. This is strenuously denied by many late writers, who are enemies to the doctrine of original sin, and particularly by Dr. Taylor.[1]

The way we come by the idea of any such thing as disposition or tendency, is by observing what is constant or general in event; especially under a great variety of circumstances; and above all, when the effect or event continues the same through great and various opposition, much and manifold force and means used to the contrary not prevailing to hinder the effect. I don't know that such a prevalence of effects is denied to be an evidence of prevailing tendency in causes and agents; or that it is expressly denied by the opposers of the doctrine of original sin, that if, in the course of events, it universally or generally proves that mankind are actually corrupt, this would be an evidence of a prior corrupt propensity in the world of mankind; whatever may be said by some, which, if taken with its plain consequences, may seem to imply a denial of this; which may be considered afterwards. But by many the fact is denied: that is, it is denied, that corruption and moral evil is commonly prevalent in the world. On the contrary, it is insisted on, that good preponderates, and that virtue has the ascendant.

To this purpose Dr. Turnbull says,[2]

> With regard to the prevalence of vice in the world, men are apt to let their imagination run out upon all the robberies, piracies, murders, perjuries, frauds, massacres, assassinations they have either heard of, or read in history; thence concluding all mankind to be very wicked. As if a court of justice were a proper place to make an estimate of the morals of mankind, or an hospital of the healthfulness of the climate. But ought they not to consider, that the number of honest citizens and farmers far surpasses that of all sorts of criminals in any state, and that the innocent and kind actions of even criminals themselves surpass their crimes in numbers; that it is the rarity of crimes, in comparison of innocent or good actions, which engages our attention to them, and makes them to be recorded in history, while honest, generous domestic actions are overlooked, only because they are so common? As one great danger, or one month's sickness shall become a frequently repeated story during a long life of health and safety. Let not the vices of mankind be multiplied or magnified. Let us make a fair estimate of human life, and set over against the shocking, the astonishing instances of barbarity and wickedness that have been perpetrated in any age, not only the exceeding generous and brave actions with which history shines, but the prevailing innocency, good-nature, industry, felicity and cheerfulness of the

greater part of mankind at all times; and we shall not find reason to cry out, as objectors against providence do on this occasion, that all men are vastly corrupt, and that there is hardly any such thing as virtue in the world. Upon a fair computation, the fact does indeed come out, that very great villainies have been very uncommon in all ages, and looked upon as monstrous; so general is the sense and esteem of virtue.[3]

It seems to be with a like view that Dr. Taylor says, "We must not take the measure of our health and enjoyments from a lazar-house, nor of our understanding from Bedlam, nor of our morals from a gaol."[4]

With respect to the propriety and pertinence of such a representation of things, and its force as to the consequence designed; I hope we shall be better able to judge, and in some measure to determine whether the natural disposition of the hearts of mankind be corrupt or not, when the things which follow have been considered.

But for the greater clearness, it may be proper here to premise one consideration, that is of great importance in this controversy, and is very much overlooked by the opposers of the doctrine of original sin in their disputing against it; which is this—

That is to be looked upon as the true tendency of the natural or innate disposition of man's heart, which appears to be its tendency when we consider things as they are in themselves, or in their own nature, without the *interposition of divine grace.* Thus, that state of man's nature, that disposition of the mind, is to be looked upon as evil and pernicious, which, as it is in itself, tends to extremely pernicious consequences, and would certainly end therein, were it not that the free mercy and kindness of God interposes to prevent that issue. It would be very strange, if any should argue that there is no evil tendency in the case, because the mere favor and compassion of the Most High may step in and oppose the tendency, and prevent the sad effect tended to. Particularly, if there be anything in the nature of man, whereby he has an universal, unfailing tendency to that moral evil, which according to the real nature and true demerit of things, as they are in themselves, implies his utter ruin, that must be looked upon as an evil tendency or propensity; however divine grace may interpose, to save him from deserved ruin, and to overrule things to an issue contrary to that which they tend to of themselves. Grace is a sovereign thing, exercised according to the good pleasure of God, bringing good out of evil; the effect of it belongs not to the nature of things themselves, that otherwise have an ill tendency, any more than the remedy belongs to the disease; but is something altogether independent on it, introduced to oppose the natural tendency, and reverse the course of things. But the event that things tend to, according to their own demerit, and according to divine justice, that is the event which they tend to in their own nature; as Dr. Taylor's own words fully imply. "God alone," says he, "can declare whether he will pardon or punish the ungodliness and unrighteousness of mankind, which is in its own nature punishable."[5] Nothing is more precisely according to the truth of things, than divine justice; it weighs things in an even balance; it views and estimates things no otherwise than they are truly in their own nature. Therefore undoubtedly that which implies a tendency to ruin according to the estimate of divine justice, does indeed imply such a tendency in its own nature.

And then it must be remembered, that it is a *moral depravity* we are speaking of; and therefore when we are considering whether such depravity don't appear by a tendency to a bad effect or issue, 'tis a *moral tendency* to such an issue, that is what is to be taken into the account. A moral tendency or influence is by desert. Then it may be said, man's nature or state is attended with a pernicious or destructive tendency, in a moral sense, when it tends to that which deserves misery and destruction. And therefore it equally shews the moral depravity of the nature of mankind in their present state, whether that nature be universally attended with an effectual tendency to destructive vengeance actually executed, or to their deserving misery and ruin, or their just exposedness to destruction, however that fatal consequence may be prevented by grace, or whatever the actual event be.

One thing more is to be observed here, viz. that the topic mainly insisted on by the opposers of the doctrine of original sin, is the justice of God; both in their objections against the imputation of Adam's sin, and also against its being so ordered that men should come into the world with a corrupt and ruined nature, without having merited the displeasure of their Creator by any personal fault. But the latter is not repugnant to God's justice, if men can be, and actually are, born into the world with a tendency to sin, and to misery and ruin for their sin, which actually will be the consequence, unless *mere grace* steps in and prevents it. If this be allowed, the argument from *justice* is given up; for it is to suppose that their liableness to misery and ruin comes in a way of justice; otherwise there would be no need of the interposition of divine grace to save 'em. Justice alone would be sufficient security, if exercised, without grace. 'Tis all one in this dispute about what is just and righteous, whether men are born in a miserable state, by a tendency to ruin, which actually follows, and that justly; or whether they are born in such a state as tends to a desert of ruin, which might justly follow, and would actually follow, did not grace prevent. For the controversy is not, what grace will do, but what justice might do.

I have been the more particular on this head, because it enervates many of the reasonings and conclusions by which Dr. Taylor makes out his scheme; in which he argues from that state which mankind are in by divine grace, yea, which he himself supposes to be by divine grace; and yet not making any allowance for this, he from hence draws conclusions against what others suppose of the deplorable and ruined state, mankind are in by the fall.[6] Some of his arguments and conclusions to this effect, in order to be made good, must depend on such a supposition as this; that God's dispensations of grace are rectifications or amendments of his foregoing constitutions and proceedings, which were merely legal; as though the dispensations of grace, which succeed those of mere law, implied an acknowledgement, that the preceding legal constitution would be unjust, if left as it was, or at least very hard dealing with mankind; and that the other were of the nature of a satisfaction to his creatures, for former injuries, or hard treatment: so that put together, the injury with the satisfaction, the legal and injurious dispensation taken with the following good dispensation, which our author calls grace, and the unfairness or improper severity of the former amended by the goodness of the latter, both together made up one righteous dispensation.

The reader is desired to bear this in mind, which I have said concerning the interposition of divine grace, its not altering the nature of things, as they are in themselves; and accordingly, when I speak of such and such an evil tendency of things, belonging to the present nature and state of mankind, understand me to mean their tendency *as they are in themselves,* abstracted from any consideration of that remedy the sovereign and infinite grace of God has provided.

Having premised these things, I now proceed to say, that mankind are all naturally in such a state, as is attended, without fail, with this consequence or issue; that they universally run themselves into that which is, in effect, their own utter eternal perdition, as being finally accursed of God, and the subjects of his remedy-less wrath, through sin.

From which I infer, that the natural state of the mind of man is attended with a propensity of nature, which is prevalent and effectual, to such an issue; and that therefore their nature is corrupt and depraved with a moral depravity, that amounts to and implies their utter undoing.

Here I would first consider the truth of the proposition; and then would shew the certainty of the consequences which I infer from it. If both can be clearly and certainly proved, then I trust, none will deny but that the doctrine of original depravity is evident, and so the falseness of Dr. Taylor's scheme demonstrated; the greatest part of whose book, that he calls *The Scripture-Doctrine of Original Sin* etc. is against the doctrine of innate depravity. In p. 383 he speaks of the conveyance of a corrupt and sinful nature to Adam's posterity as the grand point to be proved by the maintenance of the doctrine of original sin.

In order to demonstrate what is asserted in the proposition laid down, there is need only that these two things should be made manifest: one is this fact, that all mankind come into the world in such a state, as without fail comes to this issue, namely, the universal commission of sin; or that every one who comes to act in the world as a moral agent, is, in a greater or lesser degree, guilty of sin. The other is, that all sin deserves and exposes to utter and eternal destruction, under God's wrath and curse; and would end in it, were it not for the interposition of divine grace to prevent the effect. Both which can be abundantly demonstrated to be agreeable to the word of God, and to Dr. Taylor's own doctrine.

That every one of mankind, at least of them that are capable of acting as moral agents, are guilty of sin (not now taking it for granted that they come guilty into the world) is a thing most clearly and abundantly evident from the holy Scriptures. (I Kings 8:46), "If any man sin against thee, for there is no man that sinneth not." (Eccles. 7:20), "There is not a just man upon earth that doth good, and sinneth not." (Job 9:2-3), "I know it is so of a truth" (i.e. as Bildad had just before said, that God would not cast away a perfect man, etc.), "but how should man be just with God? If he will contend with him, he cannot answer him one of a thousand." To the like purpose (Ps. 143:2), "Enter not into judgment with thy servant; for in thy sight shall no man living be justified." So the words of the Apostle (in which he has apparent reference to those words of the Psalmist, Rom. 3:19-20), "That every mouth may be stopped, and all the world become guilty before God. Therefore by the deeds of the law there shall no flesh be justified in his sight: for by the law is the knowledge of sin." So Gal. 2:16; I John 1:7-10: "If we walk in the light, the blood of Christ cleanseth us from all sin. If we say that we have no sin, we deceive ourselves, and the truth is not in us. If we confess our sins, he is faithful and just to forgive us our sins, and to cleanse us from all unrighteousness. If we say that we have not sinned, we make him a liar, and his word is not in us." As in this place, so in innumerable other places, confession and repentance of sin are spoken of as duties proper for all; as also prayer to God for pardon of sin; and forgiveness of those that injure us, from that motive, that we hope to be forgiven of God. Universal guilt of sin may also be demonstrated from the appointment, and the declared use and end, of the ancient sacrifices; and also from the ransom, which everyone that was numbered in Israel, was directed to pay, to make atonement for his soul (Exod. 30:11-16). All are represented, not only as being sinful, but as having great and manifold iniquity (Job 9:2, 3; James 3:1, 2).

There are many scriptures which both declare the universal sinfulness of mankind, and also that all sin deserves and justly exposes to everlasting destruction, under the wrath and curse of God; and so demonstrate both parts of the proposition I have laid down. To which purpose, that in Gal. 3:10 is exceeding full. "For as many as are of the works of the law are under the curse; for it is written, cursed is every one that continueth not in all things which are written in the book of the law, to do them." How manifestly is it implied in the Apostle's meaning here, that there is no man but what fails in some instances of doing all things that are written in the book of the law, and therefore as many as have their dependence on their fulfilling the law, are under that curse which is pronounced on them that do fail of it. And hence the Apostle infers in the next verse, "that no man is justified by the law in the sight of God"; as he had said before in the preceding chapter, vv. 16, 17. "By the works of the law shall no flesh be justified" and that all that "seek to be justified by the works of the law, are found sinners." The Apostle shews us that he understands, that by this place which he cites from Deuteronomy, the Scripture hath concluded, or shut up, all under sin; as in ch. 3:22. So that here we are plainly taught, both that every one of mankind is a sinner, and that every sinner is under the curse of God.

To the like purpose is that, Rom. 4:14, and also II Cor. 3:6, 7, 9, where the law is called "the letter that kills, the ministration of death, and the ministration of condemnation." The wrath, condemnation and death which is threatened in the law to all its transgressors, is final perdition, the second death, eternal ruin; as is very plain, and is confessed. And this punishment which the law threatens for every sin, is a just punishment; being what every sin truly deserves; God's law being a righteous law, and the sentence of it a righteous sentence.

All these things are what Dr. Taylor himself confesses and asserts. He says, that the law of God requires perfect obedience. (*Note on Rom.* 7:6, pp. 391, 392), "God can never require imperfect obedience, or by his holy law allow us to be guilty of any one sin, how small soever. And if the law as a rule of duty were in any respect abolished, then we might in some respects transgress the law, and yet not be guilty of sin. The moral law, or law of nature, is the truth, everlasting, unchangeable; and therefore, as such, can never be abrogated. On the contrary, our Lord Jesus Christ has promulgated it anew under the gospel, fuller and clearer than it was in the Mosaical constitution, or anywhere else; [. . .] having added to its precepts the sanction of his own divine authority." And many things which he says imply that all mankind do in some degree transgress the law. In p. 228, speaking of what may be gathered from Rom. 7 and 8, he says, "We are very apt, in a world full of temptation, to be deceived, and drawn into sin by bodily appetites, etc. And the case of those who are under a law threatening death to every sin, must be quite deplorable, if they have no relief from the mercy of the law-giver." But this is very fully declared in what he says in his *Note on Romans* 5:20, pp. 378, 379. His words are as follows: "Indeed, as a rule of action prescribing our duty, it (the law) always was, and always must be a rule ordained for obtaining life; but not as a rule of justification, not as it subjects to death for every transgression. For if it could in its utmost rigour have given us life, then, as the Apostle argues, it would have been against the promise of God. For if there had been a law, in the strict and rigorous sense of law, *which could have made us live,* verily justification should have been by the law. But he supposes, no such law was ever given: and therefore there is need and room enough for the promises of grace; or as he argues (Gal. 2:21), it would have frustrated, or rendered useless the grace of God. For if justification came by the law, then truly Christ is dead in vain, then he died to accomplish what was, or *might have been effected* by law it self, without his death. Certainly the law was not brought in among the Jews to be a rule of justification, or to recover 'em out of a state of death, and to procure life by their sinless obedience to it: for in this, as well as in another respect, it was *weak;* not in itself, but through the *weakness* of our flesh. (Rom. 8:3). The law, I conceive, is not a dispensation suitable to the infirmity of the human nature in our present state; or it doth not seem congruous to the goodness of God to afford us no other way of salvation, but by *law: which if we once transgress, we are ruin'd forever. For who then from the beginning of the world could be saved?* How clear and express are these things, that no one of mankind from the beginning of the world can ever be justified by law, because every one transgresses it?[7]

And here we also see, Dr. Taylor declares, that by the law men are sentenced to everlasting ruin for one transgression. To the like purpose he often expresses himself. So, p. 207: "The law requireth the most extensive obedience, discovering sin in all its branches. It gives sin a deadly force, subjecting every transgression to the penalty of death; and yet supplieth neither help nor hope to the sinner; but leaveth him under the power of sin, and sentence of death." In p. 213 he speaks of the law as extending to lust and irregular desires, and to every branch and principle of sin; and even to its latent principles, and minutest branches. Again (*Note on Rom.* 7:6, p. 391), to every sin, how small soever. And when he speaks of the law subjecting every transgression to the penalty of death, he means eternal death, as he from time to time explains the matter. In p. 212 he speaks of the law in the condemning power of it, as binding us in everlasting chains. In p. 396 he says that death which is the wages of sin, is the second death: and this (p. 78) he explains of [as] final perdition. In his *Key,* p. 155, no. 264 he says, "The curse of the law subjected men for every transgression to eternal death." So in *Note on Rom.* 5:20, p. 371, ·"The law of Moses subjected those who were under it to death, meaning by death eternal death." These are his words.

He also supposes, that this sentence of the law, thus subjecting men for every, even the *least sin,* and every minutest branch, and *latent principle of sin,* to so dreadful a punishment, is just and righteous, *agreeable to truth and the nature of things,* or to the natural and *proper demerits of sin.* This he is very full in. Thus in p. 21 "It was sin," says he, "which subjected to death by the law, justly threatening sin with death. Which law was given us, that sin might appear; might be set forth in its proper colours; when we saw it subjected us to death by a law perfectly holy, just, and good; that sin by the commandment, by the law, might be represented what it really is, an exceeding great and deadly evil." So in *Note on Rom.* 5:20, p. 380. "The law or ministration of death, as it subjects to death for every transgression, is still of use to shew the natural and proper demerit of sin." (Ibid., p. 371, 372), "The language of the law, dying thou shalt die, is to be understood of the demerit of the transgression, that which it deserves." (Ibid., p. 379), The law was added, saith Mr. Locke on the place, because the Israelites, the posterity of Abraham, were transgressors as well as other men, to shew them their sins, and the punishment and death, which in strict justice they incurred by them. And this appears to be a true comment on Rom. 7:13—Sin, by virtue of the law, subjected you to death for this end, that sin, working death in us by that which is holy, just & good, perfectly consonant to everlasting truth and righteousness.... Consequently every sin is in strict justice deserving of wrath and punishment; and the law in its rigour was given to the Jews, to set home this awful truth upon their consciences, to shew them the evil and pernicious nature of sin; and that being conscious they had broke the law of God, this might convince them of the great need they had of the favour of the lawgiver, and oblige them, by faith in his goodness, to fly to his mercy for pardon and salvation.

If the law be holy, just and good, a constitution perfectly agreeable to God's holiness, justice and goodness; then he might have put it exactly in execution, agreeably to all these his perfections. Our author himself says (p. 409), "How that constitution, which establishes a law, the making of which is inconsistent with the justice and goodness of God, and the executing of it inconsistent with his holiness, can be a righteous constitution, I confess, is quite beyond my comprehension."

Now the reader is left to judge whether it ben't most plainly and fully agreeable to Dr. Taylor's own doctrine, that there never was any one person from the beginning of the world, who came to act in the world as a moral agent, and that it is not to be hoped there ever will be any, but what is a sinner or transgressor of the law of God; and that therefore this proves to be the issue and event of things, with respect to all mankind in all ages, that, by the natural and proper demerit of their own sinfulness, and in the judgment of the law of God, which is perfectly consonant to truth, and exhibits things in their true colors, they are the proper subjects of the curse of God, eternal death, and everlasting ruin; which must be the actual consequence, unless the grace or favor of the lawgiver interpose, and mercy prevail for their pardon and salvation. The reader has seen also how agreeable this is to the doctrine of the Holy Scripture.

And if so, and what has been observed concerning the interposition of divine grace be remembered, namely, that this alters not the nature of things as they are in themselves, and that it don't in the least affect the state of the controversy we are upon, concerning the true nature and tendency of the state that mankind come into the world in, whether grace prevents the fatal effect or no; I say, if these things are considered, I trust, none will deny, that the proposition that was laid down, is fully proved, as agreeable to the word of God, and Dr. Taylor's own words; viz. that mankind are all naturally in such a state, as is attended, without fail, with this consequence or issue, that they universally are the subjects of that guilt and sinfulness, which is, in effect, their utter and eternal ruin, being cast wholly out of the favor of God, and subjected to his everlasting wrath and curse.

### Section 2

The proposition laid down being proved, the consequence of it remains to be made out, viz. that the mind of man has a *natural tendency* or propensity to that event, which has been shewn universally and infallibly to take place (if this ben't sufficiently evident of itself, without proof), and that this is a *corrupt* or *depraved* propensity.

I shall here consider the former part of this consequence, namely, whether such an universal, constant, infallible event is truly a proof of the being of any tendency or propensity to that event; leaving the evil and corrupt nature of such a propensity to be considered afterwards.

If any shall say, they don't think that its being a thing universal and infallible in event, that mankind commit some sin, is a proof of a prevailing tendency to sin; because they don't only sin, but also do good, and perhaps more good than evil: let them remember, that the question at present is not, how much sin there is a tendency to; but whether there be a prevailing propensity to that issue, which it is allowed all men do actually come to, that all fail of keeping the law perfectly, whether there ben't a tendency to such imperfection of obedience, as always without fail comes to pass; to that degree of sinfulness, at least, which all fall into; and so to that utter ruin, which that sinfulness implies and infers. Whether an effectual propensity to this be worth the name of depravity, because of the good that may be supposed to balance it, shall be considered by and by. If it were so, that all mankind, in all nations and ages, were at least one day in their lives deprived of the use of their reason, and run raving mad; or that all, even every individual person, once cut their own throats, or put out their own eyes; it might be an evidence of some tendency in the nature or natural state of mankind to such an event; though they might exercise reason many more days than they were distracted, and were kind to and tender of themselves oftener than they mortally and cruelly wounded themselves.[8]

To determine whether the unfailing constancy of the above-named event be an evidence of tendency, let it be considered, what can be meant by tendency, but a prevailing liableness or exposedness to such or such an event? Wherein consists the notion of any such thing, but some stated prevalence or preponderation in the nature or state of causes or occasions, that is followed by, and so proved to be effectual to, a stated prevalence or commonness of any particular kind of effect? Or, something in the permanent state of things, concerned in bringing a certain sort of event to pass, which is a foundation for the constancy, or strongly prevailing probability, of such an event? If we mean this by tendency (as I know not what else can be meant by it, but this, or something like this) then it is manifest, that where we see a stated prevalence of any kind of effect or event, there is a tendency to that effect in the nature and state of its causes. A common and steady effect shews, that there is somewhere a preponderation, a prevailing exposedness or liableness in the state of things, to what comes so steadily to pass. The natural dictate of reason shews, that where there is an effect, there is a cause, and a cause sufficient for the effect; because, if it were not sufficient, it would not be effectual: and that therefore, where there is a stated prevalence of the effect, there is a stated prevalence in the cause: a steady effect argues a steady cause.[9] We obtain a notion of such a thing as tendency, no other way than by observation: and we can observe nothing but events: and 'tis the commonness or constancy of events, that gives us a notion of tendency in all cases. Thus we judge of tendencies in the natural world. Thus we judge of the tendencies or propensities of nature in minerals, vegetables, animals, rational and irrational creatures. A notion of a stated tendency or fixed propensity is not obtained by observing only a single event. A stated preponderation in the cause or occasion, is argued only by a stated prevalence of the effect. If a die be once thrown, and it falls on a particular side, we don't argue from hence, that that side is the heaviest; but if it be thrown without skill or care, many thousands or millions of times going, and constantly falls on the same side, we have not the least doubt in our minds, but that there is something of propensity in the case, by superior weight of that side, or in some other respect. How ridiculous would he make himself, who should earnestly dispute against any tendency in the state of things to cold in winter, or heat in the summer; or should stand to it, that although it often happened that water quenched fire, yet there was no tendency in it to such an effect?

In the case we are upon, the human nature, as existing in such an immense diversity of persons and circumstances, and never failing in any one instance, of coming to that issue, viz. that sinfulness which implies extreme misery and eternal ruin, is as the die often cast. For it alters not the case in the least, as to the evidence of tendency, whether the subject of the constant event be an individual, or a nature and kind. Thus, if there be a succession of trees of the same sort, proceeding one from another, from the beginning of the world, growing in all countries, soils and climates, and otherwise in (as it were) an infinite variety of circumstances, all bearing ill fruit; it as much proves the nature and tendency of the kind, as if it were only one individual tree that had remained from the beginning of the world, had often been transplanted into different soils etc. and had continued to bear only bad fruit. So, if there were a particular family, which, from generation to generation, and through every remove to innumerable different countries and places of abode, all died of a consumption, or all run distracted, or all murdered themselves, it would be as much an evidence of the tendency of something in the nature or constitution of that race, as it would be of the tendency of something in the nature or state of an individual, if some one person had lived all that time, and some remarkable event had often appeared in him, which he had been the agent or subject of, from year to year and from age to age, continually and without fail.[10]

Thus a propensity attending the present nature or natural state of mankind, eternally to ruin themselves by sin, may certainly be inferred from apparent and acknowledged fact. And I would now observe further, that not only does this follow from facts that are acknowledged by Dr. Taylor, but the things he asserts, the expressions and words which he uses, do plainly imply that all mankind have such a propensity; yea, one of the highest kind, a propensity that is *invincible,* or a tendency which really amounts to a fixed constant unfailing *necessity.* There is a plain confession of a propensity or proneness to sin (p. 143). "Man, who drinketh in iniquity like water; who is attended with so many sensual appetites, and so apt to indulge them." And again (p. 228), "We are very apt, in a world full of temptation, to be deceiv'd, & drawn into sin by bodily appetites." If we are very apt or prone to be drawn into sin by bodily appetites, and sinfully to indulge them, and very apt or prone to yield to temptation to sin, then we are *prone to sin:* for to yield to temptation to sin, is sinful. In the same page he represents, that on this account, and on account of the consequences of this, the case of those who are under a law threatening death for every sin, must be quite deplorable, if they have no relief from the mercy of the law-giver. Which implies, that their case is hopeless, as to an escape from death, the punishment of sin, by any other means than God's mercy. And that implies, that there is such an aptness to yield to temptation to sin, that 'tis hopeless that any of mankind should wholly avoid it. But he speaks of it elsewhere, over and over, as truly impossible, or what can't be; as in the words which were cited in the last section, from his *Note on Romans* 5:20, where he repeatedly speaks of the law, which subjects us to death for every transgression, as what cannot give life; and represents that if God offered us no other way of salvation, no man from the beginning of the world could be saved. In the same place he with approbation cites Mr. Locke's words, in which, speaking of the Israelites, he says, "All endeavours after righteousness was lost labour, since any one slip forfeited life, & it was impossible for them to expect aught but death."[11]  Our author speaks of it as impossible for the law requiring sinless obedience, to give life, not that the law was weak in itself, but through the weakness of our flesh. Therefore, he says, he conceives the law not to be a dispensation suitable to the infirmity of the human nature in its present state. These things amount to a full confession, that the proneness in men to sin, and to a demerit of and just exposedness to eternal ruin by sin, is universally invincible, or, which is the same thing, amounts to absolute invincible necessity; which surely is the highest kind of tendency, or propensity: and that not the less for his laying this propensity to our infirmity or weakness, which may seem to intimate some defect, rather than anything positive: and 'tis agreeable to the sentiments of the best divines, that all sin originally comes from a defective or privative cause. But sin don't cease to be sin, or a thing not justly exposing to eternal ruin (as is implied in Dr. Taylor's own words) for arising from infirmity or defect; nor does an invincible propensity to sin cease to be a propensity to such demerit of eternal ruin, because the proneness arises from such a cause.

It is manifest, that this tendency which has been proved, don't consist in any particular external circumstances, that some or many are in, peculiarly tempting and influencing their minds; but is *inherent,* and is seated in that *nature* which is common to all mankind, which they carry with them wherever they go, and still remains the same, however circumstances may differ. For it is implied in what has been proved, and shewn to be confessed, that the same event comes to pass in all circumstances, that any of mankind ever are or can be under in the world. In God's sight no man living can be justified; but all are sinners, and exposed to condemnation. This is true of persons of all constitutions, capacities, conditions, manners, opinions and educations; in all countries, climates, nations and ages; and through all the mighty changes and revolutions, which have come to pass in the habitable world.

We have the same evidence, that the propensity in this case lies in the nature of the subject, and don't arise from any particular circumstances, as we have in any case whatsoever; which is only by the effects appearing to be the same in all changes of time and place, and under all varieties of circumstances. It is in this way only we judge, that any propensities, which we observe in mankind, are such as are seated in their nature, in all other cases. 'Tis thus we judge of the mutual propensity betwixt the sexes, or of the dispositions which are exercised in any of the natural passions or appetites, that they truly belong to the nature of man; because they are observed in mankind in general, through all countries, nations and ages, and in all conditions.

If any should say, though it be evident that there is a tendency in the state of things to this general event, that all mankind should fail of perfect obedience, and should sin, and incur a demerit of eternal ruin; and also that this tendency don't lie in any distinguishing circumstances of any particular people, person or age—yet it may not lie in man's nature, but in the general constitution and frame of this world, into which men are born—though the nature of man may be good, without any evil propensity inherent in it; yet the nature and universal state of this earthly world may be such as to be full of so many and strong temptations everywhere, and of such a powerful influence on such a creature as man, dwelling in so infirm a body etc. that the result of the whole may be, a strong and infallible tendency in such a state of things, to the sin and eternal ruin of every one of mankind.

To this I would reply, that such an evasion will not at all avail to the purpose of those whom I oppose in this controversy. It alters not the case as to this question, whether man is not a creature that in his present state is depraved and ruined by propensities to sin. If any creature be of such a nature that it proves evil in its proper place, or in the situation which God has assigned it in the universe, it is of an evil nature. That part of the system is not good, which is not good in its place in the system: and those inherent qualities of that part of the system, which are not good, but corrupt, in that place, are justly looked upon as evil inherent qualities. That propensity is truly esteemed to belong to the *nature* of any being, or to be inherent in it, that is the necessary consequence of its nature, considered together with its proper situation in the universal system of existence, whether that propensity be good or bad. 'Tis the nature of a stone to be heavy; but yet, if it were placed, as it might be, at a distance from this world, it would have no such quality. But seeing a stone is of such a nature, that it will have this quality or tendency, in its proper place, here in this world, where God has made it, 'tis properly looked upon as a propensity belonging to its nature: and if it be a good propensity here in its proper place, then it is a good quality of its nature; but if it be contrariwise, it is an evil natural quality. So, if mankind are of such a nature, that they have an universal effectual tendency to sin and ruin in this world, where God has made and placed them, this is to be looked upon as a pernicious tendency belonging to their nature. There is, perhaps, scarce any such thing in beings not independent and self-existent, as any power or tendency, but what has some dependence on other beings, which they stand in some connection with, in the universal system of existence: propensities are no propensities, any otherwise, than as taken with their objects. Thus it is with the tendencies observed in natural bodies, such as gravity, magnetism, electricity etc. And thus it is with the propensities observed in the various kinds of animals; and thus it is with most of the propensities in created spirits.

It may further be observed, that it is exactly the same thing, as to the controversy concerning an agreeableness with God's moral perfections of such a disposal of things, that man should come into the world in a depraved ruined state, by a propensity to sin and ruin; whether God has so ordered it, that this propensity should lie in his nature considered alone, or with relation to its situation in the universe, and its connection with other parts of the system to which the Creator has united it; which is as much of God's ordering, as man's nature itself, most simply considered.

Dr. Taylor (pp. 188, 189), speaking of the attempt of some to solve the difficulty of God's being the author of our nature, and yet that our nature is polluted, by supposing that God makes the soul pure, but unites it to a polluted body (or a body so made, as tends to pollute the soul); he cries out of it as weak and insufficient, and too gross to be admitted: For, says he, who infused the soul into the body? And if it is polluted by being infused into the body, who is the author and cause of its pollution? And who created the body etc? But is not the case just the same, as to those who suppose that God made the soul pure, and places it in a polluted world, or a world tending by its natural state in which it is made, to pollute the soul, or to have such an influence upon it, that it shall without fail be polluted with sin, and eternally ruined? Here, mayn't I also cry out, on as good grounds as Dr. Taylor, Who placed the soul here in this world? And if the world be polluted, or so constituted as naturally and infallibly to pollute the soul with sin, who is the cause of this pollution? And, who created the world–?

Though in the place now cited, Dr. Taylor so insists upon it, that God must be answerable for the pollution of the soul, if he has infused or put the soul into a body that tends to pollute it; yet this is the very thing which he himself supposes to be fact, with respect to the soul's being created by God, in such a body as it is, and in such a world as it is; in a place which I have already had occasion to observe, where he says, "We are *apt,* in a world full of temptation, to be drawn into sin by bodily appetites." And if so, according to his way of reasoning, God must be the author and cause of this aptness to be drawn into sin. Again (p. 143), we have these words, "Who drinketh in iniquity like water; who is attended with so many sensual appetites, and so apt to indulge them." In these words our author in effect says that the individual thing that he cries out of as so gross, viz. the tendency of the body, as God has made it, to pollute the soul, which he has infused into it. These sensual appetites, which incline the soul, or make it apt to a sinful indulgence, are either from the body which God hath made, or otherwise a proneness to sinful indulgence is immediately and originally seated in the soul itself, which will not mend the matter, for Dr. Taylor.

I would lastly observe, that our author insists upon it (pp. 317, 318). That this lower world where we dwell, in its present state, "Is as it was, when, upon a review, God pronounced it, and all its furniture, very good. [. . .] And that the present form and furniture of the earth is full of God's riches, mercy & goodness, and of the most evident tokens of his love & bounty to the inhabitants." If so, there can be no room for such an evasion of the evidences from fact, of the universal infallible tendency of man's nature to sin and eternal perdition, as, that the tendency there is to this issue, don't lie in man's nature, but in the general constitution and frame of this earthly world, which God hath made to be the habitation of mankind.

## Section 3

The question to be considered, in order to determine whether man's nature is not depraved and ruined, is not whether he is not inclined to perform as many *good deeds* as *bad ones,* but, which of these two he preponderates to, in the frame of his heart, and state of his nature, a state of innocence and righteousness, and favor with God; or a state of sin, guiltiness and abhorrence in the sight of God. Persevering sinless righteousness, or else the guilt of sin, is the alternative, on the decision of which depends (as is confessed) according to the nature and truth of things, as they are in themselves, and according to the rule of right and perfect justice, man's being approved and accepted of his Maker, and eternally blessed as good; or his being rejected, thrown away and cursed as bad. And therefore the determination of the tendency of man's heart and nature with respect to these terms, is that which is to be looked at, in order to determine whether his nature is good or evil, pure or corrupt, sound or ruined. If such be man's nature, and state of his heart, that he has an infallibly effectual propensity to the latter of those terms; then it is wholly impertinent, to talk of the innocent and kind actions, even of criminals themselves, surpassing their crimes in numbers; and of the prevailing innocence, good nature, industry, felicity and cheerfulness of the greater part of mankind. Let never so many thousands, or millions of acts of honesty, good nature, etc. be supposed; yet, by the supposition, there is an unfailing propensity to such moral evil, as in its dreadful consequences infinitely outweighs all effects or consequences of any supposed good. Surely that tendency, which, in effect, is an infallible tendency to eternal destruction, is an infinitely dreadful and pernicious tendency: and that nature and frame of mind, which implies such a tendency, must be an infinitely dreadful and pernicious frame of mind. It would be much more absurd, to suppose that such a state of nature is good, or not bad, under a notion of men's doing more honest and kind things, than evil ones; than to say, the state of that ship is good, to cross the Atlantick Ocean in, that is such as cannot hold together through the voyage, but will infallibly founder and sink by the way; under a notion that it may probably go great part of the way before it sinks, or that it will proceed and sail above water more hours than it will be sinking: or to pronounce that road a good road to go to such a place, the greater part of which is plain and safe, though some parts of it are dangerous, and certainly fatal to them that travel in it; or to call that a good propensity, which is an inflexible inclination to travel in such a way.

A propensity to that sin which rings God's eternal wrath and curse (which has been proved to belong to the nature of man) is not evil, only as it is calamitous and sorrowful, ending in great *natural evil;* but it is *odious* too, and *detestable;* as, by the supposition, it tends to that *moral evil,* by which the subject becomes odious in the sight of God, and liable, as such, to be condemned, and utterly rejected and cursed by him. This also makes it evident, that the state which it has been proved mankind are in, is a corrupt state in a moral sense, that it is inconsistent with the fulfillment of the law of God, which is the rule of moral rectitude and goodness. That tendency, which is opposite to that which the moral law requires and insists upon, and prone to that which the moral law utterly forbids, and eternally condemns the subject for, is doubtless a corrupt tendency, in a moral sense.

So that this depravity is both odious, and also pernicious, fatal and destructive, in the highest sense, as inevitably tending to that which implies man's eternal ruin; it shews, that man, as he is by nature, is in a deplorable and undone state, in the highest sense. And this proves that men don't come into the world perfectly innocent in the sight of God, and without any just exposedness to his displeasure. For the being by nature in a lost and ruined state, in the highest sense, is not consistent with being by nature in a state of favor with God.

But if any should still insist on a notion of men's good deeds exceeding their bad ones, and that seeing the good that is in men more than counter-vails the evil, they can't be properly denominated evil; all persons and things being most properly denominated from that which prevails, and has the ascendent in them: I would say further, that

I presume it will be allowed, that if there is in man's nature a tendency to guilt and ill-desert, in a vast over-balance to virtue and merit; or a propensity to that sin, the evil and demerit of which is so great, that the value and merit that is in him, or in all the virtuous acts that ever he performs, are as nothing to it; then truly the nature of man may be said to be corrupt and evil.

That this is the true case, may be demonstrated by what is evident of the infinite heinousness of sin against God, from the nature of things. [12] The heinousness of this must rise in some proportion to the obligation we are under to regard the Divine Being; and that must be in some proportion to his worthiness of regard; which doubtless is infinitely beyond the worthiness of any of our fellow creatures. But the merit of our respect or obedience to God is not infinite. The merit of respect to any being don't increase, but is rather diminished in proportion to the obligations we are under in strict justice to pay him that respect. There is no great merit in paying a debt we owe, and by the highest possible obligations in strict justice are obliged to pay; but there is great demerit in refusing to pay it.

That on such accounts as these there is an infinite demerit in all sin against God, which must therefore immensely outweigh all the merit which can be supposed to be in our virtue, I think, is capable of full demonstration; and that the futility of the objections, which some have made against the argument, might most plainly be demonstrated. But I shall omit a particular consideration of the evidence of this matter from the nature of things, as I study brevity, and lest any should cry out, "Metaphysicks!" as the manner of some is, when any argument is handled, against any tenet they are fond of, with a close and exact consideration of the nature of things. And this is not so necessary in the present case, inasmuch as the point asserted, namely, that he who commits any one sin, has guilt and ill-desert which is so great, that the value and merit of all the good which it is possible he should do in his whole life, is as nothing to it; I say, this point is not only evident by metaphysics, but is plainly demonstrated by what has been shewn to be *fact,* with respect to God's own constitutions and dispensations towards mankind: as particularly by this, that whatever acts of virtue and obedience a man performs, yet if he trespasses in one point, is guilty of any the least sin, he, according to the law of God, and so according to the exact truth of things and the proper demerit of sin, is exposed to be wholly cast out of favor with God, and subjected to his curse, to be utterly and eternally destroyed. This has been proved; and shewn to be the doctrine which Dr. Taylor abundantly teaches. But how can it be agreeable to the nature of things, and exactly consonant to everlasting truth and righteousness, thus to deal with a creature for the least sinful act, though he should perform ever so many thousands of honest and virtuous acts, to countervail the evil of that sin? Or how can it be agreeable to the exact truth and real demerit of things, thus wholly to cast off the deficient creature, without any regard to the merit of all his good deeds, unless that be in truth the case, that the value and merit of all those good actions bear no proportion to the heinousness of the least sin? If it were not so, one would think, that however the offending person might have some proper punishment, yet seeing there is so much virtue to lay in the balance against the guilt, it would be agreeable to the nature of things, that he should find some favor, and not be altogether rejected, and made the subject of perfect and eternal destruction; and thus no account at all be made of all his virtue, so much as to procure him the least relief or hope. How can such a constitution represent sin in its proper colors and according to its true nature and desert (as Dr. Taylor says it does) unless this be its true nature, that it is so bad, that even in the least instance it perfectly swallows up all the value of the sinner's supposed good deeds, let 'em be ever so many? So that this matter is not left to our metaphysics or philosophy; the great Lawgiver and infallible Judge of the universe has clearly decided it, in the revelation he has made of what is agreeable to exact truth, justice and the nature of things, in his revealed law or rule of righteousness.

He that in any respect or degree is a transgressor of God's law, is a wicked man, yea, wholly wicked in the eye of the law; all his goodness being esteemed nothing, having no account made of it, when taken together with his wickedness. And therefore, without any regard to his righteousness, he is, by the sentence of the law, and so by the voice of truth and justice to be treated as worthy to be rejected, abhorred and cursed forever; and must be so, unless grace interposes, to cover his transgression. But men are really, in themselves, what they are in the eye of the law, and by the voice of strict equity and justice; however they may be looked upon, and treated by infinite and unmerited mercy.

So that, on the whole, it appears, all mankind have an infallibly effectual propensity to that moral evil, which infinitely outweighs the value of all the good that can be in them; and have such a disposition of heart, that the certain consequence of it is, their being, in the eye of perfect truth and righteousness, wicked men. And I leave all to judge, whether such a disposition be not in the eye of truth a depraved disposition.

Agreeable to these things, the Scripture represents all mankind, not only as having guilt, but immense guilt, which they can have no merit or worthiness to countervail. Such is the representation we have in Matt. 18:21, to the end. There, on Peter's inquiring how often his brother should trespass against him and he forgive him, whether until seven times? Christ replies, "I say not unto thee, until seven times, but until seventy times seven"; apparently meaning, that he should esteem no number of offenses too many, and no degree of injury it is possible our neighbor should be guilty of towards us, too great to be forgiven. For which this reason is given in the parable there following, that if ever we obtain forgiveness and favor with God, he must pardon that guilt and injury towards his majesty, which is immensely greater than the greatest injuries that ever men are guilty of, one towards another, yea, than the sum of all their injuries put together; let 'em be ever so many, and ever so great: so that the latter would be put as an hundred pence to ten thousand talents: which immense debt we owe to God, and have nothing to pay; which implies that we have no merit, to countervail any part of our guilt. And this must be because, if all that may be called virtue in us, be compared with our ill-desert, it is in the sight of God as nothing to it. The parable is not to represent *Peter's* case in particular, but that of all who then were, or ever should be Christ's disciples. It appears by the conclusion of the discourse; *"So likewise shall my heavenly Father do . . . if ye, from your hearts, forgive not every one his brother their trespasses."*

Therefore how absurd must it be for Christians to object, against the depravity of man's nature, a greater number of innocent and kind actions, than of crimes; and to talk of a prevailing innocency, good nature, industry, and cheerfulness of the greater part of mankind? Infinitely more absurd, than it would be to insist, that the domestic of a prince was not a bad servant, because though sometimes he contemned and affronted his master to a great degree, yet he did not spit in his master's face so often as he performed acts of service; or, than it would be to affirm, that his spouse was a good wife to him, because, although she committed adultery, and that with the slaves and scoundrels sometimes, yet she did not do this so often as she did the duties of a wife. These notions would be absurd, because the crimes are too heinous to be atoned for, by many honest actions of the servant or spouse of the prince; there being a vast disproportion between the merit of the one, and the ill-desert of the other: but in no measure so great, nay infinitely less than that between the demerit of our offenses against God and the value of our acts of obedience.

Thus I have gone through with my first argument; having shewn the evidence of the truth of the proposition I laid down at first, and proved its consequence. But there are many other things, that manifest a very corrupt tendency or disposition in man's nature in his present state, which I shall take notice of in the following sections.

## Notes

[1] [See above, Intro., Sec. 4.]

[2] [Ibid.]

[3] *Mor[al] Phil[osophy]*, pp. 289-90.

[4] [John Taylor, *The Scripture-Doctrine of Original Sin, Proposed to Free and Candid Examination* (3d ed., Belfast, 1746)], p. 353. [See above, Intro., Sec. 3, esp. p. 36.]

[5] [John Taylor, *Key to the Apostolic Writings, with a Paraphrase and Notes on the Epistle to the Romans* (Dublin, 1746). JE refers to this work variously as the *Key, Notes on Romans,* and *Pref. to Par. on Rom.*], p. 187.

[6] [When JE refers to Taylor's writings simply by page, the reference is to the *Scripture-Doctrine of Original Sin.*]

He often speaks of death and affliction as coming on Adam's posterity in consequence of his sin; and in pp. 20-21 and many other places, he supposes that these things come in consequence of his sin, not as a punishment or a calamity, but as a benefit: but in p. 23 he supposes, these things would be a great calamity and misery, if it were not for the resurrection; which resurrection he there, and in the following pages, and many other places, speaks of as being by Christ; and often speaks of it as being by the grace of God in Christ.

pp. 63-64. Speaking of our being subjected to sorrow, labor and death, in consequence of Adam's sin; he represents these as evils that are reversed, and turned into advantages, and that we are delivered from through grace in Christ. And in pp. 65-67, he speaks of God's thus turning death into an advantage through grace in Christ, as what vindicates the justice of God in bringing death by Adam.

pp. 152, 156. 'Tis one thing which he alleges against this proposition of the Assembly of Divines [Westminster Assembly, 1645-46] that we are by nature bond-slaves to Satan; that God hath been providing, from the beginning of the world to this day, various means and dispensations, to preserve and rescue mankind from the devil.

pp. 168, 169, 170. One thing alleged, in answer to that objection against his doctrine, that we are in worse circumstances than Adam, is the happy circumstances we are under by the provision and means furnished, through free grace in Christ.

p. 228. Among other things which he says, in answering that argument against his doctrine, and brought to shew men have corruption by nature, viz, that there is a law in our members . . . bringing us into captivity to the law of sin and death, spoken of in Rom. 7. He allows that the case of those who are under a law threatening death for every sin (which law he else-where says, shews us the natural and proper demerit of sin, and is perfectly consonant to everlasting truth and righteousness) must be quite deplor-able, if they have no relief from the mercy of the lawgiver.

pp. 367-370. In opposition to what is supposed of the miserable state mankind are brought into by Adam's sin, one thing he alleges, is the noble designs of love manifested by advancing a new and happy dispensation, founded on the obedience and righteousness of the son of God; and that although by Adam we are subjected to death, yet in this dispensation a resurrection is provided; and that in Adam's posterity are under a mild dispensation of grace, etc.

pp. 388, 389. He vindicates God's dealings with Adam, in placing him at first under the rigor of law, transgress and die (which, as he expresses it, was putting his happiness on a foot extremely dangerous) by saying, that as God had before determined in his own breast, so he immediately established his covenant upon a quite different bottom, namely upon grace.

pp. 398, 399. Against what R. R. [Isaac Watts, *The Ruin and Recovery of Mankind* in *Collected Works* by David Jennings and Philip Doddridge, 1753] says, that God forsook man when he fell, and that mankind after Adam's sin were born without the divine favor, etc. He alleges among other things, Christ's coming to be the propitiation of the sins of the whole world . . . and the riches of God's mercy in giving the promise of a Redeemer to destroy the works of the devil, that he caught his sinning falling creature in the arms of his grace. In his *Note on Rom.* 5:20, p. 379 [Taylor, *Key*] he says as follows: "The law, I conceive, is not a dispensa-tion suitable to the infirmity of the human nature in our present state; or it doth not seem congruous to the goodness of God, to afford us no other way of salvation but by law, which if we once transgress we are ruined forever. For who then from the beginning of the world could be saved? And therefore it seems to me, that the law was not absolutely intended to be a rule for obtaining life, even to Adam in paradise: grace was the dispensation God intended mankind should be under: and therefore Christ was foreordained before the foundation of the world." There are various other passages in this author's writings of the like kind.

[7] I am sensible, these things are quite inconsistent with what he says elsewhere, of sufficient power in all mankind constantly to do the whole duty which God requires of 'em, without a necessity of breaking God's law in any degree (pp. 339, 340, 344, 348). But I hope the reader will not think me accountable for his inconsistencies.

[8] [Here JE appears to argue that a single event, occasion, or act provides evidence of a tendency. But this is inconsistent with the principal thrust of the argument which elsewhere (p. 108 and Pt. I, Ch. 1, sec. 9) insists on the need for continued observation for the establishment of a "fixed pro-pensity."]

[9] [On JE's controversial use of the term "cause" see Yale ed., *I*, 34-5, 118.]

[10] Here may be observed the weakness of that objection, made against the validity of the argument for a fixed propensity to sin, from the constancy and universality of the event, that Adam sinned in one instance, without a fixed propensity. Without doubt a single event is an evidence, that there was some cause or occasion of that event: but the thing, we are speaking of, is a fixed cause: propensity is a stated continued thing. We justly argue, that a stated effect must have a stated cause; and truly observe, that we obtain the notion of tendency, or stated preponderation in causes, no other way than by observing a stated prevalence of a particular kind of effect. But who ever argues a fixed propensity from a single effect? And is it not strange arguing, that because an event which once comes to pass, don't prove any stated tendency, therefore the unfailing constancy of an event is an evidence of no such thing?—But because Dr. Taylor makes so much of this objection, from Adam's sinning without a propensity, I shall hereafter consider it more particularly, in the beginning of the 9th section of this chapter; where will also be considered what is objected from the fall of the angels.

[11] [Originally "ought."]

[12] [See above, Intro., Sec. 3, "The Fact and Nature of Sin."]

**Gustave F. Wiggers**

# The Pelagian View of Original Sin

According to the Pelagian doctrine, there is absolutely no original sin, i. e. no sin which passes, by generation, from the first man to his posterity, and of which they have to bear the punishment. This is a main point in which Pelagianism differs from Augustinism, as is shown by all the memorials of those contests now extant. In these, it is worthy of remark, that the Pelagians, when they speak of Augustine's original sin, instead of the term *original sin,* used by Augustine, employ rather the expression *natural sin* (peccatum naturale), or the expression *natural evil* (malum naturale, Op. Imp. I. 101), probably in order to render the more striking the contradiction that is involved in a *natural sin.* And on this account, Augustine protested against this expression, and when it was used by the Pelagians, commonly substituted his own *peccatum originale.* There may be, says he, indeed, a sin of nature (peccatum naturae), but not a natural sin (peccatum naturale). In a certain sense, however, he defended this term (Op. Imp. V. 9, 40), only he regarded the expression, *original sin,* as more

From *An Historical Presentation of Augustinism and Pelagianism from the Original Sources* (Andover, N.Y.: Gould, Newman and Saxton, 1840), pp. 83-88.

definite, because by it, the idea of God being the author of any sin, is removed. Augustine employed the expression *original sin,* besides, as synonymous with *hereditary* evil (hereditarium vitium, Ep. 194. c. 6), and also originale vitium. Ep. 157. c. 3.

We have already seen, that it was brought as an objection to Caelestius at Carthage, that he denied original sin; and that he did not directly deny the objection, though he would not condemn the doctrine. But in his confession of faith already mentioned, he denied it flatly. "A sin propagated by generation (peccatum ex traduce), is totally contrary to the catholic faith. Sin is not born with man, but is committed afterwards by man. It is not the fault of nature, but of free will.—The mystery of baptism must not be so interpreted as to imply, to the prejudice of the Creator, that evil is transferred by nature to man, before it is committed by him." De Pec. Orig. 6.—That Pelagius also admitted of no original sin, in the sense declared, is proved by his explanation of Paul's epistles, before composed at Rome, in which he expressly refers that passage in Romans to the imitation of Adam's sin, in which, according to Augustine's acceptation, it is said, that in Adam all his posterity sinned. Afterwards, however, (as he would not own as his those propositions which were charged upon Caelestius, at the synod of Diospolis, but condemned such as taught anything in that way, viz. that "Adam would have died, whether he had sinned or not: His sin injured himself only, not his posterity: And new-born infants are in the same condition as Adam was before the fall," De Pec. Orig. 11), he might indeed consider Adam's death as a punishment for *himself,* though only as a natural necessity for his *posterity.* Respecting both the other propositions, he explained himself against his scholar, after that synod (De Pec. Orig. 15), and condemned the propositions, because Adam did injure his posterity, in as much as he gave them the first example of sin; and because new born infants are so far in a different condition from that of Adam before transgression, that they cannot yet perform what is commanded, but he could; and they cannot yet use that free intelligent will, without which no command could have been given to Adam.—A transfer of Adam's sin, and an imputation of it, and consequently original sin, Pelagius did not admit, and did not explain himself in favor of it at Diospolis. But Julian was most zealous, as appears from the passages already quoted respecting the object of baptism, against the assumption that man comes into the world corrupted through Adam's sin, and loaded with its guilt and punishment. "We believe that God has made men, and without any fault at all, full of natural innocence, and capable of voluntary virtues." Op. Imp. III. 82.

The Pelagian idea of original sin may be reduced still more definitely to the following propositions.

1. A propagation of sin by generation, is by no means to be admitted. This physical propagation of sin, can be admitted only when we grant the propagation of the soul by generation. But this is a heretical error. Consequently there is no original sin; and nothing in the moral nature of man has been corrupted by Adam's sin.

Besides the passages already adduced, the following may suffice as proof, that this was a Pelagian tenet.

In his commentary on Romans 7:8, Pelagius remarks: "They are insane who teach, that the sin of Adam comes on us by propagation (per traducem)." In another passage, (which indeed is not now to be found in that very interpolated work, but which Augustine quotes from it verbatim, De Pec. Mer. III. 3), Pelagius says: "The soul does not come by propagation, but only the flesh, and so this only has the propagated sin (traducem peccati), and this only deserves punishment. But it is unjust, that the soul born to-day, that has not come from the substance of Adam, should bear so old and extrinsic a sin." And the Pelagians discarded the propagation of souls by generation, which seemed to lead to materialism, and assumed, that every soul is created immediately by God. In Pelagius's confession of faith, it is said: "We believe that souls are given by God, and say, that they are made by himself." From the first book of Pelagius on free will, Augustine quotes the following declaration of his opponent (De Pec. Orig. 13): "All good and evil, by which we are praise or blameworthy, do not originate together with us, but are done by us. We are born capable of each, but not filled with either. And as we are produced without virtue, so are we also without vice; and before the action of his own free will, there is in man only what God made." But the transmission of sin (peccatum ex traduce), was most vehemently and keenly assailed by Julian who, on account of this assumption, gave Augustine the nickname of *Traducianus.* Augustine's second book against Julian, and also the first book of his Imperfect Work, are filled with acute arguments of that Pelagian against the propagation of sin by physical generation, to which Augustine could make no very pertinent reply.

2. Adam's transgression was imputed to himself, but not to his posterity. A reckoning of Adam's sin as that of his posterity, would conflict with the divine rectitude. Hence bodily death is no punishment of Adam's imputed sin, but a necessity of nature.

From the commentary of Pelagius on Romans, Augustine quotes his words thus (De Pec. Mer. III. 3): "It can in no way be conceded that God, who pardons a man's own sins, may impute to him the sins of another." In his book "on nature," Pelagius says: "How can the sin be imputed by God to the man, which he has not known as his own?" De Nat. et Gr. 30.—If God is just, (this is amply shown by Julian, according to the first book of the Imperfect Work), he can attribute no foreign blame to infants.— "Children (filii), so long as they are children, that is, before they do anything by their own will, cannot be punishable (rei)." Op. Imp. II. 42.—"According to the Apostle, by one man, sin came into the world, and death by sin: because the world has regarded him as a criminal and as one condemned to perpetual death. But death has come upon all men, because the same sentence reaches all transgressors of the succeeding period; yet neither holy men nor the innocent have had to endure this death, but only such as have imitated him by transgression." II. 66. The Pelagians, therefore, could regard the bodily death of Adam's descendants no otherwise than as a natural necessity. And if Pelagius himself admitted that it may have been a punishment in the case of Adam, (as we should rather believe by his explanation at Diospolis, though a passage quoted by Augustine from the writings of Pelagius, is against this view, De Nat. et Gr. 21); yet his adherents were of a different opinion, and believed that Adam was *created* mortal. But all must have agreed in this, that the bodily death which comes on Adam's *posterity,* is not a punishment of his sin, but a necessity of nature. "The words—till thou return to the earth from which thou wast taken, for earth thou art and to earth shalt again return—belong not to the curse, but are rather words of consolation to the man. The sufferings, toils, and griefs shall not endure forever, but shall one day end. If the dissolution of the body was a part of the punishment of sin, it would not have been said—thou shalt return to the earth, *for earth thou art;* but, thou shalt return to the earth, *because thou hast sinned and broken my command.*" Op. Imp. VI. 27. "If therefore fruitfulness, according to the testimony of Christ (Matt. 22:30) who instituted it, was produced in order to replace what death takes away, and this was ordained as the design of marriage before the fall, it is manifest that mortality has no respect to the transgression, but to nature, to which marriage also has respect." VI. 30. "Adam himself, say the Pelagians, would have died, as to the body, though he had not sinned; and hence he did not die in consequence of his guilt, but by the necessity of nature." Aug. de Haer. c. 88, and in innumerable other places.

3. Now, as sin itself has no more passed over to Adam's posterity, than has the punishment of sin, so every man, in respect to his *moral* nature, is born in just the same state in which Adam was first created.

Augustine quotes (De Nat. et Gr. 21) from Pelagius's book, a passage in which it is said: "What do you seek? They [infants] are well, for whom you seek a physician. Not only are Adam's descendants no weaker than he, but they have even fulfilled more commands, since he neglected to fulfil so much as one." In the letter to Demetrias, Pelagius depicts the prerogatives of human nature, without making any distinction between Adam's state before the fall and after it. Take only the description of conscience, in the fourth chapter. "A good conscience itself decides respecting the goodness of nature. Is it not a testimony which nature herself gives of her goodness, when she shows her displeasure at evil?—There is in our heart, so to express myself, a certain natural holiness, which keeps watch, as it were, in the castle of the soul, and judges of good and evil."—"Human nature," says Julian (C. Jul. III. 4) "is adorned in infants with the dowry of innocence." "Freewill is as yet in its original uncorrupted state, and nature is to be regarded as innocent in every one, before his own will can show itself." Op. Imp. II. 20. According to Julian, the sinner becomes, by baptism, from a bad person a perfectly good one; but the innocent, who has no evil of his own will, becomes from a good a still better person. "That has corrupted *the innocence which he received at his origin,* by bad action; but this, without praise or blame of his will, has only what he has received from God his creator. He is more fortunate as, in his early and uncorrupted age, he cannot have corrupted the goodness of his simplicity. He has no merit of acts, but only retains what he has possessed by the good pleasure of so great an architect." I. 54.

But with this Pelagian view of the uncorrupted state of man's nature, the admission of a moral corruption of men in their present condition, by the continued habit of sinning, stood in no contradiction. This Pelagius taught expressly. According to the eighth chapter of his letter to Demetrias, he explicitly admits, that, by the protracted *habit* of sinning, sin appears in a measure to have gained a dominion over human nature, and consequently renders the practice of virtue difficult. "While nature was yet new, and a long continued habit of sinning had not spread as it were a mist over human reason, nature was left without a [written] law, to which the Lord, when it was oppressed by too many vices and stained with the mist of ignorance, applied the file of the law, in order that, by its frequent admonitions, nature might be cleansed again and return to its lustre. And there is no other difficulty of doing well, but the long continued habit of vice, which has contaminated us from youth, up, and corrupted us for many years, and holds us afterwards so bound and subjugated to herself, that she seems, in a measure, to have the force of nature." Here Pelagius also mentions the bad education by which we are led to evil.—But this habit of sinning, however, affects only adults, and that by their own fault. According to the Pelagian theory, man is *born* in the same state, in respect to his *moral* nature, in which Adam was created by God.

# 13

## Reinhold Niebuhr

# Sin and Man's Responsibility

### Temptation and Inevitability of Sin

The full complexity of the psychological facts which validate the doctrine of original sin must be analysed, first in terms of the relation of temptation to the inevitability of sin. Such an analysis may make it plain why man sins inevitably, yet without escaping responsibility for his sin. The temptation to sin lies, as previously observed, in the human situation itself. This situation is that man as spirit transcends the temporal and natural process in which he is involved and also transcends himself. Thus his freedom is the basis of his creativity but it is also his temptation. Since he is involved in the contingencies and necessities of the natural process on the one hand and since, on the other, he stands outside of them and foresees their caprices and perils, he is anxious. In his anxiety he seeks to transmute his finiteness into infinity, his weakness into strength, his dependence into independence. He seeks in other words to escape finiteness and weakness by a quantitative rather than qualitative development of his life. The quantitative antithesis of finiteness is infinity. The qualitative possibility of human life is its obedient subjection to the will of God. This

From *The Nature and Destiny of Man* (New York: Charles Scribner's Sons, 1941), pp. 251-64. Used by permission.

possibility is expressed in the words of Jesus: "He that loseth his life for my sake shall find it." (Matt. 10:39).

It will be noted that the Christian statement of the ideal possibility does not involve self-negation but self-realization. The self is, in other words, not evil by reason of being a particular self and its salvation does not consist in absorption into the eternal. Neither is the self divided, as in Hegelianism, into a particular or empirical and a universal self; and salvation does not consist in sloughing off its particularity and achieving universality. The Christian view of the self is only possible from the standpoint of Christian theism in which God is not merely the *x* of the unconditioned or the undifferentiated eternal. God is revealed as loving will; and His will is active in creation, judgment and redemption. The highest self-realization for the self is therefore not the destruction of its particularity but the subjection of its particular will to the universal will.

But the self lacks the faith and trust to subject itself to God. It seeks to establish itself independently. It seeks to find its life and thereby loses it. For the self which it asserts is less than the true self. It is the self in all the contingent and arbitrary factors of its immediate situation. By asserting these contingent and arbitrary factors of an immediate situation, the self loses its true self. It increases its insecurity because it gives its immediate necessities a consideration which they do not deserve and which they cannot have without disturbing the harmony of creation. By giving life a false centre, the self then destroys the real possibilities for itself and others. Hence the relation of injustice to pride, and the vicious circle of injustice, increasing as it does the insecurity which pride was intended to overcome.

The sin of the inordinate self-love thus points to the prior sin of lack of trust in God. The anxiety of unbelief is not merely the fear which comes from ignorance of God. "Anxiety," declares Kierkegaard, "is the dizziness of freedom,"[1] but it is significant that the same freedom which tempts to anxiety also contains the ideal possibility of knowing God. Here the Pauline psychology is penetrating and significant. St. Paul declares that man is without excuse because "the invisible things of him from the creation of the world are clearly seen, being understood by the things that are made, even his eternal power and Godhead" (Romans 1:20). The anxiety of freedom leads to sin only if the prior sin of unbelief is assumed. This is the meaning of Kierkegaard's assertion that sin posits itself.[2]

The sin of man's excessive and inordinate love of self is thus neither merely the drag of man's animal nature upon his more universal loyalties, nor yet the necessary consequence of human freedom and self-transcendence. It is more plausibly the consequence of the latter than of the former because the survival impulse of animal nature lacks precisely those boundless and limitless tendencies of human desires. Inordinate self-love is occasioned by the introduction of the perspective of the eternal into natural and human finiteness. But it is a false eternal. It consists in the transmutation of "mutable good" into infinity. This boundless character of human desires is an unnatural rather than natural fruit of man's relation to the temporal process on the one hand and to eternity on the other. If man knew, loved and obeyed God as the author and end of his existence, a proper limit would be set for his desires including the natural impulse of survival.[3]

The fact that the lie is so deeply involved in the sin of self-glorification and that man cannot love himself inordinately without pretending that it is not his, but a universal, interest which he is supporting, is a further proof that sin presupposes itself and that it is neither ignorance nor yet the ignorance of ignorance which forces the self to sin. Rather it "holds the truth in unrighteousness."

The idea that the inevitability of sin is not due merely to the strength of the temptation in which man stands by reason of his relation to both the temporal process and eternity, is most perfectly expressed in the scriptural words: "Let no man say when he is tempted, I am tempted of God: for God cannot be tempted with evil, neither tempteth he any man: But every man is tempted, when he is drawn away of his own lust, and enticed. Then when lust hath conceived, it bringeth forth sin: and sin, when it is finished, bringeth forth death."[4] But on the other hand the idea that the situation of finiteness and freedom is a temptation once evil has entered it and that evil does enter it prior to any human action is expressed in Biblical thought by the conception of the devil. The devil is a fallen angel, who fell because he sought to lift himself above his measure and who in turn insinuates temptation into human life. The sin of each individual is preceded by Adam's sin: but even this first sin of history is not the first sin. One may, in other words, go farther back than human history and still not escape the paradoxical conclusion that the situation of finiteness and freedom would not lead to sin if sin were not already introduced into the situation. This is, in the words of Kierkegaard, the "qualitative leap" of sin and reveals the paradoxical relation of inevitability and responsibility. Sin can never be traced merely to the temptation arising from a particular situation or condition in which man as man finds himself or in which particular men find themselves. Nor can the temptation which is compounded of a situation of finiteness and freedom, plus the fact of sin, be regarded as leading necessarily to sin in the life of each individual, if again sin is not first presupposed in that life. For this reason even the knowledge of inevitability does not extinguish the sense of responsibility.

## Responsibility Despite Inevitability

The fact of responsibility is attested by the feeling of remorse or repentance which follows the sinful action. From an exterior view not only sin in general but any particular sin may seem to be the necessary consequence of previous temptations. A simple determinism is thus a natural characteristic of all social interpretations of human actions. But the interior view does not allow this interpretation. The self, which is privy to the rationalizations and processes of self-deception which accompanied and must accompany the sinful act, cannot accept and does not accept the simple determinism of the exterior view. Its contemplation of its act involves both the discovery and the reassertion of its freedom. It discovers that some degree of conscious dishonesty accompanied the act, which means that the self was not deterministically and blindly involved in it. Its discovery of that fact in contemplation is a further degree of the assertion of freedom than is possible in the moment of action.

The remorse and repentance which are consequent upon such contemplation are similar in their acknowledgment of freedom and responsibility and their implied assertion of it. They differ in the fact that repentance is the expression of freedom and faith while remorse is the expression of freedom without faith. The one is the "Godly sorrow" of which St. Paul speaks, and the other is "the sorrow of this world which worketh death." It is, in other words, the despair into which sin transmutes the anxiety which precedes sin.

There are of course many cases in which the self seems so deeply involved in its own deceptions and so habituated to standards of action which may have once been regarded as sinful that it seems capable of neither repentance nor remorse. This complacency is possible on many levels of life from that of a natural paganism in which the freedom of spirit is not fully developed, to refined forms of Pharisaism in which pride as self-righteousness obscures the sin of pride itself. It is not true, however, that habitual sin can ever destroy the uneasy conscience so completely as to remove the individual from the realm of moral responsibility to the realm of unmoral nature.[5]

The religious sacrifices of nature religions, in which primitive peoples express an uneasy conscience and assume that natural catastrophe is the expression of their god's anger against their sins, is a proof of the reality of some degree of freedom even in primitive life.[6] The brutality with which a Pharisee of every age resists those who puncture his pretensions proves the uneasiness of his conscience. The insecurity of sin is always a double insecurity. It must seek to hide not only the original finiteness of perspective and relativity of value which it is the purpose of sin to hide, but also the dishonesty by which it has sought to obscure these. The fury with which oligarchs, dictators, priest-kings, ancient and modern, and ideological pretenders turn upon their critics and foes is clearly the fury of an uneasy conscience, though it must not be assumed that such a conscience is always fully conscious of itself.

An uneasy conscience which is not fully conscious of itself is the root of further sin, because the self strives desperately to ward off the *dénouement* of either remorse or repentance by accusing others, seeking either to make them responsible for the sins of the self, or attributing worse sins to them. There is a certain plausibility in this self-defense, because social sources of particular sins may always be found and even the worst criminal can gain a certain temporary self-respect by finding some one who seems more deeply involved in disaster than he is. On the other hand such social comparisons always increase the force of sin, for they are efforts to hide a transaction between the self and God, even though God is not explicitly known to the sinner. While all particular sins have both social sources and social consequences, the real essence of sin can be understood only in the vertical dimension of the soul's relation to God because the freedom of the self stands outside all relations, and therefore has no other judge but God.[7] It is for this reason that a profound insight into the character of sin must lead to the confession, "Against thee, thee only, have I sinned, and done this evil in thy sight" (Ps. 51). All experiences of an uneasy conscience, of remorse and of repentance, are therefore religious experiences, though they are not always explicitly or consciously religious. Experiences of repentance, in distinction to remorse, presuppose some knowledge of God. They may not be consciously related to Biblical revelation but yet they do presuppose some, at least dim, awareness of God as redeemer as well as God as judge. For without the knowledge of divine love remorse cannot be transmuted into repentance. If man recognizes only judgment and knows only that his sin is discovered, he cannot rise above the despair of remorse to the hope of repentance.

The vertical dimension of the experience of remorse and repentance explains why there is no level of moral goodness upon which the sense of guilt can be eliminated. In fact the sense of guilt rises with moral sensitivity: "There are only two kinds of men," declares Pascal, "the righteous who believe themselves sinners; the rest, sinners, who believe themselves righteous." Pascal does not fully appreciate, at least as far as this statement is concerned, how infinite may be the shades of awareness of guilt from the complacency of those who are spiritually blind to the sensitivity of the saint who knows that he is not a saint. Yet it is obviously true that awareness of guilt arises with spiritual sensitivity and that such an awareness will be regarded as morbid only by moralists who have no true knowledge of the soul and God. The saint's awareness of guilt is no illusion. The fact is that sin expresses itself most terribly in its most subtle forms. The sinful identification of the contingent self with God is less crass on the higher levels of the spiritual life but it may be the more dangerous for being the more plausible. An example from the realm of political life may explain why this is true. The inevitable partiality of even the most impartial court is more dangerous to justice than the obvious partiality of contending political factions in society, which the impartiality of the court is intended to resolve. The partiality of the contending forces is so obvious that it can be discounted. The partiality of the court, on the other hand, is obscured by its prestige of impartiality. Relative degrees of impartiality in judicial tribunals are important achievements in political life. But without a judgment upon even the best judicial process from a higher level of judgment, the best becomes the worst.[8]

The fact that the sense of guilt rises vertically with all moral achievement and is, therefore, not assuaged by it nor subject to diminution or addition by favourable and unfavourable social opinion, throws a significant light on the relation of freedom to sin. The ultimate proof of the freedom of the human spirit is its own recognition that its will is not free to choose between good and evil. For in the highest reaches of the freedom of the spirit, the self discovers in contemplation and retrospect that previous actions have invariably confused the ultimate reality and value, which the self as spirit senses, with the immediate necessities of the self. If the self assumes that because it realizes this fact in past actions it will be able to avoid the corruption in future actions, it will merely fall prey to the Pharisaic fallacy.

This difference between the self in contemplation and the self in action must not be regarded as synonymous with the distinction between the self as spirit and the self as natural vitality. To regard the two distinctions as identical is a plausible error, and one which lies at the root of all idealistic interpretations of man. But we have already discovered that the sins of the self in action are possible only because the freedom of spirit opens up the deterministic causal chains of the self in nature and tempts the self to assume dignities, to grasp after securities and to claim sanctities which do not belong to it. The contemplating self which becomes conscious of its sins does not therefore view some other empirical self which is not, properly speaking, its true self. There is only one self. Sometimes the self acts and sometimes it contemplates its actions. When it acts it falsely claims ultimate value for its relative necessities and falsely identifies its life with the claims of life *per se*. In contemplation it has a clearer view of the total human situation and becomes conscious, in some degree, of the confusion and dishonesty involved in its action. It must not be assumed, however, that the contemplating self is the universal self, judging the finite and empirical self. At its best the contemplating self is the finite self which has become conscious of its finiteness and its relation to God as the limit and the fulfillment of its finiteness. When the self in contemplation becomes contritely aware of its guilt in action it may transmute this realization into a higher degree of honesty in subsequent actions. Repentance may lead to "fruits meet for repentance"; and differences between the moral quality in the lives of complacent and of contrite individuals are bound to be discovered by observers. But the self cannot make too much of them; for its real standard is not what others do or fail to do. Its real standard is its own essential self and this in turn has only God's will as norm. It must know that judged by that standard, the experience of contrition does not prevent the self from new dishonesties in subsequent actions. The self, even in contemplation, remains the finite self. In one moment it may measure its situation and discover its sin. In the next moment it will be betrayed by anxiety into sin. Even the distinction between contemplation and action must, therefore, not be taken too literally. For any contemplation which is concerned with the interests, hopes, fears and ambitions of this anxious finite self belongs properly in the field of action; for it is a preparation for a false identification of the immediate and the ultimate of which no action is free.

We cannot, therefore, escape the ultimate paradox that the final exercise of freedom in the transcendent human spirit is its recognition of the false use of that freedom in action. Man is most free in the discovery that he is not free. This paradox has been obscured by most Pelagians and by many Augustinians. The Pelagians have been too intent to assert the integrity of man's freedom to realize that the discovery of this freedom also involves the discovery of man's guilt. The Augustinians on the other hand have been so concerned to prove that the freedom of man is corrupted by sin that they have not fully understood that the discovery of this sinful taint is an achievement of freedom.

### Literalistic Errors

The paradox that human freedom is most perfectly discovered and asserted in the realization of the bondage of the will is easily obscured. Unfortunately the confusion revealed in the debate between Pelagians and Augustinians has been further aggravated by the literalism of the Augustinians. In countering the simple moralism of the Pelagians they insisted on interpreting original sin as an inherited taint. Thus they converted the doctrine of the inevitability of sin into a dogma which asserted that sin had a natural history. Thereby they gave their Pelagian critics an unnecessary advantage in the debate, which the latter have never been slow to seize.[9]

While Augustinian theology abounds in doctrines of original sin which equate it with the idea of an inherited corruption and which frequently make concupiscence in generation the agent of this inheritance, it is significant that Christian thought has always had some suggestions of the representative rather than historical character of Adam's sin. The idea of Adam as representative man allowed it to escape the historical-literalistic illusion. The very fountain-source of the doctrine of original sin, the thought of St. Paul, expresses the idea of original sin in terms which allow, and which possibly compel the conclusion that St. Paul believed each man to be related to Adam's sin in terms of "seminal identity" rather than historical inheritance. The Pauline words are: "Wherefore as by one man sin entered the world and death by sin; and so death passed to all men *for that all have sinned.*"[10] The idea of a mystical identity between Adam and all men is found in Irenaeus and is explicitly formulated in Ambrose.[11] Even Augustine, who insists on the theory of an inherited corruption, inserts an interesting qualification which points in the same direction when he quotes the Pauline passage, Romans 3:23, so that it reads: " 'For all have sinned'—*whether in Adam or in themselves*—'and come short of the glory of God.' " The same idea struggles for, and achieves partial, expressions in some of the explanations of original sin in Calvin, even while he insists on the idea of inheritance.[12]

It is obviously necessary to eliminate the literalistic illusions in the doctrine of original sin if the paradox of inevitability and responsibility is to be fully understood; for the theory of an inherited second nature is as clearly destructive of the idea of responsibility for sin as rationalistic and dualistic theories which attribute human evil to the inertia of nature.[13] When this literalistic confusion is eliminated the truth of the doctrine of original sin is more clearly revealed; but it must be understood that even in this form the doctrine remains absurd from the standpoint of a pure rationalism, for it expresses a relation between fate and freedom which cannot be fully rationalized, unless the paradox be accepted as a rational understanding of the limits of rationality and as an expression of faith that a rationally irresolvable contradiction may point to a truth which logic cannot contain. Formally there can be of course no conflict between logic and truth. The laws of logic are reason's guard against chaos in the realm of truth. They eliminate contradictory assertions. But there is no resource in logical rules to help us understand complex phenomena, exhibiting characteristics which seem to require that they be placed into contradictory categories of reason. Loyalty to all the facts may require a provisional defiance of logic, lest complexity in the facts of experience be denied for the sake of a premature logical consistency. Hegel's "dialectic" is a logic invented for the purpose of doing justice to the fact of "becoming" as a phenomenon which belongs into the category of neither "being" nor "nonbeing."

The Christian doctrine of original sin with its seemingly contradictory assertions about the inevitability of sin and man's responsibility for sin is a dialectical truth which does justice to the fact that man's self-love and self-centredness is inevitable, but not in such a way as to fit into the category of natural necessity. It is within and by his freedom that man sins. The final paradox is that the discovery of the inevitability of sin is man's highest assertion of freedom. The fact that the discovery of sin invariably leads to the Pharisaic illusion that such a discovery guarantees sinlessness in subsequent actions is a revelation of the way in which freedom becomes an accomplice of sin. It is at this point that the final battle between humility and human self-esteem is fought.

Kierkegaard's explanation of the dialectical relation of freedom and fate in sin is one of the profoundest in Christian thought. He writes: "The concept of sin and guilt does not emerge in its profoundest sense in paganism. If it did paganism would be destroyed by the contradiction that man becomes guilty by fate. . . . Christianity is born in this very contradiction. The concept of sin and guilt presupposes the individual as individual. There is no concern for his relation to any cosmic or past totality. The only concern is that he is guilty; and yet he is supposed to become guilty through fate, the very fate about which there is no concern. And thereby he becomes something which resolves the concept of fate, and to become that through fate! If this contradiction is wrongly understood it leads to false concepts of original sin. Rightly understood it leads to a true concept, to the idea namely that every individual is itself and the race and the later individual is not significantly differentiated from the first man. In the possibility of anxiety freedom is lost, for it is overwhelmed by fate. Yet now it arises in reality but with the explanation that it has become guilty."[14]

## Notes

[1] *Begriff der Angst*, p. 57.

[2] *Ibid.*, p. 27.

[3] Failure to understand the difference between a natural and an unnatural though inevitable characteristic of human behaviour confuses otherwise clear analyses such as that of Bertrand Russell's: He declares: "Between man and other animals there are various differences some intellectual and some emotional. One chief emotional difference is that human desires, unlike those of animals, are essentially boundless and incapable of complete satisfaction." *Power*, p. 9.

Thus Mr. Russell is forced to regard the boundless will-to-power as natural in his analysis of human nature and as the very principle of evil in his analysis of society.

[4] James 1:13-15.

This word succinctly expresses a general attitude of the Bible which places it in opposition to all philosophical explanations which attribute the inevitability of sin to the power of temptation. One of the most ingenious of these is the theory of Schelling, who, borrowing from the mystic system of Jacob Boehme, declares that God has a "foundation that He may be"; only this is not outside himself but within him and he has within him a nature which though it belongs to himself is nevertheless different from him. In God this foundation, this "dark ground," is not in conflict with His love, but in man it "operates incessantly and arouses egotism and a particularized will, just in order that the will to love may arise in contrast to it." Schelling, *Human Freedom*, trans. by J. Gutman, pp. 51-53. Thus in this view sin is not only a prerequisite of virtue but a consequence of the divine nature.

[5] James Martineau erroneously regards the state of habitual sin as a reversion to natural necessity. He writes: "The forfeiture of freedom, the relapse into automatic necessity, is doubtless a most fearful penalty for persistent unfaithfulness; but once incurred it alters the complexion of all subsequent acts. They no longer form fresh constituents in the aggregate of guilt but stand outside in a separate record after its account is closed. . . . The first impulse of the prophets of righteousness when they see him thus is, 'he cannot cease from sin' and perhaps to predict for him eternal retribution; but looking a little deeper, they will rather say, 'he has lost the privilege of sin and sunk away from the rank of persons into the destiny of things.' " *A Study of Religion*, II, 108.

[6] *Cf.* W. E. Hocking, *The Meaning of God in Human Experience*, p. 235.

[7] *Cf.* I Cor. 4:3f.: "But with me it is a very small thing that I should be judged of you, or of man's judgement: yea, I judge not mine own self. For I know nothing against myself; yet am I not hereby justified: but he that judgeth me is the Lord."

[8] Surely this is the significance of the words of Isaiah: "He maketh the judges of the earth as vanity" (Isa. 40:23). In one of the great documents of social protest in Egypt, "The Eloquent Peasant," the accused peasant standing in the court of the Grand Visier declares: "Thou hast been set as a dam to save the poor man from drowning, but behold thou art thyself the flood." *Cf.* J. H. Breasted, *The Dawn of Conscience*, p. 190.

[9] One can never be certain whether Pelagian and Semi-Pelagian criticisms of the Pauline doctrine are primarily directed against the literalistic

corruptions of it or against its basic absurd but profound insights. A good instance of such a criticism is to be found in a modern Anglo-Catholic treatise on the subject: "Nor is it necessary to do more than point out the absurdity of the theory of 'original guilt,' which asserts that human beings are held responsible to an all-just Judge for an act which they did not commit and for physiological and psychological facts which they cannot help. . . . Those (if there be any such) who demand formal disproof of the belief that what is *ex hypothesi* an inherited psychological malady is regarded by God in the light of a voluntarily committed crime, may be referred to the scathing satire of Samuel Butler's *Erewhon."* N. P. Williams, *Ideas on the Fall and Original Sin,* p. 381.

[10] *Cf.* C. H. Dodd, *Epistle to the Romans,* p. 79.

[11] He writes: "So then Adam is in each one of us, for in him human nature itself sinned." *Apol. David altera,* 71.

[12] *Cf. Institutes,* Book II, Ch. i, par. 7. "We ought to be satisfied with this, that the Lord deposited with Adam the endowments he chose to confer on human nature; and therefore that when he lost the favours he had received *he lost them not only for himself* but for us all. Who will be solicitous about a transmission of the soul when he hears that Adam received the ornaments that he lost, *no less for us* than for himself? That they were given, not to one man only, *but to the whole human nature."* It must be admitted that Calvin confines Adam's identity with human nature to the original endowments. The loss of these endowments is conceived in terms of an hereditary relation between Adam and subsequent men, for Calvin continues: "For the children were so vitiated in their parent that they became contagious to their descendants; there was in Adam such a spring of corruption that it is transfused from parents to children in a perpetual stream."

[13] Harnack declares: "The doctrine of original sin leads to Manichean dualism, which Augustine never surmounted, and is accordingly an impious and foolish dogma. . . . His doctrine of concupiscence conduces the same view." *History of Dogma,* Vol. V, p. 217. Harnack's criticisms must of course be discounted, as those of other Christian moralists, because he is as unable to understand the doctrine of original sin, when stripped of its literalistic errors, as when stated in its crude form. His assertion that "turn as he will, Augustine affirms an evil nature and therefore a diabolical creator of the world" is simply not true.

[14] *Begriff der Angst,* p. 105.

# The Result of Sin: Guilt

**14**

## James Orr

## Sin as Guilt— The Divine Judgment

Hitherto, though constantly implied in what has preceded, the character of "guilt" in sin has not received any independent investigation. The feeling of guilt, indeed, in weaker or stronger degree, is an element in the consciousness of every moral being who knows himself as a wrong-doer. It is there naturally and spontaneously, a spring of disquiet and remorse, neither waiting on theoretical considerations for its justification, nor capable of being got rid of by theoretical reasonings the most subtle and plausible. All serious literature treats it as a terrible fact, and finds its weirdest interest in depicting the agonies of the guilt-afflicted conscience, and in tracking the Nemesis that surely awaits the transgressor.[1]

Still, the idea of guilt depends, for its proper apprehension, on presuppositions in the general doctrine of sin, which had first to be made good before the nature and bearings of this idea could be intelligently approached. If guilt is a reality, and not simply a deceptive play of consciousness with itself—an illusion, disease, or figment of the mind—it seems self-evident that certain things about it must be postulated. There must be assumed the existence and freedom of the moral agent, the reality of

From *Sin as a Problem of Today* (New York: Hodder and Stoughton, 1910), pp. 252-82.

moral law, with its intrinsic distinctions of right and wrong, some
authority, be it only in society, to which the wrong-doer is accountable for
infringements of that law—in religion, the existence of God as Moral Ruler
and Holy Judge of men. Suppose, on the other hand, the view taken—as it
is taken by some—that man has not real freedom, that, in words of
Mr. Spencer before quoted, freedom is "an inveterate illusion"[2]—suppose,
again, it is held that sin, or what is called such, is a natural and necessary
stage in man's development—a step to the good,—which seems the implication in most metaphysical and evolutionary theories,—suppose it is
thought, as by many, that good and evil are but relative to the finite
standpoint, and have no existence for the Absolute or for the universe as a
whole, or, as by naturalism, that morality is only a social convention, and
moral ideas the product of casual association and education ("homo
mensura"),—suppose, finally, the Personality, Holiness, or Moral Government of God is denied, or the idea of "law" is held to be inapplicable to
the relations of God to men,—it seems plain that the logical ground is
taken from the conception of "guilt" in any serious sense. The term either
ceases to have meaning, or is weakened down to the expression of an
affrighted state of the individual feeling, without any objective reality to
correspond. There is "guilt-consciousness," as a subjective experience, but
not a "guilt" of which God and the universe must take account.

Is "guilt," then, a reality, and in what does its nature consist? How is it
related to the divine order of the world, and to that "judgment of God"
which, St. Paul assures us, "is according to truth against them that
practise" evil?[3]

In asking, first, what "guilt" *is,* we may start, with Mr. Bradley, in his
older book, *Ethical Studies,* with the idea of *"answerableness"*–
*imputability.*[4] The sense of guilt arises, primarily, in connexion with the
acts which a man imputes to himself as proceeding from his own will in
the exercise of his freedom.[5] These, if wrong, i.e., involving the transgression of some principle of duty, he attributes to himself as their cause,
feels that he is "answerable" for them, takes blame to himself on their
account, and is conscious that he deserves blame from others. As conditions of such self-reprobation, certain things, as already hinted, are
implied—the agent's consciousness of his self-identity and freedom, some
knowledge of moral distinctions, the awareness that he *ought* to have
acted otherwise than he has done, a perception of demerit in the act he has
performed.[6] The sense of guilt, therefore, originates in a *moral judgment*
of a condemnatory kind passed by the agent upon himself for acts which
he knows to be wrong.

Attention must now be fixed more particularly on this idea of *demerit,*
or *ill-desert,* attaching to the wrong act and to its doer. Hitherto we have
been dealing with sin as something in its nature intrinsically evil—opposed
in principle to the good, a source of disorder and impurity, hateful in its
manifestations, ruinous in its spiritual results. In this light sin bears the
aspect of a *disease;* is something foul, malignant, repulsive, the cause of

disturbance, misery, and death. Thus also it appears in Scripture. It is uncleanness, impurity: the abominable thing which God hates.[7] To this aspect of sin some, in their inquiries, would almost entirely confine themselves, ignoring everything which involves what they regard as a *legal* or *juristic* element. But there is another aspect of sin which accompanies all these internal phases of it. Besides possessing the character now described—because, indeed, of its possession of this character—sin has the quality of *evil desert*—of *punishableness*.[8] Sin is not simply a hateful, it is likewise a *condemnable* thing; not something only that *may* be punished, but something that *deserves* to be punished[9]—that could not emerge in a morally-constituted universe and be lawfully passed over as indifferent. This character of the evil desert of sin asserts itself instinctively in every conscience; as conscience develops and grows more sensitive it asserts itself only the more unconditionally. Our feeling regarding a wrong act is, not only that it is something which we blame ourselves for, and are perhaps ashamed of, but something, further, for which we may justly be called to account, and made to *suffer*.

The distinction here made between sin as disease, and sin as entailing evil desert, is one which, as earlier noted, presents itself likewise in ordinary ethical theory. Some schools it is well known, prefer to look on virtue on the *aesthetic* rather than on what is sometimes called the *juristic* side. Virtue is, in this view, the beautiful (τὸ καλόν), the harmonious, the lovable in character; vice, by contrast, is the inharmonious, the turbulent, the irregular, the morally ugly and repulsive. Thus, e.g., in Plato and Shaftesbury. Other moralists, as Kant, start from the side of law, and, emphasising the judicial function of conscience, dwell on the evil desert and punishableness of transgression. One view has regard more to the quality of character; the other to the acts in which character is expressed. Both aspects, however, have their rightful place in a complete view of the facts. The prejudice against a "forensic" view of morality may easily be carried too far. Universal speech endorses the conception of conscience as a court of arraignment for the evil-doer;[10] and heavy and unrelenting, often, are the sentences which this court pronounces.

The relation of guilt and punishment waits closer examination, but one current misconception may here be guarded against. One reason why the term "juristic" is an unfortunate one in this connexion is, that it conveys, or is apt to convey, the impression that ill-desert belongs to, and takes its origin from, statutory law; that it is enough, therefore, to brand the *legal* standpoint in religion as low and imperfect to get rid of the notion of a judicial dealing with sin altogether. Ritschl, e.g., in denying punitive justice to God, proceeds on this idea.[11] Certainly, however, it is a mistaken one. The presence of law is, indeed, presupposed in ill-desert; but ill-desert itself, as an inherent quality of the sinful act or disposition, cleaves, by an intuitive "value-judgment," to the consciousness of wrong-doing prior to any recognition of it by prescriptive law. If it were not already there, law could not make it. It would be there, were that conceivable, even were there no power or authority to call to account for it. Statute law itself, with its imperfect justice, is not an arbitrary thing, but rests, or professes to rest, on principles of right which depend on conscience for their sanction. It would be truer to say that the inner tribunal of conscience is the model on which courts of law are founded, than that it is they which furnish the pattern, and give sanctity to the decisions, of conscience.

Even to the natural consciousness, therefore, guilt is a terrible and woeful reality—not a feeling or alarm of the transgressor's own heart merely (a guilt-*consciousness*), but a guilt that is objectively *there,* and has to be taken account of by the wrong-doer himself and by others. Thus it is regarded in the secret judgments of the soul; thus it is treated in the moral estimates of men by their fellows; thus, when it takes the form of "crime" against society, it is judged by human law.[12]

This, however, still leaves us far outside the full *Christian* estimate of guilt. If guilt has this serious character even in ordinary ethics, infinitely more is its ill-desert apparent when transgression is lifted up into the *religious* sphere, and judged of in its proper character as *sin.* Sin, we have already seen, is much more than simple breach of moral law; it concerns the whole spiritual relation to God. In this higher relation, its demerit is measured not only by the law of conscience—at best a weak and pale reflection of the divine judgment,[13] —but by the majesty of the holiness against which the offence is committed, the absoluteness of the divine claim on our obedience, and the potency of evil perceived to be involved in sin's principle, trivial as may seem, on our lower scale of judging, its immediate manifestation. For here, again, is a fallacy to be avoided. In measuring the evil of sin, we are too apt to be misled by what, in our levity, we call the insignificance of the act (untruth, selfishness, unforgivingness, displays of anger, etc.);[14] our judgments are unhappily out of proportion because our own standpoint is habitually so far below the level of a true spirituality. It seems to us dreadful, no doubt, that a man should commit forgery, or betray a trust; but the fact that any one's (or our own) heart is alienated from God, and insensible to His goodness; that the spiritual balance of the nature is upset—the flesh strong, the spirit weak; that things below, not things above, enchain the affections,—in brief, that the *centre* of life is a wrong one, and that, judged by the standard of *holiness,* almost every thought and act invite condemnation,—this appears to us not so very evil, and occasions comparatively little concern. It is precisely these standards of judgment, however, which religion inverts, and which we, too, must invert, if we are to see things with God's eyes. It will hardly be denied, at least, that, in the Christian Gospel, the demerit, turpitude, ill-desert of sin throughout assume this more awful aspect. The sin of a world turned aside from God is there judged, not by human, but by divine, standards. Guilt is a reality not to be gainsaid. "All the world" is "brought under the judgment of God."[15] A condemnation rests upon it, which no effort of man's own can remove. [16] This, however, introduces us to a further circle of conceptions, the nature and legitimacy of which must now be considered.

Sin is *punishable;* this belongs to its essence. But what is the ground of this connexion between sin and punishment? How is punishment itself to be regarded in its nature and end? And what place has this conception in a religion like the Christian, which proceeds on a principle of *love?*

Eliminating from punishment, as one must do, the idea of personal vengeance—the simple requiting of injury with injury—the question comes to be: Is punishment *retributive,* i.e., due to sin on its own account? or is it only *disciplinary* or *deterrent*—a "chastisement" inflicted from a motive of benevolence, or a means to the prevention of wrong-doing in others? The latter is the "eudaemonistic" or "utilitarian" view of punishment so severely criticised by Kant.[17] As, however, no one denies that punishment may be used, and in God's providence largely is used, for disciplinary ends,[18] the question really turns on the other point of the acknowledgment or denial of its *retributive* aspect. This, on various grounds, is contested. Dr. Moberly, in his interesting discussion of the subject in his *Atonement and Personality,* takes what may be regarded as a mediating view. He grants that punishment *may* be retributive, but holds that its primary purpose is disciplinary, and that only as it fails in its object of producing inward penitence does it acquire the retributive character.[19] But this is a difficult position to maintain. To be productive of any good, disciplinary suffering must always, in the first instance, be recognised as *just,* as *deserved*—one's *due,* and in reasonable proportion to the offence. That is to say, it must include the retributive element.[20] Neither is it easy to understand how a punishment *not* at first due on its own account, can afterwards become retributive simply through its failure to effect a moral change. *Solely* retributive, in contrast with previous moral uses, or more *severely* retributive, with increased hardening in sin, it possibly may become; but essentially the retributive character must have inhered in it from the beginning.[21]

Objection is taken to the retributive aspect of punishment on the ground that God, in Christ's revelation, is no longer looked on as Judge, but as *Father.* Ritschl, going deeper, would deny punitive justice to God as contradictory of His character as love.[22] Neither objection can be readily sustained. St. Paul also, while upholding retribution,[23] knew well that God was Father;[24] Jesus, revealing the Father, gave sternest expression to the truth that God is likewise Judge.[25] God is indeed Father: Fatherhood is expressive of His inmost heart in relation to a world of beings made originally in His own image. But Fatherhood is not the whole truth of God's relation to the world. There is another relation which He sustains than that of Father—the relation of Moral Ruler and Holy Judge—Founder, Upholder, Vindicator, of that moral order to which our own consciences and the whole constitution of things bear witness,—and it is this relation which, once sin has entered, comes into view, and claims to have its rights accorded to it.[26] It was not as Father that St. Paul wrote of God, "Then how shall God judge the world?"[27] "The wrath of God is revealed from heaven against all ungodliness and unrighteousness of men."[28]

What, then is the ground of the punishment of sin? It would lead us too far afield to enter into what may be termed the metaphysics of this difficult question. May it not be enough at present to say, what the foregoing has sought to make clear, that transgression, as in principle a break with that moral order of the world on conformity to which all claim on life and its blessings depends, carries in itself the forfeiture of right to these blessings, and the desert of their opposite, loss and pain? Thus Kant would put it;[29] religion goes deeper in seeing in God's will the last principle of that order, and in sin the turning of the creature will from God in violation of the fundamental demand of moral law, unison of will with God. How then shall it be that a divine holiness shall not react against transgression?

One thing certain is that the presence and working of a retributive justice in men's lives and in the history of the world have ever had a place among the deepest and most solemn convictions of the noblest portions of our race. The Bible need not be appealed to: its testimony is beyond dispute.[30] It is ever, indeed, to be remembered that in this world retribution never acts alone,—that it is crossed, restrained, on all hands, by an abundant mercy,[31] —is counteracted by remedial and redemptive forces,— is changed even where grace prevails (here is the truth of Dr. Moberly's contention), as far as it continues, into the discipline of a loving Father.[32] But retribution, nevertheless, stern and terrible, there is, interweaving itself with every strain of sinful existence; this universal conscience testifies. It is the underlying idea in the Hindu solution of the inequalities of life—the doctrine of transmigration; it is the meaning of the Buddhist doctrine of "Karma"—that invisible law of moral causation infallibly binding act to consequence, even in the production of a new being, when the original agent has ceased to be at death;[33] it is the dread background to the sunny gaiety of ordinary Greek life (Erinnys, Nemesis, Ate), and lends their atmosphere of terror and abiding power over mind and conscience to the great creations of Greek Tragedy (Oedipus, Antigone, Orestes, etc.), not, as will be seen after, without their softer note of mediation and forgiveness;[34] it is equally the informing soul of modern tragedy (Macbeth, Hamlet; in Ibsen), and of a great part of our nobler fiction (e.g., Geo. Eliot, Hawthorne),[35] even of fiction that is less noble (Dumas, Zola, Balzac, etc.). It is the implication of Schiller's "The history of the world is the judgment of the world"; of Matthew Arnold's all too impersonal "Power, not ourselves, that makes for righteousness." All this, falling though it does below the height of the Christian conception, with its Personal Holy Ruler of the world, and its law of righteousness, stretching in its effects into the life beyond, is a witness, impossible to be explained away, to the reality of a law of moral retribution, inbuilt inexorably into the very structure of our universe.[36]

Sin, it has been seen, in its very nature, cuts the bond of fellowship with God, but, further, as entailing guilt, creates in man a feeling of alienation and distrust, and calls forth a reaction of the divine holiness against itself—what Scripture speaks of as the "wrath" (ὀργή) of God—

which expresses itself in "judgment" (κρίμα; "condemnation," κατάκριμα), or punishment. The punishment of sin is no more "fate," or "destiny," or impersonal, self-acting "law," without connexion with a moral Will, as in popular writing it is often represented, but has in it and behind it the intensity of a divine righteousness. The truth to be firmly grasped here is, that this is no arbitrary relation of God to the sin of the world. It is grounded in His very nature, and cannot be laid aside by any act of will, any more than the moral law itself can be reversed or annulled. Sin is that against which the Holy One and Upholder of the moral order of the universe, *must* eternally declare Himself in judgment. To do otherwise would be to deny that He is God. This, however, again gives rise to important questions as to the *manner* and *forms* in which the divine judgment takes effect, and on this point, in view of certain one-sided tendencies in current thought, a little must now be said.

It is a true, if not a complete, thought, that a large part of the punishment of sin—therefore, one form of the judgment of God—lies in the *immanent action* of God in the laws He has established in the worlds of nature and of mind. The first and often least bearable part of the punishment of sin is *internal*,—in the case of greater offences in the miseries of conscience, the pangs of regret, the horror, shame and self-loathing, that make the guilt-laden soul a hell,—but always in the moral and spiritual degradation, discord, and bondage that sin inevitably brings with it. Illustrations might be endlessly multiplied—the class of works already mentioned abounds in them—of the mental torture which the consciousness of guilt can inflict.[37] Not in the inner life of the soul only, however, but *objectively,* in nature and society, the transgressor encounters the punishment of his misdoings. Law is at work here also. Wrong-doing puts the transgressor out of harmony with his environment, as well as with himself, and plunges him into countless troubles. Nature, as Butler said, is constituted for virtue, not for vice, and transgression brings the wrong-doer into collision with its order. Witness, e.g., the effects on health of the indulgence in sinful passions (envy, malice, etc.), or of a life of vice. Society is in arms against the man who violates its laws, or even its proprieties. Everywhere, despite apparent exceptions,[38] the saying is verified, "the way of transgressors is hard."[39]

It is therefore an important truth that God judges sin through the operation of spiritual and natural laws. But this truth, as already suggested, is in danger of becoming a serious error when it is turned round to mean that laws, automatically acting, *take the place of God* in His judgment of sin, and exclude His personal, volitional action in connexion with it. This idea of inherent, "self-acting" laws, which take the punishment of sin, as it were, out of God's hands into their own, needs to be protested against as an undue exaggeration of the truth of God's immanence.[40] Laws are, after all, but God's ministers, and God remains the supreme, personal Power, acting above as well as within spirit and nature, omnipresently governing and directing both. Even in the internal punishment of sin, it is not always remembered, when self-acting laws are spoken of, how largely a personal element enters into such experience in the sinner's consciousness of the hostile judgment passed on him by others. It is this personal element of the disesteem of his fellows which, not infrequently, enters most deeply and with most withering effect into his soul, drying up its springs of happiness and rest. More terrible is it, in relation to God, to realise that it is not self-acting laws the sinner has to do with, but a Holy Judge, whose searching glance no transgression can escape, and who "will bring every work into judgment, with every hidden thing, whether it be good, or whether it be evil."[41]

In nature, again, it is not simply self-acting laws which the transgressor has to deal with. We fail of a complete view if, with Martineau and others, we think of nature as a system of physical agencies which moves on its unbending way without any regard to moral character.[42] Nature, equally with mind, is the sphere of a divine providence. It is not simply that the sinner suffers through his collision with the established natural order; but nature, under the direction of God, takes up a hostile attitude towards the sinner. This, which is undoubtedly the teaching of Scripture,[43] is surely the truer view philosophically as well as religiously. Laws alone do not explain nature. To explain the actual course of nature there is needed, besides, what J. S. Mill, borrowing from Dr. Chalmers, called the "collocation" of laws—the manner in which laws are combined and made to work together.[44] To this is due the fine threadings and conjunctions in life which, with other factors, make up what we rightly speak of as its providential meaning for us.[45] Things, in other words, do not fall out by hap-hazard; they are part of a divine ordering that takes all the conditions—natural and moral—into account. The agencies of nature, therefore, can well be used, and are used, of God, as His instruments in the punishment of sin.

The word in which Scripture sums up, comprehensively, the penalty of sin is *"death."* "The wages of sin is death."[46] Death, in this relation, certainly includes a moral element; it has sin behind it as its cause.[47] The intimacy of spiritual and physical is maintained here also. The real dying is *inward,*—the result of disobedience, severing from fellowship with God, and issuing, save as grace prevents, in corruption and subjection to evil powers.[48] Death is not, therefore, simply physical dissolution. On the other hand, it seems impossible to deny that physical dissolution,—the separation of soul and body, in contradiction of man's true destiny[49] —is, in the Scriptural idea,[50] included in it. The meaning of death for man, in its scientific relations, was considered in a previous chapter, and need not be further dwelt upon. With death, however, in its universal prevalence,[51] and, as involved in this, the whole question of hereditary evil, is connected another dark and difficult problem, the possibility of a *hereditary or racial,* as distinct from a purely individual, *guilt.* From what has been said in elucidation of guilt, it would seem as if the very nature of guilt lay in its being individual. I cannot be guilty of another's sin. On the other side, the fact has to be faced that, because of the organic connexion—the *solidarity*—of the race, the penalties of transgression rarely are confined to the individual transgressor, but overflow on all connected with him. They descend from generation to generation,[52] even to the extent of the inheritance of a polluted nature, and, on the above showing, of universal subjection to death.

How is this antinomy to be solved? It plainly cannot be on the ground of pure individualism. It was before seen, however, that the individual point of view is not the only one; the *social* and *racial* aspects of man's existence have likewise to be regarded, and these entail responsibilities.

1. It is to be recalled that, while personal guilt, obviously, there can be none for the acts of another, this does not preclude even the innocent from the suffering of *painful consequences* which are truly the penalties of that other's transgression.

2. Next, it cannot be denied that, while purely personal action entails only individual responsibility, there are *public* and *corporate responsibilities,* in which all concerned must take their share, though the acts by which they are affected are not their own. A firm is responsible for the defalcations of a clerk or of one of its own members; an employer is responsible for his servant's carelessness; a nation may be involved in prolonged war through a rash word spoken or a blow struck. There is not here, indeed, a sharing of the guilt, but there is of the *liabilities* which the wrong act entails—a fruit of the common responsibility.

3. A deeper case is where, besides outward association, there is *kindredship in disposition* with the transgressors—participation in, and heirship of, the *spirit* that prompted the evil deeds. Jesus held the Pharisees responsible for the deeds of their fathers, of whose spirit they were partakers. He spoke of the blood of all the prophets coming on Jerusalem.[53] The French Revolution, as depicted by Carlyle, is a modern illustration of the same avenging law. Guilt, accumulating for centuries, discharges its terrible load upon a later generation. In these cases continuity of spirit knits the generations together into one guilty whole.

All these principles, it may be held, meet in their application to the *race.* Guilt, as well as sin, has a racial aspect. The race is not innocent. Sprung from a sinful root, itself gone far astray,[54] it shares in the disabilities which sin entails. Without prejudice to individual responsibility, we can speak of a common "guilt" of humanity.

The great, the solemn, inquiry yet remains—Does sin's penalty exhaust itself in this life? Or is it carried over into *the Beyond,* and with what issues? Does death end all? The question must here be reserved, but it is that on which everything depends for a satisfying solution of the moral problems of the world. There is, it has been seen, a divine moral administration in this life,—a judgment of sin, inward and outward, continually going on,—but the mind is easily contented which can regard this temporal dispensation of God's justice as either perfect or final. The manifest incompleteness of the earthly system of things, in relation both to the good and to the evil, is, in fact, the loudest plea for a Hereafter, and one of the strongest reasons for believing in its existence. The present, too, it is needful again to remind ourselves, is a Day of Grace even more than a scene of Judgment. A remedial system is in operation, the bearings of which on sin are manifold and far-reaching. Rarely, if ever, is sin permitted to work out its full effects; never, in this life is it visited with its full penalty. This, manifestly, is not final. A day is awaited when the veil will fall, when everything will be revealed in its true light, and meet with its due reward. Gospel as it is of all-embracing love, Christianity joins with conscience in announcing "judgment to come."[55]

## Notes

[1] "Raro antecedentem scelestum/Deseruit pede poena claudo."—Horace, *Odes,* iii. 2.

[2] Cf. his *Psychology,* i. pp. 500ff.

[3] Rom. 3:2.

[4] *Op. cit.,* pp. 3ff. What is it to be morally responsible? "We see in it at once the idea of a man's appearing to answer. He answers for what he has done, or has neglected and left undone. And the tribunal is a moral tribunal; it is the court of conscience, imagined as a judge, divine or human, external or internal" (p. 3).

[5] Hence the use of αἰτία for guilt, in such phrases as "to hold one guilty," "to acquit of guilt."

[6] Mr. Bradley puts the matter thus: "The first condition of the possibility of my guiltiness, or of my becoming a subject for moral imputation, is my self-sameness; I must be throughout one identical person. . . . In the first place, then, I must be the very same person to whom the deed belonged; and, in the second place, it must have belonged to me—it must have been mine. . . . The deed must issue from my will; in Aristotle's language, the ἀρχή must be in myself. . . . Thirdly, responsibility implies a *moral* agent. No one is accountable who is not capable of knowing (not, who *does* not know) the moral quality of his acts" (*Op. cit.,* pp. 5-7).

[7] E.g., Ps. 14:3; Isa. 6:5; Jer. 44:4; Ezek. 36:29; II Cor. 7:1; Eph. 4:19; 5:4; James 1:2; Rev. 22:11.

[8] Cf. Kant, *Crit. of Pract. Reason* (Abbott's trans., *Theory of Ethics,* pp. 127ff.). "Finally, there is something further in the idea of our practical reason, which accompanies the transgression of a moral law—namely, its *ill-desert*" (p. 127).

[9] Mr. Bradley says: "What is really true for the ordinary consciousness; what it clings to, and will not let go; what marks unmistakably, by its absence, a 'philosophical' or a 'debauched' morality, is the necessary connexion between responsibility and liability to punishment, between punishment and desert, or the finding of guiltiness before the law of the moral tribunal. For practical purposes we need make no distinction between responsibility, accountability, and liability to punishment" (*Op. cit.,* p. 4).

[10] Rom. 2:15.

[11] In this theory of Ritschl's, see below. In criticism, cf. Dorner, *Syst. of Doct.*, E.T., iv. pp. 60-3.

[12] Cf. T. H. Green, *Works*, ii. pp. 489ff. Mr. Green perhaps errs in seeking the ground of punishment too exclusively in the harm done to society, but he insists strongly on the punishment being a *just* one—one truly *deserved*. "It demands retribution in the sense of demanding that the criminal should have his due, should be dealt with according to his deserts, should be punished justly. . . . When the specified conditions of just punishment are fulfilled, the person punished himself recognises it as just, as his due or desert, and it is so recognised by the onlooker who thinks himself into the situation" (pp. 491-2).

[13] I John 3:20.

[14] Cf. Christ's estimate of these things (Matt. 5:22; 6:15; 12:36; etc.).

[15] Rom. 3:19, ὑπόδικος.

[16] Rom. 3:19, 20, 23, etc.

[17] Cf. passage above cited.

[18] Ch. 2 of the Book of Hosea is a fine example of how God's severest judgments on Israel had an end of discipline and mercy.

[19] *Op. cit.*, ch. 1. "This purpose of beneficent love is, we may venture to suggest, the proper character and purpose of punishment" (p. 14; cf. p. 24). It is allowed that in human justice the retributive aspect is primary; but this, it is said, belongs to it "not as it is justice, but as it is human . . . to the necessary imperfectness of such corporate and social justice as is possible on earth" (p. 9).

[20] Cf. the remarks in W. F. Lofthouse's *Ethics and Atonement*, p. 102.

[21] This is partially conceded in the use of the word "latent" (on p. 14). Another difficulty for Dr. Moberly is that, as he rightly holds, the "penitence" he desiderates is "impossible" apart from the saving interposition of Christ (pp. 44-5). But an aspect of punishment (the disciplinary) which is dependent on redemption cannot be thought of as primary; unless, indeed, it is contended that there would have been no punishment of sin, had grace not entered.

[22] Cf. the writer's *Ritschlian Theology*, pp. 110, 146-9.

[23] Rom. 2:3-11.

[24] God is "the God and Father of our Lord Jesus Christ" (II Cor. 1:3; Eph. 1:3), "our Father" (Eph. 1:2), "the Father from whom every family in heaven and earth is named" (Eph. 3:14), etc. In a wider regard all are His "offspring" (Acts 17:28).

[25] Matt. 10:28; 11:22, 24; 12:36-37; 21:44; 24:35; etc.

[26] Cf. on this T. G. Selby, *Theology in Modern Fiction*, on Geo. Macdonald, pp. 151ff.

[27] Rom. 3:5.

[28] Rom. 1:18. It is interesting to observe how St. Peter combines and yet distinguishes the two notions: "If ye call on Him as Father, who without respect of persons judgeth according to each man's work" (I Peter 1:17).

[29] Cf., e.g., the Fragment of a "Moral Catechism" in Kant's *Methodology of Ethics* (Semple's trans., Ed. 1869, p. 290ff.).

[30] Isaiah: "Say ye of the righteous, that it shall be well with him. . . . Woe unto the wicked! it shall be ill with him," etc. (2:10, 11); Jesus and Jerusalem (Matt. 23:32-39). St. Paul has been already cited.

[31] "His goodness, and forbearance, and long-suffering" (Rom. 3:4).

[32] Heb. 12:5ff.

[33] Prof. Huxley, *Evolution and Ethics* (Works, ix. pp. 61-2), connects the idea of "Karma" with heredity. It is really very different—an abstract, impersonal law, which has no relation to biological transmission. Its persistence past death Huxley speaks of as transmission "from one phenomenal association to another by a sort of induction" (p. 67).

[34] Cf. Plumptre, *Sophocles,* Introd., p. lxxxiii.

[35] This part of the subject is well illustrated in the book above named, T. G. Selby's *Theology in Modern Fiction* (Fernley Lects., 1896). One thinks here of the teaching of George Eliot's *Silas Marner, Adam Bede, Felix Holt, Romola,* and of Hawthorne's *Scarlet Letter* and *Twice Told Tales.* Mr. Selby says of George Eliot: "Working through all her plots is a stern, intelligent, unforgetting principle of retribution which brings even the secret things of darkness into judgment" (p. 9).

[36] Prof. Huxley's strong words on the punishment of at least "certain actions" were quoted in the previous chapter, (p. 228).

[37] Two examples may be taken from antiquity:—
Juvenal, in his 13th Sat. (191-8), asks: "Yet why suppose that those have escaped punishment whom conscience holds in constant fear and under the noiseless lash—the mind her own tormentor? Sore punishment it is—heavier far than those of stern Caedicius or Rhadamanthus—night and day to carry one's own accuser in the breast."
Tacitus in his *Annals* (vi. 6) depicts the guilty agonies of Tiberius. In a letter to the Senate the emperor writes: "What to write you, conscript fathers, or how to write, or what *not* to write, may all the gods and goddesses destroy me worse than I feel they are daily destroying me, if I know." "With such retribution," adds the historian, "had his crimes and atrocities recoiled upon himself."

[38] Ps. 37:35-36; 73:12-20.

[39] Prov. 13:15.

[40] Dr. Dale in his work on *the Atonement* (Lect. viii.) criticises this theory of "self-acting" moral laws in its relation to forgiveness as expounded by an older writer, Dr. John Young, in his *Life and Light of Men.*

"God simply looks on. The vast machine of the moral universe is self-acting." Cf. Mr. Selby's remarks on recent views in his *Theol. of Modern Fiction,* pp. 168ff. He justly says: "A God who has put a huge body of inviolable natural or moral laws between Himself and His creatures is imperfectly personal" (p. 168).

[41] Eccles. 12:14.

[42] Cf. Martineau, *Seat of Authority in Religion,* p. 105: "The *physical* agency of God . . . can take no separate notice of human life and character, nor of the differences which distinguish us from each other in our lot and in our mind. . . . An administration which, still intellectual, is *un*moral, and carries its inexorable order through, and never turns aside, though it crushes life and hope, and even gives occasion to guilt and abasement."

[43] Deut. 28:15ff.; Isa. 1:4ff.; Hos. 2; Amos 4; Rev. 8; etc.

[44] *Syst. of Logic,* Bk. iii. 12. 2.

[45] Cf. McCosh, *Method of Div. Govt.,* Bk. ii. ch. 2. "The inquiring mind will discover designed combinations, many and wonderful, between the various events of divine providence. . . . What singular unions of two streams at the proper place to help on the exertions of the great and good! What curious intersections of cords to catch the wicked as in a net, when they are prowling as wild beasts! By strange, but most apposite correspondences, human strength, when set against the will of God, is made to waste away under His indignation, as, in heathen story, Meleager wasted away as the stick burned which his mother held in the fire" (p. 198). Mr. Selby, illustrating from George Eliot, says: "The gathering up of all these tangled threads after years of oblivion implies an over-watching providence of judgment in human life" (*op. cit.,* p. 52).

[46] Rom. 6:23.

[47] Gen. 2:17; 3:19; Rom. 5:12.

[48] On death as spiritual, cf. John 5:24; Rom. 8:6; Eph. 2:1, 5; 5:14; I Tim. 5:16; I John 3:14.

[49] Cf. the writer's *God's Image in Man,* pp. 53, 251ff.

[50] This is contested by many, e.g., by Principal E. Griffith-Jones, in his *Ascent Through Christ,* pp. 174ff. But fair exegesis cannot get rid of this idea of Paul's teaching (Rom. 5:12; I Cor. 15:21, 22; etc.). Ritschl grants that Paul taught the doctrine, but holds that Paul's thought is no rule for us (*Justif. and Recon.,* E.T., p. 359).

[51] Cf. Rom. 5:12-15.

[52] Exod. 20:5.

[53] Matt. 23:29-39. On the same principle we speak of the sin *of the world* as crucifying Christ Himself. The Jews cried: "His blood be on us and on our children" (Matt. 27:25).

[54] Isa. 53:6.

[55] Acts 24:25; Rom. 2:5, 16; II Cor. 5:10; Heb. 6:1, 2; etc.

# 15

## Charles G. Finney

# Accounting for Moral Depravity

The term "moral" is from the Latin *mos,* manners. The term "depravity," as has been shown, is from *de* and *pravus,* crooked. The terms united, signify crooked manners, or bad morals. The word ἁμαρτια, *amartia,* rendered sin, as has been said, signifies to miss the mark, to aim at the wrong end, a deviation from the divine law. In this discussion I must,

(1.) Remind you of some positions that have been settled respecting moral depravity.

(2.) Consult the oracles of God respecting the nature of moral depravity, or sin.

(3.) Consult the oracles of God in respect to the proper method of accounting for the existence of sin.

(4.) Show the manner in which it is to be accounted for as an ultimate fact.

(1.) *Some positions that have been settled.*

(i.) It has been shown that moral depravity resolves itself into selfishness.

(ii.) That selfishness consists in the supreme choice of self-indulgence.

From *Lectures on Systematic Theology* (Oberlin, Ohio: James M. Fitch, 1846), pp. 394-404.

(iii.) That self-indulgence consists in the committal of the will to the gratification of the sensibility, as opposed to obeying the law of the reason, and of God.

(iv.) That sin, or moral depravity, is a unit, and always consists in this committed state of the will to self-gratification, irrespective of the particular form or means of self-gratification.

(v.) It has also been shown, that moral depravity does not consist in a sinful nature.

(vi.) And, also that actual transgression cannot justly be ascribed to a sinful constitution.

(vii.) We have also seen that all sin is actual, and that no other than actual transgression can justly be called sin.

(2.) *We are to consult the oracles of God respecting the nature of moral depravity, or sin.*

Reference has often been made to the teachings of inspiration upon this subject. But it is important to review our ground in this place, that we may ascertain what are the teachings, and what are the assumptions, of the Bible in regard to the nature of sin. Does it assume that as a truth, which natural theology teaches upon the subject? What is taught in the Bible, either expressly, or by way of inference and implication, upon this subject?

(i.) The Bible gives a formal definition of sin. I John 3:4, "Sin is a transgression of the law"; and 5:17, "All unrighteousness is sin." As was remarked on a former occasion, this definition is not only an accurate one, but it is the only one that can possibly be true.

(ii.) The Bible everywhere makes the law the only standard of right and wrong, and obedience to it to be the whole of virtue, and disobedience to it the whole of sin. This truth lies everywhere upon the face of the Bible. It is taught, assumed, implied, or expressed, on every page of the Bible.

(iii.) It holds men responsible for their voluntary actions alone, or more strictly for their choices alone, and expressly affirms, that "if there be a willing mind, it is accepted according to what a man hath, and not according to what he hath not." That is, willing as God directs is accepted as obedience, whether we are able to execute our choices or not.

(iv.) The Bible always represents sin as something done or committed, or wilfully omitted, and never as a part or attribute of soul or body. We have seen, that the texts that have been relied on, as teaching the doctrine of constitutional sinfulness, when rightly understood, mean no such thing.

(v.) The Bible assures us, that all sin shall pass in review at the solemn judgment, and always represents all sin then to be recognized, as consisting in "the deeds done in the body." Texts that support these assertions are too numerous to need to be quoted, as every reader of the Bible knows.

(3.) *We are to consult the Bible in respect to the proper method of accounting for moral depravity.*

(i.) We have more than once seen that the Bible has given us the history of the introduction of sin into our world; and that from the narrative, it is plain, that the first sin consisted in selfishness, or in consenting to indulge the excited constitutional propensities in a prohibited manner. In other words, it consisted in yielding the will to the impulses of the sensibility, instead of abiding by the law of God, as revealed in the intelligence. Thus the Bible ascribes the first sin of our race to the influence of temptation.

(ii.) The Bible once, and only once, incidentally intimates that Adam's first sin has in some way been the occasion, not the necessary physical cause, of all the sins of men. Rom. 5:12-19.

(iii.) It neither says nor intimates anything in relation to the manner in which Adam's sin has occasioned this result. It only incidentally recognizes the fact, and then leaves it, just as if the *quo modo* was too obvious to need explanation.

(iv.) In other parts of the Bible we are informed how we are to account for the existence of sin among men. For example, James 1:15, "When lust ('desire,' $\epsilon\pi\iota\theta\upsilon\mu\iota\alpha$) has conceived, it bringeth forth sin." Here sin is represented, not as the desire itself, but as consisting in the consent of the will to gratify the desire.

James says again, that a man is tempted when he is drawn aside of his own lusts, ($\epsilon\pi\iota\theta\upsilon\mu\iota\alpha\iota$ "desires") and enticed. That is, his lusts, or the impulses of his sensibility, are his tempters. When he or his will is overcome of these, he sins.

(v.) Paul and other inspired writers represent sin as consisting in a carnal or fleshly mind, in the mind of the flesh, or in minding the flesh. It is plain that by the term flesh they mean what we understand by the sensibility, as distinguished from intellect, and that they represent sin as consisting in obeying, minding the impulses of the sensibility. They represent the world, and the flesh, and Satan, as the three great sources of temptation. It is plain that the world and Satan tempt by appeals to the flesh, or to the sensibility. Hence, the apostles have much to say of the necessity of the destruction of the flesh, of the members, of putting off the old man with his deeds, &c. Now, it is worthy of remark, that all this painstaking, on the part of inspiration, to intimate the source from whence our sin proceeds, and to apprise us of the proper method of accounting for it, and also of avoiding it, has probably been the occasion of leading certain philosophers and theologians who have not carefully examined the whole subject, to take a view of it which is directly opposed to the truth intended by the inspired writers. Because so much is said of the influence of the flesh over the mind, they have inferred that the nature and physical constitution of man is itself sinful. But the representations of Scripture are, that the body is the occasion of sin. The law in his members, that warred against the law of his mind, of which Paul speaks, is manifestly the impulse of the sensibility opposed to the law of the reason. This law, that is, the impulse of his sensibility, brings him into captivity, that is, influences his will, in spite of all his convictions to the contrary.

In short, the Bible rightly interpreted, everywhere assumes and implies, that sin consists in selfishness. It is remarkable, if the Bible be read with an eye to its teachings and assumptions on this point, to what an extent this truth will appear.

(4.) How moral depravity is to be accounted for.

(i.) It consists, remember, in the committal of the will to the gratification or indulgence of self—in the will's following, or submitting itself to be governed by, the impulses and desires of the sensibility, instead of submitting itself to the law of God revealed in the reason.

(ii.) This definition of the thing shows how it is to be accounted for, namely; the sensibility acts as a powerful impulse to the will, from the moment of birth, and secures the consent and activity of the will to procure its gratification, before the reason is at all developed. The will is thus committed to the gratification of feeling and appetite, when first the idea of moral obligation is developed. This committed state of the will is not moral depravity, and has no moral character, until the idea of moral obligation is developed. The moment this idea is developed, this committal of the will to self-indulgence must be abandoned, or it becomes selfishness, or moral depravity. But, as the will is already in a state of committal, and has to some extent already formed the habit of seeking to gratify feeling, and as the idea of moral obligation is at first but feebly developed, unless the Holy Spirit interferes to shed light on the soul, the will, as might be expected, retains its hold on self-gratification. Here alone moral character commences, and must commence. No one can conceive of its commencing earlier. Let it be remembered, that selfishness consists in the supreme and ultimate choice, or in the preference of self-gratification as an end, or for its own sake, over all other interests. Now, as the choice of an end implies and includes the choice of the means, selfishness, of course, causes all that outward life and activity that makes up the entire history of sinners.

This selfish choice is the wicked heart—the propensity to sin—that causes what is generally termed actual transgression. This sinful choice is properly enough called indwelling sin. It is the latent, standing, controlling preference of the mind, and the cause of all the outward and active life. It is not the choice of sin itself, distinctly conceived of, or chosen as sin, but the choice of self-gratification, which choice is sin.

Again: It should be remembered, that the physical depravity of our race has much to do with our moral depravity. A diseased physical system renders the appetites, passions, tempers, and propensities more clamorous and despotic in their demands, and of course constantly urging to selfishness, confirms and strengthens it. It should be distinctly remembered that physical depravity has no moral character in itself. But yet it is a source of fierce temptation to selfishness. The human sensibility is, manifestly, deeply physically depraved; and as sin, or moral depravity, consists in committing the will to the gratification of the sensibility, its physical depravity will mightily strengthen moral depravity. Moral depravity is then universally owing to temptation. That is, the soul is tempted to self-indulgence, and yields to the temptation, and this yielding, and not the temptation, is sin or moral depravity. This is manifestly the way in which Adam and Eve became morally depraved. They were tempted, even by undepraved appetite, to prohibited indulgence, and were overcome. The sin did not lie in the constitutional desire of food, or of knowledge, nor in the excited state of these appetites or desires, but in the consent of the will to prohibited indulgence.

Just in the same way all sinners become such, that is, they become morally depraved, by yielding to temptation to self-gratification under some form. Indeed, it is impossible that they should become morally depraved in any other way. To deny this were to overlook the very nature of moral depravity. It is remarkable, that President Edwards, after writing five hundred pages, in which he confounds physical and moral depravity; in answer to an objection of Dr. Taylor of England, that his view made God the author of the constitution, the author also of sin, turns immediately round, and without seeming aware of his own inconsistency, ascribes all sin to temptation, and makes it consist altogether in obeying the propensities, just as I have done. His words are—

"One argument against a supposed native, sinful depravity, which Dr. Taylor greatly insists upon, is, 'that this does, in effect, charge Him who is the author of our nature, who formed us in the womb, with being the author of a sinful corruption of nature; and that it is highly injurious to the God of our nature, whose hands have formed and fashioned us, to believe our nature to be originally corrupted, and that in the worst sense of corruption.'

"With respect to this, I would observe, in the first place, that this writer, in handling this grand objection, supposes something to belong to the doctrine objected against, as maintained by the divines whom he is opposing, which does not belong to it, nor follow from it. As particularly, he supposes the doctrine of original sin to imply, that nature must be corrupted by some positive influence; 'something, by some means or other, infused into human nature; some quality or other, not from the choice of our minds, but like a taint, tincture, or infection, altering the natural constitution, faculties, and dispositions of our souls! That sin and evil dispositions are implanted in the *foetus* in the womb.' Whereas truly our doctrine neither implies nor infers any such thing. In order to account for a sinful corruption of nature, yea, a total native depravity of the heart of man, there is not the least need of supposing any evil quality infused, implanted, or wrought into the nature of man, by any positive cause or influence whatsoever, either from God, or the creature; or of supposing that man is conceived and born with a fountain of evil in his heart, such as is anything properly positive. I think a little attention to the nature of things will be sufficient to satisfy any impartial, considerate inquirer, that the absence of positive good principles, and so the withholding of a special divine influence to impart and maintain those good principles—leaving the common natural principles of self-love, natural appetite, &c., to themselves, without the government of superior divine principles, will certainly be followed with the corruption, yea, the total corruption of the heart, without occasion for any positive influences at all. And that it was thus in fact, that corruption of nature came on Adam immediately on his fall, and comes on all his posterity as sinning in him, and falling with him.

"The case with man was plainly this: When God made man at first he implanted in him two kinds of principles. There was an inferior kind which may be natural, being the principles of mere human nature; such as self-love, with those natural appetites and passions which belong to the nature of man, in which his love to his own liberty, honour, and pleasure, were exercised. These, when alone, and left to themselves, are what the scriptures sometimes call flesh. Besides these, there were superior principles, that were spiritual, holy, and divine, summarily comprehended in divine love; wherein consisted the spiritual image of God, and man's righteousness and true holiness; which are called in scripture the divine nature. These principles may, in some sense, be called supernatural, being (however concreated or connate, yet) such as are above those principles that are essentially implied in, or necessarily resulting from, and inseparably connected with, mere human nature: and being such as immediately depend on man's union and communion with God, or divine communications and influences of God's Spirit, which though withdrawn, and man's nature forsaken of these principles, human nature would be human nature still; man's nature, as such, being entire without these divine principles, which the scripture sometimes calls spirit, in contradistinction to flesh. These superior principles were given to possess the throne, and maintain absolute dominion in the heart; the other to be wholly subordinate and subservient. And while things continued thus, all was in excellent order, peace, and beautiful harmony, and in a proper and perfect state. These divine principles thus reigning, were the dignity, life, happiness, and glory of man's nature. When man sinned and broke God's covenant, and fell under his curse, these superior principles left his heart; for, indeed, God then left him, that communion with God on which these principles depended, entirely ceased; the Holy Spirit, that divine inhabitant, forsook the house, because it would have been utterly improper in itself, and inconsistent with the constitution God had established, that he should still maintain communion with man, and continue, by his friendly, gracious, vital influences, to dwell with him and in him, after he was become a rebel, and had incurred God's wrath and curse. Therefore, immediately the superior divine principles wholly ceased; so light ceases in a room when the candle is withdrawn; and thus man was left in a state of darkness, woeful corruption, and ruin; nothing but flesh without spirit. The inferior principles of self-love and natural appetite, which were given only to serve, being alone, and left to themselves, of course became reigning principles; having no superior principles to regulate or control them, they became the absolute masters of the heart. The immediate consequence of which was a fatal catastrophe, a turning of all things upside down, and the succession of a state of the most odious and dreadful confusion. Man immediately set up himself, and the objects of his private affections and appetites, as supreme, and so they took the place of God. These inferior principles were like fire in a house; which we say is a good servant, but a bad master; very useful while kept in its place, but if left to take possession of the whole house, soon brings all to destruction. Man's love to his own honour, separate interests, and private pleasure, which before was wholly subordinate unto love to God, and regard to his authority and glory, now disposes and impels him to pursue those objects, without regard to God's honour or law; because there is no true regard to these divine things left in him. In consequence of which, he seeks those objects as much when against God's honour and law, as when agreeable to them. God still continuing strictly to require supreme regard to himself, and forbidding all undue gratification of these inferior passions; but only in perfect subordination to the ends, and agreeable to the rules and limits which his holiness, honour, and law prescribe; hence, immediately arises enmity in the heart, now wholly under the power of self-love; and nothing but war ensues, in a course against God. As when a subject has once renounced his lawful sovereign, and set up a pretender in his stead, a state of enmity and war against his rightful king necessarily ensues. It were easy to show, how every lust, and depraved disposition of man's heart, would naturally arise from this privative original, if here were room for it. Thus it is easy to give an account, how total corruption of heart should follow on man's eating the forbidden fruit, though that was but one act of sin, without God putting any evil into his heart, or implanting any bad principle, or infusing any corrupt taint, and so becoming the author of depravity. Only God's withdrawing, as it was highly proper and necessary that he should, from rebel man, and his natural principles being left to themselves, is sufficient to account for his becoming entirely corrupt, and bent on sinning against God.

"And as Adam's nature became corrupt, without God's implanting or infusing of any evil thing into it; so does the nature of his posterity. God dealing with Adam as the head of his posterity, as has been shown, and treating them as one, he deals with his posterity as having all sinned in him. And therefore, as God withdrew spiritual communion, and his vital, gracious influence from all the members, as they come into existence; whereby they come into the world mere flesh, and entirely under the government of natural and inferior principles; and so become wholly corrupt, as Adam did."–*Edwards' Works,* pp. 532-538.

To sum up the truth upon this subject in few words, I would say–

1. Moral depravity in our first parents was induced by temptation addressed to the unperverted susceptibilities of their nature. When these susceptibilities became strongly excited, they overcame the will; that is, the human pair were over-persuaded, and fell under the temptation. This has been repeatedly said, but needs repetition in a summing up.

2. All moral depravity commences in substantially the same way. Proof:–

(1.) The impulses of the sensibility are developed, and gradually commencing from the birth, and depending on physical developement and birth.

(2.) The first acts of will are in obedience to these.

(3.) Self-gratification is the rule of action previous to the developement of reason.

(4.) No resistance is offered to the will's indulgence of appetite, until a habit of self-indulgence is formed.

(5.) When reason affirms moral obligation, it finds the will in a state of habitual and constant committal to the impulses of the sensibility.

(6.) The demands of the sensibility have become more and more despotic every hour of indulgence.

(7.) In this state of things, unless the Holy Spirit interpose, the idea of moral obligation will be but dimly developed.

(8.) The will of course rejects the bidding of reason, and cleaves to self-indulgence.

(9.) This is the settling of a fundamental question. It is deciding in favour of appetite, against the claims of conscience and of God.

(10.) Light once rejected, can be afterwards more easily resisted, until it is nearly excluded altogether.

(11.) Selfishness confirms, and strengthens, and perpetuates itself by a natural process. It grows with the sinner's growth, and strengthens with his strength; and will do so for ever, unless overcome by the Holy Spirit through the truth.

### Remarks

1. Adam, being the natural head of the race, would naturally, by the wisest constitution of things, greatly affect for good or evil his whole posterity.

2. His sin in many ways exposed his posterity to aggravated temptation. Not only the physical constitution of all men, but all the influences under which they first form their moral character, are widely different from what they would have been, if sin had never been introduced.

3. When selfishness is understood to be the whole of moral depravity, its *quo modo,* or in what way it comes to exist, is manifest. Clear conceptions of the thing will instantly reveal the occasion and manner.

4. The only difficulty in accounting for it, has been the false assumption, that there must be, and is, something lying back of the free actions of the will, which sustains to those actions the relation of a cause, that is itself sinful.

5. If holy Adam, and holy angels, could fall under temptations addressed to their undepraved sensibility, how absurd it is to conclude, that sin in those who are born with a physically depraved constitution, cannot be accounted for, without ascribing it to original sin, or to a nature that is in itself sinful.

6. Without divine illumination, the moral character will of course be formed under the influence of the flesh. That is, the lower propensities will of course influence the will, unless the reason be developed by the Holy Spirit, as was said by President Edwards, in the extract just quoted.

7. The dogma of constitutional moral depravity, is a part and parcel of the doctrine of a necessitated will. It is a branch of a grossly false and heathenish philosophy. How infinitely absurd, dangerous, and unjust, then, to embody it in a standard of Christian doctrine, to give it the place of an indispensable article of faith, and denounce all who will not swallow its absurdities, as heretics. O, shame!

8. We are unable to say precisely at what age infants become moral agents, and of course how early they become sinners. Doubtless there is much difference among children in this respect. Reason is developed in one earlier than in another, according to the constitution and circumstances.

A thorough consideration of the subject, will doubtless lead to the conviction, that children become moral agents much earlier than is generally supposed. The conditions of moral agency are, as has been repeatedly said in former lectures, the possession of the powers of moral agency, together with the developement of the ideas of the good or valuable, of moral obligation or oughtness—of right and wrong—of praise and blameworthiness. I have endeavoured to show, in former lectures, that mental satisfaction, blessedness or happiness, is the ultimate good. Satisfaction arising from the gratification of the appetites, is one of the earliest experiences of human beings. This no doubt suggests or developes, at a very early period, the idea of the good or the valuable. The idea is doubtless developed, long before the word that expresses it is understood. The child knows that happiness is good, and seeks it in the form of self-gratification, long before the terms that designate this state of mind are at all understood. It knows that its own enjoyment is worth seeking, and doubtless very early has the idea, that the enjoyment of others is worth seeking, and affirms to itself, not in words, but in idea, that it ought to please its parents and those around it. It knows, in fact, though language is as yet unknown, that it loves to be gratified, and to be happy, that it loves and seeks enjoyment for itself, and doubtless has the idea that it ought not to displease and distress those around it, but that it ought to endeavour to please and gratify them. This is probably among the first ideas, if not the very first idea, of the pure reason that is developed, that is, the idea of the good, the valuable, the desirable; and the next must be that of oughtness, or of moral obligation, or of right and wrong, &c. I say again, these ideas are, and must be developed, before the signs or words that express them are at all understood, and the words would never be understood except the idea were first developed. We always find, at the earliest period at which children can understand words, that they have the idea of obligation, of right and wrong. As soon as these words are understood by them, they recognize them as expressing ideas already in their own minds, and which ideas they have had further back than they can remember. Some, and indeed most persons, seem to have the idea, that children affirm themselves to be under moral obligation, before they have the idea of the good; that they affirm their obligation to obey their parents before they know, or have the idea of the good or of the valuable. But this is, and must be a mistake. They may and do affirm obligation to obey their parents, before they can express in language, and before they would understand, a statement of the grounds of their obligation. The idea, however, they have, and must have, or they could not affirm obligation. It is agreed, and cannot be denied, that moral obligation respects acts of will, and not strictly outward action. It is agreed, and cannot be denied, that obligation respects intelligent actions of will. It is also agreed, and cannot be denied, that all intelligent acts of will, and such as those to which moral obligation belongs, must respect ends or means. If, therefore, one has any true idea of moral obligation, it must respect acts of will or intentions. It must respect the choice of an end, or of means. If it respect the choice of a means, the idea of the end must exist. It cannot justly affirm obligation of anything but choice or intention, for, as a matter of fact, obligation belongs to nothing else. The fact is, the child knows that it ought to please its parent, and seek to make its parent happy. This it knows, that it ought to intend, long before it knows what the word intention means. Upon this assumption it bases all its affirmations in respect to its obligation to obey its parents and others that are around it. It regards its own satisfaction or enjoyment as a good, and seeks it, before it knows what the words mean that express this state of mind. It also knows, that the enjoyment of others is a good, and affirms not in word, but in idea, that it ought to seek the enjoyment of all. This idea is the basis upon which all affirmations of obligation rest, and if it be truly an idea of real obligation, it is impossible that the idea of the good, or of the value of enjoyment, should not be its base. To assert the contrary, is to overlook the admitted fact, that moral obligation must respect choice, and the choice of an end; that it must respect intention. It is absurd to suppose, that a being can truly affirm moral obligation, in respect to outward action before he has the idea of the obligation to will, or intend, an end. The idea of an end may not be developed in words, that is, the word expressive of the idea may not be understood, but the idea must be in the mind, in a state of developement, or there can be no affirmation of obligation. The fact is, there is a logical connection between the idea of the good, and the idea of moral obligation, of right and wrong, of praise and blameworthiness. These latter ideas cannot exist without the first, and the existence of that necessitates the developement of these. These are first truths of reason. In other words, these ideas are universally and necessarily developed in the minds of moral agents, and indeed their developement is the condition of moral agency. Most of the first truths are developed in idea, long before the language in which they are expressed is or can be understood. Thus the ideas of space, of time, of causality, of liberty of will, or ability, of the good, of oughtness, or obligation of right and wrong, of praise or blameworthiness, and many others, are developed before the meaning of those words is at all understood. Human beings come gradually to understand the words or signs that represent their ideas, and afterwards, so often express their ideas in words, that they finally get the impression that they received the idea from the word, whereas, in every instance, in respect to the first truths of reason, they had the idea long before they understood, or perhaps ever heard, the word that represents it, and was coined to express it.

9. Those persons who maintain the sinfulness of the constitutional appetites, must of course deny, that man can ever be entirely sanctified in this life, and must maintain, as they do, that death must complete the work of sanctification.

10. False notions of moral depravity lie at the foundation of all the objections I have seen to the doctrine of entire sanctification in this life.

11. A diseased nervous system is a fierce temptation. Some forms of disease expose the soul to much trial. Dyspeptic and nervous persons need superabounding grace.

12. Why sin is so natural to mankind. Not because their nature is itself sinful, but because the appetites and passions tend so strongly to self-indulgence. These are temptations to sin, but sin itself consists not in these appetites and propensities, but in the voluntary committal of the will to their indulgence. This committal of the will is selfishness, and when the will is once given up to sin, it is very natural to sin. The will once committed to self-indulgence as its end, selfish actions are in a sense spontaneous.

13. The doctrine of original sin, as held by its advocates, must essentially modify the whole system of practical theology. This will be seen as we proceed in our investigations.

14. The constitution of a moral being as a whole, when all the powers are developed, does not tend to sin, but strongly in an opposite direction; as is manifest from the fact that when reason is thoroughly developed by the Holy Spirit, it is more than a match for the sensibility, and turns the heart to God.

15. The difficulty is, that the sensibility gets the start of reason, and engages the attention in devising means of self-gratification, and thus retards, and in a great measure prevents, the developement of the ideas of the reason which were designed to control the will.

16. It is this morbid developement that the Holy Spirit is given to rectify, by so forcing truth upon the attention, as to secure the developement of the reason. By doing this, he brings the will under the influence of truth. Our senses reveal to us the objects correlated to our animal nature and propensities. The Holy Spirit reveals God and the spiritual world, and all that class of objects that are correlated to our higher nature, so as to give reason the control of the will. This is regeneration and sanctification, as we shall see in its proper place.

16

**Louis Berkhof**

# The Transmission of Sin

Scripture and experience both teach us that sin is universal, and according to the Bible the explanation for this universality lies in the fall of Adam. These two points, the universality of sin, and the connection of Adam's sin with that of mankind in general, now call for consideration. While there has been rather general agreement as to the universality of sin, there have been different representations of the connection between the sin of Adam and that of his descendants.

## Historical Review

### Before the Reformation

The writings of the Apologists contain nothing definite respecting original sin, while those of Irenaeus and Tertullian clearly teach that our sinful condition is the result of Adam's fall. But the doctrine of the direct imputation of Adam's sin to his descendants is foreign even to them. Tertullian had a realistic conception of mankind. The whole human race

From *Systematic Theology* (Grand Rapids: William B. Eerdmans, 1938), pp. 237-43. Used by permission.

was potentially and numerically present in Adam, and therefore sinned when he sinned and became corrupt when he became corrupt. Human nature as a whole sinned in Adam, and therefore every individualization of that nature is also sinful. Origen, who was profoundly influenced by Greek philosophy, had a different view of the matter, and scarcely recognized any connection between the sin of Adam and that of his descendants. He found the explanation of the sinfulness of the human race primarily in the personal sin of each soul in a pre-temporal state, though he also mentions some mystery of generation. Augustine shared the realistic conception of Tertullian. Though he also spoke of "imputation," he did not yet have in mind the direct or immediate imputation of the guilt of Adam to his posterity. His doctrine of original sin is not entirely clear. This may be due to the fact that he hesitated to choose between traducianism and creationism. While he stresses the fact that all men were seminally present in Adam and actually sinned in him, he also comes very close to the idea that they sinned in Adam as their representative. However, his main emphasis was on the transmission of the *corruption of sin.* Sin is passed on by propagation, and this propagation of Adam's sin is at the same time a punishment for his sin. Wiggers states the idea very briefly in these words: "The corruption of human nature, in the whole race, was the righteous punishment of the transgression of the first man, in whom all men already existed."[1] Augustine's great opponent, Pelagius, denied such a connection between the sin of Adam and those of his posterity. As he saw it, the propagation of sin by generation involved the traducianist theory of the origin of the soul, which he regarded as a heretical error; and the imputation of Adam's sin to anyone but himself would be in conflict with the divine rectitude.

The Pelagian view was rejected by the Church, and the Scholastics in general thought along the lines indicated by Augustine, the emphasis all the while being on the transmission of the pollution of Adam's sin rather than on that of his guilt. Hugo St. Victor and Peter the Lombard held that actual concupiscence stains the semen in the act of procreation, and that this stain in some way defiles the soul on its union with the body. Anselm, Alexander of Hales, and Bonaventura stressed the realistic conception of the connection between Adam and his posterity. The whole human race was seminally present in Adam, and therefore also sinned in him. His disobedience was the disobedience of the entire human race. At the same time generation was regarded as the *sine qua non* of the transmission of the sinful nature. In Bonaventura and others after him the distinction between original guilt and original pollution was more clearly expressed. The fundamental idea was, that the guilt of Adam's sin is imputed to all his descendants. Adam suffered the loss of original righteousness, and thereby incurred the divine displeasure. As a result all his descendants are deprived of original righteousness, and as such the objects of divine wrath. Moreover, the pollution of Adam's sin is in some way passed on to his posterity, but the manner of this transmission was a matter of dispute among the Scholastics. Since they were not traducianists, and therefore could not say that the soul, which is after all the real seat of evil, was passed on from father to son by generation, they felt that something more had to be said to explain the transmission of inherent evil. Some said that it is passed on through the body, which in turn contaminates the soul as soon as it comes in contact with it. Others, sensing the danger of this explanation sought it in the mere fact that every man is now born in the state in which Adam was before he was endowed with original righteousness, and thus subject to the struggle between the unchecked flesh and the spirit. In Thomas Aquinas the realistic strain again appears rather strongly, though in a modified form. He pointed out that the human race constitutes an organism, and that, just as the act of one bodily member—say, the hand—is regarded as the act of the person, so the sin of one member of the organism of humanity is imputed to the whole organism.

### After the Reformation

While the Reformers did not agree with the Scholastics as to the nature of original sin, their view of its transmission did not contain any new elements. The ideas of Adam as the representative of the human race, and of the "immediate" imputation of his guilt to his descendants are not yet clearly expressed in their works. According to Luther we are accounted guilty by God because of the indwelling sin inherited from Adam. Calvin speaks in a somewhat similar vein. He holds that, since Adam was not only the progenitor but the root of the human race, all his descendants are born with a corrupt nature; and that both the guilt of Adam's sin and their own inborn corruption are imputed to them as sin. The development of the federal theology brought the idea of Adam as the representative of the human race to the foreground, and led to a clearer distinction between the transmission of the guilt and of the pollution of Adam's sin. Without denying that our native corruption also constitutes guilt in the sight of God, federal theology stressed the fact that there is an "immediate" imputation of Adam's guilt to those whom he represented as the head of the covenant.

Socinians and Arminians both rejected the idea of the imputation of Adam's sin to his descendants. Placeus, of the school of Saumur, advocated the idea of "mediate" imputation. Denying all immediate imputation, he held that because we inherit a sinful nature from Adam, we are deserving of being treated as if we had committed the original offense. This was something new in Reformed theology, and Rivet had no difficulty in proving this by collecting a long line of testimonies. A debate ensued in which "immediate" and "mediate" imputation were represented as mutually exclusive doctrines; and in which it was made to appear as if the real question was, whether man is guilty in the sight of God solely on account of Adam's sin, imputed to him, or solely on account of his own inherent sin. The former was not the doctrine of the Reformed Churches, and the latter was not taught in them before the time of Placeus. The teachings of the latter found their way into New England theology, and became especially characteristic of the New School (New Haven) theology. In modern liberal theology the doctrine of the transmission of sin from

Adam to his posterity is entirely discredited. It prefers to seek the explanation of the evil that is in the world in an animal inheritance, which is not itself sinful. Strange to say, even Barth and Brunner, though violently opposed to liberal theology, do not regard the universal sinfulness of the human race as the result of Adam's sin. Historically, the latter occupies a unique place merely as the first sinner.

## The Universality of Sin

Few will be inclined to deny the presence of evil in the human heart, however much they may differ as to the nature of this evil and as to the way in which it originated. Even Pelagians and Socinians are ready to admit that sin is universal. This is a fact that forces itself upon the attention of every one.

### The History of Religions and of Philosophy Testify to It

The history of religions testifies to the universality of sin. The question of Job, "How shall a man be just with God?" is a question that was asked not merely in the realm of special revelation, but also outside of it in the Gentile world. The heathen religions testify to a universal consciousness of sin and of the need of reconciliation with a Supreme Being. There is a general feeling that the gods are offended and must be propitiated in some way. There is a universal voice of conscience, testifying to the fact that man falls short of the ideal and stands condemned in the sight of some higher Power. Altars reeking with the blood of sacrifices, often the sacrifices of dear children, repeated confessions of wrong-doing, and prayers for deliverance from evil,—all point to the consciousness of sin. Missionaries find this wherever they go. The history of philosophy is indicative of the same fact. Early Greek philosophers were already wrestling with the problem of moral evil, and since their day no philosopher of name was able to ignore it. They were all constrained to admit the universality of it, and that in spite of the fact they were not able to explain the phenomenon. There was, it is true, a superficial optimism in the eighteenth century, which dreamt of the inherent goodness of man, but in its stupidity flew in the face of the facts and was sharply rebuked by Kant. Many liberal theologians were induced to believe and to preach this inherent goodness of man as gospel truth, but to-day many of them qualify it as one of the most pernicious errors of the past. Surely, the facts of life do not warrant such optimism.

### The Bible Clearly Teaches It

There are direct statements of Scripture that point to the universal sinfulness of man, such as I Kings 8:46; Ps. 143:2; Prov. 20:9; Eccles. 7:20; Rom. 3:1-12, 19, 20, 23; Gal. 3:22; James 3:2; I John 1:8, 10. Several passages of Scripture teach that sin is the heritage of man from the time of his birth, and is therefore present in human nature so early that it cannot possibly be considered as the result of imitation, Ps. 51:5; Job

14:4; John 3:6. In Ephesians 2:3 Paul says of the Ephesians that they "were *by nature* children of wrath, even as the rest." In this passage the term "by nature" points to something inborn and original, as distinguished from what is subsequently acquired. Sin, then, is something original, in which all men participate, and which makes them guilty before God. Moreover, according to Scripture, death is visited even upon those who have never exercised a personal and conscious choice, Rom. 5:12-14. This passage implies that sin exists in the case of infants prior to moral consciousness. Since infants die, and therefore the effect of sin is present in their case, it is but natural to assume that the cause is also present. Finally, Scripture also teaches that all men are under condemnation and therefore need the redemption which is in Christ Jesus. Children are never made an exception to this rule, cf. the preceding passages and also John 3:3, 5; I John 5:12. This is not contradicted by those passages which ascribe a certain righteousness to man, such as, Matt. 9:12, 13; Acts 10:35; Rom. 2:14; Phil. 3:6; I Cor. 1:30, for this may be either civil righteousness, ceremonial or covenant righteousness, the righteousness of the law, or the righteousness which is in Christ Jesus.

### The Connection of Adam's Sin with That of the Race

#### The Denial of This Connection

Some deny the causal connection of the sin of Adam with the sinfulness of the human race either wholly or in part.

a. Pelagians and Socinians deny absolutely that there is any necessary connection between our sin and the sin of Adam. The first sin was Adam's sin only and does not concern his posterity in any way. The most they will admit is that the evil example of Adam led to imitation.

b. Semi-Pelagians and the earlier Arminians teach that man inherited a natural inability from Adam, but is not responsible for this inability, so that no guilt attaches to it, and it may even be said that God is somewhat under obligation to provide a cure for it. The Wesleyan Arminians admit that this inborn corruption also involves guilt.

c. The New School (New Haven) theory teaches that man is born with an inherent tendency to sin, in virtue of which his moral preference is invariably wrong; but that this tendency cannot itself be called sin, since sin always consists exclusively in conscious and intentional transgression of the law.

d. The Theology of crisis stresses the solidarity of sin in the human race, but denies that sin originated in an act of Adam in paradise. The fall belongs to pre- or super-history, and is already a thing of the past when the historical Adam appears upon the scene. It is the secret of God's predestination. The story of the fall is a myth. Adam appears as the type of Christ in so far as it can be seen in him that life without sin is possible in communion with God. Says Brunner: "In Adam all have sinned—that is the Biblical statement; but how? The Bible does not tell us that. The doctrine of original sin is read into it."[2]

### Different Theories to Explain the Connection

a. *The realistic theory.* The earliest method of explaining the connection between the sin of Adam and the guilt and pollution of all his descendants was the realistic theory. This theory is to the effect that human nature constitutes, not only generically but numerically as well, a single unit. Adam possessed the whole human nature, and in him it corrupted itself by its own voluntary apostatizing act in Adam. Individual men are not separate substances, but manifestations of the same general substance; they are numerically one. This universal human nature became corrupt and guilty in Adam, and consequently every individualization of it in the descendants of Adam is also corrupt and guilty from the very beginning of its existence. This means that all men *actually* sinned in Adam before the individualization of human nature began. This theory was accepted by some of the early Church Fathers and by some of the Scholastics, and was defended in more recent times by Dr. Shedd. However, it is open to several objections: (1) By representing the souls of men as individualizations of the general spiritual substance that was present in Adam, it would seem to imply that the substance of the soul is of a material nature, and thus to land us inevitably in some sort of materialism. (2) It is contrary to the testimony of consciousness and does not sufficiently guard the interests of human personality. Every man is conscious of being a separate personality, and therefore far more than a mere passing wave in the general ocean of existence. (3) It does not explain why Adam's descendants are held responsible for his first sin only, and not for his later sins, nor for the sins of all the generations of forefathers that followed Adam. (4) Neither does it give an answer to the important question, why Christ was not held responsible for the *actual* commission of sin in Adam, for He certainly shared the same human nature, the nature that *actually* sinned in Adam.

b. *The doctrine of the covenant of works.* This implies that Adam stood in a twofold relationship to his descendants, namely, that of the natural head of all mankind, and that of the *representative head* of the entire human race in the covenant of works. (1) *The natural relationship.* In his natural relationship Adam was the father of all mankind. As he was created by God he was subject to change, and had no rightful claim to an unchangeable state. He was in duty bound to obey God, and this obedience did not entitle him to any reward. On the other hand, if he sinned, he would become subject to corruption and to punishment, but the sin would be only his own, and could not be placed to the account of his descendants. Dabney holds that, according to the law that like begets like, his corruption would have passed on to his descendants. But however this may be—and it is rather useless to speculate about it—they certainly could not have been held responsible for this corruption. They could not have been considered guilty in Adam merely in virtue of the natural relationship in which Adam stood to the race. The usual Reformed representation is a different one. (2) *The covenant relationship.* To the natural relationship in which Adam stood to his descendants God graciously added a covenant relationship containing several positive elements: (a) *An element of repre-*

*sentation.* God ordained that in this covenant Adam should not stand for himself only, but as the representative of all his descendants. Consequently, he was the head of the race not only in a parental, but also in a federal sense. (b) *An element of probation.* While apart from this covenant Adam and his descendants would have been in a continual state of trial, with a constant danger of sinning, the covenant guaranteed that persistent perseverance for a fixed period of time would be rewarded with the establishment of man in a permanent state of holiness and bliss. (c) *An element of reward or punishment.* According to the terms of the covenant Adam would obtain a rightful claim to eternal life, if he fulfilled the conditions of the covenant. And not only he, but all his descendants as well would have shared in this blessing. In its normal operation, therefore, the covenant arrangement would have been of incalculable benefit for mankind. But there was a possibility that man would disobey, thereby reversing the operation of the covenant, and in that case the results would naturally be correspondingly disastrous. Transgression of the covenant commandment would result in death. Adam chose the course of disobedience, corrupted himself by sin, became guilty in the sight of God, and as such subject to the sentence of death. And because he was the federal representative of the race, his disobedience affected all his descendants. In His righteous judgment God imputes the guilt of the first sin, committed by the head of the covenant, to all those that are federally related to him. And as a result they are born in a depraved and sinful condition as well, and this inherent corruption also involves guilt. This doctrine explains why only the first sin of Adam, and not his following sins nor the sins of our other forefathers, is imputed to us, and also safeguards the sinlessness of Jesus, for He was not a human person and therefore not in the covenant of works.

c. *The theory of mediate imputation.* This theory denies that the guilt of Adam's sin is *directly* imputed to his descendants, and represents the matter as follows: Adam's descendants derive their innate corruption from him by a process of natural generation, and only on the basis of that inherent depravity which they share with him are they also considered guilty of his apostasy. They are not born corrupt because they are guilty in Adam, but they are considered guilty because they are corrupt. Their condition is not based on their legal status, but their legal status on their condition. This theory, first advocated by Placeus, was adopted by the younger Vitringa and Venema, by several New England theologians, and by some of the New School theologians in the Presbyterian Church. This theory is objectionable for several reasons: (1) A thing cannot be mediated by its own consequences. The inherent depravity with which the descendants of Adam are born is already the result of Adam's sin, and therefore cannot be considered as the basis on which they are guilty of the sin of Adam. (2) It offers no objective ground whatsoever for the transmission of Adam's guilt and depravity to all his descendants. Yet there must be some objective legal ground for this. (3) If this theory were consistent, it ought to teach the mediate imputation of the sins of all previous generations to those following, for their joint corruption is passed on by generation. (4) It also proceeds on the assumption that there can be no moral corruption that is not at the same time guilt, a corruption that does not in itself make one liable to punishment. (5) And finally, if the inherent corruption which is present in the descendants of Adam can be regarded as the *legal* ground for the explanation of something else, there is no more need of any mediate imputation.

## Notes

[1] *Augustinism and Pelagianism*, p. 88.

[2] *Man in Revolt*, p. 142.

## 17

**Russell Shedd**

# Paul's Conception
# of Human Solidarity

## Introduction

The study of the Old Testament and Jewish thought in the general period of the Second Temple has been conducted for the purpose of disclosing the sources of the conceptions of solidarity which are reflected in the Epistles of Paul. Our present task is to present the Pauline ideas of unity and their relationship to these source materials.

At the outset we must justify this portion of our investigation by considering the implications of the conversion experience of the Apostle. But for that event, the rest of our study would not only be unnecessary, but impossible. Saul of Tarsus might have been another of the illustrious Rabbis of his day.[1] As a matter of fact, because of his experience on the Damascus Road, a re-orientation of thought transpired. (1) Many ideas were completely reversed; these are exemplified in the controversies with Judaizers and elsewhere. (2) Other ideas were incorporated into his system of thought unchanged. (3) Still another category of conceptions was subjected to the principle of "stimulus diffusion." This term refers to an old

From *Man in Community* (Grand Rapids: William B. Eerdmans, 1964), pp. 93-125. Used by permission.

idea given a new orientation or content; the old and the new agree in form only.[2] Of these three classifications, the latter two alone concern us.

Before we proceed to the central objective in Part Two, it will be necessary to explain the omission of various Hellenistic systems of thought which have been proposed as the background of Paul's conception of human solidarity by an influential segment of scholarship. We will discuss briefly the most plausible Hellenistic sources and objections to them.

## Stoicism

Because there was a Stoic "school" in Tarsus,[3] a presumption is lodged that Paul must have been influenced by this philosophy. But the objections overrule the evidence. In the Stoic system, man was a part of nature, or more accurately a member.[4] Man was declared to be mortal by reason of his body, which decayed, but immortal by reason of his οὐσιώδης ἄνθρωπος ("essential humanity").[5] The fundamental unity of the cosmos constituted a living being, an organic unity.[6] The life which animates the cosmic organism is the true reason (λόγος ὀρθός),[7] or alternatively τὸ τοῦ κόσμου πνεῦμα ("the spirit of the world").[8] Reason is the essence of the divine. Since it is the common possession of all men, humanity is the incarnation of God, a portion of the universal pantheism;[9] in Epictetus' memorable phrase the soul is "a fragment of God."[10] It is this feature of the Greek system which most radically contrasts with the fundamental Hebraic distinction between God and Man. The Stoic conception of the immanence of the divine would have been utterly revolting to a Jew.

As a Jewish theist, Paul maintains the impassable gulf between the Creator, who in self-consciousness is free to will into existence that which is, and man, the creature, as the object of the divine creative will.[11] The bond of Paul's human solidarity is not divine immanence or a metaphysical unity. It is only through a mediated κοινωνία ("fellowship"), that the one God may be imparted to mankind.[12] The basic division between God and man in Paul's view, justifies our search for the source-background of his thought in his Hebraic heritage, rather than in Stoicism,[13] Platonism,[14] or other less important Greek philosophical systems. In these, abstract thought is paramount in contrast to the empirical conclusions of the Jewish mind.[15] For this reason great caution must be exercised in the interpretation of words and ideas in the Epistles which might be assumed to bear their normal Hellenistic association.

## Gnosticism

Other scholars have sought to trace Pauline dependence on Gnostic mythology, particularly in his doctrine of the organic unity of the race.[16] But this position raises numerous problems in its attempt to correlate the Gnostic view of sin and redemption with Pauline theology. For the former system evil is not primarily a moral phenomenon but purely natural; it becomes identical with the imperfect, the relative, and the finite.[17] The dualism presupposed by such an understanding of evil, is far closer to

Philo's thought (in which the realm of settled being and the world of becoming had by nature tendencies frequently at variance with the good of the totality)[18] than it is to Paulinism.[19] Docetism and dualism of a Hellenistic variety (the evil matter captivating a good spirit) is not only unknown in the Epistles, but it is actively controverted by Paul.[20] The dualism of Pauline theology is exclusively moral, not metaphysical.[21] We shall have occasion to return to this contention in the last chapter where a fuller discussion of the differences of the conception of solidarity in Paul from Gnostic mythology will be presented.

## The Mystery Religions

A third source for the Pauline doctrines of redemption and anthropology has been sought in the Hellenistic Mystery Religions. The importance of these Cults in the Roman Empire of the first century in conjunction with the similarity of the Pauline terminology, has given the case considerable plausibility in the minds of notable sponsors such as R. Reitzenstein,[22] W. Bousset,[23] K. Lake,[24] among a number. The similarities have been well summarized by H. A. A. Kennedy:

> Like the Mystery religions, he proclaimed a great "redemption." Like them he could point to a "knowledge" of God which meant not intellectual apprehension but practical fellowship. Like them he could think of a transformation into the Divine likeness which was the very goal of being. . . . But his presuppositions were different. Redemption from *sin* was primary with him, not redemption from *fate*.[25]

There are other reasons for denying any essential relationship between Christianity according to Paul and the Mysteries. W. D. Davies has suggested some of the most fundamental divergencies.[26] (1) The Mysteries were individualistic while Christianity is social—incorporation into a Community, the Body of Christ.[27] (2) The Hellenistic religious experience depended on mythological creations and speculative reconstruction; Christianity was founded on recent historical events and persons. Its founding was witnessed by individuals then alive. (3) There is no mystical absorption in Christianity such as the Mysteries promulgated. (4) There is no counterpart to faith (in the Pauline sense) in the Mystery religions. (5) The whole atmosphere of Christianity is radically different from that of the Mysteries.

As in other areas of thought and experience, the clue to a proper understanding of the relationship between Paul and alien religious ideas is found in "stimulus diffusion." In the Apostle's search for a meaningful terminology, he was obliged to adopt terms with which his audience was acquainted; but, he gave new meanings to them in the new context of Christianity.[28] In Paul, mysticism is always subordinate to monotheism.[29] The human plight is not immersion in an irresponsible εἱμαρμένη, but a moral solidarity in sin. Redemption is not mystical absorption into an esoteric and consequently irresponsible Mystery; justification is cast in ethical terms of holiness and absolute moral purity (cf. Eph. 5:27; 4:17-5:16).[30]

The procedure to be followed in this chapter is the presentation of the basis of Paul's view of human solidarity and the implications which are derived from it in the Epistles. Of primary importance in the first section are both the unity of God and the origin of mankind from one ancestor. The second part of the chapter will examine the representative character of Adam and the corporate personality of the race in Adam. The implications of the corporate judgement of Adam and racial involvement in the Old Aeon will be treated in that context as a preparation for the discussion of the last chapter and the conception of the solidarity of the redeemed and re-created humanity.

## The Foundations of the Solidarity of the Race

The unity of all mankind is a presupposition transferred without challenge from Judaism and the Old Testament into the theology of the Epistles of Paul. The conception is of such a fundamental nature that one searches almost in vain for explicit declarations of the proposition. While there is no argument for what W. Wrede calls "an undefinable coherence between the race and the individual,"[31] the assumed unity of the race is the only possible explanation in Paul's mind for the universality of sin and all the determining factors in human existence apart from the obvious inter-relationship of cause and effect (e.g. environmental or personal influence, etc.). This presupposition was not held by Paul in isolation or superimposed by him upon the contemporary scene, but it was a solidarity which he perceived to be rooted in the original creation of man.

### The Implications of the Unity of God

The threshold of Paul's doctrine of the unity of mankind, is the unity of God or his Jewish monotheism.[32] Without recourse to the pantheism of current pagan cults and philosophy, the Apostle's doctrine adheres to the unity of the Creator as the cause and ground for the unity of the race. It was impossible for him to conceive of men as the atomistic offspring or creations of sundry deities. Individual men are the branches of a human tree growing in its historical dimension from a single seed. It was God who had created and planted that seed which makes of men an organic unity.

The most explicit reference to human unity in its derivation from the Creator, is made in the Mars Hill address. Paul declares that humanity as a whole is the offspring (γένος) of God (Acts 17:28-29)[33] implying a common unity akin to the Jewish conception of the corporate sonship of Israel. Although it is impossible to determine any direct relationship between the two ideas, the underlying conception is the same. Both predicate a corporate divine sonship[34] to a group without denying the creation of that group in history (cf. Col. 1:16-17 with Deut. 32:6, 18).[35] The intention of Paul in using this terminology was two-fold. On the one hand, it implies the unity of the race; on the other, a common responsibility incurred through the total family relationship to the Creator. In a less defined form, this same idea is found in Ephesians 3:15. Referring to God as the Father in the preceding verse, Paul continues: "From whom every family in heaven and on earth is named. . . ." The term Father in the same context, and the Hebraic connotation of the term, "name," suggests the idea of a family possessed by God and its consequent responsibility. The reference to the Fatherhood of God is not clear in another passage in Ephesians (4:6: ". . . One God and Father of us all, who is above all and through and in all") as to its scope. Whether it is restricted to the Church or not, however, all of these passages seek to establish the unity of the corporate son or family while they declare the united responsibility of the race to God.

It is in this relationship of man to God that Paul's conception of righteousness finds its basic application. Neither sin nor perfection can be judged by a human standard. "There is not one righteous among men" (cf. Acts 17:30; Rom. 3:19, 23; 5:12)[36] makes reference to the corporate and individual failure of man to fulfil the requirements of the divine standard.[37]

The basis for Paul's doctrine of responsibility is man's creation by one holy and personal God. The nature of human responsibility is dual; there is the duty towards God and a concomitant duty toward fellow men. The two areas of responsibility interpenetrate each other in such a way that they are not always distinguishable. Paul felt no obligation to argue for this point on the basis of man created in the *Imago Dei*. In the existence of the law and man's rationality, the dual responsibility of the race is self-evident. Mankind is universally faced with the requirement of maintaining a moral standard which is his through creation by God.[38] The revelation of this standard to man was made in two distinct ways, involving corresponding dimensions of human solidarity.

(1) The Special Revelation given to Israel.—Paul teaches that it is the former Jewish law which embodies the revealed will of God for His creatures (Rom. 2:18). It provided the gauge by which man must be judged (Rom. 2:12; Gal. 3:10).[39] The Jews, however, despite their boasting the privileged role as bearers of God's standard (Rom. 3:2) and doers of His will (Rom. 2:17), had fallen far short of its requirements. In brief, they had done the same things for which they had condemned Gentile sinners outside the law (Rom. 2:1, 18-29). The conclusion of the argument is the corporate guilt of Israel and its consequent condemnation before God (Rom. 3:9).

(2) The Natural Revelation given to Mankind.—The objection might have been raised that the law could only determine the responsibility of those to whom it was accessible. This problem was recognized by Paul. In his estimation, it provided the primary distinction between the Jew and the Gentile. Yet the Gentile was not without law of some kind. This conclusion was confirmed in the Apostle's mind by the fact that non-Jews in some cases fulfilled the basic principles of the law. It was written on the heart, witnessed to by the συνείδησις ("conscience"), and provided the

basis for the comparative judging of one man by another (Rom. 2:14-15).[40]

Roughly equivalent to the conscience is the νοῦς. This term is used to designate that element in man which knows the good and apparently would accomplish it, were it accorded the sufficient power (cf. Rom. 7:22-23, 25).[41] But both conscience and mind may be defiled, cancelling any good which they might otherwise instigate (see Titus 1:15; cf. 3:11). It is quite possible that this innate element opposed to τὸ φρόνημα τῆς σαρκός represents the Rabbinic *yetzer hatob*.[42] But the mind, unaided, is strictly limited in its ability to understand and respond to the wisdom of God.[43] But even as the Jews have fallen short of their duty in observing the revealed law, the Gentiles have violated the innate law written on the heart. "The fearful vices which beset the Gentile world are due to the rejection of τὴν φυσικὴν χρῆσιν for τὴν παρὰ φύσιν χρῆσιν" (Rom. 1:26).[44] This natural law, apprehensible to the "mind," is undoubtedly equivalent to the Jewish Rabbinical preceptive code known as the Noachian commandments. This name denotes their universality through humanity's common descent from Noah.[45] These precepts, given to Adam under similar circumstances to the revelation of the Torah to Israel, were indelibly inscribed in the hearts of all Adam's descendants. It is described by Paul as the revelation to all men from the foundation of the world, the "truth held in unrighteousness" (Rom. 1:18-32). It further serves as the basis of man's inexcusability (Rom. 1:20) and universal guilt apart from the question of the possession of the Mosaic Torah (a more external and expanded form of the innate law—Rom. 2:12).[46]

It is of supreme importance to recognize at this juncture that any conception of an inherent or universal law can be predicated only on the basis of the solidarity of the race. If a Stoic or Hellenistic conception of the cosmic spirit is rejected on the grounds of Paul's doctrine of creation as the source of the common unity of the race, we are left with no alternative to the Hebraic postulation of the unity of the race through creation and heredity. The corollary of this conviction in both Judaism and Paul's mind is the corporate responsibility of the race to God in a vertical dimension and to one another on a horizontal level.

Although Paul postulated the conception of a racial solidarity, it does not imply that a common unity amongst men could be found in his day. The universal kinship of mankind should have found its expression in a universal *koinonia;* but, with the severance of the covenantal bond of unity with God (Rom. 1:18-32) came an inevitable dissolution of the external bond of love which should have united all men.[47] The incursion of sin (i.e. failure in responsibility to God) brought strife and factions into the human scene. For this reason Paul condemned the Christians of Corinth for walking as (κατά) men in their tolerance of schismatic splinters within the Church (I Cor. 3:3; cf. verse 4: οὐκ ἀνθρωποί ἐστε). As Israel had broken the special covenant (cf. Jer: 11:10; 22:9), the Gentiles have broken the "natural" covenant, especially in idolatry and immorality (cf. Rom. 1:23-24 with Isa. 24:5).

## The Implication of Common Descent from One Man

The clearest declaration of the means by which the solidarity of the race is secured is not found in the Epistles but in Paul's sermon on the Areopagus (Acts 17:22-31). It was apparently a fundamental feature of his earliest message to a Gentile audience to emphasize the unity of the race because of its descent from the first man to be created. In any case, we are not left to speculation in Paul's message to the Athenians. In this sermon Paul establishes the organic unity of the race and a concomitant responsibility of each individual on the basis of the universal human descent from one ancestor.[48] In the record preserved by Luke he says: "And (God) has made of one (man)[49] every race ($\pi\hat{\alpha}\nu$ ἔθνος) of men to live on all the face of the earth, having determined allotted periods and the boundaries of their habitation, that they should seek God . . ." (Acts 17:26-27). The implication of the postulate is no less than the universal kinship of all men. It is the logical expansion and conclusion of the Old Testament conception of the family, in which either the kin-group immediately, or a whole nation, was designated a *miš*[e]*pāhāh* on the basis of common descent. The exclusivism which prevented Judaism from capitalizing on the postulation of a universal brotherhood of mankind was contradicted in the teaching of Jesus to which Paul became heir (cf. e.g. John 10:16; Matt. 5:22, 23-24, 47; 7:3-5; 18:15, 21, 35). Paul further relates the proposition of a common kinship to descent from one man. This provides the first element in the involved teaching of the Epistles which conceives of Adam as the ancestor and head of the race. Mankind is consequently a corporate unit. It is a totality of an identical character to that of Israel in the Old Testament and early Jewish thought. As Abraham was ascribed the determining role of an ancestor of the nation bearing his name, Adam's character and decisions have implicated his race.[50] This means that the human race composes a corporate personality in Paul's theology and that Adam as its ancestral head and realistic representative is its determinative figure.

The importance of the Apostle's adoption of the conception of the corporate personality of the kin-group without qualification from the Old Testament is readily seen. Far from being the application of a principle which was endorsed by human psychological and social exigencies, Paul establishes the basis of this solidarity in the eternal counsels of God. Herein is the justification of divine election and predestination. As long as Esau is Edom and *vice versa*, there is no injustice in the indistinguishable hatred of the one or animosity toward the other (Rom. 9:11-13; cf. Mal. 1:3-4). The expanded application of the principle of corporate personality by Paul has long since been proposed by H. W. Robinson,[51] and adopted by C. H. Dodd,[52] A. Nygren,[53] and most fully by E. Best,[54] to explain the problematic Pauline mysticism. As we proceed, it will become increasingly apparent that the whole of Paul's anthropology and soteriology is built on Hebraic conceptions of the solidarity of the race.

Within the scope of Paul's general conception of Adam and the corporate personality of the race are two distinctions which, upon their recognition, aid in the understanding of his thought. The first is the role of

Adam as the ancestor of the race, involving his historicity as the first man to be created (cf. Acts 17:26; I Cor. 15:45, 47-50).[55] The second is Adam as the realistic representative of the race, cast in the role of a collective personality (cf. Rom. 5:12-21; I Cor. 15:21-22). The race is identified with Adam and Adam with the race in such a manner that the experience and consequent judgement of both are mutual.[56] The collective totality (*the many*) has both a horizontal and vertical extension, so that all men are "in Adam" (*the one,* I Cor. 15:22) at any given point in history as well as throughout all history. These two distinctions are not to be treated as though they were mutually exclusive but have been adopted primarily for convenience.

## The Fatherhood of Adam and the Terrestrial Character of His Progeny

On the basis of our presupposition that Paul accepted the historicity of Adam, it will be necessary to examine briefly the account of the creation of man in the Old Testament. The Genesis narrative establishes the formation of Adam from the dust (*āpār*) of the earth (Gen. 2:7), creation in the image and likeness of God (1:27; 5:1), his animation by living breath (2:7), his naming in conjunction with Eve as *ādām* ("man") (Gen. 5:2), his unique position in the creation as lord (1:26; cf. 2:15, 19-20), his unique role as the progenitor of the race (1:28; cf. 3:20). By noting the nature of Adam through creation and the nature of humanity as it is, Paul concluded that the latter is a derivation from the former. For this reason, the three basic characteristics of natural humanity have been determined by the solidarity of all mankind with Adam who was the original human creation. But the implications of human generic relationship to Adam must be distinguished from Adam's realistic representative role. Generically, the historical Adam has determined the human possession of a perishable, "soulish," and fleshly body.

### The Perishable Body

The first implication which we shall consider is the corruptibility of the human body. In the words of Paul:

> The first man was from the earth (γῆς; cf. *āpār*, Gen. 2:7), a man of dust (χοϊκός). . . . As was the (man) of dust, so are those who are of dust (οἱ χοϊκοί). . . . Just as we have borne the image (εἰκόνα) of the man of dust, we shall also bear the image of the man of heaven. I tell you this, brethren: flesh and blood cannot inherit the kingdom of God, nor does the perishable inherit the imperishable (I Cor. 15:47-50; cf. Rom. 1:23).

In this passage, the Apostle compares the body of the first man with that of all men. He recognizes the incontrovertible fact that human flesh is subject to the laws of natural decay. Thus, the mortality of the flesh is one of its essential characteristics (I Cor. 15:44, 50; cf. II Cor. 4:11, 16; 5:1;

Rom. 6:12). Man is a part of the changeable physical order.[57] His finitude is equivalent to the Old Testament description of man as grass (cf. e.g. Isa. 40:6-7; Ps. 103:15). This was common knowledge to both Paul and the troubled Corinthian Christians. It is the Apostle's vehement argument that there is a logical necessity for the resurrection because of the perishable nature of man's body which cannot exist in the New Order; rather, the body must be re-created after the pattern of Christ's glorious body (I Cor. 15:49; cf. II Cor. 5:1).

It is more than incidental to Paul's case that there is no definite allusion to the relationship of mankind to Adam through natural descent; if there had been, it would have destroyed the parallel between Adam and Christ and their respective communities. It is apparent in the context that the medium of the actualization of the old creation is the natural process of birth,[58] while the New Humanity is created through a supernatural process of inclusion into Christ (II Cor. 5:17).

## The Psychic Body

In a further refinement of his point Paul describes the natural body as ψυχικόν ("soulish"). "If there is a 'soulish' body, there is also a spiritual body. So also it is written, the first man, Adam became a living soul" (I Cor. 14:44-45).[59] This is an extension of the comparison between humanity and Adam. Not only is the human body corporeal, but the life principle which animates it derives its finite character from the original *nepeš ḥayyâ* of Adam. All men partake of this creative life principle which stands over against the new life principle of the New Creation (τὸ πνευματικόν), which is not temporal but eternal (I Cor. 15:45-46). Again, the explanation for the common possession of a "soulish" body, is the natural process of procreation. "As the same flesh and blood, so also, so to speak, the same soul essence is propagated through the human race."[60]

## The Body of Flesh

The third basic element in Paul's anthropology is mankind as σάρξ. A considerable amount of confusion has centred around conjectures introduced to explain the Apostle's broad and enigmatic use of this term.[61] Burton suggests seven distinctive uses of the term from the reference to the merely physical nature of man's body, all the way to an "element that makes for sin."[62] For our purposes, a simpler classification suggested by Wahlstrom is quite adequate: (1) the ordinary sense of the material flesh (cf. e.g. Gal. 4:13; I Cor. 15:39); (2) σάρξ used as the symbol of human existence.[63] It is vital for our study to further sub-divide the second category into human nature apart from any connotation of sin, and σάρξ as a symbol of man's involvement in the Old Aeon.[64] In this sub-division, we may note a very distinct echo from the Old Testament conception of *bāśār*.[65] On the one hand, it defined the kin-group constituted of one flesh through generic descent. On the other, *bāśār* was used to describe a relationship which could be acquired, such as one might secure through the union of marriage (cf. Gen. 2:24 with Eph. 5:29) which was essentially spiritual in its character. When "flesh" denoted an acquired relationship, it was often given an ethical connotation. Thus, it was "flesh" which corrupted itself (i.e. morally, cf. Gen. 6:12) in all the earth.

Corresponding to the distinctions in the Old Testament, σάρξ is used by Paul to refer to a purely racial or physical symbol (cf. Col. 2:5 [note I Cor. 5:3]; Gal. 4:14 [note I Cor. 6:13]); however, in the context of the Old Age, the "flesh" has a very definite ethical connotation, a characteristic achieved through acquisition.[66] We shall discuss this latter usage under the implications of the corporate judgement of Adam.

## Conclusion

We have sought in this section to present the implications which natural descent had for the human race as the progeny of Adam. The three terms, body, soul, and flesh, are variously used by the Apostle to describe the creaturely finitude of mankind. We have also contended that the universality of these characteristics is an evidence of the Old Testament conception of the family, in which the succeeding generations share in the *bāśār* of the ancestor. There is more. As in the Old Testament, flesh is a totality denomination which is descriptive of the solidarity of the group; so in Paul, ". . . σάρξ stands for man, in the solidarity of creation in his distance from God."[67] Such an idea of a universal totality comes primarily from the Old Testament period of Hebrew thought.

There may be some intimations of a Rabbinic doctrine of the creation of the race in Adam. As the summary of Davies shows, there was a type of mythological unity of the race mediated through its origin:

> That doctrine implied that the very constitution of the physical body of Adam and the method of its formation was symbolic of the real oneness of mankind. In that one body of Adam, east and west, north and south were brought together, male and female, as we have seen. The "body" of Adam included all mankind.[68]

The Jewish doctrine of human reproduction maintained that the physical and natural body was the heritage from the parents. The soul was infused directly by God. If we are restricted in this particular section to treating the naturally inherited characteristics of the race, it would be correct to see a coincidence between the Old Testament and Judaism as the background. On the other hand, Paul's emphasis on the universal kinship of all men, savours more of the ancient conception of the race as the extension of the flesh or the soul of the ancestor.

## Adam's Realistic Representation of the Race

### *The Corporate Transgression*

Our detailed study of the conception of corporate personality in the Old Testament indicated that realistic representation of a group might devolve on the head of that group. It might in one case be the father, in others, a master, priest, or king. Paul did not choose to emphasize the hereditary relationship in his doctrine of mankind's corporate involvement in sin and death.[69] His sole purpose in mentioning the relationship of Adam to his progeny is to draw a direct antithetical parallel between Adam, including his community, and Christ, including the New Humanity.[70] If we heed Barth's warning to interpret Adam as merely the type of the real thing, that is, the Christ-collectivity,[71] we are forced to allow that realistic representation is the primary element in Paul's Adam-typology.

Paul's discussion of Adam's representative role in the introduction of sin is confined in large to two passages: (1) Romans 5:12-21 is central. (2) In a more contracted form, the same theme occurs in I Corinthians 15:21-22: "Wherefore since by ($\delta\iota\acute{\alpha}$) (one) man is death, also through (one) man is the resurrection of the dead. For as in Adam all die, so also in Christ shall all be made to live."

The theme of these passages is the relationship of the one to the many. One man (in this case, Adam) sinned. Because of his realistic representation of the race, his original transgression was not isolated, but corporately involved the whole of the race.[72] It is Adam's position as the archetypal head of the race, which he embodies as a corporate personality, that makes his rebellion against God the revolt of his group. Under such a conception (particularly as it is found in the Old Testament) it was quite possible for Paul to see the individual and the group as identical. This identity is evident in such a phrase as, e.g. "in Adam" (cf. I Cor. 15:22), which is the direct converse of the phrase, "in Christ."

But does Paul actually intend that his readers should understand that in Adam's disobedience all men in some mystical manner participated? This question has both perplexed and divided interpreters down through the history of Pauline exegesis.[73] If we examine this passage in the light of the principle of corporate personality a two-fold answer is probably justified.

(1) Yes, we must in the first analysis admit that Adam's sin was corporate or shared by all men.[74] The use of the aorist, $\mathring{\eta}\mu\alpha\rho\tau o\nu$, is an indication in this direction.[75] In the words of A. Nygren: "If we are to keep the translation, 'because all have sinned,' we shall have to understand it as Augustine did, 'all men have sinned in Adam.' "[76] A confirmation of this conclusion is found in Romans 5:19, where a direct antithesis is drawn between the disobedience of Adam and the obedience of Christ. In II Corinthians 5:14 this act is explicitly defined as the corporate death of Christ: "For the love of Christ constrains us, this judging, that one died for all; then indeed all died" ($\mathring{\alpha}\pi\acute{\epsilon}\theta\alpha\nu o\nu$). On the basis of the realistic representation of the heads of the two respective types of humanity, Paul affirms that the two corresponding groups have actually participated in the archetypal acts of human history. Only on such a basis, can any adequate parallel be drawn between the original transgression of Adam and the obedience of the Second Adam.

(2) The second aspect of Paul's answer rests on the empirical fact of

the universal human endorsement of Adam's representative act. The aspect of oscillation in the Hebrew conception of corporate personality comes into view as the focus turns to examine mankind. It is noteworthy that Paul does not even begin his theology of Romans with a reference to the corporate transgression of Adam; on the contrary, it is his conclusion.[77] In the interest of establishing the universal involvement of the human race in sin, no mention is made of Adam at all. It is the unfolding of the sordid human story, the increasing corruption within the group and individual relationships through following one's free choice.[78] Nor was Paul's introduction of Adam as the source of sin intended in any sense to detract from man's responsibility for sin. It is of the very essence of Paul's argument to maintain the complete inexcusability of man. This individual option is particularly evident in Romans 7. There Paul depicts every man as "the Adam of his own soul" since the powerful influence of sin comes to overcome and deceive him, yet not apart from the self-determinate will of the individual.[79]

For Paul, our division of the answer to the original question into two opposing aspects, would savour of a scholastic distinction. As long as the one is the many, and the many are the one, no distinction is necessary between the sin of the representative and that of his group.[80] In itself, the whole issue was less problematic than the corporate treatment of the sin of Achan or David would have been; there is a vindication of God's treatment of Adam's sin as a racial act in the universal human adoption of his way. In the particular conception of solidarity which Paul applies to the whole race, the archetypal action of the representative is indistinguishable from the innumerable acts of members within the human totality.[81] But this is not true only because of the solidarity of mankind. As we have already discovered in the Old Testament and Judaism, sin was itself unconfined to the individual. It was organic, contagious, invariably involving the group in guilt.[82] Like dye when poured into a body of water discolours the whole, so the original pollution has spread from the fountain-head to sully the entire human stream. In this manner, Adam's Fall and the universal guilt and propensity to sin are inseparably bound together.[83] Both the unity of the race and the impossibility of maintaining sin's immurement produce the confirmation of Paul's doctrine.

### The Corporate Judgement

A further confirmation of the doctrine of the corporate sin of the race was deduced by Paul from the corporate judgement of the race. Holding an unmitigated conception of the justice of God, there assuredly could be no punishment where there was neither guilt nor sin. On the basis of the fact that sin can be imputed only on the ground of a transgression of law (Rom. 5:13; cf. 4:15) and the second consideration that there was no law existent between Adam and Moses, the universal punishment of the race with death implies the corporate sin of the race in Adam (Rom. 5:13-14).[84] Since there could be no sin as individual transgression between the original injunction laid upon Adam and the revelation of the

Torah, it is Paul's conclusive argument that the race sinned in Adam. Despite the absence of sin as individual transgression, death reigned over all; it was the application of corporate justice at the provocation of a corporate transgression.[85]

In the whole of this discussion we are forced to see the Jewish heritage of Paul. In both the Old Testament and the postcanonical Jewish writings, the conception of a divine corporate justice is frequently encountered. As the group might be punished with or for the sin of a member who represents the group realistically, the whole race is involved in the judgement of Adam's archetypal act. It is the expansion of the idea of demerit from its normal restriction to Israel, and a re-application to the human totality. One is further impressed by the organic nature of Paul's thinking. Inseparably related to the proposition of a corporate sin is the individual's free choice of evil. The corporate judgement of God, applied on the basis of the solidarity or corporate personality of the race, is vindicated by the individual's willingly entangling himself in guilt. For these reasons, it is quite unrealistic to maintain stubbornly that Paul is dependent upon specific Jewish documents such as *IV Ezra* or *II Baruch,* or even the opinions of certain Rabbis. The principles were right at hand. That which is unique in the Apostle's thought, apparently, are contrasting deductions arising out of his soteriological doctrine of Christ's realistic representation of the New Humanity.[86]

## The Solidarity of Humanity in the Old Aeon

### Introduction

We have already attempted to establish the contention that Paul applied the Hebraic ideas of kinship and corporate personality to the entire race of men. This, however, does not exhaust the Apostle's conception of the solidarity of the race. Other passages, as well as those which have been examined, posit the mysterious conception of an Old Aeon or Age (αἰών). The connotation of the term involves both the solidarity of the creation and a corresponding continuity of humanity under subjection to powerful forces which control all material existence. O. Cullmann has made a noteworthy contribution to a biblical understanding of the Aeon in his book *Christ and Time.* He correctly shows that in the Hebraic conception of man, humanity is not isolated in the Creation. On the contrary, man holds a representative position over all that God has made.[87] In the New Testament man's exalted role of lordship in the Creation lies behind the solidarity which is inferred to exist between man and nature (cf. Rom. 8:19-23. See Gen. 3:17-19 and Jewish views, pp. 73-6 *supra*). For this reason, the curse of corporate humanity in Adam implicates the rest of creation.[88]

In man's miserable failure to effect the destiny which was designed for him by God, he is actually allying himself with the nefarious forces of the Old Age in open rebellion against the universal authority of God. United together, it has become the formation of an enemy stronghold within

God's universal state. If we were to ask how this all came about, the accusing finger again points to Adam, who was responsible for bringing the race into this alien alliance. As the Apostle does not in stated terms ascribe this initiatory role to Adam, this point is clear only as it can be derived from the Adam-Christ parallel.

In this parallel, certain facts may be deduced. In the relationship of the redeemed to Christ (who is the Figure under discussion, Adam's antitype), there is no question of a hereditary connexion. Rather, it is the One taking the place of the many, including them in Himself (note the reiteration of this idea in Rom. 5:8-21; I Cor. 15:19-28, 45-49). The Community is related to Christ through faith and personal choice in such a manner that He, as their Representative, does in and for them what they could not do for themselves (cf. Rom. 5:8). An identically inclusive role is played by Adam, who as the first man is the universal archetype of all men, a sort of comprehensive personality.[89] As Christ implicated the New Humanity in the New Age, Adam has involved his race in the Old.

### The Nature of the Old Aeon

The root of the aeon-concept lies buried in the ancient astrological observation of time-cycle patterns. The variation in the seasons due to the miscalculation of the length of a year and the omission of any compensatory leap year, provided the basis for a calculation of the World Year. This period of 1460 years became known as an aeon or age. How it came about that Judaism assumed only two aeons (the postulation of seven is more common) is not easily explained. [90] It is probable that the aeon-conception was modified by the doctrine of the Fall, the antithesis of Satan and God, and the eschatological expectation of the restoration of Israel. M. Dibelius has established that in the aeon-concept, there was an integration of the astral and the spirit-world. Since a star-spirit rules the world during any stated epoch, there is an apparent alliance between the aeon-theory and the belief in a world-ruler.[91]

In the Epistles of Paul the terminology used to denote the Old Aeon is both varied and confusing. For our purposes it will be sufficient to confine our discussion to $\alpha i\omega\nu$ and $\kappa \delta\sigma\mu\sigma\varsigma$. The terms $\alpha i\omega\nu\sigma\varsigma$ $\tau o\hat{\upsilon}\tau o\varsigma$ "this age" (cf. Rom. 12:2; I Cor. 1:20; 2:6, 8; 3:18; II Cor. 4:4; Eph. 1:21) or $\tau o\hat{\upsilon}$ $\alpha i\hat{\omega}\nu\sigma\varsigma$ $\tau o\hat{\upsilon}$ $\dot{\epsilon}\nu\epsilon\sigma\tau\hat{\omega}\tau\sigma\varsigma$ (Gal. 1:4), or $\dot{o}$ $\nu\hat{\upsilon}\nu$ $\alpha i\hat{\omega}\nu$ (I Tim. 6:17; II Tim. 4:10; Titus 2:12), is a total concept which refers to both time and sphere.[92] At the same time, the term $\kappa \delta\sigma\mu\sigma\varsigma$ may denote the total relationship between the creation and the age (cf. I Cor. 3:19; 7:31).[93] J. Weiss says succinctly: "The fundamental conception that this present world will be replaced by a new world, a 'new creation' (II Cor. 5:17; Gal. 6:15), while the former itself 'passes away' (I Cor. 7:31), is the basic apocalyptic pattern of Paul's thinking."[94]

The $\kappa \delta\sigma\mu\sigma\varsigma$ and the $\alpha i\hat{\omega}\nu$ have a very definite relationship to spiritual beings. Paul refers to being made a spectacle ($\theta\epsilon\dot{\alpha}\tau\rho\sigma\nu$) in the cosmos as becoming the gazing-stock of both men and angels (I Cor. 4:9). The formulae $\dot{\epsilon}\pi\sigma\upsilon\rho\alpha\nu i\omega\nu$ $\kappa\alpha\dot{\iota}$ $\dot{\epsilon}\pi\iota\gamma\epsilon i\omega\nu$ $\kappa\alpha\dot{\iota}$ $\kappa\alpha\tau\alpha\chi\theta\sigma\nu i\omega\nu$ (Phil. 2:10), and $\tau\dot{\alpha}$

πάντα ἐν τοῖς οὐρανοῖς καὶ ἐπὶ τῆς γῆς, τὰ ὁρατὰ καὶ τὰ ἀόρατα (Col. 1:16; cf. 1:20), show the same corresponding inclusion of the spirit-world and the material creation under the term κτίσις (κτίζω) (cf. Col. 1:15 with 1:16) which in turn is similar in its connotations to κόσμος.[95]

In Paul's use of the problematic phrase στοιχεῖα τοῦ κόσμου there may be the idea of the inter-relation of metaphysical, spiritual, and material elements.[96] Apparently, this phrase carries a connotation of spirits and demons which are in active opposition to the original intention of the Creation (cf. Gal. 4:3, 9; Col. 2:8, 20). There is in this phrase the suggestion of the spirits which control the heavenly bodies of the universe and determine the succession of seasons and days.[97] In Galatians 4:8-9, Paul evidently relates the στοιχεῖα to the heathen deities (which according to I Cor. 10:19-20 have a real existence as demons), in that he refers to Christians having formerly been subjected to them. In the opinion of E. Y. Hinks, there is nothing in the Pauline theology which conflicts with his expressed opinion that the elemental forces of the world were spirits.[98]

In still other passages one encounters apparent reference to the spirit-rulers who govern the cosmos. In I Corinthians 2:6, 8 Paul asserts that the wisdom of God was unknown to the ἀρχόντων τοῦ αἰῶνος τούτου, which is now generally conceded to mean angelic or spiritual powers.[99] Cullmann maintains that the ἐξουσίαι are spirit-authorities,[100] but the nature of their loyalty is not always clearly distinguished (cf. I Cor. 15:24). Colossians 2:15 clearly illustrates the relationship of the evil ἐξουσίαι to the Aeon. Their authority has been effectively challenged by the death and victory of Christ.[101] The importance of these invisible powers of the Old Aeon is clear from Ephesians 6:12, in which Paul declares that the Christian's warfare is in reality against τὰς ἀρχάς, τὰς ἐξουσίας, τοὺς κοσμοκράτορας τοῦ σκότους τούτου, τὰ πνευματικὰ τῆς πονηρίας ἐν τοῖς ἐπουρανίοις (cf. Eph. 1:21; Col. 1:16), not flesh and blood (i.e. mankind). The idea behind these formulae is a gauged hierarchy of demonic forces[102] that have allied themselves in a rebellious mutiny against the supreme Authority of the universe. In this alliance they have become identified with the Aeon, and indeed, are the cosmic authorities and rulers of the universe. So effective is their control over nature, that Paul sees the creation in thraldom, that is, in subjection to the forces which control it (cf. Rom. 8:19-23).[103] The Christian is warned against their insidious activity, particularly as it reveals itself in erroneous doctrines (cf. I Tim. 4:1: πνεύμασιν . . . διδασκαλίαις δαιμονίων).

Over all the intermediary hierarchy of inimical forces is the sinister figure of Satan, ὁ ἄρχων τῆς ἐξουσίας τοῦ ἀέρος (Eph. 2:2).[104] Such a title implies the headship of all the personal opposition to God in the Old Aeon. He is king of legion intermediary and lesser cosmic spirits (cf. Matt. 12:26; Mark 3:22; Luke 11:15-23)[105] adding unity and destiny to opposition against God. He demands complete subordination to himself within the Aeon. I Corinthians 2:12 mentions τὸ πνεῦμα τοῦ κόσμου in antithesis to the "Spirit from God." The inference may be justified that Paul has Satan in mind.[106] If this is the case, there is a comparable relationship of the devil to unredeemed humanity, as there is in the manifestation of the Holy Spirit in the believer. In Ephesians 2:2 there is an explicit reference to Satan as the "spirit which is now working in the sons of disobedience." Thus, for Christians to leave the faith is equivalent to "turning after Satan" (I Tim. 5:15. Contrast Heb. 6:4-5, where partaking of the Holy Spirit is to participate in the power of the Age to Come), or falling into the judgement, snare, and reproach of the devil (I Tim. 3:6-7). In a striking reference to Satan as ὁ θεὸς τοῦ αἰῶνος τούτου (II Cor. 4:4), the blindness of the thoughts of unbelievers is ascribed to his devilish activity. He is distinct from the "rulers" (I Cor. 2:6, 8, note the plural τῶν ἀρχόντων) and "sons of disobedience" (Eph. 2:2), but he acts in and through them to effect the extension and maintenance of his dominion over the Old Aeon.[107] To secure this objective, he is transformed into an angel of light even as the "false apostles" are transformed into "apostles of Christ" (II Cor. 11:13-14). In a passage fraught with exegetical difficulty, Paul told the Corinthian Church that the worship of idols or heathen deities was in actuality the worship of demons (I Cor. 10:20-21).[108] In all probability the deity of Satan is of this same character, namely, an assumed and derived divinity, secured through the homage subscribed by lesser spirits and men.[109] Certainly, Paul did not hold to Satan's deity in any comparable sense to that of God; both Satan and his demonic retinue had been created by Jesus Christ (Col. 2:16). The devil merely stands as a puppet over the Old Aeon; God still rules over the whole Creation.[110] Consequently, Paul sees Satan as under the obligation to serve God, as when the incestuous man is delivered into the power of the devil for the destruction of the flesh (I Cor. 5:5), or as Hymenaeus and Alexander are committed into Satan's tutelage to unlearn blasphemous speech (I Tim. 1:20). Therefore, the dualism of the New Testament is only mediated and temporal (cf. I Thess. 2:18; 3:5; II Thess. 2:3-9), not metaphysical.[111]

A problem is introduced in positing an alliance of spirit-forces in opposition against God and against the original *good* creation. The only commendable answer is the Fall of Satan and his cohorts, although there is no direct statement to that effect. The Fall of Adam was neither coincident with, nor did it precipitate the Fall of the evil spirits;[112] rather, it was the occasion through which the world was brought into subjection to them.[113] Through Adam's original transgression not only was sin able to gain a strangle-hold on mankind, but the whole cosmos (man and nature) became part of the Old Aeon. Thus, evil spirits, mankind, and the material creation were united in the direct violation of the original intention of the Creation. Paul refers to this thraldom as the subjection of the creation (κτίσις) to vanity (ματαιότης); it is in the "bondage of corruption" (Rom. 8:20-21). "Vanity" at once suggests a connexion with the heathen deities, in that μάταιος is a standing term for the gods of the Gentiles in the Septuagint.[114] An actual relationship was seen by Paul to exist between the demons, the heathen deities, and rest of creation. Man's subjection to the power of sin is the counterpart to the wilful offering of allegiance to pagan deities and its consequent corruption.[115] It is here that the true nature of sin appears as self-asserted rebellion against God.[116] For this reason, Paul saw the cosmos and all of its constituents involved in sin.

Κόσμος may have a narrower meaning than αἰών in some instances. It is used to designate the world of men as a totality (cf. Rom. 5:12; 3:6; I Cor. 6:2; 11:32; II Cor. 5:19; 1:12). The identification of the cosmos with the Aeon is clear from the fact that the term still bears the connotation of sinfulness.[117] The emphasis does not lie on humanity as such, but on man as a part of αἰών οὗτος,[118] and consequently sinful. For this reason, κόσμος is used as the antithesis to the New Humanity in a number of instances (cf. e.g. I Cor. 1:20-21, 27-28; Eph. 2:2; I Cor. 6:2). The significance of the believer's deliverance from the forces of the cosmos is readily seen in the earliest Christian confessions which refer to the defeat and subjection of these powers by Jesus.[119] Paul, therefore, warns against collusion with the "world" lest his believing audience be included in its judgement (I Cor. 11:32). Says R. Bultmann very much to the point:

> This means that "Kosmos" is an eschatological concept. It denotes the world of men and the sphere of human activity as being, on the one hand, a temporary thing hastening toward its end, and on the other hand, the sphere of anti-godly power under whose sway the individual who is surrounded by it has fallen. It is the sphere of "the rulers of this age" (I Cor. 2:6, 8) and of "the god of this age" (II Cor. 4:4).[120]

### The Implication of Mankind in the Old Aeon Through Adam

#### *Mankind's Betrayal into the Domain of Death*

We have already discussed the corporate judgement of Adam, the decree that he and his posterity should all die. But the full significance of this judgement cannot be realized without seeing with Paul that sin and death are the bonds by which humanity is held in the thraldom of the Old Age. Death (as sin) was personalized in such a manner in the mind of Paul that he speaks of its domain as a realm over which it rules autocratically (cf. ἐβασίλευσεν in Rom. 5:14, 17). This realm includes Adam's corporate race.[121] Since it is the real ruler of man's particular part of the Aeon, it is called the "last enemy."

The Apostle further characterizes death as a sphere in which men are immersed. To be in the position of the heathen is to be dead in trespasses and sins (Eph. 2:1-5; Col. 2:13. In this passage it is parallel to "uncircumcision" indicating separation, cf. Eph. 2:11-12). The scope of death's kingdom is world-wide including the animate and inanimate creation (Rom. 8:20). Jews and Gentiles (the conclusion of the argument in Rom. 1:18-3:20) and the Aeon itself are dominated by death (cf. I Cor. 15:22-23). Sin and death, which are, from the human standpoint, the fundamental characteristics of the Age, were united and established in Adam.[122] Only in Christ, the Last Adam, is the dominion of death relinquished in its moral (i.e. separation from God) and physical aspects. Because of Christ's victory over the power of death, Paul exults, ποῦ σου θάνατε τὸ νῖκος; ποῦ σου θάνατε τὸ κέντρον (I Cor. 15:55) and foresees the abolishment of death altogether (II Tim. 1:10).

## Man's Subjection to the Power of Sin

Besides the dominion of death in the Old Aeon, Paul posits regal authority to sin (Rom. 5:21; cf. 6:12, 14; 7:9, 11). Sin is the sting, goad, or weapon (κέντρον) which is the means of death's continued dominion over mankind (I Cor. 15:56). "Like a harsh tyrant (it) holds men enslaved (Rom. 6:6, 20; 7:14), paying men for its service the miserable wage of death" (Rom. 6:23).[123] While one might be prone to consider the choice of evil as an evidence of human freedom, "sin" actually took the part of determinism (Rom. 7:17-20).[124] Consequently, the significance of God's giving men up (Rom. 1:24, 26, 28) is that they were released into the power of sin which in turn leads to destruction. We must be aware that Paul does not have in mind sinful acts or unrighteousness as a quality, but an active, powerful, external principle that organically produces its fruit, the evil deed (Rom. 7:17).[125]

Sin, by its very nature, acts in an organic way. Just as *IV Ezra* saw the evil seed sown in the heart of Adam growing to bear the fruit of corruption in his progeny, Paul saw all human sin as the development of the details of the original transgression. It has organization and structure. It provides a spiritual κοινωνία of darkness (Eph. 5:8, 11; cf. I Tim. 5:22; I John 1:6; II John 11)[126] which exists in radical opposition to the light. It forms a kingdom whose extent embraces the whole human race. It is a force[127] which rules in such a manner that Paul may refer to the "law of sin in my members" (Rom. 7:25). Sin, moreover, produces a sphere in which the unredeemed dwell (ἐπιμένω, Rom. 6:1); this realm is the domain of Satan (Acts 26:18) and therefore identifiable with the Old Age.

Sin is the primary characteristic of the Old Aeon. Αἰών οὗτος is thoroughly and irremediably wicked; hence, redemption must be extended from without (Gal. 1:4; Eph. 2:5; Rom. 8:2; Col. 1:13).[128] Sin is the expression and power of the age, providing the bonds whereby its subjects are brought into and kept in thraldom (cf. Rom. 5:12, 21; 3:9; Gal. 3:22). In Romans 6-8, a glance will confirm the conclusion that Paul considered sin to be man's master. Slavery, bondage, legal power, among other ideas, characterize the nature of sin's control.

It is only in this context that one may see the significance of Paul's doctrine of sin and redemption. Again, it was his conception of the solidarity of mankind which allowed him to postulate the view that Adam was responsible for man's implication in the Aeon and his subjection to its external powers (Rom. 5:12). It is not Original Sin,[129] in its usual exposition, but mankind betrayed and betraying itself into the control of sin in the cosmos, which is Paul's doctrine.

## "Flesh" Implicated in the Old Aeon

We pick up now where we left off, to examine the second aspect of

Paul's usage of the term σάρξ. Beyond the connotation of "flesh" as a physical substance or human relationship is a designation of σάρξ as a continuum, a type of cohesive being which is the captive and seat of sin. This aspect concerns the flesh as a part of the Aeon and consequently its standing in opposition to God.[130] The flesh comes to symbolize mankind in thraldom to the ruling power of sin in the Aeon. Thus, to be ἐν σαρκί is to say that one is subject to the powers which control the flesh. "In Romans 7:6, 'that wherein we were holden' refers to the σάρξ: it is that by virtue of which the powers have their grip over us."[131] ἐν σαρκί is far removed from the Greek idea of the flesh as the material body or even the Old Testament where man is a manifestation of the totality of all flesh. In Paul's theology, "flesh" is a sphere controlled by alien powers. As long as one remains in it, he is subjected to these forces. The end of life κατὰ σάρκα is death (Rom. 8:12). With the acquisition of the new life in Christ, the believer is no longer in the flesh but in the Spirit (Rom. 8:9; cf. Rom. 7:5). "Flesh" and "Spirit" are not two spheres in which one can live at the same time. Only one of these entities can determine man's existence.[132] Thus, Paul tells the Roman Christians that they are no longer "in the flesh" but "in the Spirit" (8:9; cf. Gal. 5:13). Formerly, existence ἐν τῇ σαρκί meant the dominion of the passions of sin in our members (cf. Gal. 5:19-21) resulting in death (Rom. 7:5); now, however, there is no longer any condemnation for us who do not walk κατὰ σάρκα (Rom. 8:1, 4).

The enmity of the Aeon against God is also ascribed by Paul to the σάρξ (Rom. 8:7; Gal. 5:17; cf. Rom. 2:28-29; 7:6). It is for this reason that Paul describes the flesh as σαρκὸς ἁμαρτίας (Rom. 8:3). Surely, to be "in the flesh" obviates any possibility of pleasing God (Rom. 8:8; Gal. 3:3), and sowing to the flesh can only culminate in corruption (Gal. 6:8).

It is a most essential element in Paul's doctrine to conceive of the flesh (i.e. the sphere of human existence) as a sort of living or organic whole. When the Apostle comes to expound his doctrine of the atonement of Christ, he stresses the humanity of Christ. Through His assumption of a body and death, sin's control of the flesh was successfully challenged; consequently, those that are included in Him are extracted from the Old Aeon and its malignant powers, sin, death, and the Law (Rom. 8:3; 7:4).[133] By this particular type of redemption, Christ was able to reverse the subjection of the flesh to sin which Adam inaugurated. This is the core of Paul's theology, a core so often misunderstood because our thought is so completely dominated by traditional Western individualism. Throughout the exposition of his doctrine, Paul's mind must be seen in its determination by Old Testament[134] and Early Jewish conceptions.

Paul's doctrine of man in the flesh, under the dominion of sin and death, is not merely a re-statement of the Old Testament and Jewish conceptions. The plight of man's involvement through the solidarity of the race in its distance from God[135] is more poignant to the Apostle because of the light which is cast upon it by the New Age. The striking nature of the human dilemma apart from redemption is two-fold. (1) Man, because of the weakness of the flesh, is completely unable to fulfil his responsibility to God. (2) Man, besides being frail, is engulfed in his solidarity with the race within the domain of powers too great for him to master. Both ideas characterize Paul's conception of the Aeon, the evil inversion of the New Aeon inaugurated by Jesus Christ. It is this same inversion which must explain the true nature of the Adam-Christ typology. Adam involved the race in the Aeon by virtue of his determinative headship; Christ, by incorporating the New Humanity into Himself, brings them into the New Age (II Cor. 5:17; Rom. 8:21; I Cor. 15:51-57).

## *"Law" Implicated in the Old Aeon*

As strange as it might at first appear, Paul, who taught that the Law which originated with divine approval and whose commands were holy, just, and good (Rom. 7:12; cf. 7:14; 17; 18; I Tim. 1:8-10. Note also the practice of Paul according to Acts 16:3; 21:18-27), also thought of the Law as being implicated in the Old Age. In this context the Law was one of the forces of the Aeon that had joined with sin and death in the subjection of mankind.[136] In the words of J. A. T. Robinson: "If sin is the accomplice of death, the *law* is the instrument of sin."[137] Paul calls the Law (subjectively, not objectively) "the power ($\delta\acute{\nu}\nu\alpha\mu\iota\varsigma$, I Cor. 15:56) of sin" that beguiled him (Rom. 7:11). The Law $\kappa\alpha\tau\epsilon\rho\gamma\acute{\alpha}\zeta\epsilon\tau\alpha\iota$ "works" wrath, for without it sin could not exist except in a submerged form.[138] The Law secures the bridgehead or footing ($\dot{\alpha}\phi\rho\rho\mu\acute{\eta}$, Rom. 7:8, 11) whereby sin gains control over the whole man, thereby causing sin to abound (Rom. 5:20). It gives sin's reign full power. It deceives those that put their confidence in it with the intent of securing eternal life through the fulfilment of its injunctions (Gal. 3:11-12). And with this failure of the Law to give life, Paul found an empirically conclusive argument that subjection to the Law is worse than useless, an emphatic confirmation that it is one of the partners of the Old Aeon.

Paul does not hesitate to posit that, just as man is enslaved by sin and death, he is equally the thrall of the Law (Gal. 4:1-7; 5:1), under it (Gal. 4:21; Rom. 6:14), and subject to its curse (Gal. 3:13). This latter point corresponds to the sentence of death under which all men in the Old Aeon live.[139] This contention is confirmed by Colossians 2:14-15, where an unmistakable relationship is drawn between the "principalities and powers" on the one hand, and the "ordinances" (i.e. Law) on the other.[140] W. Morgan suggests that the presiding of these powers over the Law implies a malicious interest in prosecuting both its demands and its condemnation to man's undoing.[141] Thus, Paul sees that the Torah, of divine origin, instead of acting to deliver man from the clutches of sin, is itself the instrument of the forces which delight in the destruction of man. As in the cases of the other powers of the Aeon, man's release from the bondage and curse of the law is effected through Christ.[142] Consequently, death (cf. $\dot{\alpha}\pi\acute{\epsilon}\theta\alpha\nu\rho\nu$, and its parallel identification with the crucifixion of Christ, Gal. 2:20) to the Law is the beginning of life unto God (Gal. 2:19).

But in what sense did Paul see Adam as the means by which mankind was implicated in the bondage and condemnation of the law? Although there are no explicit statements in the Epistles that Adam did involve man in legal subjection directly, at least symbolically, if not actually, Paul attributes to Adam the corporate responsibility for the legal subjection of mankind. Adam knew the will of God (although the Torah was not given until Moses, Rom. 5:14) which made transgression a possibility.[143] With Adam's betrayal of the race into the power of sin, the Law could have no other effect than to produce an antagonism to the will of God. It is interesting in this context to note that the major part of Romans 7 appears to be a personal paraphrase of the Eden temptation.[144] In any case, Paul does not divide responsibility for the subjection of mankind to the powers of the Old Age. Sin, death, flesh, and the Law are all inextricably interconnected in the Aeon in such a manner that the admission of one brings in the rest.

## Conclusion

Our intended goal in this general section has been to unravel three dissimilar lines of thought which, more than likely, were not distinguished in Paul's mind.

(1) The first is Adam as the father of the race. As its ancestor, he is the origin (*Ursprung*) of all those general racial characteristics which distinguish mankind from the rest of Creation. One might profitably compare the race to a tree, which although possessing distinct leaves, gives to each leaf a common life and character, since the foliage is organically interrelated through the stem and the trunk.

(2) The second line of thought concerns Adam's role as the realistic representative of the race. This role implies the Hebrew conception of the corporate personality of the race in such a manner that all mankind is identifiable with one man; in Paul's doctrine this man is Adam. Because of his representation of the race, Paul posits a universal participation of the race in the original and archetypal transgression of Adam, culminating in the corporate judgement of the totality of men.

(3) The third aspect of Paul's doctrine may combine the first two lines of thought, but adds the horizontal solidarity of man under sin in united opposition to God. The Jewish idea of the two Aeons reached a heightened development in Paul's mind because he had personally experienced the contrast between the Old and the New (cf. Gal. 3:22: ". . . συνέκλεισεν ἡ γραφὴ τὰ πάντα ὑπὸ ἁμαρτίαν").

Throughout our presentation of the Pauline views on the solidarity of the race, his dependence on the Old Testament and current Jewish thought has been more or less self-evident. Probably the most important single principle of solidarity used by Paul was the Old Testament conception of the corporate personality of the group. The application of this principle made it possible for Paul to go far beyond the current ideas of his day to postulate a doctrine of total human implication in sin as the foundation for his all-embracing doctrine of redemption. The debt of the Apostle to current theories of corporate justice, transferable demerit, the horizontal extension of life and flesh (which to the ancient Hebrew would correspond to the extension of personality)[145] as frail and yet a totality which may have more or less a psychic or organic life,[146] is self-evident. It is a debt which is primarily one of background. Paul may not be accused of parroting ideas of his Jewish contemporaries. Indeed, he makes more direct use of Old Testament conceptions than those of the Rabbis. But "stimulus diffusion" is the phrase which best describes Paul's application of Old Testament and Early Jewish conceptions of the solidarity of the human race.

## Notes

[1] Cf. H. F. Rall, *According to Paul* (New York, 1947), p. 3 note 2; A. C. Headlam, *St Paul and Christianity* (London, 1913), pp. 14, 18-21.

[2] Cf. C. C. McCown, *Munera Studiosa,* ed. M. H. Shepherd and S. H. Johnson (Cambridge, Mass., 1946), in T. S. Kepler, *Contemporary Thinking about Paul* (New York, 1950), p. 121.

[3] Cf. T. A. Lacey, *The One Body and the One Spirit* (London, 1925), p. 233; T. R. Glover, *Paul of Tarsus* (London, 1925), p. 5.

[4] C. H. Dodd, *Man in God's Design* (Newcastle, 1952), p. 11; T. A. Lacey, op. cit. p. 233.

[5] C. H. Dodd, op. cit. p. 13.

[6] S. Hanson, *The Unity of the Church in the New Testament,* p. 52.

[7] Ibid. Cf. W. Morgan, *The Religion and Theology of Paul* (Edinburgh, 1917), pp. 134-5.

[8] T. A. Lacey, op. cit. p. 233. Cf. W. Morgan, op. cit. p. 28.

[9] Cf. C. H. Dodd, *The Meaning of Paul for Today* (London, 1920), p. 139.

[10] Cf. H. R. Willoughby, *Pagan Regeneration* (Chicago, 1929), p. 294.

[11] Cf. L. S. Thornton, *The Incarnate Lord* (London, 1928), pp. 111-12; T. A. Lacey, op. cit. pp. 62-3; C. H. Dodd, *Man in God's Design,* op. cit. pp. 14-15. See C. S. Lewis, *Surprised by Joy* (London, 1955), p. 21.

[12] Cf. Wm. Robinson, *The Biblical Doctrine of the Church* (St Louis, 1948), pp. 15-34.

[13] Cf. J. B. Lightfoot, "St Paul and Seneca," *St Paul's Epistle to the Philippians* (London, 1868), pp. 291-333.

[14] A. C. Headlam, op. cit. p. 125. For the Platonic conception of man, see C. N. Cochrane, *Christianity and Classical Culture* (Oxford, 1940), p. 79.

[15] Cf. C. H. Dodd, *Man in God's Design,* p. 17.

[16] Notably R. Bultmann; cf. *Theology of the New Testament,* trans. K. Grobel, Vol. I (London, 1952), 174, 250; and "New Testament and Mythology," in *Kerugma and Myth,* ed. H. W. Bartsch, trans. R. H. Fuller

(London, 1953), p. 15; L. G. Rylands, *The Beginnings of Gnostic Christianity* (London, 1940), pp. 210-11.

[17] Cf. H. L. Mansel, *The Gnostic Heresies of the First and Second Centuries* (London, 1875), p. 13.

[18] Cf. E. R. Goodenough, *By Light, Light* (New Haven, 1935), p. 394.

[19] Cf. J. M. Creed, "The Heavenly Man," *JTS*, Vol. XXVI (1925), p. 133; E. R. Goodenough, op. cit. p. 394. See W. D. Davies's excellent discussion of the whole issue of dualism in the teaching of Paul, *Paul and Rabbinic Judaism*, pp. 17ff.

[20] Cf. B. Weiss, *Biblical Theology of the New Testament*, trans. D. Eaton, Vol. I (Edinburgh, 1882), 339-40.

[21] J. S. Stewart, *A Man in Christ* (London, 1938), p. 104. Cf. J. A. T. Robinson, *The Body*, pp. 24-6; R. Bultmann, "New Testament and Mythology," p. 17.

[22] Cf. e.g. *Die Hellenistischen Mysterienreligionen* (3 Aufl., Leipzig, Berlin, 1927); *Poimandres* (Leipzig, 1904).

[23] Cf. e.g. *Kurios Christos* (2nd edn., Göttingen, 1921).

[24] Cf. e.g. *The Earlier Epistles of St Paul*, p. 215.

[25] *The Theology of the Epistles* (London, 1919), p. 25.

[26] Op. cit. pp. 89-100. W. L. Knox agrees in general with this conclusion in *St Paul and the Church of Jerusalem* (Cambridge, 1925), p. 147; so also A. Schweitzer, *The Mysticism of Paul the Apostle*, trans. W. Montgomery (London, 1931), *passim*.

[27] C. A. A. Scott, *Christianity According to St Paul*, p. 22.

[28] Cf. ibid. pp. 127-33; C. Chavasse, *The Bride of Christ*, p. 19.

[29] See E. Best, *One Body in Christ* (London, 1955), *passim*.

[30] Contrast W. L. Knox, *St Paul and the Church of the Gentiles*, p. 107.

[31] *Paul*, trans. E. Lummis (London, 1907), p. 82.

[32] On the unity of God, see S. Hanson, *The Unity of the Church in the New Testament*, p. 57. The explicit phrase εἷς θεός is found in Rom. 3:30; I Cor. 8:4, 6; Gal. 9:20; I Tim. 2:5. It is the direct antithesis to the pantheon "who are called gods" (I Cor. 8:5).

[33] This passage is a quotation from Aratus, a Stoic of Cilicia. Cf. T. A. Lacey, op. cit. p. 233. This manner of speaking is an apt illustration of the principle of "stimulus diffusion." There is no more of a confusion of the human and the divine in this passage than elsewhere. God is the Creator (Acts 17:26), not "Infuser." This point applies with equal force to the alleged Stoic formula found in Rom. 11:36, ὅτι ἐξ αὐτοῦ καὶ δι' αὐτοῦ καὶ εἰς αὐτὸν τὰ πάντα (so also with variations, I Cor. 8:6. Cf. Eph. 4:6; Col. 1:16). E. Norden has established the currency of this formula in the early centuries of the era. See *Agnostos Theos* (Leipzig, Berlin, 1913), pp. 240-50, 374. Cf. E. C. Rust, *Nature and Man in Biblical Thought*,

pp. 207, 212; T. W. Manson, *The Teaching of Jesus* (Cambridge, 1931), p. 91; A. Schweitzer, *Paul and His Interpreters,* trans. W. Montgomery (London, 1912), pp. 96, 239.

[34] L. S. Thornton, *The Common Life in the Body of Christ* (2nd edn, London, 1944), p. 115 note 1.

[35] Cf. E. Brunner, *Man in Revolt,* trans. O. Wyon (London, 1939), pp. 108-13; G. S. Duncan, *Jesus, Son of Man* (London, 1947), p. 44.

[36] For the attestation of an identical view in the Old Testament, see Quell, "Sin," *Bible Key Words (TWNT),* pp. 17-21.

[37] Cf. E. H. Wahlstrom, *The New Life in Christ* (Philadelphia, 1950), pp. xi, 7.

[38] Cf. I Cor. 11:14: "... ἡ φύσις αὐτὴ διδάσκει. ..." See R. Bultmann, *Theology of the New Testament,* p. 250.

[39] For the Jewish conception of sin, see "Sin," *Bible Key Words (TWNT),* p. 39. Cf. R. Bultmann, *Jesus and the Word,* trans. L. P. Smith, E. Huntress (London, 1935), pp. 66-72.

[40] Cf. F. Prat, *The Theology of St Paul,* II.50. The idea of a conscience in man originated in Stoicism, but was evidently adopted by Judaism and given a covenantal basis.

[41] Cf. B. Weiss, op. cit. I.348.

[42] The difference and similarities between the Pauline νοῦς, συνείδησις and the *yetzer hatob* suggest another instance of "stimulus diffusion."

[43] Cf. F. Prat, op. cit. II.50-1. This is a point of contrast between Paul and the Hellenistic conception of the νοῦς.

[44] W. D. Davies, op. cit. p. 116.

[45] Cf. ibid. p. 114. See *Sanh* 56a-b. Cf. K. Lake, op. cit. pp. 55-8. Note that these commandments are reflected in the precepts given to Gentile converts and endorsed by Paul in Acts 15:28-30.

[46] Note that there is a universal recognition of the good implied in Romans 12:17: "... Provide things honest in the sight of all men." Cf. W. D. Davies, op. cit. p. 327. It is the basis of the argument in Romans 13:1-7.

[47] Cf. E. Brunner, op. cit. p. 141.

[48] Cf. N. Söderblom, *The Mystery of the Cross,* trans. A. G. Hebert (London, 1933), p. 29; T. W. Manson, op. cit. pp. 332-3.

[49] The word αἵματος must be omitted as S. Hanson has well contended and confirmed by the best texts—op. cit. p. 103. That ἑνός signifies "one man" is supported by the parallel drawn with Christ in this passage (17:31) and elsewhere (cf. Rom. 5:18). Cf. M. Burrows, *An Outline of Biblical Theology,* p. 322.

[50] W. Wrede (op. cit. p. 81) relates Paul's view of Adam to the ancient conception of what happens first in history is repeated in succeeding series

or cycles. F. V. Filson, (*St Paul's Conception of Recompense*, p. 11) sees a reflection of the Rabbinic doctrine of merit and demerit. Both are correct in part only.

[51] Cf. *The Christian Doctrine of Man*, p. 121; "Hebrew Psychology," *The People and the Book*, p. 378; *The Cross of the Servant*, p. 34.

[52] Cf. *The Epistle of Paul to the Romans* (London, 1932), pp. 79-80, 86.

[53] Cf. *Commentary on Romans*, trans. C. C. Rasmussen (Philadelphia, 1949), p. 213.

[54] Op. cit. *passim*.

[55] Historicity is not only of primary importance out of deference to the scriptural account, but it is fundamental to a nondualistic explanation of evil. Cf. C. N. Cochrane, op. cit. p. 240.

[56] This distinction corresponds in general to G. B. Stevens's phrase "mystical realism," *The Pauline Theology* (London, 1892), pp. 32-40.

[57] Cf. A. Robertson and A. Plummer, *The First Epistle of St Paul to the Corinthians, ICC* (Edinburgh, 1911), pp. 370, 373.

[58] That is, the organic principle of biological reproduction which requires that that which is born be of the same kind as the parent (cf. Gen. 1:11-12, 21, 24; Matt. 7:16-18; Gal. 6:7-8).

[59] The contrast between Paul and Philo is readily seen at this juncture. The latter sets σάρξ and ψυχή in sharp antithesis. Cf. H. A. A. Kennedy, op. cit. p. 34 note 3.

[60] B. Weiss, op. cit. p. 338 note 8.

[61] These conjectures follow two general lines: (1) those who interpret the "flesh" as the point of sin's attack, and (2) those who find a basic dualism in Paul's use of the term. In this view, flesh is, like the Hellenistic conception of matter, evil in itself.

[62] See his discursus in *The Epistle to the Galatians, ICC* (New York, 1920), pp. 492-5.

[63] Op. cit. p. 9.

[64] See pp. 121-3 *infra*. Cf. P. C. Boylan, *St Paul's Epistle to the Romans* (Dublin, 1934), p. 83; F. Prat, op. cit. II.402-3.

[65] See J. A. T. Robinson's whole discussion in *The Body*, pp. 11-16.

[66] The usage of σάρξ, in the Epistles, is distributed in a proportion of 56 cases of the former, and 35 of the latter. H. W. Robinson, *The Christian Doctrine of Man*, p. 114; W. D. Davies, op. cit. p. 19.

[67] J. A. T. Robinson, op. cit. p. 31.

[68] W. D. Davies, op. cit. p. 57.

[69] E. Brunner objects strenuously to Augustine's first argument for Original Sin, i.e. a hereditary bias stemming from Adam. Brunner main-

tains that to accept this view is to ground something personal in a natural fact. Op. cit. pp. 121-2; cf. *The Christian Doctrine of Creation and Redemption* (*Dogmatics* II), trans. O. Wyon (London, 1952), p. 82.

[70] Cf. P. Wernle, *The Beginnings of Christianity*, trans. G. A. Bieneman (London, 1903), I.230.

[71] *Christus und Adam nach Röm* 5 (Zurich, 1952), p. 11. Cf. idem, *The Epistle to the Romans*, trans. E. Hoskyns (London, 1933), pp. 170-1.

[72] Cf. S. Hanson, op. cit. p. 68; A. Nygren, op. cit. p. 213.

[73] See discussions by F. Prat, op. cit. I.218; Sanday and Headlam, *Romans* (*ICC*), p. 134; and S. Hanson, for more recent views, op. cit. pp. 66-8.

[74] Cf. F. R. Tennant, *SDFOS*, p. 261; A. B. Bruce, *St Paul's Conception of Christianity* (New York, 1907), p. 130; H. Weinel, *Biblische Theologie des Neuen Testaments* (Tübingen, 1911), p. 245; W. Beyschlag, *New Testament Theology*, trans. N. Buchanan (Edinburgh, 1896), II.60; W. D. Davies, op. cit. p. 32; G. B. Stevens, *The Theology of the New Testament* (Edinburgh, 1899), pp. 357-8. Contrast the opinion of Sanday and Headlam, op. cit. p. 134; K. Barth, *Romans*, p. 172; H. C. Sheldon, *New Testament Theology* (New York, 1911), p. 212; C. Weizsäcker, *The Apostolic Age of the Christian Church*, trans. J. Millar (London, 1894), I.149-50; E. Best, op. cit. p. 34.

[75] Contrast H. C. Sheldon, op. cit. p. 211, who sees an escape from this view in the possible use of the aorist with a perfect sense.

[76] Op. cit. pp. 214-15.

[77] Cf. H. F. Rall, op. cit. pp. 36-7. H. Weinel contrasts the metaphysical (Rom. 5) with the empirical (Rom. 1-2). Op. cit. p. 370.

[78] Cf. A. S. Peake, *The Quintessence of Paulinism* (Manchester, 1916), pp. 27, 30; F. R. Tennant, *The Concept of Sin* (Cambridge, 1912), pp. 40-2; J. Weiss, *The History of Primitive Christianity*, ed. in E. trans., F. C. Grant (London, 1937), p. 607.

[79] Some scholars point to ἐφ' ᾧ πάντες ἥμαρτον (Rom. 5:12) as an example of this idea (cf. W. D. Davies, op. cit. p. 32), but it is not well substantiated. The same idea is found in II Thess. 2:9-12, where men are deceived by the "lawless man" but at the same time love unrighteousness and hate the truth. Cf. J. Weiss, p. 435.

[80] A similar failure to notice any paradox in an inherent bias to sin, and individual responsibility was noted in IV Ezra (cf. H. A. A. Kennedy, op. cit. p. 40; P. Feine, *Theologie des Neuen Testaments* [Leipzig, 1910], p. 272) and II Baruch. Even the Rabbis at times reflect this conception. But Paul's teaching on sin is unique in its predication of a corporate sin of the race in Adam. This is nowhere to be found in our Jewish sources.

[81] Cf. W. P. Dickson, *St Paul's Use of the Terms Flesh and Spirit* (Glasgow, 1883), p. 318; E. Burton, op. cit. pp. 422-3.

[82] Cf. E. Brunner, *The Christian Doctrine of Creation and Redemption*, p. 96; C. H. Dodd, *Romans*, p. 80.

83 Cf. "Sin," *Bible Key Words* (*TWNT*), p. 78.

84 Cf. P. Wernle, op. cit. p. 229; W. Beyschlag, op. cit. II.59; F. R. Tennant, *SDFOS*, op. cit. p. 257. Paul affirms the less apparent universality of sin from the undeniable inevitability of death in these verses (cf. F. C. Baur, *Paul: His Life and Works*, trans. A. Menzies, Vol. 11 [London, 1875], p. 185; A. B. Bruce, op. cit. p. 129).

85 This point may be further attested by the death of infants.

86 Note, e.g. Romans 8:10: "And if Christ be in you, the body is dead because of sin" (i.e. of Adam; cf. L. S. Thornton, *The Common Life*, p. 143); "but the Spirit is life because of righteousness" (i.e. of Christ).

87 Cf. Gen. 1:28, Ps. 8:5-8 for the lordship of Adam and humanity.

88 O. Cullmann, *Christ and Time*, trans. F. V. Filson (London, 1951), pp. 101, 115-18. Cf. S. A. Cook, *The Cambridge Ancient History*, III.443.

89 Cf. J. Weiss, op. cit. p. 434; S. Hanson, op. cit. p. 68.

90 Cf. J. Weiss, op. cit. p. 603 note 15; E. D. Burton, op. cit. pp. 427-31. The latter claims that Paul provides the earliest evidence of the acceptance of this idea among Christians.

91 *Die Geisterwelt im Glauben des Paulus* (Göttingen, 1909), pp. 193-4.

92 Cf. E. C. E. Owen, "αἰών and αἰώνιος," *JTS*, Vol. XXXVII (1936), pp. 266-8, where he lists a parallel usage in the LXX; e.g. "a generation, race of men" (Sap 14:6), "this world" (Ps. 89 [90]:8; Eccles. 3:11; Ecclus. 38:34; in the sense of the sensible, material, sinful world). There is more than one example of the use of αἰών in the plural (cf. I Cor. 10:11, τὰ τέλη τῶν αἰώνων; 2:7; Gal. 1:5; Col. 1:26; Eph. 3:9; II Tim. 1:9; Titus 1:2); but this usage has a less technical meaning, i.e. successive periods of time, ages.

93 Cf. Eph. 2:2: κατὰ τὸν αἰῶνα τοῦ κόσμου τούτου. The phrase represents a single Hebrew phrase often encountered in the Rabbis. Cf. J. Armitage Robinson, *St Paul's Epistle to the Ephesians* (London, 1903), p. 48.

94 Op. cit. p. 604.

95 Ibid. p. 596. The terms κτίσις and κόσμος by no means always imply a connexion with evil (cf. e.g. Col. 1:15). There were, of course, the good angels for both Judaism and Paul, which, although part of the universal creation, were free from the corruption of sin (cf. I Cor. 15:52; I Thess. 4:16; Gal. 3:19; I Cor. 13:1).

96 Cf. E. C. Rust, op. cit. pp. 235-6. The connexion of the στοιχεῖα with the aeon may be no more than terminological. Burton claims that apparently there is no evidence that στοιχεῖον meant "spirit," "angel," or "demon" earlier than the *Test Sal*, which is probably late (cf. E. Y. Hinks, "The Meaning of the phrase τὰ στοιχεῖα τοῦ κόσμου in Gal. 4:3 and Col. 2:8," *JBL*, XV.191). Burton continues his contention that Paul does not accept the demonic connotation but refers merely to imperfect teaching (cf. op. cit. pp. 514-15, so also J. B. Lightfoot, *The Epistles of St Paul to*

the *Colossians and Philemon* [London, 1886], pp. 180-1; F. Prat, op. cit. II.422-3).

[97] Cf. E. Y. Hinks, op. cit. p. 190.

[98] Op. cit. p. 190.

[99] J. Weiss, op. cit. p. 494; A. S. Peake, op. cit. pp. 28-9. Contrast Robertson and Plummer, op. cit. pp. 39-40.

[100] *Christ and Time,* p. 194; cf. J. B. Lightfoot, *Colossians and Philemon,* p. 154. This notion is particularly important in I Corinthians 6:3 where Paul denounces the Christians' practice of going to court in suits against each other. "Know ye not that we shall judge angels?" The courts, as the states which authorize them, are unconsciously controlled by spiritual forces. See O. Cullmann, op. cit. p. 193; J. Weiss, op. cit. p. 600. In Titus 3:1 Christians are encouraged to be in subjection to the ἀρχαῖς ἐξουσίαις, probably as a temporary measure.

[101] Cf. J. B. Lightfoot, *Colossians and Philemon,* p. 190.

[102] Cf. J. Armitage Robinson, op. cit. p. 49; H. A. A. Kennedy, op. cit. p. 40. In the words of G. H. C. Macgregor: ". . . κοσμοκράτορες is the very word which is used in the hellenistic mystical writings of the seven supreme astral deities; it occurs in Orphic hymns, in inscriptions, in Gnostic writings, and even in Rabbinic literature." "Principalities and Powers: the Cosmic Background of Paul's Thought," *New Testament Studies* (Cambridge, 1954), I.21.

[103] Cf. E. Y. Hinks, op. cit. p. 191. Note that Stephen affirms that God ". . . turned and gave them up (i.e. Israel) to serve the astral host" (Acts 7:42).

[104] Note the parallel phrase, ὁ ἄρχων τοῦ κόσμου τούτου (John 12:31; 16:11). See further, G. H. C. Macgregor, op. cit. p. 18.

[105] The demonic view of Paul is the same as that of the Synoptics. N. P. Williams, *The Ideas of the Fall and of Original Sin,* p. 160. Cf. B. Weiss, op. cit. I.104, 332.

[106] So B. Weiss, op. cit. I.332. Cf. H. W. Robinson, *Mansfield College Essays,* presented to A. M. Fairbairn (London, 1909), p. 285.

[107] Note II Tim. 2:26: ". . . and they (those that oppose themselves) may recover themselves out of the snare of the devil, having been taken captive by him unto his will." Cf. II Cor. 11:4.

[108] Cf. H. A. A. Kennedy, op. cit. p. 40; N. P. Williams, op. cit. p. 160; W. Morgan, *The Religion and Theology of Paul* (Edinburgh, 1917), p. 13. A similar relationship between demons and pagan gods is found in the Old Testament. "They sacrificed unto demons (*šēd,* 'evil spirit, demon,' according to L. Koehler and W. Baumgartner, *Lexicon in Veteris Testamenti Libros* [Leiden, 1953], p. 949), not to God; to gods whom they knew not, to new gods that came newly up, whom your fathers feared not" (Deut. 32:17).

[109] Note the parallel idea in II Thess. 2:4; cf. Rev. 13:4.

[110] This idea may be clearly grasped by comparing II Cor. 4:4 with I Cor. 15:24. Satan's dominion over humanity was instituted through Adam (Rom. 5:12-21) who traitorously delivered the cosmos (i.e. humanity) into Satan's domain, the Old Aeon. Christ, the Second Adam, through His singular victory on the Cross (Col. 2:15) wrested humanity (Paul calls it the "kingdom") from the Aeon and from Satan (cf. Rom. 16:20) to deliver it back to its rightful Owner (I Cor. 15:24).

[111] Cf. O. Cullmann, *Christ and Time,* p. 196; J. S. Stewart, "On a Neglected Emphasis in New Testament Theology," *SJT,* Vol. IV (1951), p. 300.

[112] The Genesis account of the Fall clearly maintains that evil existed before Adam's disobedience. Paul concurs apparently in saying that "sin entered into the world" (Rom. 5:12) and asserting that Eve was subjected to external temptation (I Tim. 2:14). H. J. Holtzmann, *Lehrbuch der Neutestamentlichen Theologie* (Tübingen, 1911), II.47, regards the phrase, "sin deceived me," as a conscious reference to the Fall-story in conjunction with II Cor. 11:3, ". . . the Serpent deceived Eve." Cf. J. E. Thomas, *The Problem of Sin in the New Testament* (London, 1927), p. 80. In any case, as Brunner says, man is not astute enough to have invented sin; *The Christian Doctrine of Creation and Redemption,* p. 108.

[113] This view was held both before and contemporaneously with Paul by Jews; (J. Armitage Robinson, op. cit. p. 49).

[114] Cf. W. L. Knox, *St Paul and the Church of the Gentiles,* op. cit. p. 107.

[115] This is the theme of Romans 1:18-32. "God gave them up" repeatedly emphasizes the passing of man from the dominion of God to that of idolatry and sin. Cf. C. H. Dodd, *The Meaning of Paul for Today,* p. 59.

[116] "Sin" in *Bible Key Words* (*TWNT*), p. 78.

[117] A. Nygren, "Christ and the Forces of Destruction," *SJT,* Vol. IV (1951), p. 336.

[118] Cf. E. C. Rust, op. cit. p. 199; B. Weiss, op. cit. p. 331. We may well agree with the latter that the pre-Messianic age (. . .) of current Jewish thought affords the background of Paul's conception of the Aeon, since for Judaism also, this period was ungodly and wicked; ibid. pp. 331-2.

[119] O. Cullmann, *Christ and Time,* p. 103.

[120] *Theology of the New Testament,* p. 256.

[121] E. H. Wahlstrom, op. cit. pp. 26, 61; Sanday and Headlam, op. cit. p. 143. J. A. T. Robinson says appropriately: "The universality of death as the destiny of man is thus not a natural fact like the mortality of the σάρξ"; op. cit. p. 35.

[122] A. Schweitzer, *Paul and His Interpreters,* p. 221.

[123] J. Weiss, op. cit. p. 515.

[124] Cf. J. A. T. Robinson, op. cit. p. 36.

125 Cf. O. Pfleiderer, *Paulinism*, trans. E. Peters (London, 1877), I.38; *Primitive Christianity*, trans. W. Montgomery (London, 1906), I.289-90; J. S. Stewart, *A Man in Christ*, p. 105.

126 L. S. Thornton, op. cit. p. 13.

127 Cf. C. Weizsäcker, op. cit. I.148; H. Weinel, op. cit. p. 244; C. A. A. Scott, op. cit. p. 47. For the passages in point see "Sin" in *Bible Key Words* (*TWNT*), p. 51.

128 A. Schweitzer, *Paul and His Interpreters*, p. 57. C. A. A. Scott, op. cit. p. 29.

129 See J. Caird's brilliant analysis of the problem in his Gifford Lectures, *Fundamental Principles of Christianity* (Glasgow, 1899), I.210-11.

130 See J. A. T. Robinson's admirable treatment, op. cit. pp. 24f.

131 J. A. T. Robinson, op. cit. p. 22. By the flesh, the individual is connected with the cosmos; J. Weiss, op. cit. p. 606.

132 R. Asting, *Die Heiligkeit im Urchristentum* (Göttingen, 1930), p. 193. The carnal Christian (σαρκίνοις, σαρκικοί, I Cor. 3:1, 3) is living as though he still remained in the thraldom of the Aeon in spite of the redemption of Christ, which not only makes such an existence unnecessary, but utterly reprehensible (cf. Rom. 6:1-23; 7:6; 8:1-13; Gal. 5:15-21).

133 Cf. J. Weiss, op. cit. p. 434.

134 Of supreme importance is the conception of the σάρξ as a totality (cf. H. A. A. Kennedy, op. cit. p. 129) which harks back to the Old Testament conception of bāsār (cf. *supra*, pp. 28-9). But more than this is the concurrence of Paul and the Old Testament in the ascription of an ethical quality to the flesh, an idea altogether undeveloped by the Rabbis. W. D. Davies says: "There are no expressions in Rabbinic Judaism which literally correspond to the use of σάρκινος, σαρκικός and πνευματικός and ψυχικός in Paul" (op. cit. p. 20). There are passages in Jewish literature which establish a connexion between the *yetzer* and the body in such a manner that the latter is completely under the domination of the former (cf. W. D. Davies, op. cit. p. 27, and *supra*, pp. 85-7). The Old Testament distinction between *nephesh* and *ruah* is analogous in some ways to the conflict between the σάρξ and πνεῦμα (Gal. 5:17); and ψυχικός and πνευματικός (I Cor. 2:14-15). Cf. T. A. Lacey, op. cit. p. 243.

135 Cf. J. A. T. Robinson, op. cit. p. 31. That is what N. Söderblom has called a mysterious solidarity of the individual and the race which is a "solidarity of woe and of a curse"; op. cit. p. 10; cf. p. 27.

136 Cf. S. Hanson, op. cit. p. 63; A. C. Headlam, op. cit. p. 127; W. Bousset, *Kurios Christos*, p. 193.

137 Op. cit. p. 36. Cf. T. Zahn, *Introduction to the New Testament* (Edinburgh, 1901), I.362.

138 Cf. Rom. 3:20; N. P. Williams, op. cit. p. 132. "Wrong actions done

without knowledge that they are wrong are not imputed to the doer";
Sanday and Headlam, op. cit. p. 144.

139 Cf. H. Weinel, op. cit. p. 248.

140 Gal. 4:3 further indicates a relationship between the Law and the
Aeon, in that it is identified with the στοιχεῖα τοῦ κόσμου. It has been
impressed into the service of the forces of the Aeon; therefore, Paul says,
ὅτε ἦμεν νήπιοι, ὑπὸ τὰ στοιχεῖα τοῦ κόσμου ἤμεθα δεδουλωμένοι.

141 Op. cit. p. 71.

142 Cf. A. B. Bruce, op. cit. p. 173; D. Somerville, *St Paul's Conception
of Christ* (Edinburgh, 1897), p. 166.

143 J. A. T. Robinson, op. cit. p. 35 note 1.

144 So P. Feine, op. cit. p. 275. In that case, sin is equivalent to the
serpent which tempts, deceives, and brings death (Rom. 7:8-11). The
divine will is embodied in a commandment (ἐντολή, 7:8, 9-12. It may be
significant that Paul does not use νόμος as he normally does).

145 Cf. J. A. T. Robinson, op. cit. p. 14; E. C. Rust, op. cit. p. 97.

146 Cf. H. W. Robinson, *Mansfield College Essays,* op. cit. p. 286.

PART THREE

# The Person of Christ

## Editor's Introduction

When we consider the person of Jesus Christ, we are dealing with the very center of the Christian faith. The questions are: Who is Jesus? What is He like? And what can He do for us?

These questions concerned the church quite early. After the earliest generation of believers died, these questions could no longer be settled on the basis of a personal acquaintance with Jesus. Differing viewpoints arose and disputes resulted. The church realized that issues of life and death were involved—the life and death of the faith of the church. A series of ecumenical councils considered the alternative ways of regarding Jesus. This series culminated with the council convened at Chalcedon in 451. From this issued a formula that summed up the decisions made in earlier councils and that added to them. This formula insisted that Jesus was fully God and fully man, possessing two distinct natures (He was not some sort of hybrid), but that at the same time He was a single person, not a split or dual person.

In recent years this type of thinking has come in for considerable criticism. Some argue that such thinking is speculation, that it imposes Greek metaphysical categories on Biblical (Hebraic) thought. Chalcedon was a fifth-century cultural phenomenon, and its conclusions have been supplanted by more modern ways of thinking. For some, the question of what Jesus was and is like has become an improper question.

**J. Theodore Mueller** considers this question. Writing from an orthodox Lutheran perspective, he maintains that the purpose of the Chalcedonian formula is still in need of fulfillment. While Nestorius and Eutyches have long since passed from the scene, their successors are very much with us. The value of the Chalcedonian formula is its warning that here is "a divine mystery which reason cannot fathom, but which faith must proclaim."

While different periods of church history have emphasized either the humanity or the deity of Jesus, sometimes neglecting the other, both aspects of His reality are equally important. **Leon Morris** develops from the Scripture the idea of Jesus' full humanity, noting that the characteristics and the behavior usually found in men also were found in Him. **F. F. Bruce** and **William J. Martin** recount for us the Biblical evidences for the deity of Jesus Christ. This includes an examination of the titles of Jehovah ascribed to Jesus, as well as the works or actions peculiar to Him.

**Harry Emerson Fosdick**, the popularizer of a particular type of liberal Christianity in the twenties and thirties, suggests a different approach to the question—to get back to the history of Jesus and see Him as He truly was. This means not so much asking who Jesus is (this will lead to uncertainties) but examining what He has done. Fosdick concludes that Jesus must have been the type of person who could have done what He did. He was, in other words, divinely appointed. We can even say that He was the *Messiah*, a Hebrew category of function and purpose. But there was in this practical concept no speculative philosophical idea of divine substance, equality with the Father, or anything of that type.

Another attempt to understand the mystery of Jesus is found in **Donald Baillie**'s classic, *God Was in Christ*. The title indicates Baillie's thesis. Rather than saying Christ was God, Baillie suggests that God was present and active in Jesus' person and life. This is to be understood on the analogy of the activity of God in the life of the Christian. This, of course, poses questions about Jesus' uniqueness. Was it merely quantitative, whereby God was in Christ to a greater degree than He is in us, or was there a unique quality about Him?

Finally, we look at a selection from **Wolfhart Pannenberg**'s *Jesus—God and Man*. In contrast with theologies that begin from above, from dogma and faith, Pannenberg believes that Christology must be done "from below"—based upon firm and objective historical reasoning. The deity of

Jesus Christ is derived from the fact of His resurrection, a fact that can be proved, says Pannenberg, like any other fact of history.

The apparent tension or at least polarity between the divine and human natures of Jesus comes to a sharp focus in the question of His sinlessness. If Jesus was truly and fully God, certainly He could not have sinned. On the other hand, however, if He was genuinely man, there had to have been the real possibility of sin. These issues in turn have soteriological significance. If Jesus was not really man, His death cannot avail for our benefit, for He was an outsider to the human race, scarcely able to represent it. On the other hand, if He was not really God, His death cannot really have the infinite value it must have if it is to be an atonement for all mankind.

**Louis Berkhof** presents the case for what is sometimes termed the impeccability of Jesus. By this he means not merely that Jesus could avoid sinning, but further that He could not possibly have sinned. He cites numerous Scriptures that testify to Jesus' sinlessness.

**Nels Ferre**, on the contrary, emphasizes the completeness of Jesus' humanity. Jesus, he points out, had weaknesses, ignorance, finitude, and mortality. This was an accompaniment of full humanity. But did this, and need this, involve His committing sin as well? Certainly, if by sin we mean gross acts of misconduct, Jesus cannot be accused of such. Ferre, indeed, dislikes applying the term *sinfulness* to Jesus because it suggests a great deal of sin. He does find hints in Scripture of the "unsinlessness" of Jesus, however. If sin is the lack of perfect confidence in God and the presence of anxiety, then Hebrews 5:7 seems to suggest that Jesus was not completely sinless.

A mediating position between these two is found in the selection from **Hugh R. Mackintosh**. If Jesus was fully human and was genuinely tempted as we are, so that He could be our "high priest," then presumably He could have sinned. The sinlessness of Jesus resides not in the impossibility of His sinning, but rather in the fact that He did not sin. He successfully resisted temptation in every case. Mackintosh does not speculate about what would have happened to the incarnation if Jesus had sinned. It is enough for him that Jesus did not.

The virgin birth is a topic that has at times in the past provoked sharp and even acrimonious debate. It was one of the major subjects of contention in the fundamentalist-modernist controversy which raged from approximately 1910 to 1930 in the United States. Here the issue was often considerably broader than just the virgin birth. Liberals frequently rejected the virgin birth because their whole view of reality was somewhat naturalistic. It could not really accommodate or account for a miracle such as this. To the fundamentalist, the virgin birth was the seal or proof or testimony of the uniqueness of the deity of Jesus Christ. This series of articles on the virgin birth presents virtually the whole gamut of opinion, from those who feel it is indispensible to those who consider it incredible.

**Carl F. H. Henry** most closely approximates the traditional fundamentalist position. His contention is that without the virgin birth there scarcely could have been a genuine incarnation. The one can be affirmed without the other, but the connection is so close that if the virgin birth is denied, it is likely that either the incarnation would be called into question or affirmed in a form different from that which it has in Scripture and historic teaching.

**Edward J. Carnell** takes a somewhat more moderate view. He rejects the argument that the deity or the sinlessness of Jesus requires the virgin birth. Rather the virgin birth was a sign strengthening and supporting the faith of believers, including even Mary and Joseph. While God could have accomplished the incarnation in a different fashion, He chose to do it in this way. We should be thankful for this and appropriate its benefits.

**L. Harold De Wolf** is not hostile to the doctrine of the virgin birth. He does not consider such an event impossible. He merely questions the adequacy of the evidence for it and asks what real practical difference it made or now makes. The doctrine is, in other words, dispensable.

**Reginald J. Campbell**, on the other hand, finds in the virgin birth something of an obstacle to faith. He insists that he is not denying anything that Christian devotion ever affirmed regarding Jesus. It is simply that he affirms the same things of humanity as a whole, but in a differing degree. The virgin birth cannot therefore be something that radically separates Jesus from the rest of the human race. The virgin birth cannot be sustained by Scripture, he feels. It was evidently unknown to the primitive church, for the earliest New Testament writings make no mention of it. Isaiah 7:14 does not apply to the birth of Jesus. The doctrine conflicts with the inclusion of Joseph's genealogy in Matthew and is indifferent to Christian faith. Actually it is a hindrance to it. The real meaning of the virgin birth is that the lower acting upon the lower cannot produce the higher; that can come only from above.

# The Incarnation

18

## J. Theodore Mueller

# Have We Outmolded Chalcedon?

Of the great ecumenical creeds of the Christian Church, the Chalcedonian Formula is perhaps least familiar to the rank and file of its members. While it does not contain any Christological tenet other than what has already been set forth in the Apostles' Creed and that of Nicaea, its particular emphasis rests upon the doctrine of two unconfounded and undivided natures in the person of Christ.

### The Chalcedonian Formula

The Formula was adopted by the fourth ecumenical council held in 451 A.D. at Chalcedon, a city in Bithynia on the Bosporus, opposite Constantinople. Today the town is a Turkish bathing resort, known as Kadiköy. After the conquest of Constantinople in 1453, the magnificent Chalcedonian cathedral was torn down by Moslem invaders and used as building material for the erection of the so-called "Blue Mosque," which is generally regarded as the most beautiful Mohammedan temple in the

From *Christianity Today*, 7 December 1959, pp. 9-10. Used by permission.

world. No doubt the many Christological controversies in the fifth century gradually paved the way for the Islamic view that reduced Christ to a merely human and rather subordinate prophet.

The Chalcedonian Formula reads:

> Following the holy fathers, we all with one voice teach men to confess that the Son and our Lord Jesus Christ is one and the same, that he is perfect in godhead and perfect in manhood, truly God and truly man, of a reasonable soul and body, consubstantial with the Father as touching his godhead and consubstantial with us as to his manhood, in all things like unto us, without sin; begotten of the Father before all worlds according to his godhead; but in these last days, for us and for our salvation, of the Virgin Mary, the Theotokos, according to his manhood (humanity), one and the same Christ, Son, Lord, only-begotten Son, in two natures, unconfusedly, immutably, indivisibly, inseparably; the distinction of natures being preserved and concurring in one person and hypostasis, not separated or divided into two persons, but one and the same Son and Only-begotten, God the Word, the Lord Jesus Christ, as the prophets from the beginning have spoken concerning him.

The Chalcedonian Formula, which moderns may find somewhat wordy and repetitious, directs itself above all against two antipodal errors which for a long time greatly troubled the Christian Church: Eutychianism and Nestorianism. Of these two heresies the former confounded the two natures in Christ (the divine and the human) into a new nature, while the latter ultimately separated them into two distinct persons. Against them, as Augustus H. Strong, in his *Systematic Theology* (Vol. II, p. 673), points out, the Formula asserts with great emphasis the reality and integrity of the two natures and at the same time also their intimate union in the one person of our Lord. Thus the Christian doctrine forbids men either to confound the natures or to divide the person, since Christ is the God-man.

### Eutychianism and Nestorianism

Eutychianism, so named after the Alexandrian presbyter and archimandrite Eutyches, apparently in the interest of our Lord's divinity, denied the distinction and coexistence of the two natures in Christ and averred a mingling of the two into a *tertium quid*. The human nature, as he taught, by the Incarnation, was changed into the divine and, ignoring our Lord's true humanity, he maintained that it was the Logos who was born, and who suffered and died on Calvary's cross (cf. Charles Hodge, *Systematic Theology*, Vol. II, 102ff.).

Eutychianism was an extreme view to which its founder was moved by the opposite extreme of Nestorianism, so called after Nestorius, patriarch of Constantinople. This prominent church leader, perhaps in the interest of opposing the ever-increasing trend toward Mariolatry, affirmed a twofold personality of Christ and represented the divine Logos as dwelling in the man Christ similar to the Spirit's indwelling in the believer. Thus Nestorianism endangered the true divinity of our Lord. While Eutyches mingled the two natures, Nestorius divided the divine person. Mary, he contended, should not be called the "Mother of God" but only the "Mother of Christ." To safeguard this expression the Formula designated Mary as the "Theotokos" according to Christ's humanity. Though Nestorius deprecated many conclusions that were deduced from his premise, Nestorianism ultimately denied the reality of the Incarnation, its Christ being a deified man rather than God incarnate (cf. Strong, *op. cit.*, p. 671f.). In passing, we may add that Nestorianism gradually spread throughout Arabia and then toward the East as far as India and China. Despite fierce persecution by many enemies, in modern times especially by the Turks, Nestorianism still counts about three thousand adherents in Kurdistan, Persia, and other Eastern countries.

## The Mystery of the Incarnation

Eutychianism and Nestorianism were attempts at solving the "mystery of godliness" of which Paul writes: "And without controversy great is the mystery of godliness; He who was manifested in the flesh" (I Tim. 3:16). These attempts began with Ebionism (about 107 A.D.) which denied the reality of Christ's divine nature and regarded him as a mere man. At the same time Docetism (influential from 70 to 170 A.D.) denied the integrity of our Lord's human nature, and asserted that Christ was only seemingly a human being and not one in reality. Arianism (about 325 A.D.) denied Christ's deity by holding that he was not true God but merely the first and highest of created beings. Apollinarianism (about 381 A.D.) denied the integrity of Christ's human nature by teaching that he indeed had a human body and soul but not a human spirit, the place of which was filled by the Logos. Monothelitism, closely related to Eutychianism, denied Christ's human will and held that he possessed only the divine will. Against all these doctrinal deviations the Chalcedonian Formula defends the scriptural doctrine of Christ's two natures coexisting in the one divine person without confusion or division. The mystery of the Incarnation cannot be solved by finite man; it is either believed or rejected.

## Modern Christological Aberrations

Modern attempts at solving the mystery of Christ's incarnation have resulted in the same heretical reduction of our Lord to a mere man. H. R. Mackintosh, in his well-known work, *Types of Modern Theology*, accuses Schleiermacher, commonly known as the "father of modernism," of coming close to Docetism because he denied the reality of his temptations (*op. cit.*, p. 69). But Schleiermacher also denied Christ's essential deity, as a careful study of his *Christlicher Glaube* shows. According to his teaching Christ is divine only inasmuch as in him was found the highest consciousness of God. No wonder that he denied also our Lord's supernatural conception, vicarious atonement, resurrection, ascension, and second advent.

From a somewhat different viewpoint, but nevertheless just as emphatically, Albrecht Ritschl denied Christ's essential deity by negating his eternal pre-existence. Ritschl regarded the confession of our Lord's godship as a mere value-judgment based on moral perception (Macintosh, *op. cit.,* p. 69). J. L. Neve, in his valuable *History of Christian Doctrine,* says of him: "He effected the transfer of Christ into an ideal man who was made by divine providence to be the perfect revealer of God's love" (Vol. II, p. 151).

Ernst Troeltsch, one of the founders and the chief dogmatician of the religio-historical school, went still further by placing Christ on the same level with other human religious teachers and so paving the way for religious humanism which ultimately ended in complete agnosticism, if not atheism.

We mention these men as outstanding liberal leaders in the modern age who left their theological imprint upon scores of modernists in Great Britain and our own country. No matter how greatly they may differ from one another, they all agree in rejecting the Chalcedonian Formula in its central affirmation that Christ is true God and true man in one person. Nor has neo-orthodoxy stemmed the trend of denying Christ's deity; in fact, also existential theology has failed to return to a clear and unmistakable confession of Christian orthodoxy as set forth in the ecumenical creeds of the Christian Church. When, for example, Brunner ventures the utterly unwarranted statement that "Jesus said nothing openly about his eternal being with the Father" (*The Mediator,* p. 192), his departure from Scripture and the Chalcedonian Formula becomes apparent.

### Chalcedonian Formula Not Outmoded

As long as men seek to solve the mystery involved in the undivided yet also unconfounded union of the two natures in the person of our Lord, the Chalcedonian Formula stands as a warning that we are here dealing with a divine mystery which reason cannot fathom, but which faith must proclaim. That is the great task of the Christian Church.

Our perishing world needs a Savior who is both God and man: man, in order that he might be our substitute and atone for our sins; God, in order that we might be purchased with God's own blood (Acts 10:28). Unless the Christian Church teaches the divine-human Christ of Scripture it has no Saviour who can save that which is lost. It is this very Gospel which the Chalcedonian Formula seeks to guard and preserve. Anchored in Scripture, it can never be outmoded because it proclaims the central message of Scripture in answer to the ever-existential question: "What think ye of Christ?" The Chalcedonian Formula stands as the Church's official and final reply to that paramount query.

**19**

**Leon Morris**

# Jesus the Man

Greek mythology abounds in stories of gods who walked the earth giving the impression that they were men. They looked like men. They acted like men. But when the need arose they cast off pretence, put forth their powers, and revealed their divinity. They were not really men, but gods in disguise. Some early Christians, the Docetists (who are not without their modern cousins!), thought of Jesus in this way. He was God, looking like man, but not really man. But the Christian Church decisively rejected all such views, and labelled them rank heresy. Jesus was truly a man.

We do not know a great deal about His early life, but such evidence as there is shows a normal growth and development. The first and third Gospels preserve genealogies, which point to human descent. He was born as others are. (The Virgin "Birth" is actually a misnomer. It was the conception that was miraculous; we know of nothing abnormal about the birth.) Twice over Luke tells of the way Jesus grew (Luke 2:40, 52), and both times we get the impression of a perfectly normal life.

Jesus knew Himself to be a man, as His response to the first temptation shows, "Man shall not live by bread alone" (Matt. 4:4). He was subject to

From *The Lord from Heaven* (Grand Rapids: William B. Eerdmans, 1958), pp. 42-52. Used by permission.

all the limitations that compass our mortal frame, He knew weariness (John 4:6), hunger (Matt. 21:18; Luke 4:2), and thirst (John 19:28). Bodily life has its joys and its sorrows, and He knew them both.

But human life includes more than bodily experiences. Our emotional lives are a very important part of our being. And, as we can see, Jesus had emotions just like all other men. He could be joyful (John 15:11), or sorrowful (Matt. 26:37). He experienced love for others (Mark 10:21), and compassion (Matt. 9:36). It was astonishment which marked His reaction to the faith of the centurion (Luke 7:9) and to the unbelief of the men of Nazareth (Mark 6:6). On occasion He was indignant (Mark 10:14). And at times He could be angry and grieved (Mark 3:5).

Then we should notice some striking passages where He is spoken of as being troubled in one way or another. If He were not Man as well as God it would be impossible to speak of Him in this kind of language. Take, for example, His behaviour at the tomb of Lazarus. There He "groaned in the spirit." John uses a very down-to-earth expression, for the verb is one that is used of horses snorting! Jesus was troubled, and He wept (John 11:33, 35).

Similarly He was troubled at the prospect of His death. Luke speaks of Him as being "straitened" ("under constraint") till His sufferings should be accomplished (Luke 12:50), and John tells us that His soul was troubled (John 12:27). In Gethsemane He longed for human companionship (Matt. 26:37f.). As He prayed there He was in an agony (Luke 22:44). There is an air of human desolation about the cry from the cross, "My God, my God, why hast thou forsaken me?" (Mark 15:34). It is a very human Jesus that we see undergoing these experiences.

His whole manner of life was genuinely human. He was in subjection to Mary and Joseph (Luke 2:51). He paid taxes (Matt. 17:24ff.). People mistakenly called Him, "a man gluttonous, and a winebibber" (Matt. 11:19). Often He asked questions. We are not unfamiliar with the person who asks questions when he already knows the answers, e.g. a schoolteacher; but Jesus does not appear to be acting like this. When, for example, He asked the father of the epileptic, "How long is it ago since this came unto him?" (Mark 9:21) the impression we get is that He wanted the information.

Few of us would spontaneously refer to Jesus as "a religious man." Yet the Gospels show us that He was just that. He was regular in His attendance at public worship (Luke 4:16). He did not neglect private prayer, for there are many references to it (Mark 1:35; 6:46; Luke 3:21; etc.). Sometimes He prayed all night (Luke 6:12), which is eloquent of His sense of need. Even His enemies bore witness to His trust in God (Matt. 27:43). He practised those acts of worship and communion with God which we must practise. In this, as in all things, He has set the example we must follow.

We see, then, that the Gospels paint a picture of a real incarnation. When the Son of God came to earth He did not play at being man. He became man in the fullest sense as D. M. Baillie, for example, has made abundantly clear in his fascinating essay *God Was in Christ*. The mechanics of the process are hid from us, but of the fact the Bible leaves us in no doubt. We may be totally unable to explain how the second Person of the Trinity could be exercising His cosmic functions and at the same time be the Babe of Bethlehem. But that does not give us license to reject that part of the evidence which displeases us. The facts of the previous chapters point us to the deity of our Lord. Those of this chapter indicate no less clearly His manhood. We may notice something of the problem thus posed by considering at greater length two parts of the evidence for His manhood, His human ignorance and His temptations.

## The Limitations of Jesus' Knowledge

We have already noted that Jesus asked questions, and that the most natural way of understanding this is to say that He did so because He wanted to find out the answers. He did not know. On one point, the date of His second coming, we are left in no doubt at all. Jesus explicitly said that He did not know when this would be (Mark 13:32). There is thus no doubt that His knowledge was limited in some way.

This seems inevitable if there is to be a real incarnation. It is of the essence of human life that we do not know quite a lot of things. Think how very different life would be for the student if he knew from the beginning of the year what questions would turn up in his examination paper! What vistas of bliss and ease the prospect opens up! Again, it is of the very essence of the matter when we are weighing up alternative courses of action that we do not *know* how either will turn out. We must make our decision on the basis of our understanding of the probabilities. It hardly seems necessary to labour the point. Ignorance is an inevitable accompaniment of the only human life that we know. It compasses us round at every turn. It is a foe against which we must wage constant warfare. Knowledge must be acquired through the discipline of toil and effort.

Sometimes one meets people who overlook this aspect of Jesus' life. They picture Him as going on a serene way, knowing all the time all the secrets of the universe, knowing the thoughts of everyone about Him, knowing the outcome of every course of action in which He or they were engaging. If this was the manner of it, then the life Jesus lived was not a human life. It lacked a necessary quality of human life, even human life at the highest level. And it is out of harmony with the Gospels. As we have seen, the evangelists portray for us a Jesus who was genuinely human.

So far, I think, most students would agree. Difficulties arise as to the extent of this ignorance. Here it must be borne in mind that Jesus did show a most remarkable knowledge on occasions when we might have thought that a merely human individual would have been ignorant. Thus He knew the thoughts of His friends (Luke 9:47) and of His enemies (Luke 6:8, etc.). John tells us that He knew the secret experience of Nathaniel (John 1:47f.), the past life of the woman of Samaria (John 4:29), and even "what was in man" (John 2:25).[1]

This kind of thing has led E. J. Bicknell to postulate a difference between His "discursive knowledge," that which is gained "either by the operation of our mind, by processes of reasoning or argument, or else by receiving information from others," and His "intuitive knowledge," that gained "not piecemeal, but by a direct and immediate perception." He was limited like all other men as regards the former, but not as regards the latter.[2]

There may be something in this, but it does not seem to account for all the facts. It does not explain, for example, His knowledge of the past of the woman of Samaria. Nor of the fact that Lazarus was dead (John 11:11-14). Probably we are to understand this in the light of His mission. He had come to accomplish the divine purpose, and such knowledge, of whatever kind, as was necessary for the discharge of this function was afforded Him. But in all other matters His genuine humanity forbids us to think that He was in better case than we.

The crux of the problem here arises when we think of the possibility of error. Many modern scholars find no difficulty in the thought that Jesus was quite wrong in many things, being, in fact, just as much a child of His age as we are of ours. They feel that He was in error in the matter of the date of the second coming, the authorship of the Pentateuch, and other matters.

But to others it seems crystal clear that ignorance is not the same thing as error, and that whereas we must think of Jesus as being ignorant on many matters there is not the same compulsion about error. Thus Orr writes: "Ignorance is not error, nor does the one thing necessarily imply the other. That Jesus should use the language of His time on things indifferent, where no judgment or pronouncement of His own was involved, is readily understood; that He should be the victim of illusion, or false judgment, on any subject on which He was called to pronounce, is a perilous assertion."[3] Leonard Hodgson points out that the assumption that error is a necessary part of human life makes the mistake of measuring Christ's manhood by ours rather than ours by His.[4]

There is no finality in the matters which are urged as proving Him to have been mistaken. Thus some contend that He expected the second coming to take place within the lifetime of the disciples. But this is met by His own statement, to which we have already referred, that He did not know when this would be (Mark 13:32). Others suggest that He was wrong in His views on the authorship of the Pentateuch, and the events in the life of Jonah. But, no matter how certain some modern scholars may be in their own minds as to the truth in these matters, it is impossible in the nature of the case to produce conclusive proof. Nothing in the available evidence can be taken as *proving* that the Master was in error.

There is a tendency today for men to be so convinced of the manhood of Jesus that His Godhead is to all intents and purposes lost sight of. In stressing His humanity there are not wanting those who practically bring Him down to our level. He becomes a typical man of the first century, wrong about very many things, though right in some of His insights into the nature of God. In holding fast His community with us they have surrendered His community with God.

It must be plainly asserted that Jesus was man. Nothing must be allowed to obscure the condescension involved in a full incarnation. But it must be as plainly asserted that He was not only man. His limitations must be understood in the light of this. Admittedly we are faced with a mystery here. The incarnation is unique. We have nothing to compare it with, and finite minds cannot grasp all that is involved in it or how it took place. But the point is that it is a real incarnation. It was God who became man. The manhood must not be so understood as to rule out a real Godhead.

## The Temptations of Jesus

At the beginning of His ministry Jesus was tempted in the wilderness, and at the end, in Gethsemane. He was tempted also on other occasions as we see from Luke's statement that the devil left Him "for a season" (Luke 4:13). The temptations are important evidence of the true humanity of Jesus, for, as James tells us, "God cannot be tempted with evil" (James 1:13). The fact that He was subjected to real temptations shows that the incarnation was a real assumption of manhood, and not a playing with the human frame.

Sometimes people object that the temptations of Jesus cannot have been real, since He was a sinless Being. Christians have felt throughout the ages that the sinlessness of Jesus is something important, and that it is not to be thought of as more or less fortuitous, as though He might have sinned or He might not have, and it just happened that He did not. Such a position would never satisfy the Christian understanding of Jesus. Nothing must be said which will leave His sinlessness a matter more or less of chance.

Nevertheless, when full allowance has been made for this, the possibility of real temptation remains. Concerning the idea that Jesus was genuinely tempted and yet could not yield to the temptation William Temple has said: "This is not even a paradox to any one who has seriously considered what is involved in the temptation felt by a man of high character to an act contrary to his character: he is attracted by the wrong course; he has to keep a hold on himself; he knows he is making a real choice; yet (being himself) he could not yield. The effort needed to overcome the temptation is a real effort, but it is also a necessary effort because his character, being such as it is, must so react to the situation."[5] The rightness of such a statement can hardly be doubted. And if this may be the case even with a moral man, how much more in the case of such a one as Jesus.

The objection that if Jesus was sinless He could not have experienced real temptation rests on the assumption, in the words of A. E. Taylor, "that *if* a man does not commit certain transgressions . . . it must be because he never felt the appeal of them."[6] As soon as we face it we see that this is just not true in the case of men like ourselves. And we have no warrant for affirming it of Jesus.

The reality of Jesus' temptations is highlighted by the story of Gethsemane. There we read that He was "in an agony" and that "his sweat was as it were great drops of blood falling down to the ground" (Luke 22:44). It makes nonsense of this to say that there was no real struggle, that Jesus did not really experience a natural human shrinking from the horror of the cross which He yet knew to be the Father's will, that His final "thy will be done" does not represent a victory won the hard way (notice that in Matt. 26:39 He prays that if possible the cup should pass from Him, but in verse 42 the inevitability of the cup is accepted). The story is meaningless unless Jesus wrestled with a real temptation.

It is true that Jesus' experience lacked one element of ours, namely, the consciousness of past sin. But this does not mean that He was not tempted. Adam was genuinely tempted, though before that first temptation he had no experience of sin. We must not make the mistake of taking our imperfect lives as the standard, and regarding Christ as human only as He conforms to our failures. He is the standard, and He shows us what a genuine humanity can be.

There is also the thought that, far from sinlessness meaning something less in the way of temptation, human experience suggests that it means more. "The resistance of temptation may be torture to a good man, whereas a bad man yields easily."[7] The man who yields to a particular temptation has not felt its full power. He has given in while the temptation has yet something in reserve. Only the man who does not yield to a temptation who, as regards that particular temptation, is sinless, knows the full extent of that temptation. Thus Jesus, the sinless One, is the only one who really knows the full extent of temptation's power, and He knows it precisely because He did not yield. If I Cor. 10:13 is correctly interpreted as affording a correlation between the temptation and the power to endure, then Christ's temptations must have been of an intensity inconceivable to us.

Bodily life seems necessarily to involve the possibility of temptation. Bodily appetites carry with them the temptation to misuse. Thus hunger points to the possibility of gluttony, the need for rest to the possibility of slothfulness, and so on. The mission of Jesus could be truly forwarded only by right means. But wrong means often look plausible if the end is right, and the temptation narrative shows that Jesus felt this temptation, too. All this highlights such a statement as that of Moberly, "There was a hypothetical or conceivable selfishness,—the possible imagination of a rebellious self,—not actual indeed, nor actually possible without chaos: yet something to be, by moral strain, controlled and denied; something which made self-denial in the Incarnate, not an empty phrase, but a stupendous act or energy of victorious moral goodness."[8] It is this which must be safeguarded.

To think of Jesus as going serenely through life's way with never a ripple of real temptation to disturb His even course is to empty His moral life of real worth, and to prevent us from seeing in Him our Example. His sinlessness did not result from some automatic necessity of His nature as much as from His moment-by-moment committal of Himself to the Father.[9] He overcame. But it was a real victory, over real temptation.

## Notes

[1] See Leon Morris, *The Lord from Heaven,* pp. 97f.

[2] *A Theological Introduction to the Thirty-nine Articles of the Church of England,* London, 1933, pp. 88f.

[3] *Revelation and Inspiration,* London, 1909, pp. 150f.

[4] *And Was Made Man,* London, 1933, p. 27.

[5] *Christus Veritas,* London, 1925, p. 217. See also D. M. Baillie, "When we say *non potuit peccare,* we do not mean that He was completely raised above the struggle against sin . . . when we say that He was incapable of sinning, we mean that He was the supreme case of what we can say with limited and relative truth about many a good man." *God Was in Christ,* London, 1948, pp. 14f.

[6] *Asking Them Questions,* ed. Ronald Selby Wright, Oxford, 1942, p. 94.

[7] H. R. Mackintosh, *The Person of Jesus Christ,* Edinburgh, 1914, p. 403.

[8] *Atonement and Personality,* London, 1932, p. 106.

[9] Cf. the words of William Temple quoted in Morris, *The Lord from Heaven,* p. 24.

# 20

## F. F. Bruce
## and William J. Martin

# The Deity of Christ

The belief in the deity of Christ is derived directly from statements concerning him in the Bible. The references are so many and their meaning so plain that Christians of every shade of opinion have always regarded its affirmation as an absolute and indispensable requisite of their faith. It is proclaimed in the very first sermon of the infant Church (Acts 2:36) where Peter, to the loftiest title known to a Jew, adds a loftier still—*Lord* and Christ (Messiah); while in the last vision of the Book of Revelation the Lamb occupying *one* throne with God (Rev. 22:3) can betoken only essential oneness.

Christ's claim to be equal with God underlies his teaching right from the start. The disciples could not long have missed the implication of the change in the very frame of his message from that of the Old Testament prophets, whose familiar introduction, "Thus saith the Lord," was now replaced by "But *I* say unto you" (no fewer than nine times in the early part of the Sermon on the Mount recorded in Matthew, chapter 5).

In content and scope his teaching embraced much that was new about the nature of God. Not only the disciples but also the Jews soon recog-

From *Christianity Today*, 18 December 1964, pp. 11-17. Used by permission.

nized that he was affirming his equality with God (John 5:18). He was beginning to reveal that the "unity" of God involved a true uniting of three "persons" in the Godhead, of whom he was claiming to be one. ("Godhead" simply means "the divine nature"; "head" is an abstract ending, commonly appearing as "hood," and it was just by chance that "Godhead" became current instead of the equally proper "Godhood.")

The New Testament writers seem never to have felt the need to systematize the many statements of Christ on his unique relationship to the Father, or to define by way of a logical formulation the basis of their belief in the "Trinity." For them this doctrine was practical and implicit, rather than theoretic. Not surprisingly, therefore, the word "Trinity" itself never appears in the New Testament. To see in its absence a possible objection to the doctrine would be as illogical as to deny that theological knowledge is to be found in the New Testament since the word "theology" is nowhere used.

It is, moreover, a well-known fact that evidence for the beliefs of a community does not demand the existence of a systematic statement. No one, for instance, would question the belief of certain primitive peoples in polytheism because it lacks orderly expression.

By "trinity" is meant "three in one" and "one in three," "trinity in unity" and "unity in trinity." Thus it is not "tri-theism" or "three Gods," nor is it merely three aspects of God. The word "person" is the word that, by a process of transference, has been adopted to designate the distinctions existing in the Godhead, namely Father, Son, and Holy Spirit. It is probably the best term at our disposal to denote the possession of such decisive characteristics of personality as intercommunication and fellowship, as ascribed individually to the Father, Son, and Holy Spirit. In numerous passages in the New Testament the "trinitarian" pattern is so clearly defined that one would be compelled to invent some such word as "trinity," if it did not already exist, to describe the implications of the statements.

It was not until the Gospel had been preached for some three hundred years in New Testament terms that anyone took on himself to assail the belief of Christians in the deity of Christ. The person who did it was Arius. The novel form of his attack shows that Christians had hitherto accepted it without question. His arguments, as formulated by him, were clearly intended as an objection to the prevalent view, not as a correction of a heresy. If the state of affairs had been otherwise, that is, if Christians generally had denied the deity of Christ, then his opposition would have been meaningless. As promotion to a bishopric had been denied him, he has left himself wide open to the suspicion of having been motivated by a desire for personal revenge. He was evidently a man who knew how to exploit secular political influence to the full, and the story of his machinations makes sordid reading. As a consequence of strong political support, a controversy arose out of all proportion to the merits of his arguments. His views were finally shown to be at complete variance with Scripture and were pronounced heretical. Nevertheless, from time to time they have been revived, either deliberately or in ignorance, often peddled from door to door by text-mongers, unaware that the very passages which they have learned to quote so glibly were first used over sixteen hundred years ago by a frustrated "cleric."

Within the brief compass of this booklet it will not be possible to quote all the passages referring to the deity of Christ and to consider all the ways in which this truth is indicated in Scripture. The reader should, however, find no difficulty in adding to the references given here. In the passages quoted, the original text has been kept constantly under review, and on occasion, wording not to be found in any standard translation has been introduced, where it was felt that the meaning of the original could be made more apparent. In the section that immediately follows, the evidence is all the stronger for being of an incidental nature.

## Titles of Jehovah

One of the most remarkable things in our Lord's ministry is the quiet assurance with which he unhesitatingly applies to himself titles from the Old Testament which are there indisputably used of Jehovah. Moreover, the New Testament writers ascribe such titles to Christ.

### *"First and Last"*

A significant title assumed by the Lord Jesus in the book of Revelation is "First and Last" (chapter 1:17; 2:8; 22:13). In 22:16 the speaker says of himself: "I Jesus have sent my angel to testify unto you of these things," having already said in verse 13, "I am Alpha and Omega, the first and the last." Also in chapter 2:8, there is no doubt about the person to whom the words refer: "These things saith the first and last, who died and came to life." Now this designation "First and last" occurs three times in Isaiah (41:4; 44:6; 48:12) where on each occasion Jehovah is the speaker.

### *The "I Am"*

Jehovah, the incorrect but well-established rendering of the Hebrew consonants *YHWH,* was regarded by the Jews as too sacred to be pronounced and was replaced by a variety of substitutes, such as "Lord" (*Adonai*), or "The Name." We can no longer say with certainty how it was pronounced, but from Exodus 3:14 we know that it was derived from the verb "to be": "God said to Moses, 'I am who I am'; and he said: Say to the people of Israel 'I am' has sent you." Now on more than one occasion our Lord refers to himself by using "I am" in a way that points unmistakably to this Old Testament title of Jehovah. In a controversy with the Jews he declared: "Before Abraham was, I am" (John 8:58). Had he been merely a pre-existent Being, then he would have had to say "Before Abraham was, I was." That the amazing implication of his claim did not escape the Jews is clearly shown by the extreme violence of their reaction in attempting to stone him to death for alleged blasphemy. Another occasion on which he used it was at the time of his arrest. To his question to his approaching captors, "Whom seek ye?," they answered, "Jesus of Nazareth," to which he replied, "I am." The effect that this brief utterance had on them was dramatic: "They went backward and fell to the ground" (John 18:5, 6). The mere literal sense of these words could hardly have produced this extraordinary effect. Then again at the crucial stage of his trial, Jesus, being interrogated by the high priest as to his messianic claims, replied, "I am: and you shall see the Son of man sitting at the right hand of power and coming with the clouds of heaven" (Mark 14:62). The savage vehemence that this called forth in the high priest and the company can be explained only if it was understood by them to be a claim to personal deity, a blasphemy in their eyes of such magnitude as to be expiated only by death.

### Author of Eternal Words

The Old Testament constantly claims to be an authoritative and immutable communication from God. In Isaiah 40:8 we are told: "The grass withers and the flower fades, but the word of our God stands for ever." To this view of the Old Testament as a divine revelation our Lord unquestionably subscribes. For instance, his words in Matthew 5:18, "For truly I say unto you, until heaven and earth pass away, one jot or one tittle shall not pass away from the Law, until all things are fulfilled." For his own words he makes a substantially similar claim: "Heaven and earth will pass away, but my words shall not pass away" (Matt. 24:35).

### Light

The coming Messiah is designated in two familiar prophecies as "Light" (Isa. 9:2, compare Matt. 4:16; and Isa. 49:6, compare Luke 2:32). Five times in the first chapter of John (verses 4, 5, 7, 8, 9) this description is used. His uniqueness is stressed in verse 9: "The true light." Our Lord himself said: "I am the light of the world" (John 8:12). Now light is a well-known title of Jehovah in the Old Testament; for instance, Psalm 27:1, "The Lord is my Light and my salvation," or even more specifically in Isaiah in a context of messianic prophecies: "Jehovah will be to you an everlasting light" (Isa. 60:19 and 20). Again, following on the messianic prophecy of Isaiah 59:20 we have in 60:1 "light" designating the Messiah, equated with the glory of Jehovah. "Arise, shine [that is, Zion], for your light has come, and the glory of the Lord has dawned upon you." It is instructive to see how John in his introduction to his first epistle uses the very same epithet of God that he had already used in the opening verses of his Gospel of the incarnate Son, who is there the "light that the darkness found invincible" while in First John 1:5, "God is light and in him is no darkness at all."

### Rock

There are two words commonly used in Hebrew for "rock," as well as the word "stone." One is used for instance in Psalm 18:2, "Jehovah is my rock," the other in Psalm 95:1, "O come let us sing to Jehovah, let us make a joyful noise to the rock of our salvation." Paul in I Corinthians 10:4 interprets the "rock" of Exodus 17:6 as referring to Christ. "Stone" is used as a title of God in Genesis 49:24, and in the messianic passage in Isaiah 28:16, "Behold I am laying in Zion for a foundation a stone, a tested stone." Peter in his first letter (I Peter 2:6-8) understands this passage to be speaking of Christ as the foundation stone of the "spiritual house," the Church. Although the word here is not the one used in Matthew 16:18 ("and upon this rock I will build my church"), the similarity of function is so obvious that Peter must also have had these words in mind. This seems all the more certain from his application two verses later of "rock," a description of Jehovah taken from Isaiah 8:14, to Christ. On linguistic grounds there could be no objection to seeing in Matthew 16:18 another instance of our Lord's taking to himself a common Old Testament title of Jehovah.

### Bridegroom

The figure of a bridegroom is one that is frequently used either implicitly or explicitly of Jehovah in the Old Testament. In Hosea 2:16, for instance, Jehovah says, "You will call me 'my husband.'" Again in Isaiah 62:5, "As a bridegroom rejoicing over the bride, your God will rejoice over you." Our Lord early in his ministry and often subsequently depicts himself as a bridegroom. In a reply to the Pharisees, he says concerning himself: "Can the sons of the wedding chamber fast while the bridegroom is with them?" (Mark 2:19). Again in the parable of the "Foolish Virgins" he is the bridegroom (Matt. 25:1-13). In that great final beatific vision (Rev. 21:2) the Church is depicted "as a bride adorned for her husband."

### Shepherd

In Psalm 23:1 we read, "Jehovah is my shepherd," and in Ezekiel 34:15, "I myself will be the shepherd of my sheep." In John 10:11, our Lord uses this title of himself, "I am the good shepherd, the good shepherd lays down his life for the sheep." Peter calls him "the Shepherd and Guardian of your souls" (I Peter 2:25) and again "the chief Shepherd" (I Peter 5:4). The writer of the epistle to the Hebrews speaks of him as "the great shepherd" (Heb. 13:20). That the title is unique is clear from John 10:16, "So there shall be one flock, one shepherd."

### Forgiver of sins

In the Old Testament, God alone has the right and power to forgive sins: Jeremiah 31:34, "For I [Jehovah] will forgive their wickedness, and their sin will I remember no more." Or again Psalm 130:4, "For with Thee is forgiveness that Thou shouldest be feared." In the New Testament we find our Lord claiming this right for himself. In Luke 5:21 we read of the Pharisees protesting that only God could forgive sins. This was to them, as it would be to us, self-evident. To this Christ replied by substantiating his authority to forgive, by healing the paralytic. In Acts 5:31 Peter proclaims Christ as the One whom "God has exalted at His right hand as Prince and Saviour, to give repentance to Israel and forgiveness of sins." In Colossians 2:13 Paul speaks of God "having forgiven us all our transgressions," while in chapter 3:13, it is, "the Lord [or Christ] has forgiven you." If the right reading here is Lord, it must stand for Christ, as is clear from such a reference as "Christ Jesus the Lord" in chapter 2:6.

## Redeemer

The act of redemption is peculiar to God in the Old Testament. Two Hebrew words are in use, and both occur in Hosea 13:14, "From the power of Sheol, I will ransom them, from death I will redeem them." Again in Psalm 130:7, "For with Jehovah is grace and abundance of ransom and he will ransom Israel from all his iniquities." A direct parallel to this is found in Titus 2:13 with the difference that now Christ is identified with God (see verse 10): "Our great God and Saviour Jesus Christ, who gave himself for us, that he might ransom us from all iniquity." A different Greek verb for redemption is found in Galatians 3:13, "Christ has purchased us from the curse of the law." Again in Revelation 5:9, "For Thou [the Lamb] wast slain, and didst purchase unto God with thy blood, men of every tribe, and tongue, and people, and nation."

## Saviour, or Author of Salvation

In the Old Testament Jehovah is frequently described as Saviour or as the author of salvation: Isaiah 43:3, "For I am Jehovah, thy God, the holy One of Israel, thy Saviour"; or Ezekiel 34:22, "And I [the Lord Jehovah, verse 20] will save my flock and it will no longer be for booty and I will judge between sheep and sheep, and I will establish over them one shepherd." The resemblance to John 10:17, 16, is striking: "I [Jesus] lay down my life for the sheep" and "there shall be one flock, one shepherd." In Isaiah 45:22 a world-wide salvation is promised: "Turn to me and let yourselves be saved, all the ends of the earth," and a little later (verse 23): "To me every knee shall bow and every tongue shall swear," words taken up by Paul in Philippians 2:10, "At the name of Jesus every knee shall bow," and (verse 11) "every tongue confess that Jesus Christ is Lord." It would be impossible to quote all the passages in the New Testament that refer to the Lord Jesus as Saviour or the author of salvation. He was given the name Jesus expressly: "for he will save his people from their sins" (Matt. 1:21); in Hebrews 5:9, "He became unto all those who obey him the author of eternal salvation." In harmony with all this is the significant parallel between "our God and Saviour Jesus Christ" and "our Lord and Saviour Jesus Christ" by Peter (II Peter 1:1, 11).

## Co-Partner of Divine Glory

In Isaiah 42:8 we read: "I am Jehovah and I shall not give my glory to another," and the phrase is repeated again in Isaiah 48:11. Now in that sacredest of all his prayers recorded in John 17, our Lord speaks of the reciprocal nature of his shared glory with the Father and says: "Father, the hour is come, glorify the Son, that the Son may glorify thee" (verse 1). And again a little later: "And now glorify me, Father, with thine own self, with the glory which I had with thee before the world was" (verse 5). Paul sums all this up in an arresting phrase. When he confronts the abjection of His humiliation with the sublimity of His exaltation, the title he uses contains two superlatives. "For had they [the leaders] known it, they would not have crucified the *Lord* of *Glory*" (I Cor. 2:8).

## Judge

One of the earliest titles of Jehovah is that of universal judge. Abraham standing before him says: "Shall not the judge of all the earth execute justice?" (Gen. 18:25). And in Joel 3:12 Jehovah says: "I will sit to judge all the nations round about." Now from Matthew 25:31-46 we learn that Christ will occupy the throne of glory—and there can be none more eminent than this—and preside at the last judgment. Here it is not so much the assumption of a title as the exercising of an office. In Romans 2:3 Paul speaks of the judgment of God, but in II Timothy 4:1 it is, "Jesus Christ who shall judge the quick and the dead." It is not surprising, therefore, to find that II Corinthians 5:10 speaks of the judgment seat of Christ.

## The Person of Christ in Old Testament Prophecy

Some of the prophecies about Christ make it clear that he is more than man. Isaiah 9:6, "For to us a child is born, to us a son is given, and the princedom will be upon his shoulders, and his name will be called Wonderful, Counsellor, mighty God, Everlasting Father, Prince of Peace." No plainer words could be used to express his deity. Again, although often designated as the son of David, this implied more than an earthly descendant of David. The Lord makes this plain by quoting the words of David in Psalm 110:1, "The Lord said to my Lord, Sit at my right hand until I put thy enemies as thy footstool" (Matt. 22:43, 44). That an angelic Being is not meant is shown by Hebrews 1:13, "But to what angel has he ever said: 'Sit at my right hand, till I make thy enemies thy footstool.' " Peter also quotes this passage in his sermon on the day of Pentecost to prove the Lordship and Messiahship of Jesus (Acts 2:34, 35).

## Works or Actions Peculiar to Jehovah

Both Jehovah and Christ are said to have the power to give life. Hannah in her "Magnificat" says: "Jehovah is the one who causes to die and the one who makes alive" (I Sam. 2:6). Eleven times in Psalm 119 alone Jehovah is credited with the power to make alive. In John 5:21 Christ claims to have this power in equal measure with the Father: "For as the Father raises the dead and gives them life, so also the Son gives life to whom He will." In I Corinthians 15:45, Paul quotes Genesis 2:7, "The first man Adam became a living being," and adds, "the last Adam a life-giving spirit." And, perhaps the best-known and most often quoted passage of all, the words of Jesus to Martha: "I am the resurrection and the life; he who believes in me, though he die, yet shall he live" (John 11:25).

The Bible opens with the statement: "In the beginning God created the heavens and the earth," that is, all things.

In Isaiah 40:28, "Jehovah is the eternal God, the creator of the ends of the earth." Jeremiah calls him "The former [or creator] of all things" (Jer. 10:16). Paul speaks of Christ in similar terms. "For by [or in] him were all things created in the heavens, and upon the earth, things visible and things invisible, whether thrones or dominions or principalities or powers, all things have been created through him and for him" (Col. 1:16), and John 1:2, "He [the Logos] was in the beginning with God; all things were made through him, and without him was not anything made that was made."

## New Testament References to the Deity of Christ

No clearer expression of the fact of the Trinity could be desired than that given by the risen Christ in the baptismal formula in Matthew 28:19, with its inescapable implication of the co-equality and hence co-eternity of the three persons of the Godhead. "Go, therefore, and make disciples of all nations, baptizing them into the name of the Father and of the Son and of the Holy Spirit." Notice that our Lord said "name," not "names." There subsist three co-eternal persons, but the divine essence or substance is one. The model for this formula is probably to be found in the bene-diction given by the Lord to Moses in Numbers 6:24, "Jehovah bless thee and keep thee, Jehovah cause his face to shine upon thee and be gracious to thee, Jehovah lift up his face upon thee and give thee peace." And God adds: "That they may put my name upon the people of Israel and I will bless you." Although there are three blessings there is only one Blesser; thus it is "name," not "names."

At the end of Paul's second letter to the Corinthians he pronounces a benediction in which the three persons of the Trinity are named as part-ners with co-equal power to bless: "The grace of the Lord Jesus Christ, and the love of God, and the communion of the Holy Spirit, be with you all. Amen." The use of all of Christ's titles is significant: he is not merely Jesus Christ, he is the Lord Jesus Christ (II Cor. 13:14).

Paul again in I Corinthians 12 gives us a passage in which the "trinitarian" pattern is obvious: "Now there are diversities of gifts of grace, but the same Spirit. And there are varieties of services, but the same Lord. And there are diversities of activities but the same God, who is effecting all things in all" (verses 4-6). The mention of the same Spirit, the same Lord, the same God, demands the use of the word "trinity," or another word meaning the same thing.

In Paul's letter to the Ephesians, within a brief compass he refers to the Trinity no fewer than four times. The first mention describes the trini-tarian nature of our approach to God: "For through him [Christ] we both [Jew and Gentile] have access by one Spirit to the Father." The word for "access" is that used of bringing a subject into the presence of his king, or as we would say, "to have audience of" (Eph. 2:18).

The second reference describes the collaboration of the "Trinity" in our edification (Eph. 2:22): "In whom [Jesus Christ, the chief cornerstone, verse 20] you are builded together for a habitation of God through the Spirit." Again the same pattern: In whom—Christ; to whom—God; through whom—the Spirit.

The third passage is Ephesians 3:14-17, "For this cause I bow my knees to the Father, of whom the whole 'repatriation' in heaven and on earth is named. That he would grant unto you according to the riches of his grace, that ye may be strengthened with power through his Spirit in the inner man, that Christ may come and take up his abode in your hearts by faith." Thus for enjoyment of abiding fellowship we have the cooperation of the Father, the Holy Spirit, and Christ.

Again Paul refers to the work of the Trinity in maintaining unification in his Church (Eph. 4:4-6). "One body, and one Spirit, even as you were called in one hope of your calling; one Lord, one faith, one baptism, one God and Father of all, who is above all and through all and in all." Here we have unity in tri-unity.

In the first chapter of Colossians we have a number of significant statements concerning the person of Christ. In verse 15 we read: "who [the Son] is the image of the invisible God." "Image" by the common process of extension came to denote not only representation but manifestation. Thus in II Corinthians 4:4 we find it used in this latter sense: "that the light of the gospel of the glory of Christ, who is the image of God, should not dawn upon them." But Christ is also: "the first-born of every creature." The word first-born had long since ceased to be used exclusively in its literal sense, just as prime (from Latin *primus*—first) with us. The Prime Minister is not the first minister we have had; he is the most pre-eminent. A man in the "prime" of life has long since left the first part of his life behind. Similarly, first-born came to denote not priority in time but pre-eminence in rank. For instance in Psalm 89:27, "I have put him [given him] as first-born, higher than the kings of the earth." In a given situation even a whole company may rank as first-borns, as in Hebrews 12:23, "and church of the first-born ones, who are enrolled in heaven." But Paul leaves us in no doubt as to what he means by the word; for he proceeds: "for [because, for this reason] by him were all things created"; and the word Paul uses for "all" means without any exception whatever. Had Christ himself been a created being, Paul would have had to use the Greek word meaning "other things" or the word meaning "remainder, rest." But then Paul would not have called him first-born but "first-created," a term never applied to Christ. And verse 17 clinches the whole matter: "And he *is* before all things," not "he was." The force of this statement is equal to that of the "I am" of John 8:58.

Paul on occasions exploits language to its maximal limit to find terms in which to describe the absolute exaltation of Christ. To the believers in Rome he writes: "From whom [the Jewish nation] as concerning the flesh is Christ, who is over all, God blessed for ever" (Rom. 9:5). When speaking to the Corinthian converts about the Cross as the focal point of their salvation, he goes on to say: "To us there is one God: the Father, of whom are all things, and we unto him, and one Lord, Jesus Christ, through whom are all things, and we through him" (I Cor. 8:6). To the Ephesians, he asserts: "[He is set] far above all hierarchy, and authority, and power, and dominion, and every name that is named, not only in this world, but also in that which is to come" (Eph. 1:21). To the Colossian Christians he says: "In him dwells all the fulness of the deity bodily" (Col. 2:9). Even in his short letter to Titus he must mention it: "Expecting the blessed hope and glorious appearing of our great God and the Saviour Jesus Christ" (Titus 2:13).

In the most unlikely places in the New Testament we find the deity of Christ taken for granted. James, his brother, begins his letter with the words: "James, a servant of God, and of the Lord Jesus Christ." James must have heard our Lord often say, "No servant can serve two masters" (Luke 16:13). But the very title, too, that he gives to Christ, shows that he is placing him equal with God. And if emphasis was needed he provides it in chapter 2:1, "My brethren, hold not the faith of our Lord Jesus Christ, the Lord of Glory, with respect of persons." For a Jew, glory was an attribute of God alone.

In I John 5:6-9 (as everyone knows, verse 7 is absent from all good manuscripts) there appears again the trinitarian pattern: the witness of the *Spirit* with the witness of *God* witnessing concerning his *Son*. Before John finishes his letter he leaves us in no doubt concerning the person of the Son (verse 20): "And we know that the Son of God is come and has given us understanding that we know him that is true, and we are in him that is true, in his Son Jesus Christ, this is the true God and eternal life."

It was evident for the writers in the New Testament, as it should be for us, that Christ could not save if he were not fully divine. The all-sufficiency of his sacrifice depends on his absolute authority. Had he been a created being, he would have been in some sense under compulsion, a victim. It is his possession of absolute free will that removes the stigma of injustice from the Cross. And only of one who had himself absolute immortality could it be said that "he became obedient unto death."

Among the disciples was one who refused to believe in the resurrection of Christ without tangible proof. For him the witness of others was not sufficient in a matter of such momentous consequence. He demanded nothing less than positive proof within the domain of his own senses. When our Lord appeared to him, He did not rebuke him for his skepticism; rather He readily provided the kind of proof asked for. His confession, in words expressing the ultimate in Christian faith, could not have been a consequence of seeing someone risen from the dead, for he must surely have seen the risen Lazarus. There is no mistaking their intent: "Thomas answered and said to *him,* 'My Lord and My God.' " And our Lord did not restrain him nor rebuke him; he received this as his rightful designation (John 20:24-29).

The claims of Christ to deity, embedded in the highest ethical teaching known to man, are expressed in irreducible matter-of-fact language. Either he was a fraud, or he was God. There is no middle position.

Paul provides a simple test for the sincerity of our faith. To be able to confess Jesus as Lord, Paul says, we need the power of the Holy Spirit (I Cor. 12:3). Ask the one who places Christ any lower than the highest, if he will submit to this test. What is your own response, for this is a condition of salvation?

"Because, if you confess with your lips that Jesus is Lord, and believe in your heart that God raised him from the dead, you will be saved" (Rom. 10:9).

## Brief Notes on Some of the Texts Used by Arians

### John 1:1

Much is made by Arian amateur grammarians of the omission of the definite article with "God" in the phrase "And the Word was God." Such an omission is common with nouns in a predicative construction. To have used it would have equated the Word and the Word only with God, whereas without it the force is "And the Word was Himself God." The article is omitted, too, on occasion in other constructions; in fact, there are four instances of it in this very chapter (verses 6, 12, 13, 18), and in John 13:3, "God" is written once without and once with the article. To translate in any one of these cases "a god" would be totally indefensible (see R. Kuchner–B. Gerth, *Ausführliche Grammatik der griechischen Sprache*, Vol. I, pp. 591f., and E. Schwyzer, *Griechische Grammatik*, Vol. II, pp. 24ff.).

Strange literalistic interpretations, too, have been put on the word "beginning" in this verse, and to read as if it said "In the beginning the Word began," whereas what is affirmed is that in the beginning he was *already* existing. The reference is to something within the divine, not the human, order of things, and to apply the analogy of temporal succession and progression to the presence of God ("And the Word was *with* God") is utterly unwarranted. Equally narrow interpretations have been put on the word "Beginning" in such passages as Revelation 3:14: "the beginning of the creation of God." The context, however, demands an agent as a parallel to "witness," so the sense must be "Beginner" or "the first cause," as is the case in Revelation 21:6 where "Beginning" is applied to God himself (compare the Greek translation of Genesis 49:3, and Colossians 1:18, and Revelation 22:13). To understand what John means by "Word" (Logos) read Revelation 19:13-16 in conjunction with I Timothy 6:14-16.

### John 14:28

"My Father is greater than I." This can refer only to the self-imposed limitations of the Son in his incarnation. He has already claimed equality with God (John 5:18), and oneness with him (John 10:30); but he was not only true God, he was now also true man. In fact, rightly understood this is a claim of the highest import, for only things of the same order of magnitude can be compared. No mere man or angelic being could ever say, "God is greater than I," for created and uncreated are of different orders.

### Mark 13:32 (Matthew 26:36 RV)

"Concerning that day and hour no one knows, not even the angels in heaven, not even the Son, but the Father." This is in complete harmony with his consistent claim that he came to do the Father's will. He came to reveal the redemptive purpose of God but certainly not his whole mind (see John 17:8). There is again nothing here to contradict the many passages where his deity is positively and clearly stated; on the contrary it is in itself a very extraordinary claim, when we consider the ascending order: men, angels, Son, Father. He places himself above the category of angels (the highest created beings) and classes himself with the Father (see Hebrews 1:13).

### I Corinthians 11:3

"And the Head of Christ is God." Paul cannot imply by this inferiority, no more than in the case of the wife to the husband, which would be a contradiction of Galatians 3:28.

### I Corinthians 15:28

"And when all things are subjected to him, then the Son also himself will be subjected to him who put all things under him, that God may be all in all." Paul is speaking of the relation of the Son to the Father (verse 24) which was ever one of subjection (see John 5:30). But subjection does not imply subordination in the sense of inequality (see 1 Corinthians 14:32, "The spirits of the prophets are subject to the prophets"). The reference in verse 28 may well refer to organizational matters that do not come within the purview of revealed knowledge.

### John 17:21

This verse is quoted in an attempt to weaken the force of John 10:30, "I and the Father are one," about the meaning of which his audience were in no doubt whatever (see verse 33). In 17:21, however, the second "one" is not in the best manuscripts (see RV), thus simply, "that they also may be in us."

### Philippians 2:5-9

A fair rendering of this passage might be: "Cultivate this attitude of mind among you, which was in Christ Jesus, who being already in the form of God, did not treat it as a prize to be equal with God, but divested himself, taking the form of a servant." No one would dispute that when Paul says, Christ was in the "form" of a servant, he means that he was a servant in the truest and fullest meaning of the word. There is no ground for taking the phrase "in the 'form' of God" to mean less. Now from the nadir of his humiliation God has re-invested him with the insignia of his ineffable and divine glory, "and has given him the name that is—without exception—above every name."

## Mark 10:18

"And Jesus said to him, Why callest thou me good; but one is good, God." "Good" in the phrase "Good Master" meant in the suppliant's language (Aramaic) "benevolent," not "morally good"; hence there is no question of Christ denying that he was sinless (see H. L. Strack, P. Billerbeck, *Kommentar zum Neuen Testament aus Talmud und Midrasch*, Vol. I, pp. 808f., and Vol. II, pp. 24f.). Moreover "The Good"—Psalm 145:9 was probably cited—was one of the many Judaic titles for God (*op. cit.*, Vol. I., p. 809). The point of our Lord's remark is that a word with such hallowed association should not be used in a merely conventional manner. He is not stating that God alone is sinless, but that he is the personification of benevolence. To deduce from this an unexpressed contrary: "I am not sinless" or "I am not God," would be sheer sophistry. Besides, in all interpretation, situation and context, immediate and remote, must be taken into account. Now when Christ comes to disclose (verse 21) the full limit of benevolence (the end of selfish possessing), he demands a response that hitherto had been the prerogative of God alone: "And come, *follow* Me." No prophet had ever presumed to say this. Even the great Samuel unshakable in his integrity (I Sam. 12:3) did not suggest personal discipleship but said: "Turn not aside from following Jehovah" (verse 20). And invariably in the Old Testament "following" in a religious sense has as its object God (Num. 14:24 and *passim*). The implication is surely undeniable.

## Mark 15:34 (Matthew 27:46)

This prayer on the Cross ("My God, my God, why hast thou forsaken me?") has been seized upon as a possible refutation of Christ's claims to deity. We cannot, of course, know all that these words meant for him at that terrible moment, but there are several possible interpretations. First, he was still in communion with his Father, in spite of the past tense of the verb. Second, the meaning of these words to an attentive Jew would be that he was claiming *all* the Twenty-second Psalm for himself, for it was a common practice to name books and Psalms by their opening words, e.g., Psalm 113 was called the *"Hallel,"* from the Hebrew word with which it begins. An approximate analogy might be a dying Christian saying only: "Just as I am without one plea"; but his friends would know that the hymn as a whole was in his mind. The third possibility is that he was quoting it with the immediate context in mind, namely, forsaken with regard to present help. The fact that he did not use the Hebrew wording of the original but that of his mother-tongue serves only to bring out the poignant depth of his feeling of desolation.

The main argument of those who deny the deity of Christ seems to rest on a misconception of the full meaning of "Son." The fallacy consists of arguing from the analogy of human experience, that "son" implies a pre-existing father in time. The truth is, however, that "son" is used widely in both the Old and New Testaments divorced from the idea of "generation" or "priority," to denote relationship only. For instance in Hebrew, age is expressed by "the son of x years," and in the New Testament in such expressions as "the sons of disobedience." It was, in fact, one of the commonest ways of expressing identity. Again the phrase "only-begotten" refers to the uniqueness of Christ's relationship to the Father. The word is even applied to God himself in John 1:18, where the reading in the most ancient and textually best manuscripts is "God only-begotten" (In Hebrews 11:17 of Isaac, one of several sons, where the stress is on relationship).

## Harry Emerson Fosdick

# Jesus, the Messiah

The preacher ... who above all else is eager to make Jesus real to the thought and life of this generation, must be no literalist, reciting words like Messiah and Logos, as though they were sufficient vehicles for the Master's personality. Many modern minds do not clearly see what these words mean. The first requisite of a real preacher of the Master is insight to look through not only the church's elaborate theologies about him, but even the New Testament's first phrasings of him, and to become acquainted with, enamored of, the personality himself, around whom so many frameworks of interpretation have risen, and yet who himself is greater than them all. Just as soon however, as the preacher does this, I suspect that he will make an interesting discovery; he will find that what he wishes most to say about Jesus to his people now is at heart the same message which in the mental categories of their own time New Testament Christians were expressing when they called him Messiah and Logos.

Let the preacher try as thoroughly as he can this experiment of going back to the historic Jesus. In the last generation there has been an immense access of new information from travel, archeology, the discovery of

From *The Modern Use of the Bible* (New York: Macmillan, 1924), pp. 219-35. Used by permission.

old literatures, that has made first-century Palestine for us a living place, has lighted up the time when Jesus was alive, has reconstructed the social life, home life, schools and religious customs of the day when he walked the earth, until we can visualize his historic figure more clearly than our fathers could. People are still alive who can remember the stir caused when Dr. Seeley published Ecce Homo. It was one of the first endeavors to recover from the mists of antiquity a clear visualization of Jesus. We regard it now as a classic of our English-speaking Christianity, but it was violently hated when it first appeared, and even the good Earl of Shaftesbury called it the most pestilential book ever vomited from the jaws of hell.[1]

The endeavor to recover the historic figure of the Master, however, has gone on. There is no one of us who can escape its influence. Say "Jesus" to a medieval Christian and he instinctively would think of a king sitting 'on his throne or coming in the clouds of heaven. Say "Jesus" to a man of to-day and he instinctively thinks of that gracious and courageous Nazarene who lived and worked and taught in ancient Palestine. Once the great pictures of Jesus were of an exalted Judge, like Michelangelo's. Now a modern painter like Tissot goes to live in Palestine and paints the figure of Jesus as he must actually have looked, among people and scenes as they must actually have been. Once Te Deums, calling upon angels and archangels, seraphim and cherubim to fall before the throne, spontaneously expressed the church's imagination of the Master. Now we find it much more natural to sing with Whittier:

> In simple trust like theirs who heard,
>     Beside the Syrian sea,
> The gracious calling of the Lord,
> Let us, like them, without a word
>     Rise up and follow Thee.

When in the Gospels we hear Jesus talk of "the grass of the field, which to-day is, and to-morrow is cast into the oven," we think of the home in Nazareth where the boys went out to gather hay and stubble for the fire. When we hear him speak of the "leaven, which a woman took, and hid in three measures of meal, till it was all leavened," we see Jesus in Nazareth by Mary's side watching the mysterious bubbling of fermenting dough. When Jesus speaks of a hungry boy asking bread and given bread, not stone, we picture the hungry family as they came to a larder which Joseph and Mary labored to keep ample for their needs. When Jesus speaks of patched garments, or of sparrows that in the market-place are sold two for a penny, we see the practical difficulties which often faced the home from which Jesus came. When he talks of eagles circling about carrion, of birds returning to their nests and foxes to their holes, of hens gathering chickens under their wings, of lost sheep, of a red sunset prophesying a fair morning, of the wind blowing as it lists, how vivid the figure of the Master becomes! So from manger to Cross we naturally endeavor to picture the Master in a concrete historic situation, and the result in many minds was well expressed by a Jewish student: "I do not think he is the Messiah, but I do love him."

Nevertheless, let us look more closely at this historic figure and inquire what he has done for men. If we ask who Jesus *is,* we may be unsure, we may share our generation's doubts and uncertainties. Change the inquiry, therefore; what has Jesus done? what changes has he wrought? what contributions has he made to life? Such matters belong to history. They can be stated. And, as we state them, the recurring theme of our argument will be: Jesus must have been the kind of person who could do what he has done.

For one thing, *Jesus has given the world its most significant idea of God.* He supremely—some think he for the first time in history—took ethical monotheism in thorough earnest. He saw the world gathered up into one spiritual sovereignty; his God was the God of the whole earth and of all men; and the moral meaning of that insight he took with utter seriousness. Fatherhood in God, as Jesus taught it, was no soft and sentimental quality as much Christian preaching has represented it. The fundamental attribute of Jesus' God was universal moral will. No modern scientist, I think, ever sensed the reign of law in the physical world more grandly and austerely than Jesus in the moral world sensed the sovereign will of God. A moral grandeur is exhibited in Jesus' obedience to the divine will, from the first struggle in the desert until it led him through Gethsemane to the Cross, which to many of us makes his relationship with God the most impressive spiritual phenomenon in history.

This God of sovereign will Jesus interpreted in terms of utter goodness. All Jesus' love for men was the expression of God's will. If under the stars at night we think of the vast, incalculable universe and argue behind it a purposeful, intelligent power, we believe in God, but we have not thereby reached the characteristic and distinctive quality of Jesus' Father. If we philosophize until with intellectual satisfaction we produce an argument assuring us there is a God, we may believe in him, but we have not thereby reached the distinguishing characteristics of Jesus' Father. When, however, we love men, are merciful to the ungrateful and undeserving, forgive our enemies, reclaim the lost, and help the fallen, when, in a word, we respect personality wherever we find it as the supreme treasure, then in the eternal love behind our love, the divine will behind our service, we find Jesus' God. This idea of God, often hinted at and vaguely adumbrated, the Master took like so much rough ore, purified it, minted it, put his image and superscription on it, and made it current coin. Such thoughts of God, which had been fugitive and occasional, he clarified, made them triumphant affirmations, vivified them in a gloriously illustrative life, and published them so that what was before sporadic and dubious has become a persistent and conquering Gospel. The word God is only a picture-frame; all its value depends on the quality of portrait which the frame encloses. Into that old frame Jesus put a new picture so beautiful because of his own life, so inspiring and winsome because of his sacrificial death, that men never had so thought of God before and never since have been so moved, melted, and transformed by any other thought of him. That is an amazing thing to have done. In this world where so many have groped after God, guessed about God, philosophized concerning God, the Master has lived a life of such self-authenticating spiritual grandeur that increasing millions of men when they wish to think about God can think nothing so true, so satisfactory, so adequate, as that the God they worship is like Christ. Even Paul, who had been brought up in the Old Testament's noblest ideas of God, gained a new name for him when he had met the Master: "The God and Father of the Lord Jesus."

For another thing, *Jesus has immeasurably heightened man's estimate of his own worth and possibilities.* Professor George William Knox, who for twenty years had tried the Gospel out as a missionary in the Orient before he taught it as a philosophy at home, used to say that Jesus' faith in the spiritual nature, infinite value, permanent continuance, and boundless possibilities of human personality was his supreme contribution to man's thought. To believe in men as Jesus did was in itself a great and adventurous faith; to believe in men as Jesus did, in spite of all that men did to him, was magnificent. It was not so much by his teaching, however, as by his life that Jesus wrought this heightening of faith in humankind. In himself he carried our human nature to such heights, so unveiled in his own character what manhood was meant to be, and by his life of divine sonship so challenged men to claim their spiritual birthright as children of God, that he has created new standards of estimation about mankind's worth and possibilities. Wherever his real message has gone folk have begun to say such things as this: that they, too, are children of God; and if children, then heirs; heirs of God, and joint-heirs with Christ; that now are they children of God, and it is not yet made manifest what they will be; they know that, if he shall be manifested, they will be like him; that they will attain unto the unity of the faith, and of the knowledge of the Son of God, unto a fullgrown man, unto the measure of the stature of the fulness of Christ.[2] Men never have talked like that about themselves except where Jesus' influence has come.

Yet another thing the historic Jesus has done: *he has made men believe in the possibility of moral reclamation and renewal.* He was the great specialist in the conservation of the waste products of humanity—its prodigals and outcasts. He came at men from one angle, saw them in one light—what might they not become before he was through with them? Habitually he looked at people in terms of their possibilities. He valued men not at all for what they possessed, not primarily for what they had done, not even for what they were, but most of all for what they yet might become. Many people, noting this attitude of Jesus, ascribe it to kindness, but that misses the mark. It was not primarily kindness, but insight. When Robert Browning in the square of San Lorenzo in Florence picked up a yellow pamphlet for a lira, and saw in its sordid tale the possibility of The Ring and the Book, he was exercising not kindness but insight into values actually there. So always it is the greatest minds that see the greatest possibilities in the most unlikely places. The Master exercised this insight supremely on men, and the worth which he saw hidden in immature, perverted, wronged human nature he was sure God saw too, so that for those who would fulfil the conditions were waiting forgiveness, reconciliation, and moral power to become sons of God.

Divine forgiveness had long been taught, but Jesus made the concept thoroughly moral; he cleansed it of ceremonial elements; he made God's pardon dependent on man's right relationship with man; and in faith he supplied the power which could work the transformation. This message Jesus did not originate, but he clarified it and proclaimed it with a singleness of interest, a unity of purpose, a beauty of spirit, which make him its unique expositor. So the possibility of Roentgen Rays always had existed, latent in the radiant energy of which the universe is full, yet they will always bear Roentgen's name. He fulfilled the conditions of their production, disclosed them in their full meaning, brought them out of the darkness into light, and made them available for use. In some such way the message of moral reclamation and renewal is uniquely Christ's. He revealed its depth and range, personalized it, practised it, put the seal of his Cross upon it, and sent it out into the world. That is an amazing thing to have done. This is a hard world in which to believe at all that forgiveness and transformation of life are possible. Law and punishment are the certainties; forgiveness and renewal are the miracles. Yet Jesus has made men believe in them and, what is more, experience them. They are his specialties.

Another item must be added to the achievements of the historic Jesus: *he has given the world its loftiest ethical ideals.* A modern attack has been made upon the ethics of the Master on the ground that he expected a speedy-end of the world, that he thus foreshortened his horizon, and that the kind of living that he called for was adapted, not to the real world of slow progress, but to an utterly artificial view of the world swiftly coming to an end. Jesus presents, they say, an interim ethic fitted to the few intervening months before the kingdom should come in glory from the heavens, but not fitted to the needs and possibilities of our progressive world. Suppose that in answer we grant the charge (although I doubt its truth) that Jesus' ethical ideals were deeply affected by apocalyptic expectations. The real question still remains: what would be the nature of that effect? Jesus on this supposition was mistakenly looking forward to a speedy end of the age and the swift inauguration of the best of all possible worlds with God's will sovereign over all the relationships of life. In what direction, then, would his ethical insight turn? Surely it would turn to those absolute ideals whose realization would be the glory of the coming kingdom.

So, when Edward Bellamy wished to make clear what he conceived to be the ultimate moral values, he wrote Looking Backward. He placed himself, that is, in an imagined ideal state and in terms of what is right in such a social system defined the goals and standards of his endeavor. So, too, Plato's clearest thought of ethical values appears in his Republic where in terms of the best social order he could dream he determined what finally is good and evil. If, then, Jesus did share the apocalyptic expectations, what happened in his case was infinitely more vivid and compelling: he thought the ideal order really was at hand, that men must be ready on the moment for the coming of God's perfect kingdom on the earth.

Under such conditions he would not give men prudential maxims such as worldly wisdom might suggest but he would give them a vision of the ideal life fitted to the kingdom's coming. Perfect purity, perfect sincerity, perfect magnanimity and love, perfect devotion to the will of God—such were the ideals he would lift up. He would exalt the kind of life which would make men worthy of God's utterly righteous kingdom. That was in fact the quality of his teaching. His ethical principles leave us many a puzzling problem in this very unideal world, but they have done us more service than any prudential maxims ever could have done. By them we check our little maxims up. By them we decide whether we are going forward or backward in our personal and social life. They have gone before us and go before us still like the pillar of cloud by day and of fire by night leading the way to the Promised Land.

This first answer, however, based upon a granting of the charges, does not exhaust the matter. Personally, I think that this absolute quality would have been in Jesus' ethics whether or no. The plain fact is that wide areas of the Master's most characteristic teaching have no natural connection with apocalyptic expectations at all. The parable of the Good Samaritan or of the Prodigal Son, the Golden Rule, the teaching about anxiety, about goodwill even to enemies, about finding life by losing it, about loving the Lord our God with all our heart, soul, mind and strength, and our neighbor as ourselves—what has all this to do with Jewish apocalyptic? The Master's most characteristic teaching is essentially timeless; it would be as much at home in our century as in the first, and forty centuries from now it will be at home still.

Moreover, the real test of any ethical teaching is not made when folk discuss the frameworks of thought in which it first appeared, nor yet when they argue about its abstract rationality. The real test comes when men apply it, adventure on the basis of it, mold their lives and institutions to agree with it, and determine what it does when it is put to work. Whenever that test has been applied to Jesus' ethical teaching, that teaching has redeemed life. Christianity may well be ashamed of many things in its history, but of some things it need never be ashamed. Wherever Christ's spirit has welled up in personal character, wherever homes have been illumined by his teaching of self-sacrifice, mutual love, and boundless goodwill, wherever prison systems have been even a little affected by his attitude toward despised and outcast men, wherever his ideals have been applied, in ways however limited, to industrial and international life, we need never be ashamed. The Master's ideals are ahead of us, but they are ahead of us because they are the loftiest, most challenging conceptions of human character and relationships that mankind has ever known. They will not let us rest. They condemn us, haunt us, rally us, and lure us on. Mankind will not find itself until it works them out and makes them real in all of life. This immense achievement the Man of Nazareth has wrought.

Yet again, *the historic Jesus has given the world its most appealing and effective exhibition of vicarious sacrifice.* Vicarious sacrifice is not new in man's life. Gravitation is no more deeply built into the structure of the physical universe than is vicarious sacrifice into the essential nature of the moral world. Save when some one who need not do it voluntarily assumes the burden of man's misery and sin, there is no salvation from any want or tragedy that mankind knows. All this deepest realm of human experience, universal as it is, is summed up in the Master's Cross. He has given us so perfect and convincing an illustration of the power of a boundless love expressing itself through utter sacrifice that he has become the unique representative on earth of that universal principle and law.

The cold bare words in which we state this truth do no justice to the fact. The Cross of Christ, like every other abiding element in man's life, has passed through interpretation and reinterpretation as the thought of it has been poured from one generation's mental receptacles into another's. It has been run into thought-forms associated with old animal sacrifices; it has been made "a pious fraud" played by God upon the devil, who was promised Christ if he would give up man and who ultimately lost both;[3] it has been poured into the mold of the feudal system by Anselm[4] and into the mold of later European law by Grotius.[5] Yet, warped and distorted out of its vital significance, as it often has been, by categories that had no relation with its original meaning and were essentially unfitted to represent its deepest truth, the Cross of Christ has been the most subduing, impressive and significant fact in the spiritual history of man. Wherever one meets vicarious sacrifice—in Livingstone voluntarily assuming the burden of Africa's misery, in Father Damien becoming a leper to the lepers when he need not have done it, in Florence Nightingale taking on herself the tragedy of battlefields which she never had caused—it always is the most subduing and impressive fact mankind can face.

But when in the supreme character it is supremely exhibited, it becomes uniquely significant. To multitudes it has meant alike a revelation of the divine nature and a challenge to sacrificial living of their own which they could in no wise escape. It has bowed them in gratitude, chastened them into penitence, wakened them to hope, inspired them to devotion. It has made the one who bore the Cross not alone a religious and ethical teacher, but a personal Savior whom to meet, with whom to fall in love, by whom to be chastened, melted, subdued, forgiven, and empowered, has been the beginning of the noblest living that this world has ever seen.

This leads us to the issue of the matter: *Jesus has supplied an object of loyalty for the noblest devotions of the generations since he came.* Men do believe that this world is not a senseless chaos, that it is not "a tale told by an idiot, full of sound and fury, signifying nothing,"[6] that it does have a divine purpose running through it. But men do not fall in love with and devote themselves to the divine purpose in the abstract. It must become embodied so that they can see it. It must be lived so that they can adore it.

All through the universe the pervading purpose of God runs like blood through our bodies, but there must be at least one place where men can put their fingers on it and feel its pulse. Just that service Jesus has rendered men. He has been to them the place where they could feel the divine heart-beat; he has been the one in whom the eternal purpose came to the surface where they could be sure of it. The simplest, deepest, most searching way of expressing the finest consecrations of men since Jesus came has been devotion to him.

We need not feel this to be unimportant because it is not easy to state theologically; it is easy to state psychologically, and that is just as significant. To live a life so illustrative of all that men in their best hours aspire to be that they can find no finer way of phrasing their noblest devotion than in terms of personal allegiance to the one who lived it, is an achievement that would be utterly incredible if we did not know that it had been done. "The devotion of the leader to his men and to his cause," wrote Montefiore, the Jew, "Jesus shared it. The devotion of the led to their leader—Jesus inspired it. He kindled a flame which was to burn more brightly after his death than ever before it in his lifetime. 'For the sake of Jesus.' Of what fine lives and deaths has not this motive been the spring and the sustainment."[7]

We thus have rehearsed some of the achievements of the historic Jesus which leap first to the mind, not because we suppose for a moment that such a statement can be remotely adequate, but because even so brief a summary should make clear that, when we try to recover the historic figure of the Master behind the interpretative categories which the church has used, we do not find a diminished man, a thin and uninspiring character despoiled of its glory, a Jewish rabbi who by chance was exalted by being called Messiah. What we do find is a transcendent personality who has done for the spiritual life of man what no one else ever did. Whatever else may be said of Jesus, he must surely have been the kind of person who could do what he has done. When, therefore, I sum up even the few things we have been saying, the consequence seems impressive to the point of awe. Jesus was the kind of person who could do the things that we have said—give the world its loftiest thought of God, lift to its noblest heights man's estimate of his own worth and possibility, bring to men moral reclamation and renewal, give the world its noblest ethical ideals, its most appealing and effective outpouring of sacrificial saviorhood, its most satisfactory object of personal loyalty and devotion. These things at the very least the Master has done for men and he must have been the kind of person who could do them. And if, facing these facts, one says that Jesus was the divinely appointed agent of God's kingdom in the earth, is that too much to say? Is it not the most obvious and simple thing that we could say? I confess frankly that when I say it I do not think that I have said enough. Yet to say that is to call him the Messiah. That is the essential meaning of the New Testament when it interpreted his personality in Messianic terms. For Messiahship was simply the Hebrew category of function and purpose; it was a way of saying that God had specially anointed one to mediate his sovereignty over all mankind.

Nothing more clearly could illustrate the non-speculative character of Hebrew thinking than this fact that its highest category of personal greatness concerned a practical function. Divine substance and nature, ontological equality with God, were not involved in Messiahship at all. No ideas were there which could lead to philosophies of triunity in God or of two natures blended in one person. All that speculative theology came from the Gospel's contact with Hellenistic thought. Messiahship was characteristically and altogether Jewish. There were no philosophic discussions in the Jewish writings about Messiah's nature; his meaning consisted in what he was to do. Sometimes thought of as a Davidic sovereign, sometimes as the pre-existent Son of man, he was one who had been specially chosen to establish God's victorious kingdom in the earth. Of course, there are details associated with these Jewish pictures of the Messiah which our modern minds have no use for and cannot vitally believe. But when one thinks of the crucial matter, the conviction that in Jesus we have one divinely anointed to make real God's sovereignty over men, is not that precisely what we do believe? Messiahship is only superficially an outgrown category; essentially it is one of the most congenial ways of thinking that modern minds could use. I do not see why one should wish to be a Christian preacher if he does not easily and whole-heartedly approach the Master so. Immeasurably indebted for his unique, costly, and irreplaceable work, tracing all my choicest faiths, hopes, ideals and experience with God to him and to his Cross, convinced that he was divinely appointed to be the world's Savior and that he plays the indispensable part in establishing God's kingdom in the earth—so I, for one, return from trying to see him as he actually lived and died in Palestine. Therefore I call him Christ indeed and when I find an ancient Jewish Christian kneeling before him as Messiah I kneel also, not because I think my fellow-worshiper's category is adequate, but because I share his estimate of the Master, his gratitude, and his devotion.

## Notes

[1] See Edwin Hodder: The Life and Work of the Seventh Earl of Shaftesbury, Vol. III, 164.

[2] Cf. Romans 8:17; I John 3:2; Ephesians 4:13.

[3] St. Gregory of Nyssa: The Great Catechism, Ch. XXVI, in The Nicene and Post-Nicene Fathers, Second Series, Vol. V, 495-496.

[4] Cur Deus Homo.

[5] A Defence of the Catholic Faith concerning the Satisfaction of Christ, against Faustus Socinus.

[6] Macbeth, Act V, Sc. 5.

[7] C. G. Montefiore: Some Elements of the Religious Teaching of Jesus, 133.

## 22

**Donald Baillie**

# The Paradox
# of the Incarnation

### The Central Paradox

A far greater and deeper paradox than those which we have been considering lies at the very heart of the Christian life and vitally affects every
part of it. It is what we may call the paradox of Grace. Its essence lies in
the conviction which a Christian man possesses, that every good thing in
him, every good thing he does, is somehow not wrought by himself but by
God. This is a highly paradoxical conviction, for in ascribing all to God it
does not abrogate human personality nor disclaim personal responsibility.
Never is human action more truly and fully personal, never does the agent
feel more perfectly free, than in those moments of which he can say as a
Christian that whatever good was in them was not his but God's.

This astonishing paradox, so characteristic of Christianity, can be
widely illustrated from Christian literature of all ages. We may begin with
the familiar words of St. Paul: "By the grace of God I am what I am: and
his grace which was bestowed upon me was not found vain; but I laboured
more abundantly than they all: yet not I, but the grace of God which was
with me."[1] We may go on to St. Augustine, who after quoting the above

From *God Was in Christ* (New York: Charles Scribner's Sons, 1948),
pp. 114-32. Used by permission.

276   The Person of Christ

words makes the following comment: "O mighty teacher, confessor and preacher of grace! What meaneth this: 'I laboured more, Yet not I'? Where the will exalted itself ever so little, there piety was instantly on the watch, and humility trembled, because infirmity confessed all the truth." Again: "Therefore, blessed Paul, thou great teacher of grace, I will say it without fear of any man. . . . : Thy merits are recompensed with their own crown of reward; but thy merits are the gifts of God."[2] Again: "Even if men do good things which pertain to God's service, it is He Himself that brings it about that they do what He commanded."[3] This extraordinary doctrine of a God who not only demands obedience of us but supplies it Himself is summed up in St. Augustine's famous prayer: "Give what Thou command-est, and command what Thou wilt."[4] Or take this from St. Anselm of Canterbury in the eleventh century: "What a man has, not from himself but from God, he ought to regard as not so much his own as God's. For no one has from himself the truth which he teaches, or a righteous will, but from God."[5] To which we may add this from a prayer attributed to St. Anselm: "Whatsoever our heart rightly willeth, it is of Thy gift." Or take what Thomas à Kempis in the fifteenth century hears Christ say about His saints: "They glory not of their own merits, for they ascribe no goodness to themselves, but all to me."[6] Or take this from the West-minster Confession in the seventeenth century, concerning the good works of believers: "Their ability to do good works is not at all of themselves, but wholly from the Spirit of Christ. And that they may be enabled thereunto, besides the graces they have already received, there is required an actual influence of the same Holy Spirit to work in them to will and to do of his good pleasure."[7] Or take the familiar words of a nineteenth-century hymn:

> And every virtue we possess,
> And every victory won,
> And every thought of holiness
> Are His alone.[8]

We can never ponder enough upon the meaning of this paradoxical conviction which lies at the very heart of the Christian life and is the unique secret of the Christian character. It is this that makes so wide a gulf between the Christian way of life and any "mere morality," so that in a sense Christianity transcends morality altogether and there is no such thing as a Christian ethic. The question is often asked whether the impossible ethic of the Sermon on the Mount has any relevance to our life in this world, as a code to be practised or an ideal on which to mould our characters. But the truth is that in the last analysis a Christian does not live by practising any ethic or moulding himself on any ideal, but by a faith in God which finally ascribes all good to Him. To detach the ethic from the whole context of the Christian secret is to make it irrelevant because it is impossible. The main function of the impossible ethic is to drive us away from ourselves to God: and then there grows that peculiar kind of goodness which can never be achieved by mere moral endeavour, the Christian kind, which is all unconscious of itself and gives all the glory to God.

Thus the paradoxical Christian secret, while it transcends the moralistic attitude by ascribing all to God, does not make us morally irresponsible. That is part of the paradox. No one knows better than the Christian that he is free to choose and that in a sense everything depends upon his choice. Pelagius was quite right to insist upon that, if he thought it was being compromised by the extreme statements of the zealous Augustine. My actions are my very own, expressions of my own will, my own choice. No one else can choose for me or relieve me of the responsibility. When I make the wrong choice, I am entirely responsible, and my conscience condemns me. And yet (here is the paradox) when I make the right choice, my conscience does not applaud or congratulate me. I do not feel meritorious or glow with self-esteem—if and in so far as I am a Christian. Instead of that I say: "Not I, but the grace of God." Thus while there is a human side to every good action, so that it is genuinely the free choice of a person with a will, yet somehow the Christian feels that the other side of it, the divine side, is logically prior. The grace of God is prevenient. The good was His before it was ours. That comes first, and in a sense that even covers the whole. It is not as if we could divide the honours between God and ourselves, God doing His part, and we doing ours. It cannot even be adequately expressed in terms of divine initiative and human co-operation. It is false to this paradox to think of the area of God's action and the area of our action being delimited, each by the other, and distinguished from each other by a boundary, so that the more of God's grace there is in an action, the less is it my own personal action. That is precisely the mistake that misled the morally ardent Pelagius. From the historical and psychological standpoint the good actions of a Christian are purely his own actions. And even from the religious and Christian point of view that aspect is indispensable. Without it the other side would lose its true meaning, and the good man would be simply a perfect marionette, or an automaton, as Huxley wished he could be. We are not marionettes, but responsible persons, and never more truly and fully personal in our actions than in those moments when we are most dependent on God and He lives and acts in us. And yet the divine side is somehow prior to the human. Whatever good there is in our lives and actions (and it is but fragmentary) is "all of God," and it was His before it was ours, was divine grace before it was human achievement, is indeed a matter of God taking up our poor human nature into union with His own divine life, making us more truly personal, yet also more disposed to ascribe it all to Him.

This is the deepest paradox of our whole Christian experience, and it runs right through it, woven into its very texture. It is, moreover, virtually peculiar to Christianity. More than all the other paradoxes, it is a distinctive product of the religion of the Incarnation.

What I wish to suggest is that this paradox of grace points the way more clearly and makes a better approach than anything else in our experience to the mystery of the Incarnation itself; that this paradox in its fragmentary form in our own Christian lives is a reflection of that perfect union of God and man in the Incarnation on which our whole Christian life depends, and may therefore be our best clue to the understanding of it. In the New Testament we see the man in whom God was incarnate surpassing all other men in refusing to claim anything for Himself independently and ascribing all the goodness to God. We see Him also desiring to take up other men into His own close union with God, that they might be as He was. And if these men, entering in some small measure through Him into that union, experience the paradox of grace for themselves in fragmentary ways, and are constrained to say, "It was not I but God," may not this be a clue to the understanding of that perfect life in which the paradox is complete and absolute, that life of Jesus which, being the perfection of humanity, is also, and even in a deeper and prior sense, the very life of God Himself? If the paradox is a reality in our poor imperfect lives at all, so far as there is any good in them, does not the same or a similar paradox, taken at the perfect and absolute pitch, appear as the mystery of the Incarnation?

St. Augustine is not afraid to connect the one mystery with the other. "The Saviour, the Man Christ Jesus, is Himself the brightest illustration of predestination and grace." "Every man, from the commencement of his faith, becomes a Christian by the same grace by which *that* Man from His formation became Christ."[9] And Calvin, commenting on this, can say: "Therefore when we treat of the merit of Christ, we do not place the beginning in Him, but we ascend to the ordination of God as the primary cause."[10] St. Anselm, after writing the sentences I have quoted earlier, goes on to make the same connection. "What a man has, not from himself but from God, he ought to regard as not so much his own as God's. For no one has from himself the truth which he teaches, or a righteous will, but from God. Christ therefore came not to do His own will, but the Father's, because the righteous will which He had was not from His human but from His divine nature."[11] It might almost be said that in that passage at least St. Anselm treats the divine-human Christ as the supreme instance of the familiar Christian paradox.

### The God Who Was Incarnate

Let us leave the above argument for a moment and make another beginning from a different point—it will come to the same thing in the end.

Let us ask: With what conception of God have we embarked on our Christological quest? What do we understand by the word "God"? When endeavouring to confront, in an earlier chapter, those persons who are willing to believe in God but not in the Incarnation, I was constrained to ask: Are you sure that you know what you mean by "God"? And now I must pursue the question further. It is astonishing how lightly many people assume that they know what the word "God" means. But it is still more astonishing that even when we profess Christian belief and set out to try to understand the mystery of God becoming man, we are apt to start with some conception of God, picked up we know not where, an idol of the cave or of the market-place, which is different from the Christian conception; and then to attempt the impossible task of understanding how such a God could be incarnate in Jesus. If the Incarnation has supremely revealed God, shown Him to us in a new and illuminating light, put a fresh meaning into the very word that is His name, *that* is the meaning that we must use in facing the problem of the Incarnation, because that is what God really is. It is only as Christians that we can hope to understand the Incarnation. Why then should we as theologians work with any other conception of God than that which as Christians we believe to be true?

What then do we mean when we speak of "God"? We mean something unique, something that cannot be fully conceptualized. Thus if we rightly understand the word "God," if we give it the only meaning it ought to have, we cannot possibly speak of "Gods" or even strictly of "*a* God." The word "God," rightly understood, is (as I have said repeatedly) not a common noun but a proper name. That is why Brunner makes the idea of "the name of God" so important in his theology, and conceives of revelation as "God telling us His name," on the basis of the story of Moses and the burning bush, and many other biblical passages.[12] And yet this is not like any other proper name. It does not indicate particularity, one instance of a class, for God is not in any class.[13] Common names, say the logicians, possess connotation, but proper names possess only denotation. May it not be said, however, that "God" is the one proper name that does possess connotation? And yet it is a connotation that cannot be fully conceptualized. Its meaning cannot be expressed without paradox. What then does it mean? With what meaning shall we use the word, as we try to understand how God could be incarnate?

Does it mean, fundamentally, the Maker of all things? No, that is not enough, nor is it a true starting-point; for however truly that phrase may be used in its place, it does not, when taken by itself, give us the meaning of "God" at all. If we could say no more than that about God, we could not even say that, in its true sense. For if we could say no more than that, then it could only have been by such logical processes as the argument from design or the cosmological proof that we reached that conception. And by such routes we could only reach a pantheistic *deus sive natura,* or a *prima causa* in the natural sense at the beginning of a causal chain, or a supreme artificer, like Paley's invisible watchmaker inferred from the watch found lying on the ground. But none of these conceptions is what is meant by God. When Augustine questioned earth and sea and sky about God, they said with one accord, "He made us." But he knew that he could not have heard them say even this if he had not known of God in other and more inward ways.[14] The science of religions is showing, I think, that even in the case of pagan and primitive religion, where the word "God" has its plural, it was not by such arguments from nature, in howsoever primitive form, that the idea of the divine was reached. Christian faith does in fact praise God as Creator of all things, but such arguments from nature do not in themselves even begin to tell us what Christianity means by "God."

Does the word then mean the Source and Guardian of the moral law? That represents roughly the new approach proposed by Kant, the road of moral faith proposed in place of the speculative proofs which he found fallacious. This route looks at first far more promising; and Kant's conception can be so interpreted as to contain a great deal of truth. And yet if it is taken as an inferential argument from our moral convictions, as premises, to God the Moral Governor of the universe as conclusion, it does not give us what Christians mean by God. At best it would give us "the moral and providential order." If we took this as the essential meaning of the word, it would reduce the practice of religion to "mere morality," and it would give us a thoroughly Pelagian conception of the life of faith. From the Christian point of view this would be a falsification of morality itself. To accept it would be to forget that there is a sense in which the Christian secret transcends morality altogether. It is Christianity that has discovered and exposed what we may call "the paradox of moralism"[15]—that the attempt to be moral defeats itself, leads to "Pharisaism" instead of real goodness. Christianity has a different method, because it has a different conception of God. Christianity means a much deeper mystery, a much greater marvel, when it uses the word "God."

What, then, does the word "God" mean, in its true and full Christian use?

It means something so paradoxical that it is difficult to express in a few words. It means the One who at the same time makes absolute demands upon us and offers freely to *give* us all that He demands. It means the One who requires of us unlimited obedience and then supplies the obedience Himself. It means the One who calls us to work out our own salvation on the ground that "it is He Himself who works both the willing and the working" in our hearts and lives. It is not that He bestows His favour, His grace, upon those who render obedience to His commands. Such divine giving in response to human obedience is a sub-Christian idea, alien to the New Testament; and indeed if God's grace had to wait for man's obedience, it would be kept waiting for ever. But the Christian, when he has rendered his fullest and freest obedience, knows well that somehow it was "all of God," and he says: "It was not I, but the grace of God which was with me." This is the Creator-God who made us to be free personalities, and we know that we are most free and personal when He is most in possession of us. This is the God of the moral order who calls us every moment to exercise our full and responsible choice; but He also comes to dwell in us in such a way that we are raised altogether above the moral order into the liberty of the sons of God. That is what Christians mean by "God." It is highly paradoxical, but it is bound up with the whole message of Christianity and the whole structure of the Christian life; and it follows inevitably if we take seriously the fundamental paradox: "Not I, but the grace of God," as we are bound to do unless we are content to be Pelagians. It is God's very nature to give Himself in that way: to dwell in man in such a manner that man, by his own will choosing to do God's will (and in a sense it must depend on man's own choice) nevertheless is constrained to confess that it was "all of God."

Such is the Christian conception of God; and therefore it is with such a conception that we must work when we try to understand the Incarnation.

The question may well be asked at this point: Is this really the *distinctively* Christian conception of God? Do we not seem to have forgotten that the peculiarly Christian view of God is to be found in the doctrine of the Trinity? And if that is the case, ought not the Trinitarian conception to be our starting-point in Christology? To this I would reply: Are these two conceptions really different from each other? The conception of God that has worked itself out in the language of devotion in the foregoing pages—is it not identical with that which is expressed in doctrinal terms in the dogma of the Trinity? I shall return to this subject in the next chapter, but it seems necessary to say a word about it at this point. The Christian doctrine of the Trinity is not a mysterious mathematical statement about three-in-one, nor a metaphysical statement about a logically necessary triad. It may be difficult to understand the idea which Barth derives from Aquinas, that the numerical terms in the doctrine of the Trinity are to be taken metaphorically,[16] but the statement that God is three-in-one is virtually meaningless until we go on to indicate the relation of the three to the one concretely on a basis of the Gospel history and the Christian experience out of which the doctrine arose. What the doctrine of the Trinity really asserts is that it is God's very nature not only to create finite persons whom He could love, and to reveal and impart Himself to them, even to the point of incarnation (through His eternal Word) but also to extend this indwelling to those men who fail to obey Him, doing in them what they could not do themselves, supplying to them the obedience which He requires them to render (through His Holy Spirit). All of this, says the dogma of the Trinity, is of the eternal nature and essence of God. He is Father, Son and Holy Spirit, and the Son and the Spirit are consubstantial with the Father. And this outgoing love of God, His self-giving, is not new nor occasional nor transient, but "as it was in the beginning, is now, and ever shall be, world without end." Surely this doctrine is the objective expression of the same great paradox which finds its subjective expression in the confession: "Not I, but the grace of God."

This is the God in whom Christians believe. And this apprehension of God seems to be distinctive of Christianity. I do not say that it was never in any measure foreshadowed, for if this is the very nature of God there would naturally be some foreshadowing of the paradox wherever there was any knowledge of God at all. But the full paradox is peculiar to the religion of the Incarnation. It may be asked: What of the paradox so deeply rooted in Indian religion where the divine Brahma so dwells in man that He is both the worshipped and the worshipper, not only the hearer of prayer but the prayer itself, not only the desired but also the desire, not only the goal but also the aspirant? Yet that is very different from the Christian conviction, and indeed completely misses the depth of the paradox, because it is pantheistic, giving us a religion of identity, in which human personality is a painful illusion and its true goal is absorption and annihilation. In such a system the true idea of incarnation is impossible, just as there is no room for the paradox which combines the fullest personal freedom with the fullest divine indwelling, "I, yet not I, but the grace of God." At the other extreme stands a system like Islam, and here also there is no room for the paradox, but for the opposite reason. Islam is too moralistic for such a paradox. Its God is too sheerly transcendent, the Lawgiver, but not the Gracegiver, not the indwelling source and author of the obedience which He demands. Thus Islam is repelled by the doctrine of the Trinity, and its conception of God leaves no room for an incarnation.

There is, then, something peculiar to Christianity in the paradoxical conception of God that we have been elaborating and that has its counterpart in what I have called the central paradox of our Christian experience. That is, distinctively, what Christians mean by "God." And therefore when we try to understand the Incarnation, when we ask how God could become man and what it means, *that* is the God about whom we must ask the question.

But if so, then we have *ipso facto* begun to find an *answer* to the question, the only kind of answer that we ought to expect. In that case the doctrine that Jesus Christ is both God and Man is not sheer mystification. We can begin to understand it. Not that the reality so described becomes less wonderful. But it is not more wonderful than the God in whom we believe. I am reminded of the teaching we find in some of the Logos-theologians of the Patristic age, especially Irenaeus, to the effect that, while God is in Himself incomprehensible, unknowable, yet it is also His very nature to reveal Himself to His creatures, even to the point of Incarnation, because that is the natural activity of the Logos, and the Logos is of the essence of God. I am reminded also of Karl Barth's remark, that "while God's becoming *man* is not a matter of course, yet it can be justly considered as the most natural of all natural occurrences, because it was *God* who became man in Jesus Christ."[17] It may be objected that thus to explain the Incarnation by showing how naturally it connects with the doctrine of the Trinity, or with the paradoxical Christian conception of God, is no explanation at all, since these conceptions have themselves arisen out of the Incarnation. In one sense this is perfectly true. But it is not disconcerting. For there is a sense in which we should not expect or attempt to "explain" the Incarnation. Our theological task is to try to make sure that we know what we mean by it, what it means and what it does not mean; to try to make sure that, while it remains the *mysterium Christi,* it is not sheer meaningless mystery, but becomes a truly Christian paradox to us. And I am suggesting that this can happen because in our own experience, however poor and fragmentary, we know something of the paradoxical grace of God, something of the God who was incarnate in Jesus.

Our two lines of argument have converged upon the one point, with a view to such an understanding of the paradox of the Incarnation.

### True God and True Man

Let us try to trace more fully the connection and analogy between what I have called the paradox of grace and the paradox of the Incarnation.

Let us begin with the witness of the New Testament. It is plain that we find in the New Testament both the very highest claims for the divine revelation in Jesus and the very frankest recognition that He was a man. How far can we also find these two related to each other in a way that reminds us of the paradox by which a Christian says: "I, . . . yet not I, but God"? A very great deal has been written by biblical scholars during the last century on the question as to what Jesus held and taught about Himself and His place in God's purpose, and a common phrase which figured as the title of many discussions a generation ago was "the (messianic) self-consciousness of Jesus." The phrase was doubtless legitimate and useful.[18] And yet it has a somewhat unnatural sound, because in the Jesus of the Gospels it is not "self-consciousness" that strikes us, but God-consciousness. Throughout the story we get the impression of one who, with all His high claims, kept thinking far less of Himself than of the Father. Even in Him—or should we say, supremely in Him?—self-consciousness was swallowed up in His deep and humble and continual consciousness of God. When He worked cures, it was to His heavenly Father that He looked up for aid, and it was to God rather than to Himself that He expected people to give the glory when they were cured.[19] As regards goodness, He was not conscious of possessing it Himself independently, but looked away from Himself to God for it. When once a man addressed Him as "Good Master," he replied: "Why do you call me good? No one is good except God."[20] If we take the reply seriously, we shall surely find in it the supreme instance of that peculiar kind of humility which Christianity brought into the world. It was not self-depreciation: it was rather a complete absence of the kind of self-consciousness which makes a man think of his own degree of merit, and a dominating sense of dependence on God. The Man in whom God was incarnate would claim nothing for Himself as a Man, but ascribed all glory to God.

It is, however, when we turn to the Fourth Gospel that we find on the lips of Jesus the most remarkable expressions of this central paradox of Christian experience. I cannot in this place discuss the question as to how far the great Johannine discourses give us the *ipsissima verba* of Jesus; but it is in any case sufficiently impressive that in the Gospel which gives us the most transcendently high Christology to be found in the New Testament, Christology is more than anywhere else interwoven with the paradoxical human confession: "I, . . . yet not I, but the Father." On the one hand there is Jesus making His human choice from moment to moment, a choice on which in a sense everything depends. "He that sent me is with me: he hath not left me alone; for I do always the things that are pleasing to him."[21] "Therefore doth the Father love me, because I lay down my life, that I may take it again. No one taketh it away from me, but I lay it down of myself. I have power to lay it down, and I have power to take it again. This commandment received I from my Father."[22] But on the other hand, all His words and all His choices depended on the Father. "I can of myself do nothing: as I hear, I judge: and my judgment is righteous, because I seek not mine own will, but the will of him that sent me."[23] "Verily, verily, I say unto you, the Son can do nothing of himself, but what he seeth the Father doing: for what things soever he doeth, these the Son also doeth in like manner."[24] "My teaching is not mine, but his that sent me. . . . He that speaketh from himself seeketh his own glory: but he that seeketh the glory of him that sent him, the same is true, and no unrighteousness is in him."[25] I am not come of myself, but he that sent me is true, whom ye know not. I know him; because I am from him, and he sent me."[26] "I spake not from myself; but the Father which sent me, he hath given me a commandment, what I should say, and what I should speak."[27] "The words that I say unto you I speak not from myself: but the Father abiding in me doeth his works."[28]

In these remarkable passages we find Jesus making the very highest claims; but they are made in such a way that they sound rather like disclaimers. The higher they become, the more do they refer themselves to God, giving God all the glory. Though it is a real man that is speaking, they are not human claims at all: they do not claim anything for the human achievement, but ascribe it all to God. According to Barth, the holiness of Jesus means that He did not treat His own goodness as an independent thing, a heroic human attainment. His sinlessness consists in His renouncing all claim to ethical heroism. He did not set up at all as a man confronting God, but along with sinners—who do *not* take this attitude— He threw Himself solely on God's grace. The God-Man is the only man who claims nothing for Himself, but all for God.[29]

It hardly needs to be said the New Testament is conscious of a great gulf between what Christ is and what we are even when we are His people; and to some it may seem that this should exclude all analogy between His experience of God and ours. Especially it may occur to some that experience of the *grace* of God belongs to sinful men and does not enter at all into the mystery of divine Incarnation. According to Newman's hymn, "God's presence and His very self, And essence all-divine," in the Incarnation is "a higher gift than grace." More than one critic[30] has made the comment that there is no higher gift than grace, since the grace of God is simply His personal and loving action upon us or within us; but it is perhaps not necessary to quarrel with Newman's meaning. It does not follow, however, that we must not think of Jesus as the recipient or object of the grace of God, or that we must not take the "paradox of grace" as in any measure a pointer to the Incarnation. According to Thomas Aquinas, the grace given to Christ is twofold: *gratia habitualis,* given to Christ as man, like other men, and *gratia unionis,* given only to Christ;[31] but this seems an artificial distinction. It is relevant, however, to remember that the New Testament, while it speaks of the grace of God as given to Christ, speaks much more of the grace of Christ as given to us. And that indicates exactly the relation between His experience of God and ours, as conceived in the New Testament. Ours depends upon His. If God in some measure lives and acts in us, it is because first, and without measure, He lived and acted in Christ. And thus, further, the New Testament tends sometimes to say that as God dwells in Christ, so Christ dwells in us. St. Paul can express the paradox of grace by saying: "I live; and yet no longer I, but *Christ liveth in me*";[32] as he can say to Christians: "You are of Christ, and Christ is of God."[33] But that is only a part of the truth, and St. Paul can also speak of Christian men sharing, in a sense and in a measure, Christ's relation to God. It is God's purpose that these men should "be conformed to the image of his Son, that he might be the first-born among many brethren."[34] In the Epistle to the Hebrews we find strong emphasis laid on the analogy between Christ's human experience and the experience of those men whom He saves. "Both he that sanctifieth and they that are sanctified are all of one: for which cause he is not ashamed to call them brethren."[35] In the Fourth Gospel the risen Christ speaks of the disciples as "my brethren" and of God as "my Father and your Father, and my God and your God."[36] There also we find the purpose boldly expressed that all Christ's people should come to have the same kind of unity with Him, and through Him with the Father, as He has with the Father: "That they may all be one; even as thou, Father, art in me, and I in thee, that they also may be in us: that the world may believe that thou didst send me. And the glory which thou hast given me I have given unto them; that they may be one, even as we are one; I in them, and thou in me, that they may be perfected into one; that the world may know that thou didst send me, and lovedst them, even as thou lovedst me."[37]

"He was made what we are," wrote Irenaeus, "that He might make us what He is Himself."[38]

If then Christ can be thus regarded as in some sense the prototype of the Christian life, may we not find a feeble analogue of the incarnate life in the experience of those who are His "many brethren," and particularly in the central paradox of their experience: "Not I, but the grace of God"? If this confession is true of the little broken fragments of good that are in our lives—if these must be described on the one hand as human achieve-ments, and yet on the other hand, and in a deeper and prior sense, as *not* human achievements but things actually wrought by God—is it not the same *type* of paradox, taken at the absolute degree, that covers the whole ground of the life of Christ, of which we say that it was the life of a man and yet also, in a deeper and prior sense, the very life of God incarnate?

It seems plain that it is the presence of this paradox that has always made it so difficult to express the doctrine of the Incarnation without running into error on the one side or on the other, so as to lose either the divinity or the humanity. And it appears to me that the method of approach which I have indicated is a certain safeguard against these errors, because it can be a continual reminder of the need of holding fast the two sides of the paradox and letting them correct each other. On the one hand, there was from the beginning the "Adoptionist" or "Ebionite" type of error, by which Jesus was regarded as a man who achieved such goodness that God exalted Him to divinity or quasi-divinity. The reason why the Church could not rest content with such a view was not because they objected to the idea of deification (for the Greek Fathers tended too much to conceive even of salvation as deification) but because the Adoptionist Christology began with the human achievement of Jesus and brought God in at the end, so that it was a case of "first man, then God" or a man becoming God, instead of "first God, then man" or God becoming man. It was, of course, perfectly right to regard the life lived by Jesus as a human achievement. To deny that or to obscure or minimize it would be to fall into the opposite type of error, with Docetists, Apollinarians, and Monophysites. Jesus was a real man, subject to the conditions and limitations of humanity, with a human will that had to make its continual choices in face of life's temptations, and thus His goodness must be quite realistically regarded as a human achievement. But goodness in a human life, even in small proportions, is *never* simply a human achievement. To regard it as such would be pure Pelagianism. And "no New Testament thinker could think of Jesus in Pelagian terms."[39] All goodness in a human life is wrought by God. That is the other side, and somehow that side comes first, without destroying the human. And therefore the goodness of Jesus can ultimately be described only as the human side of a divine reality, which, so to say, was divine before it was human. The divine is always prevenient, so that however far back one may go in the life of Jesus, one can never reach a point that would meet the requirements of "Adoptionism," just as one can never reach a point of which a "Pelagian" account would be satisfactory. It is not adoption that we have to deal with, but Incarnation.

The whole problem of the Incarnation is contained in the old question, which can be asked in so many ways: Was Jesus divine because He lived a perfect life, or was He able to live a perfect life because He was divine? To put it otherwise: Did the Incarnation depend upon the daily human choices made by Jesus, or did He always choose aright because He was God incarnate? If our whole line of thought has been correct, this question does not present us with a genuine dilemma. It must, of course, be true that His choices were genuine human choices, and that in a sense everything depended upon them. "He that sent me is with me; he hath not left me alone; for (or because) I do always the things that are pleasing to him."[40] All depended on those human choices from moment to moment. And yet as soon as we have said that, we must inevitably turn round and say something apparently opposite, remembering that in the last analysis such human choice is never prevenient or even co-operative, but wholly dependent on the divine prevenience. We must say that in the perfect life of Him who was "*always* doing the things that are pleasing to God," this divine prevenience was nothing short of Incarnation, and He lived as He did because He was God incarnate. Thus the dilemma disappears when we frankly recognize that in the doctrine of the Incarnation there is a paradox which cannot be rationalized but which can in some small measure be understood in the light of the "paradox of grace." Somebody may wish to press the question in another form: Would *any* man who lived a perfect life be therefore and thereby God incarnate? But such a questioner would indeed be a Pelagian, showing by his very question that he regarded the human side of the achievement as the prevenient, the conditioning, the determinative. When we really accept the paradox of grace, when we really believe that every good thing in a man is wrought by God, when we have really understood the confession: "I . . . yet not I, but God," and have taken that divine priority in earnest, the question loses its meaning, and, like the proposed dilemma, fades away into the paradox of the Incarnation. And if we take these things in earnest, we have, as it appears to me, at least an approach to the *mysterium Christi* which will enable us to combine the most transcendent claims of a full and high Christology with the frankest recognition of the humanity of the historical Jesus.

It seems certain that whatever restatement of Christology may be necessary in the modern world, it will be in the direction of fuller and ever fuller recognition of both these sides of the truth. On the one hand there will be no abatement, but rather, if it were possible, an enhancement, of the highest predicates that Christian faith has ever given to Jesus Christ as God incarnate.

> The highest place that heaven affords
> Is His, is His by right:
> The King of kings and Lord of lords
> And heaven's eternal Light.

The Church must indeed break out continually into such lyrical notes to make up for the shortcomings of theological prose, and no expression can be too high. Nothing can be too high; and nothing can be too lowly or too human. Nothing can be too high, if only we save it from Docetic and Monophysite unreality by treating His life as in every sense a human life. A toned down Christology is absurd. It must be all or nothing—all or nothing on both the divine and the human side. That is the very extreme of paradox; but I have tried in this chapter to show how, as it seems to me, the derivative paradox which is the distinctive secret of the Christian life may help us to interpret in a truly Christian way the paradox of the Incarnation.

## Notes

[1] I Cor. 15:10.

[2] *De gest. Pelag.* cc. 35 *seq.*

[3] *De praedest. sanctorum,* c. 19.

[4] *Conf.* x, 29.

[5] *Cur Deus homo,* Book i, chap. ix.

[6] *De imit. Chr.,* iv, 58.

[7] *Westminster Confession of Faith,* XVI, iii.

[8] By Harriet Auber.

[9] Augustine, *De praedest. sanct.*, I, xv.

[10] Calvin, *Inst.*, II, xvii, i. It is only fair to add that Calvin in the context is arguing, against objectors, that there is no incompatibility between the idea of God's grace freely redeeming us and Christ's merit earning redemption for us, since Christ's merit itself derives from the grace of God.

[11] Anselm, *Cur Deus Homo,* Book I, chap. ix. Cf. chap. x.

[12] Emil Brunner, *The Mediator* (Eng. trans.), pp. 219, 231, 270, 280. See also Karl Barth, *The Doctrine of the Word of God,* pp. 364f.

[13] Cf. Thomas Aquinas: *Deus non est in aliquo genere, Summa theol.,* I, iii, 5.

[14] Augustine, *Conf.,* X, vi.

[15] Writers on ethics have often spoken of "the paradox of hedonism"—the fact that the quest of happiness defeats itself. But they have not so often noticed what I call "the paradox of moralism"—the fact that the quest of goodness defeats itself.

[16] Karl Barth, *Doctrine of the Word of God,* p. 407.

[17] Karl Barth, *The Knowledge of God and the Service of God,* p. 72.

[18] It was, of course, a translation of *Selbstbewusstsein,* which in this kind of usage seems more at home in the German language than its translation does in the English.

[19] Mark 7:34; 5:19; Luke 17:18.

[20] Mark 10:17f.

[21] John 8:29.

[22] John 10:17, 18.

[23] John 5:30.

[24] John 5:19.

[25] John 7:16, 18.

[26] John 7:28, 29.

[27] John 12:49.

[28] John 14:10.

[29] This is but a rough summary of a whole paragraph in Barth's *Kirchliche Dogmatik,* I, ii, 171ff.

[30] E.g. N. P. Williams, *The Grace of God,* p. 110.

[31] See Ottley, *The Doctrine of the Incarnation,* 4th ed., p. 527.

[32] Gal. 2:20.

[33] I Cor. 3:23.

34 Rom. 8:29. Cf. "the first-born from the dead," Col. 1:18.

35 Heb. 2:11. Weymouth translates "have all one Father."

36 John 20:17.

37 John 17:21-23.

38 *Adv. haer.*, Bk. v, Pref. (quoted by Ottley).

39 Hoskyns and Davey, *The Riddle of the New Testament*, p. 255.

40 John 8:29.

## 23

**Wolfhart Pannenberg**

# The Significance
# of Jesus' Resurrection

As we have seen, in all probability the earthly Jesus' expectation was
not directed toward, so to speak, a privately experienced resurrection from
the dead but toward the imminent universal resurrection of the dead,
which would, of course, include himself should his death precede it. Then
when his disciples were confronted by the resurrected Jesus, they no
doubt also understood this as the beginning of the universal resurrection of
the dead, as the beginning of the events of the end of history. Twenty to
thirty years after Jesus' death Paul still reckoned with the imminent, ultimate arrival of the resurrected Jesus for judgment, accompanied by the
universal resurrection of the dead; this was still supposed to happen in his
lifetime.[1] Only for the second generation of New Testament witnesses, for
Mark, Matthew, Luke, John, for the authors of the Deutero-Pauline
epistles and of Hebrews, did it become clear that the resurrection of Jesus
was not yet the beginning of the immediately continuous sequence of the
eschatological events but was a special event that happened to Jesus alone.
Now the danger arose that the connection of Jesus' resurrection to the
final occurrence of the universal resurrection of the dead and judgment

From *Jesus—God and Man* (Philadelphia: Westminster Press, 1968),
pp. 66-73. Used by permission.

would be lost from view. This danger is especially clear in Luke. Where the tension between the present and the expectation for the future is lost, the occurrence of Jesus' resurrection loses the inherent significance that it originally had, that is, the significance that was inherent in it within its original context in the history of traditions, namely, in the horizon of the apocalyptic expectation for the future. For Jesus' Jewish contemporaries, insofar as they shared the apocalyptic expectation, the occurrence of the resurrection did not first need to be interpreted, but for them it spoke meaningfully in itself: If such a thing had happened, one could no longer doubt what it meant.

The following points summarize the most important elements that characterize the immediate inherent significance of Jesus' resurrection.

(*a*) *If Jesus has been raised, then the end of the world has begun.*

The universal resurrection of the dead and the judgment are imminent. This comes to expression in Paul's expectation that the resurrection of other men, especially of believers, will immediately follow that of Jesus.[2] Jesus is "the first-born among many brethren" (Rom. 8:29). Christ is raised as the first-fruits of those who have fallen asleep (I Cor. 15:20). Correspondingly, in Col. 1:18 Jesus is called the firstborn of the dead. The same expression is found in Rev. 1:5, indicating that this is a traditional, widely circulated formulation. The designation of Jesus as "Author of life," preserved by Luke in Acts 3:15, is to be understood as materially similar.

To the nearness of the end which began with Jesus' resurrection belongs, as well, the early Christian conviction that the same Spirit of God by which Jesus has been raised[3] now already dwells in the Christians.[4] In early Christianity the Spirit had eschatological significance. The word designated nothing else than the presence of the resurrection life in the Christians.

(*b*) *If Jesus has been raised, this for a Jew can only mean that God himself has confirmed the pre-Easter activity of Jesus.*

Jesus' claim to authority, through which he put himself in God's place, was, as we saw in the discussion of the antitheses in the Sermon on the Mount, blasphemous for Jewish ears. Because of this, Jesus was then also slandered by the Jews before the Roman governor as a rebel. If Jesus really has been raised, this claim has been visibly and unambiguously confirmed by the God of Israel, who was allegedly blasphemed by Jesus. This was done by Israel's God. A Jew—and for the moment we are speaking only of Jews—could certainly not take an event of this kind as one that came to be apart from the will of his God. That the primitive Christian proclamation in fact understood Jesus' resurrection from the dead as the confirmation of his pre-Easter claim emerges above all in the speeches in Acts,[5] and perhaps also in the old expression that Jesus was shown to be justified in the Spirit.[6]

(*c*) *Through his resurrection from the dead, Jesus moved so close to the*

*Son of Man that the insight became obvious: the Son of Man is none other than the man Jesus who will come again.*

In his previously mentioned book, H. E. Tödt has shown that the earliest community, to the extent that its theological thought comes to expression in Q, had already identified Jesus with the Son of Man, although in other respects it appears only to have continued the proclamation of Jesus himself. This assertion of the post-Easter community was not simply an arbitrary act.

It lets the question about the basis of such an identification of Jesus with the Son of Man be put in a meaningful way from the perspective of the event itself as it was experienced by the first Christians. To what extent was the presentation of Jesus' relation to the Son of Man different to his disciples after his resurrection from what it had been in his pre-Easter message?

The pre-Easter Jesus had already proclaimed a correspondence in function between his own attitude toward men and the future attitude of the Son of Man: the attitude of men toward Jesus and the community which he grants to others are valid before the forum of the Son of Man. The distinction between these two figures consists only in the fact that the pre-Easter Jesus walked visibly on the earth, whereas the Son of Man was to come only in the future on the clouds of heaven and was expected as a heavenly being. This difference disappeared, however, with Jesus' resurrection. As the one who has been taken away to God, Jesus is a heavenly being. His coming from heaven, which was expected in the immediate future and was probably already initiated by the Easter appearances, will bring on the universal resurrection of the dead and judgment, just as the apocalyptic tradition had predicted of the appearance of the Son of Man on the clouds of heaven. Thus it is understandable that Jesus was no longer distinguished from the Son of Man, but was himself seen as the Son of Man whose coming was expected in the future, and the tradition about Jesus down to the details was connected with the expectation of the Son of Man. After Jesus' resurrection it must have become meaningless to expect a second figure in addition to him with the same function and the same mode of coming. By virtue of the resurrection, Jesus had moved into the role of the Son of Man.

(*d*) *If Jesus, having been raised from the dead, is ascended to God and if thereby the end of the world has begun, then God is ultimately revealed in Jesus.*

Only at the end of all events can God be revealed in his divinity, that is, as the one who works all things, who has power over everything. Only because in Jesus' resurrection the end of all things, which for us has not yet happened, has already occurred can it be said of Jesus that the ultimate already is present in him, and so also that God himself, his glory, has made its appearance in Jesus in a way that cannot be surpassed. Only because the end of the world is already present in Jesus' resurrection is God himself revealed in him.[7]

If these apocalyptic ideas are translated into Hellenistic terminology and conceptuality, their meaning is: in Jesus, God himself has appeared on earth. God himself—or God's revelatory figure, the Logos, the Son—has been among us as a man in the figure of Jesus. In this sense, in the transition of the Palestinian tradition into the Syrian sphere eschatology was translated throughout into epiphany. This Hellenistic concept of revelation prepared the basic pattern for the subsequent doctrine of incarnation.

The translation of the apocalyptic understanding of Jesus as the one in whom the glory of God is ultimately revealed, because in him the end event has already occurred in advance, into the Hellenistic concept of revelation as epiphany may also have been the path that led to the thesis of the true divinity of Jesus.[8] Jesus' divinity is already implied in some way in the conception of God's appearance in him, even though not with the later orthodox precision.

*(e) The transition to the Gentile mission is motivated by the eschatological resurrection of Jesus as resurrection of the crucified One.*

Israelite prophecy expected the self-demonstration of God, which it proclaimed, as an event that would take place before the eyes of all peoples. Not just Israel but all nations were to recognize from this future event the exclusive divinity of Israel's God. The exilic prophets Deutero-Isaiah and Ezekiel especially preached in this way. The same proclamation occurs repeatedly in the psalms.[9] This expectation corresponds to the hope, rooted in the Jerusalem tradition of the election of David and Zion, that in the end time all peoples would submit themselves to the Lordship of Yahweh and his Anointed One.[10]

Also in postexilic Judaism the expectation remained alive that the nations would one day be included in the eschatological salvation hoped for Israel.[11] However, in contrast to this stood the dominant conception which regarded the Gentiles simply as godless and which hoped for the time of God's vengeance on Israel's oppressors and their final annihilation at the arrival of the Messianic Kingdom.[12]

Thus it is clear that the beginning of the end in Jesus' resurrection signified the inclusion of the Gentiles into eschatological salvation only for those who together with Jesus himself followed the universalistic line of Israelite tradition. However, even in this line of Jewish tradition and thus also in the earliest Christian community, the consequence of a *mission* to the Gentiles in the Pauline sense was not automatic. One sees that the significance of the resurrection of Jesus in this point was less clear than in those previously considered.

Jesus himself had stood in contrast to the Jewish propaganda of his time and considered himself as sent only to the Israelites,[13] even though he also seems on occasion to have recognized the faith of non-Jews as a valid acceptance of eschatological salvation, corresponding to the unconditionedness of his assurance of salvation. Nonetheless, in contrast to apparently widely held conceptions of Jewish contemporaries, Jesus did not predict divine vengeance on the Gentiles for the *eschaton,* but the participation of many of them in eschatological salvation,[14] while he threatened the impenitent Israelites with wrathful judgment. However, he expected the "incorporation of the Gentiles into the people of God as the result of God's eschatological act of power,"[15] as a consequence of the reestablishment of Zion to which the nations would then flock, not as the result of religious propaganda among the nations. In this sense the earliest community apparently restricted its mission to Israel, without for that reason condemning the Gentiles as excluded from eschatological salvation and without having to deny to those who occasionally came acceptance into the community. A Gentile *mission* seems to have arisen for the first time as a result of the conviction that the resurrected Jesus has now already been exalted to Lordship in heaven and consequently the news of his Lordship is to be carried to all nations.[16] However, even then it apparently still remained unclarified whether the evangelization of the Gentiles did not also have to aim at the acceptance of the law by them. A change in this apparently occurred only when Paul combined Jesus' crucifixion with the curse threatened by the law (Gal. 3:13). On this basis, he had to understand the law as abrogated in view of the Sonship that appeared in Jesus' resurrection, so that the rejection of Jesus by the Jews, which was completed in the cross, led to the inclusion of the Gentiles in salvation (v. 14) through faith in the message of salvation that is accessible now apart from the law (chs. 3:14 and 2:15ff.). It is revealing that Paul did not originally justify the mission to the Gentiles by appealing to the universalistic promises of Old Testament prophets for the end time, but rather on the basis of the Christ event, specifically Christ's crucifixion (Gal. 3:13f.)[17] as understood, certainly, in the light of the resurrection. Then Paul appeals to the fact that Abraham, whom Jewish propaganda had already presented as the father of the proselytes,[18] was justified by faith, as the Gentile Christians are now, so that it is the blessing of Abraham that has been carried through to the Gentiles through Jesus' cross with its removal of the curse of the law (Gal. 3:14; Rom., ch. 4). If the Gentile mission is thus at first related to Israelite covenant history through the figure of Abraham,[19] Paul can in Romans draw upon eschatological prophesies such as Isa. 11:10 (Rom. 15:12; see also Ps. 117:1; 18:49) and Hosea 2:23 (Rom. 9:25f.; cf. I Peter 2:10) as proof from Scripture to justify the Gentile mission.[20] Still, Paul must have seen the correspondence of the eschatological meaning of the Gentiles' conversion to the eschatological character of the message about Christ which originated in Jesus' resurrection as the confirmation of his action.

Thus, even though the transition to the Gentile mission does not represent a direct consequence of the significance inherent in Jesus' resurrection by itself, it was inevitable as soon as Jesus' resurrection was understood in its connection with the crucifixion as the expression of his rejection by Israel (cf. Rom. 11:11ff. and Acts 13:45). Certainly even in Paul's own case the report of Jesus' crucifixion alone did not effect his transformation from a persecutor of the Christian community to missionary to the

Gentiles, but only his confrontation with the crucified as the resurrected Jesus. In this confrontation Paul's gospel of freedom from the law is immediately implied.

(*f*) *Particularly the last consequence throws light on the relationship between the* appearances *of the resurrected Jesus and the* words *spoken by him: what the early Christian tradition transmitted as the words of the risen Jesus is to be understood in terms of its content as the explication of the significance inherent in the resurrection itself.*

Word and event belong together in the appearances of the resurrected Jesus in such a way that they express the same content. The words of the risen Jesus add nothing new to the significance inherent in the event itself but, rather, state this significance. Only in this way can we understand Paul's claim, especially in Gal. 1:12, that he has received his gospel not from men but through the revelation of Jesus Christ. This happened in that it pleased God "to reveal his Son to me, in order that I might preach him among the Gentiles" (Gal. 1:16). Paul's gospel, one must understand, is the exegesis of the appearance of the resurrected Jesus that he experienced. The alternative, that Paul's gospel had been communicated in its completed form to him by way of audition, is to be excluded. Not the least thing speaking against it is the fact of a development in Pauline thought between the composition of First Thessalonians and Philippians.

In other cases, as for example the appearance of the resurrected Jesus to Peter, the relation between event and word is no longer accessible to us, especially since we can scarcely get a picture of the situation in which this appearance took place. To what extent the missionary command in Matt. 28:18f. or the tradition standing behind John, ch. 21, reflect something of this situation or only concentrate on the later experience of the community cannot be decided here. However, one must consider the possibility that the differing situation in which the resurrection appearances were imparted to the various witnesses also conditioned a difference in the audition that was connected to the appearance.

The unity of event and word in the resurrection appearances is important for the question of how this event can establish faith. If the resurrection or the appearances of the resurrected Jesus were only brute facts without inherent significance, then, certainly, the origin of faith would not be understandable from this event. But that event had its own meaning within its sphere in the history of traditions: the beginning of the end, the confirmation and exaltation of Jesus by God himself, the ultimate demonstration of the divinity of Israel's God as the one God of all men. Only thus can Jesus' resurrection be the basis of faith without being supplemented by an external interpretation added to it.

Naturally, the same is not true of every event one might choose. Every man experiences in the area of his everyday life that the meaning of the various occurrences in the context of our life can be more or less clear in very different degrees. There are occurrences that contain such irresistible evidence that there can be no doubt about their meaning for us. But there are also events whose meaning remains obscure for us and which, when they are incisive, give cause for constantly new reflection over their significance. Within the horizon of Jewish tradition, the event of the Easter appearances experienced as the confrontation with the resurrected Jesus belonged, apparently, more to the first group of events which are to a great extent unambiguous. Jesus' crucifixion is different. This event was apparently experienced, in a quite different way, as obscure and enigmatic and had initiated very different interpretations, which must concern us later.

## Notes

[1] I Thess. 4:15, 17; I Cor. 15:51. Only in Philippians does this become different for Paul.

[2] Rom. 5:12ff.; I Cor. 15:45ff.; but see also II Cor. 5:10. However, the judgment of the dead in the apocalyptic tradition in no sense always presupposes a resurrection of the wicked preceding their condemnation. On this, see Wolfhart Pannenberg, *Jesus–God and Man*, pp. 78ff.; for Paul, see ibid., n. 64.

[3] Rom. 1:3; II Cor. 13:4; see also I Tim. 3:16; I Peter 3:18.

[4] Rom. 8:11, as well as the entire section ch. 8:1-11.

[5] Acts 2:36; 3:15; 5:30f.; *et al.* Recently Friedrich Mildenberger has asserted that Jesus' *death* must have been understood as the confirmation of his claim. "Jesus' death, which occurred on the basis of this claim, could, however, not be understood as its refutation; rather, it must have been understood as the confirmation of this claim in analogy to the typology of the fate of the prophet as it was known in that time." ("Auferstanden am dritten Tage nach den Schriften," in *EvTh*, XXIII [1963], 265-280, quotation p. 270.) The certainty established in this way had simply come to its ultimate success in the Easter visions (p. 271). In this it is correct that Jesus' death was understood in the light of the suffering of the prophets. However, the suffering in itself does not provide the necessary confirmation, but only the unavoidable fate of the prophet and the righteous man in general in this evil world. With this, however, misfortune and destruction are not unambiguous signs of righteousness, for normally in the divine ordering of events these are the reward of the evildoer. In contrast, the apocalyptic theology of suffering could maintain this much: that *contrary to appearances* earthly failure must not in all circumstances put the prophet in the wrong. Yet the confirmation of his message through its fulfillment remains to be expected without fail. What would a prophet be whose word was not fulfilled, even though he perished so miserably? Also, with regard to Messianic pretenders, things normally quieted down after their failure. According to Mildenberger's logic, the prophets would then have had to be proclaimed and believed in as Messiah more than ever precisely because of their failure.

[6] I Tim. 3:16b. Is this idea also perhaps in the background in Rom. 4:25? Admittedly, the text now reads, "put to death for *our* trespasses and raised for *our* justification."

[7] On this, see my article in *OaG,* esp. pp. 95ff., 103ff.

[8] In terms of the history of traditions, the path to the perception of Jesus' divinity ran by way of the titles "Son of God" and *"Kyrios,"* as has been suggested (cf. F. Hahn, *Christologische Hoheitstitel*). In this process the exegesis of Ps. 110:1 (LXX) played a decisive role. However, we are led to the driving forces behind the transformation in the history of traditions only by questioning the *motives* of such exegesis, and these motives may be related to Hellenistic ideas of epiphany.

[9] In greater detail in Rolf Rendtorff in *OaG,* pp. 38f., 26f.

[10] This Jerusalem tradition occurs in Ps. 2:8; Isa. 2:2ff. (=Micah 4:1ff.); cf. Zech. 9:10; also, the universalism of salvation in Deutero-Isaiah (like that of the Yahwist before him, Gen. 12:3 *et al.*) may be connected to this tradition. The previously mentioned statements about Yahweh's universal revelation before all nations does not as such imply such a universalism of salvation. Yahweh's divinity could also be revealed to the nations not as the divinity of their God, but only of Israel's God.

[11] Paul Billerbeck, *Kommentar zum Neuen Testament aus Talmud und Midrash* (Munich: C. H. Beck'sche Verlagsbuchhandlung, 1922ff.), Vol. III, pp. 144, 150-152.

[12] References in Joachim Jeremias, *Jesus' Promise to the Nations* (Studies in Biblical Theology, 24; Alec R. Allenson, Inc., 1958), p. 41

[13] *Ibid.,* pp. 26f. on Matt. 15:24.

[14] Matt. 25:34; cf. Matt. 8:11f. and parallels; Luke 13:29. Jeremias, *ibid.,* pp. 47f. See also Ferdinand Hahn, *Mission in the New Testament,* tr. by Frank Clarke (London: SCM Press, Ltd., 1965), pp. 34ff.

[15] J. Jeremias, *Jesus' Promise to the Nations,* p. 71; cf. in general pp. 59ff. See also E. Käsemann, "Zum Thema der urchristlichen Apokalyptik," *ZThK,* LIX (1962), 257-284, esp. p. 267. Hahn supplements and corrects Jeremias by noting that the "acceptance of individual Gentiles" by Jesus must be seen together with his "promises for all nations" (*Mission in the New Testament,* p. 39; cf. pp. 31ff.), so that also in this regard the eschatological future has already become present in Jesus' activity (*ibid.,* p. 33, n. 2). Jesus had, "by proclaiming to Israel the Kingdom of God, preached the claim and the salvation of God for everyone to hear, and even the Gentiles heard the news" (*ibid.,* p. 39). Only in this way is it understandable how Jesus' message could become the starting point also for the Gentile mission of his community (*ibid.,* pp. 39f.; cf. p. 30). However, that is only convincing to the extent that it is maintained at the same time that Jesus regarded his mission as limited to Israel, so that the universal breadth of the communication of salvation to the Gentiles still remained for the future. A *direct* path to the Gentile *mission* did not lead from the message of Jesus but from his resurrection (and exaltation).

[16] F. Hahn, *ibid.,* pp. 63ff., on Matt. 28:18-20. According to Hahn, however, the idea of a mission of the disciples did not first arise from faith in the exalted Lord, but a mission given by the pre-Easter Jesus (pp. 40ff.) now became broadened to a universal mission in the conviction that with

Jesus' exaltation "an essential step towards the final completion has already been taken and that therefore the bringing in of the Gentiles can now begin" (p. 68). That the tradition standing behind Matt. 28:18-20, however, appeals only to a task given by the resurrected Jesus, as the exalted one, without recalling a mission given by the earthly Jesus or the universal breadth of his message, shows that the decisive importance for the motivation falls here on the resurrection (as exaltation). The connection with the character of Jesus' earthly activity represents more a modern possibility of reflection in terms of the history of traditions, which, to be sure, accents a continuity that *actually* exists, not, however, an argument that becomes effective for the transition of Hellenistic Jewish Christianity to the Gentile mission.

[17] Hahn in his arguments concerning Paul's understanding of mission (*Mission in the New Testament,* pp. 95-110) has not noticed this Pauline line of argumentation, so that he grasps the Pauline idea of the Gentile mission that is *independent of the law* only as an especially distinct understanding of the universal mission of the disciples implied in the concept of the exaltation of Jesus (pp. 100f.).

[18] References in Jeremias, *Jesus' Promise to the Nations,* p. 14.

[19] As proof from Scripture, Paul cites Gen. 12:3 (Gal. 3:8) and Gen. 17:5 (Rom. 4:17).

[20] In this, for modern judgment, the reference to Hos. 2:23 is just as erroneous as that to Joel 2:32 (Rom. 10:13), since both refer to Israel. Nevertheless, Paul rightly claimed the universalism of eschatological salvation in the prophets for the mission to the Gentiles.

# The Sinlessness of Christ

**24**

**Louis Berkhof**

# Scripture Proof for the Sinless Humanity of Christ

We ascribe to Christ not only natural, but also moral, integrity or moral perfection, that is sinlessness. This means not merely that Christ could avoid sinning (*potuit non peccare*), and did actually avoid it, but also that it was impossible for Him to sin (*non potuit peccare*) because of the essential bond between the human and the divine natures. The sinlessness of Christ has been denied by Martineau, Irving, Menken, Holsten, and Pfleiderer, but the Bible clearly testifies to it in the following passages: Luke 1:35; John 8:46; 14:30; II Cor. 5:21; Heb. 4:15; 9:14; I Peter 2:22; I John 3:5. While Christ was made to be sin judicially, yet ethically He was free from both hereditary depravity and actual sin. He never makes a confession of moral error; nor does He join His disciples in praying, "Forgive us our sins." He is able to challenge His enemies to convince Him of sin. Scripture even represents Him as the one in whom the ideal man is realized, Heb. 2:8, 9; I Cor. 15:45; II Cor. 3:18; Phil. 3:21. Moreover, the name "Son of Man," appropriated by Jesus, seems to intimate that He answered to the perfect ideal of humanity.

From *Systematic Theology* (Grand Rapids: William B. Eerdmans, 1938), pp. 318-19. Used by permission.

# 25

**Nels F. S. Ferre**

# Very God, Very Man

How far ... was the human nature of Jesus independent of Godhood either in preparation for the fullness of time or in the fullness of time? We know that Jesus had weaknesses, ignorance, finitude and mortality. We know that he had real temptations of great depth and power. But did he sin? Did he have to sin in order to share our full, actual humanity? If sin is thought of as gross acts of misconduct we have no need to suppose Jesus guilty of sin. We cannot even argue from his submitting to baptism for the remission of sin that he was doing more than join a great prophetic movement "to fulfil all righteousness." Nor can we argue that he was a sinner from the fact that his own prayer contained petition for the forgiveness of trespasses or debts. Even his pleading that not he, but God alone, was good can witness to the purity of his own consciousness which, by being pure, was the more humble, acknowledging as right the great Jewish act of the worship of a God so qualitatively different from man that His full will went beyond man's capacity as far as the heaven is from the earth. On the other hand, Bible claims to the effect that Jesus was sinless have most weight for the literalist. Such language, too, can be ascribed to unreflective

From *Christ and the Christian* (New York: Harper and Row, 1958), pp. 110-14. Used by permission.

piety and adoration. However much we bend over backwards to soften the statements that involve the unsinlessness[1] of Jesus, the evidence of the New Testament seems to be on both sides.

Is there, then, a theological way to settle the question? Historically we cannot go beyond ignorance as far as certain knowledge goes, except for the registering of the fact that Jesus in the most natural and indirect instances seems to have been humbly conscious of sin before God. His identification with man in this respect was natural, unaffected and complete. Possibly we can say more. Sin is not to be thought of basically in terms of discrete acts, but as a relation to God. The definition in James to the effect that "whoever knows what is right to do and fails to do it, for him it is sin" (4:17) is a moralistic rendering of sin and not to be compared to the deeper definition of Paul that "whatsoever does not proceed of faith is sin" (Rom. 14:23). Sin is the *acceptance* of anxiety; fear is therefore the external sign of sin. Now watch the fact that Hebrews claims that for fear Jesus cried day and night unto him who was able to deliver him from death (Heb. 5:7). We have no right, of course, to take such a claim for literally reported history, but we can say that such a biblical assertion tallies to some real extent with the total account of his life. Perhaps the context of this experience was Messianic, Jesus being "made sin" in the depth of his identification with both the will of God and the sins of his people.

Sin is "the set on self" which must be broken through by suffering. Jesus learned from the struggles of his moral conflicts, and through suffering accepted understanding and willing obedience. In this respect he was fully and gloriously human. In this sense the sinless God was present with the struggling Saviour, as the victorious Godman, sharing the struggle and being "made sin" for us, but winning so amazingly over sin, as God and man organically united (that is as the Godman) that he became the first in the Kingdom, "the firstborn of many brethren," "the pioneer and perfecter of our faith." One of our greatest evangelists, who is himself something of a modern St. Francis, has suggested that Jesus must himself have been born again, and have given his injunction of man's necessity to be born again from personal experience. May we not also say that in some sense, if all human beings have to be born again in order to see the Kingdom of God, so did Jesus; or else the Son of God was never made fully man. Jesus, as a human being, was born again, and experienced rapture and new levels of acceptance by God. Jesus, on the other side of his human experience, was the one who first accepted Incarnation, who fulfilled conclusively both the presence and purpose of God and the nature and destiny of man. In him therefore came the fullness of time, first of all for himself and potentially for all men. Jesus went the shortest way that we know home to the Father. *Jesus was eternity's miracle of time.*[2] In him heaven and earth met and in him is the focus and turning point of all earthly history. Jesus knew sin, in some sense, as a minimal but real experience within his own life; and as a maximal experience outside himself because of his supreme concern for men. This conclusive concern which takes upon itself man's sin is the seal of the fullness of time, God's own inbreaking as decisive presence and power, to rescue man from his sinful plight.

Theologically Jesus did not save us from sin unless he assumed it within himself; and sin, not finitude, is precisely our deepest problem. Jesus was "made sin," however, not in the sense that God could ever sin, certainly not even in human form, but that the human nature of Jesus shared our whole history of alienation from God and accepted the anxiety connected with it which is the root reality of sin. *To remove Jesus from our sin categorically is to deny the Incarnation and to destroy its reality and power.*

God is precisely He who from His highest stoops to our lowest. He used the greatest power, Agape, to destroy from within our worst enemy, sin. The holiness of God is not only a withdrawal from sin, in the sense of intrinsic and inviolable purity, but is also an outgoing purity questing to encounter sin and to slay it precisely by becoming the ally of the man who sins, against his own sins, and against the sins of man.

Incarnation is real. God became man! The Word became flesh! We need not deal with myth. Jesus as man was one of us. He knew our actual plight from within; but he was more than man, for God was in him reconciling the world unto Himself. God was there, not as in a dwelling, but organically united to, in and with man, constituting Jesus the Godman. God as Agape was present as the main Spirit of Jesus' life. God the Sinless entered our sinful world and by means of real human experience *from within* showed His power as the Sinless to defeat and to destroy sin, and along with sin, the ignorance, law and death which have come to be man's enemies because of sin. How can human pen phrase the most mysterious of all miracles: the creative and redemptive presence of God, as God, with man, as man, in the Incarnation!

*Enhypostasia* should safeguard the full humanity of Jesus and his full identification with actual human nature. We start, therefore, not with an unreal, but with a genuine human being in whom dwelt the Godhead bodily as the conclusive fulfilment of human nature and of history, actually in Jesus and potentially for all men. Jesus is the Godman who is the eternal purpose of God in the fullness of time. Therefore all things cohere in him.

When, however, did the hypostatic union take place? We cannot tell. Perhaps it is futile to analyse the event of the Incarnation. The conclusive union, in any case, came early enough for Jesus to illustrate an Agape life, to die an Agape death, to rise from death as Agape everlastingly victorious. At what point the union became the basic fact of Jesus' life we cannot know, although it seems likely that it occurred before his baptism. After that he appears triumphant in his parables and sayings. *Enhypostasia,* nevertheless, stands for the solid fact that in spite of all victories and even transfiguration experiences the struggle remained through the wilderness temptations, Gethsemane and until his dying cry of desertion by God.

## Notes

[1] I use this word because "sin*ful*ness" can hardly be applied to Jesus!

[2] "He lives among us in the identical conditions we live in. And proves that it can be done: that one can live a perfect Christian life in this world, in spite of darkness and death. He shows us that within the closed frontiers of this existence of ours one can lead a life that is entirely open towards God, entirely dependent upon God. He receives everything from God: from the Father and from himself as the Son" (Von Speyer, *The Word,* p. 139). The word "perfect" to me indicates a conclusively victorious life that finally broke through human history into the fullness of God by the presence and the power of God.

**Hugh R. Mackintosh**

# The Sinlessness of Jesus

The manhood of Jesus . . . is a manhood essentially one with ours. His life is a distinctively human phenomenon, moving always within the lines of an authentically human mind and will, and constituting thus a revelation of God in humanity, "not partly in it and partly out of it." Yet it is just when this has been made clear that we adequately realise the wholly exceptional quality of this human life. Jesus may be described as ideal or normal man; but these just epithets produce a totally wrong impression if we do not add immediately that manhood of this ideal type has existed but once in history.[1] He is unique in virtue of His sinlessness—the one quite unspotted life that has been lived within our sinful race. The deep and ineffaceable impression made by Jesus on those around Him cannot be dismissed as illusory. It is clear that His own consciousness of sin, had it existed, however faintly, must have affected His demeanour; that His followers must have observed the tokens of a bad conscience; and that such tokens, had they been present, must have profoundly modified their view of Jesus. No one doubts, then, that the disciples represented Jesus as without sin, and it is morally inconceivable that they should have held to

From *The Doctrine of the Person of Jesus Christ* (New York: Charles Scribner's Sons, 1912), pp. 400-404. Used by permission.

this belief in defiance of better knowledge. Once the fact of His sinlessness has been apprehended, however, we can put forward strong antecedent grounds for accepting it. Only a sinless person can guarantee the Divine pardon of sin. If redemption is to be achieved, the Redeemer must stand free of moral evil. As the source of victorious spiritual energy He must Himself be in utter oneness with the will of God. The perfect moral health, the unstained conscience, to which He is slowly raising others, must be present absolutely in His own life. If He shed His blood for the remission of sins, it is because He is without spot or blemish. Like to His brethren in all else, He is unlike them here. Yet it is no paradox to say that such unlikeness makes His kinship perfect; for sin had made Him not more a man, but less. Sin dehumanises, and by its entrance the perfection of His vital sympathy would have been irrecoverably lost.

Just here is our problem. As the record proves, Jesus underwent repeated and acute temptation; tempted, we feel, He must have been, if we are right in counting on His sympathy in the struggle. Yet are the temptations of the sinless real? In such a nature, what door can open and let in the base allurement? How can evil find resonance where there is neither inherited bias to evil nor weakness due to previous transgression?

Now we must distinguish clearly between temptation and sin. Temptation has become actual when the lower aim is felt as in collision with the higher; and if the lower aim be justifiable in its own time and place, as an appeal to inborn instinct, the felt shock of both within the moral consciousness is not yet sin. Not even the struggle that may ensue is sin. But sin is present when the decision for the higher fails, or comes too slowly. Now Jesus' nature, being integrally human, formed a medium through which the solicitation alike of higher and lower ends came knocking at His heart. It may well be that certain species of temptation—to forms of evil we name carnal—had virtually no existence for His mind. If it was so, His redeeming power over the slaves of sensuality is not thereby limited; for to the completeness of the Redeemer it is not essential that He should undergo each individual temptation by which men may be assailed. What is essential is that He should be "schooled" in temptation, should taste and see what it is to repel the approach of evil through a lowly trust in God. But however this may be, at least He was vulnerable in all His normal instincts, emotions, desires. The longing for triumph; the impulse to take the shortest path to power; a fear of death which is something almost wholly physical; a shrinking from close contact with sin—these natural, innocent tendencies and the like supplied very real opportunities of rebellion. They constituted what Moberly has called "the external capacity, and as it were machinery, for selfishness"; they meant a pressure on the will against which force must be exerted in steadfast resistance and with a real pain of conflict. Thus the Holy One learned obedience. For the holiness of Jesus was no automatic necessity of being. It was possessed only by being perpetually won anew, in a dependence of self-committal which had indeed no relation to a consciousness of sin, as with us, but which rested none the less on the felt need of an uninterrupted derivation of life and power from the Father. Precisely how this reality of tempted conflict can have occurred within a sinless mind is no doubt inscrutable. For us indeed it must be so; since the only psychological analogies we can use have their origin in our own sinful experience.[2]

It may be that we speak too much of Jesus' conflict, forgetting that His was a goodness altogether radiant, victorious, full of charm. Holiness in Him revealed that ease and mastery which belong to all perfection: "He did the most wonderful things as if nothing else were conceivable." Yet, on the other hand, while temptation never made appeal in Him to frailty resulting from previous sin, He was not therefore absolved from painful effort. Sinless temptations may be the most severe. The acquired appetite of the drunkard may be resisted with benefit to himself; but the natural appetite of thirst, if persistently denied satisfaction, will prove fatal. Not only so; but the resistance of temptation may be torture to a good man, whereas a bad man yields easily. In the light of these things we can see that our Lord, sinless as He was, had no exemption from keen and cruel warfare. None was ever tempted so subtly, and triumph came through agony. Thus the great High Priest of men gained an inner view of the tempted life, and can be touched with a feeling of our infirmities.

No miracle of Christ equals the miracle of His sinless life. To be holy in all thought and feeling; never to fail in duty to others, never to transgress the law of perfect love to God or man, never to exceed or to come short—this is a condition outstripping the power of imagination and almost of belief. Here is a casement opening on a Diviner world.

But it is essential that we should not leave the sinlessness of Jesus as a bare, uninterpreted fact. Plainly it is in no sense self-explanatory. It asks for deeper elucidation and analysis. And reflection proves that the ground or reason of it must be sought in our Lord's unique relation to God. The moral transcendence of Jesus' life is unintelligible save as it originated in, and was nourished by, a vital and organic connection with the Father, who alone is holy with the holiness manifest in Jesus. It is vain to speak of Him simply as different from others in degree; the difference is one of type. When we ask why He uniformly triumphed over sin, whereas we fail, the answer, as we shall see, must lie in that element of His being in virtue of which He is one with God.[3] Or, to put it otherwise, by the side of yet suffused with those qualities in Christ which we are summoned to imitate and reproduce, and which reveal Him as the pattern of filial life, we discern a yet more august quality—inimitable, solitary, supreme. It is a new and lonely type of spiritual consciousness, an unshared relation of identity with the Father. Divinity is here the source and basis of perfect manhood.

## Notes

[1] A character at once perfectly ideal and completely human is not inconceivable, as has been maintained; but how difficult the conception is may be seen from the fact that it has never been represented with success in imaginative literature. Tennyson's Arthur and George Eliot's Daniel Deronda are the best-known modern failures. Of Jesus only can it be said, *Das Unzulängliche, hier wird's Ereigniss.*

[2] Ultimately, it may be argued, the complete certainty that Jesus never sinned is given by our faith in His person; for there is no way of proving experimentally the impossibility of a fact.

[3] Cf. *infra*, chap. vii.

# The Virgin Birth

## Carl F. H. Henry

# Our Lord's Virgin Birth

Among the issues raised by the unfortunate and continuing controversy over the Virgin Birth, the implied dismissal of the biblical testimony naturally claims much of our attention. It is right that this should be so. For, while the biblical evidence is small, and attempts have been made to weaken it by emendation, variant readings, and literary dissection, even a theologian of Karl Barth's stature tells us that "no one can dispute the existence of a biblical testimony to the Virgin Birth" (*Church Dogmatics,* I, 2, p. 176). Thus, denial of the miracle entails direct and conscious rejection of the authority of Scripture and the apostolic teaching which it embodies. And the seriousness of such rejection is incontestable and incalculable.

Yet while this is true, there are also important theological implications which may be missed even by those who contend for the Virgin Birth on biblical grounds. A main argument used against it is in fact its supposed insignificance and even irrelevance. Many theologians, like Schleiermacher, have thought that they could accept a supernatural work of God without the Virgin Birth. Many others have tended to agree with Brunner that it is

From *Christianity Today,* 7 December 1959, pp. 20-22. Used by permission.

an unnecessary and inquisitive biological intrusion. Many would argue that they can confess the true deity and incarnation of Christ without it. Evangelicals often leave the impression that it is a kind of embarrassment which they are prepared to accept because it is in Scripture but which they do not find to be particularly significant or meaningful.

Now if this is indeed the case, it might be asked why the issue has been given such prominence in recent discussion. To be sure, any denial of the biblical record is a serious matter. But why should this particular denial be singled out as compared, for example, with the denial of some of the miracles performed by Jesus? On the other hand, may it not be that, in addition to its implications for the authenticity and authority of Scripture, the Virgin Birth does in fact have a wider theological significance which its opponents are quick to ignore and its proponents too slow to perceive? This, at any rate, has been the way in which dogmatics understood the matter prior to the rise of liberal Protestantism, and it is perhaps the way in which it must always be understood in truly dogmatic thinking.

It may be admitted, of course, that the Virgin Birth is not flatly identical with the Incarnation, just as the empty tomb is not flatly identical with the Resurrection. The one might be affirmed without the other. Yet the connection is so close, and indeed indispensable, that were the Virgin Birth or the empty tomb denied, it is likely that either the Incarnation or Resurrection would be called in question, or they would be affirmed in a form very different from that which they have in Scripture and historic teaching. The Virgin Birth might well be described as an essential, historical indication of the Incarnation, bearing not only an analogy to the divine and human natures of the Incarnate, but also bringing out the nature, purpose, and bearing of this work of God to salvation. Hand in hand with its biblical attestation as a fact, it thus has a theological necessity which not only supplies its vindication but also warns us that its repudiation will almost inevitably be accompanied by a movement away from truly evangelical teaching.

Thus, from the fact that Jesus is "born of the Virgin Mary," it may be seen that the work of Incarnation and Reconciliation involves a definite intervening act on the part of God himself. As Luther saw, a new beginning has to be made, a new creation initiated. It is not a beginning out of nothing. The role of Mary shows us that it is the old order which is the object of this creative work. The new man, Jesus Christ, is true man. In the words of Barth, "he is the real son of a real mother" (*ibid.*, p. 185). There is no question of a mere semblance of humanity, nor of a humanity which bears no relation to the original work of God. What God now does, he does in and on the old, natural man. Yet it is strictly and properly the creative work of God himself. There can be no pretense of an achievement or theory of man. By the exclusion of the male it is made quite clear that what is to be done is something which man of himself cannot do, not even though his work is sanctified for the purpose by God. There is a part which has to be played by man as represented by the virgin; but the active initiative is necessarily with God.

The inadequacy of man for this work is linked, of course, with the sinfulness of man. Hence the Virgin Birth carries with it not only the implication of the initiative of grace but also that of the hopeless sin and guilt of man. To be sure, this is not to be identified exclusively with the sexual act, as though this were the essence of sin and the problem of original sin would be solved by its evasion. Mary is no less a sinner than Joseph, and, while the sexual act is affected by sin like all others, the original sin of the race extends to every act as to each individual. No, the point is that though the Son of Mary as such stands in solidarity with sinners, yet his real birth is directly from God, so that unlike all others he is not himself a sinner, but has come to bear their sin in God's own work of salvation. A man born in the normal way could have been one with sinners, but he could not have been the sinless sin-bearer. The sinless sin-bearer comes into the world in such a way that he is also one with man, yet there is a decisive break with the old humanity as well as continuity with it. He is not sinful man accomplishing in a more worthy representative his own salvation. He is the second man, the Lord from heaven, the Son of Man who is also the Son of God incarnate for us men and for our salvation.

In this connection it is important to consider the importance of the fact that the human part is played by the female rather than the male. In a sense this is self-explanatory, for by nature the female is always present at generation. It is also theologically apt, for, as divines have pointed out from at least the time of Leo, Jesus has neither a mother in heaven nor a father on earth. There is also the further point, however, that it is the male who plays the active, initiatory role in generation, and therefore in a work in which the initiative necessarily lies with God "the whole action of man, the male can having no meaning" (*ibid.*, p. 194). On the other hand, it must be emphasized that, though the female provides the link with humanity, this is not because either by sex or in person she has innate qualities alien to the male, nor because she is free from sin, nor because there is a special female Mary herself immaculately conceived and destined to represent human glorification as the queen of heaven, but because she can fulfill the essentially passive role as the one in and on and through whom God acts in accomplishment of his gracious salvation.

The fact that in the life and work and person of Jesus Christ we are genuinely concerned with God in his saving action is positively emphasized by the second, or more strictly primary, element in the Virgin Birth, namely, the fact that Jesus was "conceived by the Holy Spirit." This does not, of course, give rise to the same offense as the "born of the Virgin Mary," since it may be conveniently "spiritualized" and linked with a normal human birth in various ways. Yet in conjunction with the "born of the Virgin" it has its own positive witness, first, that in the coming of Jesus we have neither a mythological marvel nor a natural possibility, but a true work of God, and second, that, as Jesus was born from above, so all members of the new humanity must be born again to newness of life in him by the sovereign action of the Spirit. In this respect there is truth in the statement of the older divines that the proper organ of conception in Mary was the ear, by which there came to her the Word of God and therefore faith. In other words, Christians are all born again by grace and faith in analogy to the birth of Jesus Christ himself as conceived by the Holy Spirit and born of the Virgin Mary. To become a Christian is no more a natural possibility than the Word's becoming flesh. It is the regenerative work of the Spirit in those who receive Christ, that is, who believe in his name.

It may be contended, of course, that these doctrines implicit in the Virgin Birth may still be held even where the factuality of the birth is rejected. In point of fact, however, it is noticeable that denial of the Virgin Birth almost invariably accompanies, or is accompanied by, a more basic theological defection in which the divine initiative, the inadequacy of man, the reality of original sin, the miraculous nature of regeneration, the primacy of the Word of God, and the importance of the faith which it brings are either abandoned in whole or part or drastically reinterpreted. Even in Roman Catholicism, which obviously retains the Virgin Birth, it is striking that the distortion of evangelical doctrine has almost inevitably produced a corruption of the biblical witness to the Virgin Birth in and by an unfounded, exaggerated, and basically Pelagianizing Mariology. In itself the abandonment of the scriptural testimony may seem to many to be of little account. But quite apart from the serious impugning of the written Word, it is a conditioning and resultant sign of more widespread abandonment of evangelical doctrine. For the Virgin Birth itself carries by implication the sum and substance of the Gospel.

We may close on an irenical note. Christmas has come again with its testimony to the Incarnation and atoning work of Christ without which there is no Gospel, faith, nor Church. All who claim the name of Christian will be turning afresh in public and private to the ancient and well-loved records: "Now the birth of Jesus Christ was on this wise. . . ."; "And it came to pass in those days, that there went out a decree from Caesar Augustus. . . ." All will be pondering afresh the tremendous reality and meaning of the incarnation of the Son of God. May we not make it our business to see that the records and the reality are in fact more intimately and irrevocably related than some ecclesiasts today assume? May we not ask ourselves whether we can really have the one without the other, whether we shall not necessarily lose the one if we deny the other, whether the substance of the Christmas Gospel and the purity of the Christmas faith are not an issue in this whole matter? May we not make it our concern to commit ourselves afresh to the reality and wholeness of the Christmas Gospel as the very carols sung from our own lips attest it, and with this Gospel humbly accept the holy miracle of the birth of Jesus which in the wisdom and power of God is so apt to denote the significance of his saving action as the incarnate Mediator, the first-begotten of the new creation and family of God?

## 28

**Edward J. Carnell**

# The Virgin Birth
# of Christ

The Bible says that Christ was born of a virgin, but it does not say why. This silence has encouraged theologians to compose reasons of their own. These reasons, at times, are more ingenuous than wise.

### Some Efforts at Explanation

Some theologians say Christ's *deity* required the Virgin Birth, but the effort is wide of the mark. Christ is divine because he is one with the Father and the Spirit. The Trinity is an eternal order of being.

Other theologians say Christ's *incarnation* required the Virgin Birth, but the effort overlooks the sovereignty of God. Since God is omnipotent, he could have united divine and human nature in any way he elected. The mode of Christ's birth is part of the economy of redemption.

Many theologians say Christ's *sinlessness* required the Virgin Birth, but the effort is weak on several counts. First, a "traducian" theory of the soul is required; a theory, namely, that the soul of a child is not immediately created by God, but is derived from its parents by ordinary generation.

From *Christianity Today,* 7 December 1959, pp. 9-10. Used by permission.

Such a theory is pure speculation; the Bible nowhere tells how the soul is formed. Second, the apostles trace Christ's sinlessness to his holy life, not to his miraculous birth; and the judgment of the apostles is normative for the Church. Third, the science of genetics has found that hereditary traits come from the mother as well as the father. Thus, the Virgin Birth would not, of itself, secure Christ's human nature from pollution.

Roman Catholicism tries to relieve the last difficulty by declaring Mary free from original sin. But the Roman expedient, taken out consistently, would imply a denial of the fall of man. Not only must Mary be immaculately conceived, but likewise her parents, her grandparents, and so on, until we reach Adam and Eve.

Protestants say Mary *was* conceived in sin, and in saying so they void any causal connection between the sinlessness of Christ and the Virgin Birth. Just as God protected Christ's human nature from the pollution of Mary, so he could have protected it from the pollution of Joseph; in which case Christ would have been born of ordinary generation, yet without sin.

### Christ the Promised Blessing

Theologians would be on much safer ground if they rested the case for the Virgin Birth on the manner in which God dealt with his covenant people in the Old Testament. Let us develop this.

When Adam sinned, he and all his seed incurred the just displeasure of God. Yet, grace triumphed over law in that very hour of woe. When all appeared lost, God said that the seed of the woman would bruise the head of the serpent (Gen. 3:15). The comfort of this prophecy was only surpassed by its mystery; for how could man, a willing servant of Satan, defeat the counsels of Satan?

God removed part of the mystery when he made a covenant with Abraham. God promised to bless all nations through the seed of Abraham. Abraham did not know how this would come to pass, but he believed God and it was reckoned to him as righteousness.

God removed more of the mystery when he instituted the Mosaic system of bloody sacrifice. The seed of Abraham would bless all nations by assuming the guilt of punishment into and upon himself. The Lamb of God, who takes away the sin of the world, was foreshadowed by the Mosaic system.

The Old Testament prophets concluded the economy of preparation by citing the name of the Saviour, the place and mode of his birth, and the manner of his life, death and resurrection. The Saviour would be born of a woman, and thus suffer the limitations of human nature. Yet, he would bear titles befitting his Messianic office: Wonderful Counselor, Mighty God, Everlasting Father, Prince of Peace (Isa. 9:6).

### The Threat of Involuntary Unbelief

Let us go one step further. Since God's promises were greater than man's capacity to receive them, God always accompanied his promises with special signs. The spirit is willing, but the flesh is weak. For example, when Abraham inquired how he might know that God would bless him, God ratified the covenant by a smoking furnace and a flaming torch. When Moses feared Pharaoh's court, God gave him a rod of power. And when Gideon shrank before the Midianite hordes, God honored the fleece. These signs, in each case, were aimed at subduing the threat of involuntary unbelief.

When we see why God gave signs to his people, we can see why Christ was born of a virgin; for if the great heroes of the faith required signs when they looked *forward* to the Saviour's coming, how much more were signs required by those into whose house the Saviour would be born? The signs of Christ's appearance had to admit of no doubt. Yet, the signs had to be secret, lest the foes of righteousness begin their nefarious work before Christ's hour had come.

### Signs of Christ's Appearance

When the angel told Mary that God had chosen her to be the mother of the Saviour, she found the tidings awesome. "And Mary said to the angel, 'How can this be, since I have no husband?' " (Luke 1:34) The angel allayed Mary's fear by naming two specific signs: first, her own child would be conceived of the Holy Spirit; second, Elizabeth would bear a child in her old age.

In due time Mary was able to confirm both of these signs. When she felt life stirring in her body, she knew that her child was a miracle sent from God. And a happy visit to the home of Elizabeth confirmed the second sign.

As time passed, however, a new cloud of difficulty gathered; for when Joseph found that Mary was with child, he "resolved to divorce her quietly" (Matt. 1:19). Joseph's Hebrew piety, let alone his male ego, prompted this resolve. Not only had Mary brought shame on Israel by conceiving out of wedlock, but she had deliberately concealed her condition. This, at least, is how Joseph viewed the matter.

The cloud of difficulty did not lift until God dispatched an angel of light. "Joseph, son of David, do not fear to take Mary your wife, for that which is conceived in her is of the Holy Spirit; she will bear a son, and you shall call his name Jesus, for he will save his people from their sins" (Matt. 1:20-21). Convinced by this sign, Joseph took Mary to be his wife. Mary was now free to tell all that was on her heart. Mutual pardon was sought and given. The holy couple then waited for God to give his gift to the world.

This pious vigil, however, did not end with the advent of Christ. The time of waiting, in fact, had hardly begun. Let us appreciate this as we ponder the Virgin Birth. Some 30 years elapsed between Christ's birth and his manifestation to Israel. During these years Joseph and Mary had no other proof of Christ's divinity than the signs surrounding his birth. Mary *prophesied* wonderful things about her Son, but she prophesied more than she understood. This is proved by the way she chided Jesus when he tarried in the temple at the age of 12. "Son, why have you treated us so?" (Luke 2:48) Jesus replied to this query with divine authority, "How is it that you sought me? Did you not know I must be in my Father's house?" (2:49)

Now few Christians are disturbed by the silence of the early Church, for neither the book of Acts nor the Epistles make any explicit reference to the Virgin Birth of Christ. The difficulty, however, is easily resolved.

The mode of Christ's birth forms no part of the "one act of righteousness" by which Christ reconciled God to the world. When Christ died on the cross, he offered up the fruit of a perfected human nature. He earned this fruit by loving God with all his heart and his neighbor as himself. Conscious, voluntary energy was required; an energy that Christ did not have as an infant, for his human faculties were undeveloped.

When the apostles preached the Gospel, therefore, they had no more reason to refer to the mode of Christ's birth than they did to his legal parents or the street on which he lived. The Gospel draws on the public ministry of Christ, a ministry that began with the Baptism and ended with the Resurrection.

The Virgin Birth is precious to the household of faith because it plays a major role in connecting the promises of the Old Testament with their fulfillment in the New Testament. "All this took place to fulfill what the Lord had spoken by the prophet: 'Behold, a virgin shall conceive and bear a son, and his name shall be called Emmanuel' " (Matt. 1:22-23 RSV). Scripture is inspired of God and has the force of law in the Church.

At this happy Christmas season, when we thank God for his inexpressible gift, let us renew our faith in the appointed means by which God made this gift to the world. God not only promised to bless all nations through the seed of Abraham, but he accompanied his promise with special signs. One of these signs was the Virgin Birth. If we disregard the Virgin Birth, we offend a confessional element that has united Christians from the first century until now.

## 29

## L. Harold De Wolf

# The Doctrine
# of the Virgin Birth

To all that has been pointed out in the Gospels making clear the humanity of Jesus some may reply by raising the question whether the teaching that he was born of a virgin by miraculous conception does not prove that he was only part man and by birth part God.

It must be replied that this teaching is nowhere in the Gospels presented as a denial of Jesus' humanity, nor has it any essential relation to the doctrine of his divinity. Indeed, though all of the Gospels teach that he was the Son of God, all likewise teach plainly that he was wholly and not partly a man subject to God's rule. Only two Gospels, Matthew and Luke, mention a virgin birth. In Matthew the significance of this miraculous birth is presented as a fulfillment of Isaiah 7:14.[1] Only in Luke is there a suggestion that this birth constitutes the meaning of his title, "Son of God," and even there the wording may mean simply that by reason of this miraculous birth his divine sonship will be attested or made known.[2]

It is plain that the development of Jesus' body from a fertilized or unfertilized or miraculously fertilized ovum is not the subject being discussed in the great councils which dealt with his divinity nor is it intrinsi-

From *A Theology of the Living Church*, 2nd ed. (New York: Harper and Row, 1968), pp. 230-32.

cally important to his moral authority, his spiritual power or the meaning of his death and resurrection. Those who have thought sexual procreation to be the one means by which original sin was passed from generation to generation have seen in the virgin birth the means of insulating Jesus from the hereditary Fall. But there is in the Scriptures little warrant for such an Augustinian view of sex and the Bible contains no such interpretation of the virgin birth. Moreover, the Roman Catholic Church, which has especially emphasized it, has been so ill satisfied with it as to have conjured up the additional doctrine of a miraculously "immaculate conception" of Mary in *her* mother's womb to place an additional barrier between Jesus and the Fall as well as further to exalt Mary herself.

On the other hand, those who profess to find either some disproof or some substantiating evidence of the virgin birth of Christ in the natural sciences might better be saved their pains. Scientists know about this essentially what everyone knows, namely, that there is no well-authenticated parallel case of an unfertilized ovum developing into a human body. All who believe in the virgin birth should not only agree with that assertion but should insist upon it, since if there were parallel cases Jesus' birth would lose its uniqueness. In other important respects the life of Jesus was unique and no natural scientist, using the powers which God gave him, can, by observing the world which his Creator made, set the limits of God's power to stir hope of such a unique life by a miraculous birth, if that were His will. When the question is raised whether or not Jesus was actually born of a virgin, the issue for a theist turns not on the limit of God's power but on the historical evidence.

The evidence in the text of the New Testament is not very convincing. The fact that only two books so much as mention such an event is important but not decisive evidence against it. The silence does indicate that it was no part of the Christian tradition as known to Paul and the authors of Mark, John, Hebrews and the other New Testament writings, or else it indicates that they were too skeptical or indifferent to record it among all the tributes they paid to the Master. But more important are other, more positive evidences. Both the genealogies, in Matthew and Luke, bear evidence of tampering. For if, as Matthew reports, the genealogy given traces only the lineage of "Joseph the husband of Mary, of whom Jesus was born,"[3] then it is not, as promised, "the genealogy of Jesus Christ, the son of David, the son of Abraham."[4] Even more suspicious is the parenthetical phrase introduced by Luke. For if Jesus was only "the son (*as was supposed*) of Joseph,"[5] then it is hard to see why a writer who knew that Joseph was *not* Jesus' father would have traced a genealogy through him. The parenthesis looks like an insertion into a genealogy already in circulation, to harmonize it, rather lamely, with the birth story which had come into the tradition at a later time. Probably the birth story itself had arisen as a further tribute to his divinity and to his fulfillment of the ambiguous prophecy in Isaiah 7:14.[6]

The same two Gospels which give the birth stories report that the neighbors in Nazareth thought Jesus to be Joseph's son and give this common assumption as one cause of their astonishment that he should speak as he did in maturity.[7] The neighbors plainly knew nothing of a virgin birth. Luke reports that Mary herself, speaking to Jesus, called Joseph his "father."[8] The same writer calls Joseph and Mary Jesus' "parents" and says that in his youth Jesus "was obedient to them."[9] In John 1:45 he is called "Jesus of Nazareth, the son of Joseph."

The pattern of life in the carpenter's family seems not to have been affected by remembrance of a miraculous birth. Whose life, then, are we to suppose was different because of it? The obvious answer, at first thought, would seem to be the life of Jesus. But in what respect is it to be supposed that God made him different as the son of one human parent than He may as well have made him as son of two human parents? His body was evidently fully mortal and human in every respect. Would a soul joined with such a human body be any different for that body's procreation by one than by two parents? Could God provide a man fit to be the Savior of men only by giving to that man a body from a virgin mother?[10]

But after raising the last question we must hasten to add that the New Testament, for all the teaching of his divinity, is unequivocal in affirming the completely human nature of Jesus, both soul and body. We have cited some testimony to that effect in the Gospels. It remains to point out other affirmations of his full humanity elsewhere in the New Testament.

### Notes

[1] Matt. 1:23. The Hebrew of Isa. 7:14 does not certainly imply virginity but may refer to a young matron.

[2] See Luke 1:35.

[3] Matt. 1:16.

[4] Matt. 1:1.

[5] Luke 3:23. Italics mine.

[6] Of course, the statement that the marriage of Jesus' parents had not been consummated (Matt. 1:25) at the time of his birth is an integral part of the birth tradition itself. The frequent claim, therefore, that to deny his birth of a virgin is to affirm his illegitimacy is even more pointless than it would otherwise be.

[7] Matt. 13:55-56; Luke 4:22.

[8] Luke 2:48.

[9] Luke 2:43, 51.

[10] Cf. Heb. 7:15-16.

# 30

## Reginald J. Campbell

# The Incarnation of the Son of God

**Jesus all that Christian devotion has believed Him to be.** So far we have
seen that the personality of Jesus is central for Christian faith. We deny
nothing about Him that Christian devotion has ever affirmed, but we
affirm the same things of humanity as a whole in a differing degree. The
practical dualism which regards Jesus as coming into humanity from
something that beforehand was not humanity we declare to be misleading.
Our view of the subject does not belittle Jesus but it exalts human nature.
Let this be clearly understood and most of the objections to it will vanish.
Briefly summed up, the position is as follows: Jesus was God, but so are
we. He was God because His life was the expression of divine love; we too
are one with God in so far as our lives express the same thing. Jesus was
not God in the sense that He possessed an infinite consciousness; no more
are we. Jesus expressed fully and completely, in so far as a finite consciousness ever could, that aspect of the nature of God which we have
called the eternal Son, or Christ, or ideal Man who is the Soul of the
universe, and "the light that lighteth every man that cometh into the
world"; we are expressions of the same primordial being. Fundamentally

From *The New Theology* (New York: Macmillan, 1907), pp. 92-109. Used
by permission.

we are all one in this eternal Christ. This is the most difficult statement of all to make clear, for the average westerner cannot grasp it; it is different from his ordinary way of looking at things. The best way of demonstrating it, as I have already shown, is to draw attention to the fact that Christian orthodoxy has all along been affirming the mystic union between Christ and the soul, and that the limited earthly consciousness of Jesus did not prevent Him from being really and truly God. Why should we not speak in a similar way about any other human consciousness? If we could only get men to do so habitually and sincerely, it would be the greatest gain to religion that could possibly be imagined. . . . I have pointed out that psychological science is doing much to help us toward this realisation. We are beginning to see, however hard it may be to understand it, that our limited individual consciousness is no barrier to the true identification of the lesser with the larger self. What Christian doctrine, therefore, has been affirming of Jesus for hundreds of years past is receiving impressive confirmation from modern science and is being seen to be true of every human being—that is, the lesser and the larger are one, however little the earthly consciousness may be able to grasp the fact. To me this is a most helpful and inspiring truth, one of the most important that has ever found a place in Christian thought; it elucidates much that would otherwise be obscure. It enables us to see how the human and divine were blended in Jesus without making Him essentially different from the rest of the human race; it enables us to realise our own true origin and to believe in the salvability of every soul that has ever come to moral consciousness. If this truth will not lift a man toward the higher life, I do not know one that will. It is the truth implied in all redemptive effort that has ever been made, and in every message that has ever gripped conscience and heart; it is, as the Nicene creed has it, "the taking of the manhood into God."

**The preëminence of Jesus.**—Lest anyone should think that this position involves in the slightest degree the diminution of the religious value and the moral preëminence of Jesus, let me say that it does the very opposite. Nothing can be higher than the highest, and the life of Jesus was the undimmed revelation of the highest. Faith to be effective must centre on a living person, and the highest objective it has ever found is Jesus. He is no abstraction but a spiritual reality, an ever-present friend and guide, our brother and our Lord. No one will ever compete with Jesus for this position in human hearts. When I speak of the eternal Christ, I do not mean someone different from Jesus, although I certainly do mean the basal principle of all human goodness; Jesus was and is that Christ, and we can only understand what the Christ is because we have seen Him. Wholehearted faith in Him has proved itself to be the most effective means to the manifestation of our own Christhood.

**Jesus and the incarnation.**—This thought at once opens up another great question to which we have already alluded, that of the incarnation of this eternal Christ or Son of God in the finite universe. According to the received theology the incarnation of God in human life was limited to the life of Jesus only, and through Him to mankind. I purposely say popular theology because the best Christian thought has always known better. Popular theology has it that Jesus, the only-begotten eternal Son of God, took human flesh and a human nature, was conceived by the Holy Ghost in the womb of a virgin, and was born into the world in a wholly miraculous way—a way which stamps Him as different from all that were ever born of woman before or since. It seems strange that belief in the virgin birth of Jesus should ever have been held to be a cardinal article of the Christian faith, but it is so even to-day. There is not much need to combat it, for most reputable theologians have now given it up, but it is still a stumbling-block to many minds. Perhaps, therefore, a brief examination of the subject may not be altogether out of place.

**The virgin birth not demonstrable from Scripture.**—The virgin birth of Jesus was apparently unknown to the primitive church, for the earliest New Testament writings make no mention of it. Paul's letters do not allude to it, neither does the gospel of St. Mark. "In the fulness of time," says the great apostle, "God sent forth His Son born of a woman." He was "of the seed of David according to the flesh," but nowhere does Paul give us so much as a hint of anything supernatural attending the mode of His entry into the world. Mark does not even tell us anything about the childhood of the Master; his account begins with the baptism of Jesus in Jordan. The fourth gospel, although written much later, ignores the belief in the virgin birth, and even seems to do so of set purpose as belittling and materialising the truth. The supposed Old Testament prophecies of the event have nothing whatever to do with it. The famous passage, "Behold a virgin shall conceive and bear a son, and shall call His name Immanuel," is a reference to contemporary events, and the word translated "virgin" simply means a young woman. It is a prophecy of the birth of a prince whose work it should be to put right for Judah what the reigning king Ahaz had been putting wrong. The story in the seventh of Isaiah is as follows: Ahaz, a rather weak ruler, was greatly concerned by the news that Rezin, king of Syria, and Pekah, king of northern Israel, had formed an alliance against him and were marching on Jerusalem. In his extremity this monarch of a petty state turned toward the mighty ruler of Assyria, the greatest military power in the world, and asked his help against the combination. Isaiah, statesman as well as prophet, saw that this was a wrong move. Assyria was aspiring to universal dominion, and to form an alliance with the military master of that mighty state would be to supply him with an excuse for further interference. The policy of Ahaz was therefore as suicidal as that of John Balliol when he called in Edward the First to adjudicate on his claim to the crown of Scotland, or the policy of Spain when she called in Napoleon. Sargon, king of Assyria, was overturning thrones in all directions, profiting by the divisions and jealousies of his foes. The great empires of Egypt and Babylonia went down before him as well as the smaller states. The condition of things in this ancient world was just like that of Europe at the beginning of the nineteenth century when the star of Napoleon was in the ascendant. For Ahaz to turn for help to Sargon was to court disaster in the end. Isaiah saw this and went out to meet Ahaz one day "at the end of the conduit of the upper pool in the highway of the fuller's field"—a vivid descriptive touch. The king was apparently preparing to stand a siege in his capital and was making sure of the water supply. Isaiah's remonstrance was in substance: You need not take so much trouble with your preparations; Syria and Israel will have more than enough to do presently to defend their own borders from Sargon. Besides, men like Rezin and Pekah are not men to be afraid of in any case; they have neither strength nor skill. But do not for heaven's sake call in Sargon; if you do you will supply him with an excuse for meddling and we shall never get rid of him. This was good counsel, but Ahaz was too short-sighted and panic-stricken to take much notice of it, so in oriental fashion Isaiah goes on to paint a picture of future disaster. The land, he says, will soon be laid waste, and future generations will rue the policy now being determined upon. In the end, of course, things will come all right, for God will not abandon His people. A better and wiser prince shall arise who shall restore prosperity to Judah. That prince is not yet born, but when he is, his name shall be called Immanuel,—God with us. In another place he describes him as Wonderful Counsellor, Divine Hero, Father Everlasting, Prince of Peace. "Butter and honey shall he eat," because there will be nothing else left after Assyria has swept over the country, but the discipline may have good results in the end, and will serve to bring Judah to her senses.

There is something strikingly modern about all this, and it is a good example of the way in which the same conditions arise over and over again in the course of human history. It is plain to be seen that the prophecy here indicated was only the shrewd common sense of a wise and patriotic man who loved his country and believed in God. But what on earth have his words to do with the birth of Jesus? It is only by a very long stretch of the pious imagination that they can be held to apply to Christianity at all. They have an interest of their own, and a very considerable interest, too, even from the point of view of religion; but Isaiah would have been considerably astonished to be told that they would have to wait seven hundred years for fulfilment. To a certain extent they were fulfilled soon afterward in the advent of the well-meaning but not very brilliant king Hezekiah. I have dwelt upon this passage at some length because it is a fair example of the way in which Old Testament literature has been pressed into the service of Christian dogma. What I am now saying, as I need hardly point out, is not my *ipse dixit;* expert biblical scholarship has been saying it for a long time, but somehow or other its bearing upon generally accepted dogmas is not popularly realised. It can hardly be maintained that Christian preachers who know the truth about these matters and refrain from stating it plainly are doing their duty to their congregations. No Old Testament passage whatever is directly or indirectly a prophecy of the virgin birth of Jesus. To insist upon this may seem to many like beating a man of straw, but if so the man of straw still retains a good deal of vitality.

**The virgin birth in the gospels.**—The only two gospels in which the virgin birth is alluded to are Matthew and Luke, and the nativity stories contained in these are very beautiful, especially those peculiar to Luke. But the two gospels are mutually contradictory in their account of the circumstances attending the miraculous birth. Each contains a genealogy which professes to be that of Joseph, not of Mary, and these are inconsistent with each other. What has the genealogy of Joseph got to do with the birth of Jesus if Jesus were not his own son? The conclusion seems probable that in the earlier versions of these gospels the miraculous conception did not find a place, or else that two inconsistent sources have been drawn upon without sufficient care being taken to reconcile them. But this is not the only discrepancy. Matthew gives Bethlehem as the native place of Joseph and Mary, Luke says Nazareth. Matthew says not a word about the census of Cyrenius as the motive for the journey to Bethlehem, but leads us to suppose that the holy family were already in residence there. Then again he tells us of the coming of the wise men from the East, their public inquiry as to the whereabouts of the holy child, the jealousy of Herod, the massacre of the innocents, and the flight into Egypt. Luke says nothing about these things, but gives us an entirely different set of wonders, including the attendance of an angelic host and the annunciation to the shepherds. So far from recording any massacre, or any hasty flight, he tells us that some time after His birth the babe was taken to the Temple at Jerusalem to be presented to the Lord, and that afterwards He and His parents "returned into Galilee to their own city Nazareth." According to Matthew Nazareth was an afterthought and only became the residence of the holy family after the return from Egypt. These accounts do not tally, and no ingenuity can reconcile them. The nativity stories belong to the poetry of religion, not to history. To regard them as narrations of actual fact is to misunderstand them. They are better than that; they take us into the region of exalted feeling and give us a vision of truth too great for prosaic statement. Christianity would be poorer by the loss of them, but they are not indigenous to Christianity. They have their parallels in other religions, some of them much older than the advent of Jesus. The beautiful legends surrounding the infancy of Gautama, for example, are startlingly similar to those contained in the first and third gospels. Like Jesus, the Buddhist messiah is stated to have been of royal descent and was born of a virgin mother. At his birth a supernatural radiance illuminated the whole district, and a troop of heavenly beings sang the praises of the holy child. Later on a wise man, guided by special portents, recognised him as the long-expected and divinely appointed light-bringer and life-giver of mankind. When but a youth he was lost for a time and was found by his father in the midst of a circle of holy men, sunk in rapt contemplation of the great mystery of existence. The parallel between these legends and the Christian version of the marvels attending the birth of Jesus is so close as to preclude the possibility of its being altogether accidental. There must have been a connection somewhere, and indeed there is no need to think otherwise, for nothing is to be gained or lost by admitting it.

328    *The Person of Christ*

**Christianity not dependent on a virgin birth.**—But why hesitate about the question? The greatness of Jesus and the value of His revelation to mankind are in no way either assisted or diminished by the manner of His entry into the world. Every birth is just as wonderful as a virgin birth could possibly be, and just as much a direct act of God. A supernatural conception bears no relation whatever to the moral and spiritual worth of the person who is supposed to enter the world in this abnormal way. The credibility and significance of Christianity are in no way affected by the doctrine of the virgin birth otherwise than that the belief tends to put a barrier between Jesus and the race and to make Him something which cannot properly be called human. Those who insist on the doctrine will find themselves in danger of proving too much, for, pressed to its logical conclusion, it removes Jesus altogether from the category of humanity in any real sense. Like many others, I used to take the position that acceptance or non-acceptance of the doctrine of the virgin birth was immaterial because Christianity was quite independent of it, but later reflection has convinced me that in point of fact it operates as a hindrance to spiritual religion and a real living faith in Jesus. The simple and natural conclusion is that Jesus was the child of Joseph and Mary and had an uneventful childhood.

**The truth in the doctrine of the virgin birth.**—And yet, as with every tenet which has held a place in human thought for any considerable length of time, there is a great truth contained in the idea of a virgin birth. It is the truth that the emergence of anything great and beautiful in human character and achievement is the work of the divine spirit operating within human limitations. This idea is very ancient, and there is no great religion which does not contain it in some form or other. One form of it, for example, can be discerned in the Babylonian creation myth with its parallel in the book of Genesis. The home of the primitive Chaldeans, the stock whence Israelites, Babylonians, Assyrians, and other Semitic communities sprang, was in the low-lying territory surrounding the Persian gulf. During the rainy seasons these lands were flooded by the overflow of the great rivers. The sun of springtime, rising upon this mass of waters which stretched in every direction as far as the eye could see, drew forth from their bosom the life and beauty of summer flowers and fruit. From observation of this regularly recurring phenomenon the primitive Semites constructed their creation myth, one version of which appeared in the first chapter of the book of Genesis, a version much later than the Babylonian, but an outgrowth of the same idea. They thought of a primeval waste of water covering everything. As the writer of the Genesis account has it: "The earth was without form and void, and darkness was upon the face of the deep." In the Babylonian version this primeval water was personified as a woman—Tiamat. They thought of the sun of heaven as impregnating this virgin matrix with the seeds of cosmic life—quite an accurate conception from the modern point of view. Later on this idea became spiritualised in a much higher degree. The religious mind came to regard the physical, mundane, or distinctively human principle as the matrix upon which the spirit of God brooded, bringing to the birth a divine idea. And this is perfectly true too, as anyone can see. Nothing great and noble in human experience can be accounted for merely in terms of atoms and molecules. That is where materialism always comes to grief, for on its own premises it cannot account for the emergence of intelligence and all the higher qualities of human nature. A divine element, a spiritual quickening, is required for the evolution of anything Godlike in our mundane sphere; it is a virgin birth. Lower acting upon lower can never produce a higher. It is the downpouring and incoming of the higher to the lower which produces through the lower the divine manhood which leaves the brute behind. This is the sense in which it is true that Jesus was of divine as well as human parentage. We do not account for Him merely by saying that He was the son of Joseph and Mary and the descendant of a long line of prophets, priests, and kings; we have to recognise that His true greatness came from above.

**True of all higher human experience.**—The same thing holds good in a lesser degree of everything worthy of Jesus in human experience. We do not account for any man's goodness or greatness by pointing to his ancestry. Heredity may account for a great deal, but it is inadequate as an explanation of genius or high moral achievement. If we go back far enough, we shall find that our ancestry was barbarous, and, judging from its tendencies, not at all likely to produce the Christ-man of future ages. Wherever the Christ-man appears, we have to acknowledge that the principal factor in his evolution is the incoming of the divine spirit. It is only another way of stating what has already been stated above, that the true man or higher self is divine and eternal, integral to the being of God, and that this divine manhood is gradually but surely manifesting on the physical plane. The lower cannot produce the higher, but the higher is shaping and transforming the lower; every moral and spiritual advance is therefore of the nature of a virgin birth—a quickening from above. The spiritual birth described in the conversation between our Lord and Nicodemus as given in the third of John is, properly speaking, a virgin birth. "That which is born of the flesh is flesh and that which is born of the spirit is spirit." "Ye must be born anew," or, literally, "quickened from above." Every man who deliberately faces towards the highest, and feels himself reënforced by the Spirit of God in so doing, is quickened from above; the divinely human Christ is born in him, the Word has become flesh and is manifested to the world.

**Human history one long incarnation.**—If now we can turn our thoughts away for a moment from the individual to the race and think of humanity as one being, or the expression of one being, we shall read this truth on a larger scale. All human history represents the incarnation or manifesting of the eternal Son or Christ of God. The incarnation cannot be limited to one life only, however great that life may be. It is quite a false idea to think of Jesus and no one else as the Son of God incarnate. It is easy to understand the loving reverence for Jesus which would lead men to regard Him as being and expressing something to which none of the rest of us can ever attain, but in affirming this we actually rob Him of a glory He ought to receive. We make Him unreal, reduce His earthly life to a sort of drama, and effect a drastic distinction in kind between Him and ourselves. If He came from the farther side of the gulf and we only from the hither; if we are humanity without divinity, and He divinity that has only assumed humanity,—perfect fellowship between Him and ourselves is impossible. But it is untrue to say that any such distinction exists. Let us go on thinking of Jesus as Christ, the very Christ of glory, but let us realise that that same Christ is seeking expression through every human soul. He is incarnate in the race in order that by means of limitation He may manifest the innermost of God, the life and love eternal. To say this does not dethrone Jesus; it lends significance to His life and work. He is on the throne and the sceptre is in His hand. We can rise toward Him by trusting, loving, and serving Him; and by so doing we shall demonstrate that we too are Christ the eternal Son.

To think of all human life as a manifestation of the eternal Son, renders it sacred. Our very struggles and sufferings become full of meaning. Sin is but the failure to realise it; it is being false to ourselves and our divine origin; it is the centrifugal tendency in human nature just as love is the centripetal. There is no life, however depraved, which does not occasionally emit some sign of its kinship to Jesus and its eternal sonship to God. Wherever you see self-sacrifice at work you see the very spirit of Jesus, the spirit of the Christ incarnate. I find it everywhere, and it interprets life for me as nothing else can. Take up any work of fiction, no matter what, and you will find the author instinctively preaching this truth. Look into any common-place, everyday life, no matter whose, and you will find it exemplified. Many a selfish bad man has one tender spot in his nature, his affection for his child, and for the sake of that child he will deny himself as he has never dreamed of doing for anything else; so far as that one influence is concerned he actually reverses the principle which governs the rest of his life. I have read of an African negress who on one occasion was beaten nearly to death by the brute to whom she was slave and paramour. Her murderer, for such he was, was arrested and placed on trial for his misdemeanour, in accordance with the rough justice of the white man in his dealings with the native. In the night the poor dying woman crawled painfully to the tree against which the ruffian lay bound, cut his cords, and set him free. It was her last act in this life; in the morning she was found lying dead on the spot whence the prisoner had fled. This particular story may or may not be true, but the same kind of thing has been true a million times in human history. What was the spirit in this benighted woman of the African wilds but the Christ spirit, the self-giving spirit seen with such unique sublimity in the life of Jesus?

Look abroad all through the world, look back upon the slow, upward progress of humanity to its home in God, and you will read the story of the incarnation of the eternal Son. Never has there been an hour so dark but that some gleams of this eternal light have pierced the murky pall of human ignorance and sin; never have bitter hate and fiendish cruelty gone altogether unrelieved by the human tenderness and self-devotion that testify of God. Indeed without the limitation, the struggle, and the pain, how would this Christ spirit ever have known itself? Granted that self-surrender had never been called for by the conditions of life, granted that our resources had always known themselves infinite, and that which is worthiest and sublimest in the nature of God and man alike could never have been revealed. This is why the eternal Son has become incarnate; this is what we are here to do, and upon the faithful doing of it depends our experience of the joy that the world can neither give nor take away. The life and death of Jesus are the central expression and ideal embodiment of this age-long process, a process the consummation of which will be the glorious return and triumphant ingathering of a redeemed and perfectly unified humanity to God. "And when all things shall be subdued unto him, then shall the Son also himself be subject unto him that put all things under him, that God may be all in all."

# PART FOUR

# The Work of Christ

## Editor's Introduction

A transition from the person of Christ (who He is) to the work of Christ (what He has done) is often made in traditional theologies by the concepts of the offices and the states of Christ, expounded here by **H. Orton Wiley**. The offices are the roles which He performed, which the Old Testament separated into prophet, priest, and king but which Christ combined in one person. As prophet, He is the revealer of God's message, the spokesman for God. As priest, He is man's representative to God and the one who offers to God the perfect sacrifice on man's behalf. As king, He reigns over all things. Yet this reign is only partly realized at present, its fullest exercise waiting for the future return of the Lord. Wiley discusses these concepts briefly.

This last observation also calls to our attention the two states of Christ: His humiliation and His exaltation. The earthly life of Jesus involved a series of steps by which He descended from the glory which was rightly His, culminating in His crucifixion, death, and burial. God, however, exalted Him in His resurrection and ascension, and ultimately will exalt Him in His victorious second coming.

The most significant work of Christ is probably that connected with His priestly role, or His atoning work. What was it that the death of Jesus accomplished? A number of theories have been developed over the years by Christians reflecting upon the Scriptures and upon their own experience of divine grace. Each theory emphasizes a different aspect of the atoning work of Christ. During different periods in the history of the church, different views have predominated, each giving way to some other.

Theology is organic in character. By this we mean that there is an interconnectedness, a wholeness, among the various elements or the different doctrines. Thus, the view one holds in one area will affect how he interprets Scriptures dealing with another doctrine. In other words, his conclusions on one doctrine constitute his presuppositions on another. Nowhere is this more apparent than with the atonement. One's understanding of man's condition cannot help but influence one's understanding of what man needs and hence of what must be done for him if the situation is to be rectified. If his problem is ignorance, or lack of confidence, then he must be given an example of obedience to God's will. If his problem is fear of God, or resentment of Him, then man needs a demonstration of God's love and good will. If, on the other hand, man is rebellious against God and is so sinful and corrupt that he neither wishes nor is able to behave so as to satisfy God, then it may be necessary for someone else to do for him what he cannot do for himself. One's understanding of man's condition is in turn related to one's conception of God. If God is indulgent and easygoing, perhaps not perfect Himself, waiting to receive man back to Himself if only man will return, then man needs only to be influenced or induced to respond. If, on the other hand, God is perfectly holy and cannot tolerate sin, expecting from man perfection like His own, then some sacrifice or appeasement must be offered to Him.

One's conception of the atonement is also intimately connected with one's doctrine of the person of Jesus Christ. If Jesus was man but not God, then He would not be able to serve as a substitute for man, or at least, His substitutionary death would be of less than infinite value. Conversely, however, if He was divine but not human, then His death could have no value for us as an example, for no human could follow the example of such a person.

Views of the atonement can be classified into types on the basis of what they are intended to effect, or toward whom the major influence or the atoning work is directed. Those that view the atonement as primarily influencing man are *subjective,* those that see its influence centering more upon God, *objective.*

Representative of the former is **Horace Bushnell**'s position, often referred to as the "moral influence" theory, as developed in *God in Christ.* According to this view the problem is not the wrath of God and His condemnation of man, but the effects of sin upon man. Instead of seeing himself and God accurately, he sees through the cloud of his own lusts. He therefore fashions the gods who are cruel and deceitful monsters.

This misconception the death of Christ removes. Here is the supreme revelation of the nature of God, for here is the fullest demonstration of the selfless love that is the fundamental attribute of God. It also shows a man his true self. In view of the perfect love of God, his own self-centeredness is more apparent. Yet awareness of sin is not enough. It may move him to will to turn from this sinfulness. To will is one thing, to do is quite another. What is needed is a vivid glimpse of God as He really is. This is what Jesus provides.

The death of Jesus Christ does not, therefore, involve the wrath and judgment of God; it has no penal character. It is merely a mystery of God's love—an indication of just how far that love moved Him on man's behalf.

**Hugo Grotius** sees the death of Christ influencing both God and man, and as the title of his treatise suggests, he considers this the Catholic (universal) faith. Christ's death exhibits the divine justice and secures the remission of sins. The former he emphasizes here, and it has given to this view the name of the governmental theory of the atonement.

If God is to be the Lord, man must obey Him. This in turn requires that man take seriously the commands of God. When a command is broken, punishment must be administered. If this were not done, two things would occur: man would lose his respect for God and His law, and the moral government of the world would break down. This is especially so when the punishment for disobedience has already been announced, as it were. Moreover, the very moral nature of God would be jeopardized if this happened. Being righteous, God must punish sin. Being loving and merciful, however, He desires to forgive sin. He fulfills both of His attributes by requiring the death of Jesus Christ. A demonstration of the seriousness of sin is the greatness of the sacrifice God required for it.

The Racovian Catechism, a product of sixteenth-century Socinianism, is representative of the example theory of the atonement. The treatment here concerns two major topics, the person and work of Christ. The statement rather resolutely opposes the traditional conception of the deity of Christ, that He is of the very same essence as God the Father, and substitutes for it the conception that the Holy Spirit dwelt in Jesus and was indissolubly united with His human nature in an influential presence.

The Catechism is particularly concerned with opposing the sacrificial view of the death of Christ, regarding it as contrary to both Scripture and reason. Rather, His death emphasizes *redemption* and *liberation,* the latter term denoting a motif that has received particular emphasis in recent times. Man is pictured as in captivity to sin, the world, the devil, and death. The redeemer is God and Christ, and the redemption provided by Christ consists in the example He gives us to emulate.

Of the several essays included here, the one with the most objective orientation is the excerpt from **Anselm**'s classic *Cur Deus Homo*. Cast in the form of a dialogue between Anselm and Boso, it begins with the question, What is sin? and concludes that sin is man's failure to pay God His due, namely, to be subject to His will. The creature has taken away the honor due the Creator, placing him in debt to God, a debt that either man must pay himself or God must take from him. Anselm also argues that the number of angels who fell must be made up from mankind. Man, however, cannot be saved without satisfaction for sin being rendered. Man cannot provide this satisfaction.

If man cannot by any action of his own restore to God what he has taken from Him, the only other possibility is that someone else should do this for him. This was done by Christ, who paid to God the price for the sin of man. This work of atonement could be done only by the God-man because the price paid had to be something greater than all the universe besides God. Anselm further demonstrates that such a being must be both perfect God and perfect man.

This view of the atonement has been developed in many different forms and has borne several different names. It has been termed the satisfaction theory, the commercial theory, the forensic theory, and the substitutionary-penal theory. Perhaps the last of these titles is the most satisfactory. In all of these variations of the Anselmic view, the essential point is that Jesus Christ's death has substituted for the payment that men ought to make. This in turn satisfies God, enabling Him to accept man back into His favor and restore him to what he was intended to be.

# The Three Offices of Christ

31

## H. Orton Wiley

# The Offices and Titles of Christ

### The Offices of Christ

The mediatorial process which began historically with the incarnation, and was continued through the humiliation and exaltation, reached its full perfection in the session at the right hand of God. The estates and offices therefore, form the transition from a consideration of the complex Person of Christ, to that of His finished work in the Atonement—the former relating the mediatorial work more directly to His Person, the latter more immediately to the Finished Work. As Mediator, the work of Christ is resolved into the threefold office of Prophet, Priest and King. Into these offices He was inducted at His baptism, and by a specific anointing with the Holy Spirit became officially the Mediator between God and man. But before directly considering the prophetical, priestly and regal offices of Christ, it will be necessary to consider some of the more general characteristics of Christ as Mediator. This will serve to prevent any misconception as to the nature of the mediatorial work as a whole.

1. Christ as mediator between God and men cannot be God only, or man only, for a mediator supposes two parties between whom he inter-

From *Christian Theology* (Kansas City, Mo.: Beacon Hill Press, 1940), 2:210-16. Used by permission.

venes. *Now a mediator is not a mediator of one, but God is one* (Gal. 3:20). *For there is one God, and one mediator between God and men, the man Christ Jesus* (I Tim. 2:5). The man to which the apostle refers is *Christ Jesus,* and therefore the theanthropic or God-man. The Logos was not actually and historically the Mediator until He assumed human nature. In the Old Testament Christ was Mediator by anticipation, and men were saved through His mediatorial work in view of His future Advent. In the New Testament the types and shadows through which the Word manifested Himself are done away, being superseded by the fuller revelation of the incarnate Word.

2. The Mediatorship of Christ is an assumed office. We must regard Creatorship as a primary function of Deity. The Son never assumed it and He will never lay it down. But the mediatorship as an office is not inherent in Deity, although we may say that it is inherent in His nature as sacrificial love (Eph. 1:4; I Peter 1:19, 20; Rev. 13:8). The Son voluntarily assumed the office of Mediator, being sent of the Father; and being found in fashion as a man, humbled Himself and became obedient even to the death of the cross (Phil. 2:5-11). Because the office was voluntary and involved the carrying out of a commission, His condescension and humiliation are deserving of reward. Wherefore, *God also hath highly exalted him, and given him a name which is above every name: that at the name of Jesus every knee should bow, of things in heaven, and things in earth, and things under the earth; and that every tongue should confess that Jesus Christ is Lord, to the glory of God the Father* (Phil. 2:9-11). Furthermore, the office of Mediator because it was assumed will also end—in this sense, that there will be a time when the work of redemption will cease. And while the God-man will forever exist, and the relations of His people to the Father will be eternally mediated through Him, the work of redeeming sinners will be superseded by the judgment of all things. *As it is appointed unto men once to die, but after this the judgment: so Christ was once offered to bear the sins of many; and unto them that look for him shall he appear the second time without sin* (that is, without a sin-offering) *unto salvation* (Heb. 9:27, 28).

3. Christ is represented as the Mediator of a Covenant. In a strict sense, there can be but two forms of a covenant—the legal and evangelical. The first is based upon justice, the second upon mercy. Man having sinned in the fall, the first became inoperative; consequently the evangelical covenant alone could be established. This is sometimes known as the covenant of redemption, and sometimes as the covenant of grace. The evangelical covenant existed first under the Old Dispensation, and as such was known as the "first covenant" (Heb. 8:6-13). It exists now in a second form under the New Testament, and is known as the "new" or "better covenant" (cf. also Heb. 8:6-8). The first was more external, and was administered through animal sacrifices and visible types and symbols. It was therefore ceremonial and national. The second is an internal covenant of life, and therefore spiritual and universal. In the first covenant the words were spoken to the people in the form of external law; in the new

covenant the law is written within, upon the hearts and minds of the people (Heb. 8:8-13; 10:16-18).

4. Christ, as the Mediator of the New Covenant, discharges three offices, that of prophet, priest, and king. Under the Old Testament, Samuel was a prophet and a priest; David a prophet and a king; and Melchisedec, a priest and a king; Christ alone, unites in Himself the three-fold office. His prophetical office is mentioned in Deut. 18:15, 18, *For Moses truly said unto the fathers, A prophet shall the Lord your God raise up unto you of your brethren, like unto me; him shall ye hear in all things whatsoever he shall say unto you* (Acts 3:22). His priestly office is foretold in Psalm 110:4, *Thou art a priest forever after the order of Melchisedec* (Heb. 5:6; 4:14, 15). Since Melchisedec was a king-priest, Christ's priesthood involved also His kingship. This is directly stated in Isaiah 9:6, 7, where He is called the *Prince of Peace;* and again in the Psalms, *I have set my king upon my holy hill of Zion* (Psalms 2:6).

## The Prophetic Office

Christ as a prophet is the perfect revealer of divine truth. As the Logos, He was the true Light, which lighteth every man that cometh into the world (John 1:9). In the Old Testament He spoke through angels, through theophanies, through types, and by means of the prophets, to whom He communicated His Holy Spirit. As the Incarnate Word He faithfully and fully revealed to men the saving will of God. He spoke with inherent authority (Matt. 7:28, 29) and was recognized as a teacher come from God (John 3:2). After His ascension He continued His work through the Holy Spirit, who now dwells in the Church as the Spirit of truth. In the world to come His prophetic work will be continued, for we are told that the *city had no need of the sun, neither of the moon, to shine in it: for the glory of God did lighten it, and the Lamb is the light thereof* (Rev. 21:23). It will be through His glorified manhood that we shall see and enjoy the vision of God to all eternity.

## The Priestly Office

The priestly office of Christ is concerned with objective mediation, and includes both sacrifice and intercession. *He offered up himself* (Heb. 7:27). He was at once the offering and the Offerer, the one corresponding to His death, the other to His resurrection and ascension, and together issuing in the Atonement. Based upon His sacrificial work is His office of Intercession and Benediction, which are together connected with the Administration of Redemption. It was on the eve of the crucifixion that our Lord formally assumed His sacrificial function—first by the institution of the Lord's Supper, and following this by His high priestly prayer of consecration (John 17:1-26). After Pentecost the priestly office became more prominent. Consequently the cross becomes the center of the apostolic gospel (I Cor. 1:23; 5:7); His death is the establishment of a new covenant (I Cor. 10:16; 11:24-26); and His sacrifice is regarded as a voluntary act of atonement and reconciliation (Eph. 5:2; I Peter 2:24; Rom. 5:10; Col. 1:20). After Pentecost the priestly work of Christ is continued through the Holy Spirit as a gift of the risen and exalted Saviour; and in the world to come our approach to God must be ever through Him as the abiding source of our life and glory.

## The Kingly Office

The kingly, or regal office of Christ is that activity of our ascended Lord which He exercises at the right hand of God, ruling over all things in heaven and in earth for the extension of His kingdom. It is based upon the sacrificial death, and therefore finds its highest exercise in the bestowment of the blessings secured for mankind by His atoning work. As our Lord formally assumed His priestly work on the eve of the crucifixion, so He formally assumed His kingly office at the time of the ascension. We must not overlook the fact, however, that by anticipation Christ assumed to Himself the office of king during His earthly life, particularly at the time just preceding His death. But at the ascension, He said, *All power is given unto me in heaven and in earth. Go ye therefore, and teach all nations, baptizing them in the name of the Father, and of the Son, and of the Holy Ghost: teaching them to observe all things whatsoever I have commanded you: and, lo, I am with you alway, even unto the end of the world. Amen* (Matt. 28:18-20). Having already proclaimed His rule over the dead in the *descensus:* and having declared it to His brethren on earth, He ascended to the throne, there to exercise His mediatorial power until the time of the judgment, when the mediatorial economy shall end. God's efforts to save men then have been exhausted, and the fate of all men, whether good or evil, will be fixed forever. This is the meaning of St. Paul, when he says, *Then cometh the end, when he shall have delivered up the kingdom to God, even the Father; when he shall have put down all rule and all authority and power. For he must reign, till he hath put all enemies under his feet* (I Cor. 15:24, 25). It is obvious that the kingly office as exercised for the redemption of mankind applies only to that era of extending and perfecting the kingdom; and the regal office in this sense will end when that era is completed. Nor does this mean that the Son shall not continue to reign as the Second Person in the Trinity; nor that His theanthropic Person shall cease. He shall forever reign as the God-man, and shall forever exercise His power for the benefit of the redeemed and the glory of His kingdom.

## The Titles of Christ

In our discussion of "The Divine Names and Predicates" we pointed out the practical value of a study of the names through which God had revealed Himself, and also the misuse which had been made of this subject by the so-called "Higher Criticism" of modern times. There is likewise a practical value in the study of "The Names and Titles of Our Lord." "It is the divine method of teaching us the doctrines of the economy of redemption; he who understands the derivation, uses and bearings of the rich cluster of terms, in their Hebrew and Greek symbols especially, . . . will have no mean knowledge of this branch of theology and of theology in general. For this study will also tend to give precision to the language of the theologian, especially the preacher, who will observe with what exquisite propriety every epithet is used by evangelists and apostles in relation to the person and work and relations of the Redeemer. There can be no better theological exercise than the study of evangelical doctrine as based upon the titles of Jesus. No study more surely tends to exalt our Lord. We cannot range in thought over the boundless names given by inspiration to our adorable Master without feeling that there is no place worthy of Him below the highest, that He cannot be less than God to our faith and reverence, and devotion and love" (Pope, *Compend. Chr. Th.,* II, p. 261ff). Dr. Pope classifies the names and titles under the following six general heads: (I) Names of the supra-human Being who became man; (II) Names that express the union of the divine and human; (III) Names that express the official aspects of Christ; (IV) Names which designate the specific offices of the Redeemer; (V) Names resulting from the changes and combinations of the titles of the Redeemer; and (VI) Names which refer to our Lord's relations with His people.

The various helps to the study of the Bible generally give lists of the Names, Titles and Offices of Christ. (Those found in the Oxford Bibles are excellent.) The following list is not intended to be exhaustive, but merely to furnish the student with a classification and guide to the direct study of the Scriptures.

Adam, the last, I Cor. 15:45, 47; Advocate, I John 2:11; Alpha and Omega, Rev. 1:8; 22:13; Amen, Rev. 3:14; Author and Finisher (or Perfecter) of our faith, Heb. 12:2; Beginning of the creation of God, Rev. 3:14; Blessed and only Potentate, I Tim. 6:15; Branch, Zech. 3:8; 6:12; Bread of God, John 6:33; Bread of Life, John 6:35; Captain of our Salvation, Heb. 2:10; Child, Holy, Acts 4:27; Child, little, Isa. 11:6; Christ, Matt. 16:16; Mark 8:29; Luke 9:20; John 6:69; Cornerstone, Eph. 2:20; I Peter 2:6; Counsellor, Isa. 9:6; David, Jer. 30:9; Dayspring, Luke 1:78; Deliverer, Rom. 11:26; Desire of all nations, Hag. 2:7; Emmanuel, Isa. 7:14; Matt. 1:23; Everlasting Father, Isa. 9:6; Faithful witness, Rev. 1:5; 3:14; First and Last, Rev. 1:17; First begotten (First-born) of the dead, Rev. 1:5; God, Isa. 40:9; I John 5:20; God blessed forever, Rom. 9:5; Good Shepherd, John 10:11; Governor, Matt. 2:6; Great High Priest, Heb. 4:14; High Priest, Heb. 5:10; Holy Child Jesus, Acts 4:27; Holy One, Luke 4:34; Holy Thing, Luke 1:35; Horn of Salvation, Luke 1:69; I AM, Exod. 3:14; Image of God, II Cor. 4:4; Jehovah, Isa. 26:4; Jesus, Matt. 1:21; I Thess. 1:10; Just One, Acts 3:14; King of Israel, John 1:49; King of the Jews, Matt. 2:2; King of kings, I Tim. 6:15; Lamb of God, John 1:29, 36; Law-giver, Isa. 33:22; Life, the, John 14:6; Light of the World, John 8:12; Light, the true, John 1:9; Lion of the tribe of Judah, Rev. 5:5; Living stone, I Peter 2:4; Lord, Matt. 3:3; Lord God, Almighty, Rev. 15:3; Lord of all, Acts 10:36; Lord of Glory, I Cor. 2:8; Lord of Lords, I Tim. 6:15;

Lord our righteousness, Jer. 23:6; Mediator, I Tim. 2:5; Messiah, Dan. 9:25; John 1:41; Mighty God, Isa. 9:6; Mighty One of Jacob, Isa. 60:16; Nazarene, Matt. 2:23; Passover, I Cor. 5:7; Priest forever, Heb. 5:6; Prince, Acts 5:31; Prince of Peace, Isa. 9:6; Prince of the kings of the earth, Rev. 1:5; Prophet, Deut. 18:15; Luke 24:19; Redeemer, Job 19:25; Righteous, the, I John 2:1; Root and offspring of David, Rev. 22:16; Root of David, Rev. 5:5; Ruler in Israel, Mic. 5:2; Same yesterday, today, and forever, Heb. 13:8; Saviour, Luke 2:11; Acts 5:31; Shepherd and Bishop of souls, I Peter 2:25; Shepherd of the sheep, Great, Heb. 13:20; Shiloh, Gen. 49:10; Son, a, Heb. 3:6; Son, the, Psalms 2:12; Son, my beloved, Matt. 3:17; Son, only-begotten, John 3:16; Son of David; Son of God, Matt. 8:29; Luke 1:35; Son of man, Matt. 8:20; John 1:51; Son of the Highest, Luke 1:32; Star, Bright and Morning, Rev. 22:16; Star and sceptre, Num. 24:17; Truth, the, John 14:6; Vine, the true, John 15:1, 5; Way, the, John 14:6; Witness, Rev. 3:14; Wonderful, Isa. 9:6; Word, John 1:1; Word of God, Rev. 19:13.

# The Atonement

32

**Horace Bushnell**

Moral Influence Theory

# The Protestant Views of the Atonement

Having stated frankly these objections to the common orthodox views of atonement, whether resting the value of Christ's death in what it *is,* or in what it *expresses,* it may be expected that I should renounce all sympathy and connection with them. This I have never been able to do. For if they are unsatisfactory, if the older and more venerable doctrine is repugnant, when speculatively regarded, to the most sacred instincts or sentiments of our moral nature, and dissolves itself at the first approach of rational inquiry, is it nothing remarkable, is it not even more remarkable, that it should have supported the spirit of so many believers and martyrs, in so many trials and deaths, continued through so many centuries? Refuted again and again, cast away, trampled upon by irreverent mockeries, it has never yet been able to die—wherefore, unless there be some power of divine life in it? So I have always believed, and I hope to show you, before I have done, where it is, or under what form it is hid; for I shall carry you into a region, separate from all speculation, or theologizing, and there, what I now dismiss, I shall virtually reclaim and restore, in a shape that provokes none of these objections. All that is real and essential to the

From *God in Christ* (New York: Charles Scribner's Sons, 1876), pp. 202-16.

power of this orthodox doctrine of atonement, however held, I hope to set forth still, as the *Divine Form* of Christianity, assigning it a place where it may still reveal its efficacy, standing ever as an Altar of penitence and peace, a Pillar of confidence to believing souls.

We come now to the double view of the atonement, or work of Christ, which it was proposed to establish. And,

I. The subjective, that which represents Christ as a manifestation of the Life, thus a power whose end it is to quicken, or regenerate the human character.

Here, as it has been already intimated, the value of Christ's mission is measured by what is expressed. And if so, then it follows, of course, that no dogmatic statement can adequately represent his work; for the matter of it does not lie in formulas of reason, and cannot be comprehended in them. It is more a poem than a treatise. It classes as a work of Art more than as a work of Science. It addresses the understanding, in great part, through the feeling or sensibility. In these it has its receptivities, by these it is perceived, or perceivable. Moving, in and through these, as a revelation of sympathy, love, life, it proposes to connect us with the Life of God. And when through these, believingly opened as inlets, it is received, then is the union it seeks consummated. Were it not for the air it might give to my representations, in the view of many, I should like, in common with Paul, (Phil. 1:9, 10.) to use the word *esthetic,* and represent Christianity as a power moving upon man, through this department of his nature, both to regenerate his degraded perception of excellence, and also to communicate, in that way, the fullness and beauty of God.

Hence, it would not be as wild a breach of philosophy itself, to undertake a dogmatic statement of the contents of a tragedy, as to attempt giving in the same manner the equivalents of the life and death of Jesus Christ. The only real equivalent we can give is the representation of the life itself. It is not absurd, however, to say something about the subject, if only we do not assume the adequacy of what we say—we could offer some theoretical views of a tragedy, but our theoretic matter would not be the tragedy. No more can we set forth, as a real and proper equivalent, any theoretic matter of ours concerning the life and death of Jesus Christ, which is the highest and most moving tragedy ever acted in this mortal sphere; a tragedy distinguished in the fact that God is the Chief Character, and the divine feeling, moved in tragic earnest—Goodness Infinite manifested through Sorrow—the passion represented.

Beginning, then, with the lowest view our subject permits, it is obvious that the life of Christ, considered only as a perfect being or character, is an embodiment in human history, of a spirit and of ideas, which are sufficient of themselves to change the destinies of the race, and even their capabilities of good. Is it too much for me to assume that Christ was such a character? Is it intimated that a very close, microscopic inspection has revealed, as some imagine, two or three flaws in his life? Be it so; I want no other evidence that he was a perfect and sinless being. Sin is never revealed microscopically, but, wherever it is, it sets its mark, as we set our flag on a new-discovered island. Show me, therefore, a character that is flawed only microscopically, and I will charge the flaws to the microscope or even to the solar beam, rather than to it. Christ, then, I assume, was a sinlessly perfect being. And how great an event, to have had one such perfect life or biography lived and witnessed in the world, and so deposited in the bosom of our human history. Here we have among us, call him either human only, or divine, what the most splendid gifts of human genius had labored in vain to sketch—a perfect life. What feelings, principles, beauties, ideas or regulative ideals, are thus imported into the world's bosom! Only to have seen one perfect life, to have heard the words and received the pure conceptions of one sinless spirit, to have felt the working of his charities, and witnessed the offering of his sinless obedience, would have been to receive the seeds of a moral revolution that must ultimately affect the whole race. This was true even of a Socrates. Our world is not the same world that it was before he lived in it. Much less the same, since the sinless Jesus lived and suffered in it. Such a character has, of necessity, an organific power. It enters into human thought and knowledge as a vital force; and, since it is perfect, a vital force that cannot die, or cease to work. It must, of necessity, organize a kingdom of life, and reign. The ideas it has revealed, and the spirit it has breathed into the air, are quick and powerful, and must live till the world itself is no more. The same sun may shine above, the same laws of nature may reign about us, but the grand society of man embodies new elemental forces, and the capacity, at some time or other, of another and a gloriously renovated state. The entering of one such perfect life into the world's history changes, in fact, the consciousness of the race; just as the most accomplished, perhaps, of all modern theologians assumes, when he undertakes to verify the truths of the gospel out of the contents of the religious consciousness of the Christian nations, as compared with the ancient consciousness, or that of heathen nations.

Again, the appearing of Jesus, the Messiah, has a much higher significance and power when taken as the manifestation of the Life—the incarnate Word, God expressed in and through the human.

I am obliged here, as in the general treatment of my subject, to assume a view of Christ's person, which you may not all be ready to admit. Any one, however, may go with me, who earnestly believes that in Christ the Life was manifested. I may use language that implies a different view of Christ's person, but as far as the doctrine of this particular subject is concerned, whoever can look upon Christ as a proper and true manifestation of God, a peculiar being distinguished from ordinary men, by the fact that a properly divine import is communicated by his life, (which, of course, makes the mere human import a matter of inferior consequence,) may well enough admit whatever I shall advance, and harmonize it, for himself, with his own particular view.

Regarding the world, then, even as an upright and sinless world, how great an event is it that the Eternal is incarnated in their history, that the King is among them, expressing, by the mysterious identification of his nature with theirs, a mystery yet more august—the possible union of their nature with His! How memorable his words, teachings, works, and condescensions! And when he withdraws into the deep recesses of spirit again, what name will be dear to them as the name of their Christ! His appearing is a new epoch in their history. He will live in their hearts, life within life. A divine light from the person of their Emanuel will stream through their history. Their words will be sanctified by his uses. Their works will be animated by his spirit. A divine vigor from the Life manifested among them will penetrate their feeling, elevating their ideas and purposes, and even their capacity of good itself.

But if we are to understand the full import of Christ's mission, we must go farther. He is not merely a perfect life embodied in history. He is not merely the Eternal Life manifested in a good and upright history. We must regard him as the Life manifested in an evil history, or that of an alienated and averted race. He finds us under sin, captives imprisoned by evil, and he comes to be our liberator. Accordingly, we are now to see in what manner he addresses himself to the moral wants and disabilities of a state of sin.

And here, glancing first of all at human society, we discover the appalling fact that sin, once existing, becomes, and even must become, a corporate authority—a law or Ruling Power, in the world, opposite to God. Entering into the fashions, opinions, manners, ends, passions of the race, it molds their institutions, legislates over their conduct, and even constructs a morality by standards of its own. And thus, acting through the mass, it becomes a law to the individual, crowning Lust and Mammon as gods, harnessing nations to the chariot of war, building thrones of oppression, kindling fires of persecution, poisoning the fountains of literature, adorning falsehood with the splendors of genius, sanctifying wrong under the plausible names of honor and fashion. Thus, or by all these methods, sin becomes a kind of malign possession in the race, a prince of the power of the air, reigning unto death. To break the organic force of social evil, thus dominant over the race, Christ enters the world, bringing into human history and incorporating in it as such, that which is Divine. The Life manifested in him becomes a historic power and presence in the world's bosom, organizing there a new society or kingdom, called the kingdom of heaven, or sometimes the church. For the church is not a body of men holding certain dogmas, or maintaining, as men, certain theologic wars for God; but it is the Society of the Life, the Embodied Word. Thus it is expressly declared to be the body of Christ, the fullness of him that filleth all in all. Hence our blessed Lord, just before his passion, considering that now the organic force of evil was to be broken, said, now is the judgment of this world, now is the prince of this world cast out. The princedom of evil is dissolved—the eternal Life, manifested in the world, organizes a new society of life, breaks the spell forever of social evil, and begins a reign of truth and love that shall finally renew the world.

While the social authority of evil is thus broken, there is also a movement on the individual, to clear the disabilities which sin has wrought in his nature, and withdraw him from the internal bondage of evil.

God is the light of our spiritual nature. Sin withdraws itself from God. Hence the condition of sin is a condition of blindness and spiritual darkness. The moral conceptions are dulled. The man lives in his senses and becomes a creature of sense. His religious ideas, separated from faith or by unbelief denied, still maintain their activity as vagaries, after they have lost their verity; and, haunted by these vagaries, he finds no rest till the God whose conception he has lost, is replaced by such as he can invent for himself. Hence the infallible connection of sin and idolatry. The glory of the incorruptible God is necessarily lost. Actuated still by a dim religious instinct, whose object and throne of worship are no longer seen, he fashions gods through the smoke of his own lusts—cruel and deceitful monsters, of course, for a God of love cannot be conceived through clouds of animosity and tempests of wrath.

What, now, shall cure this blinded condition of the race? How needful that God should meet them in the element where their soul lives, that is, in their senses. It is not so much an absolute religion—not doctrines or precepts or arguments that they want, but a production of the divine in the human, a living Presence, a manifestation of the Life. Therefore the Word is made flesh and dwells with men. The true light now shineth. God, who commanded the light to shine out of darkness, hath shined in our heart, to give the light of the knowledge of the glory of God in the face of Jesus Christ. God is here, in act, word, power, filling the molds of history, and visiting the blinded world in the palpable forms of life itself. The understanding that was darkened, being alienated from the life of God, beholds once more a light in the manifested life. Even the atheist feels a Presence here, whose simple and pure shining, as it provokes no argument, suffers no answer. While the understanding is blockaded by doubt, a God streams into the feeling, and proves His reality to the heart. The torpors of logic are melted away by the warmth of the life, and he knows God as love, before he finds him as the absolute of the reason. Thus it has been also with idolatry. No speculations or abstractions about God have ever been able to correct or overthrow idolatry. But how many idolatrous nations have yielded to the wondrous power that has invaded their feeling from the life and cross of Christ! The Word made flesh is the true light to them. The historic Christ fills them with God as a higher sense. The divinity, in him, floods their feeling, and they receive God as a Power, before they conceive his philosophic Idea.

The manifestation of the Life also revives in man, as a sinner, the consciousness of himself. It is one of the paradoxes realized by sin, that, while it makes a man everything to himself, it makes him also nothing. It smothers the spark of conscious immortality. This world is practically all to him. The grave is dark, and he has no faith to throw a light across on spiritual realities beyond it. But when he that was in the form of God comes into the human state, when we see one here who visibly is not of us, when he opens here a heart of love, and floods the world with rivers of divine feeling, when we trace him from the manger over which the hymns of heaven's joy are ringing, to the cross where his purpose to save embraces even death for man; and then, when we see that death cannot hold him, that he bursts into life again as a victor over death—following such a history transacted, in our view, we begin also to conceive the tremendous import of our own, the equally tremendous import also of our sin. If God, to renew the soul moves a plan like this, what is it to be a soul, what to desecrate and destroy a soul? The conscious grandeur of his eternity returns upon the transgressor and he trembles in awe of himself—himself the power of an endless life.

Suppose, now, to advance another stage, that a man under sin becomes reflective, conscious of himself and of evil, sighing with discontent and bitterness, because of his own spiritual disorders. Conceive him thus as undertaking a restoration of his own nature to goodness, and the pure ideal of his conscience. What can he do without some objective power to engage his affections, and be a higher nature, present, by which to elevate and assimilate his own? Sin has removed him from God; withdrawing into himself, his soul has become objectless, and good affections cannot live, or be made to live, where there is no living object left to warm and support them. He can rise, therefore, by no help from his affections, or through them. Accordingly, if he attempts to restore himself to that ideal beauty and purity he has lost, he is obliged to do it wholly by his will; possibly against the depressing bondage of his affections, now sunk in torpor and deadness, or soured by a protracted, malign activity. Having all this to do by his will, he finds, alas! that if to will is present, how to perform is not. He seems, to himself, like a man who is endeavoring to lift himself by pulling at his feet. Hence, or to remove this disability, God needs to be manifested as Love. The Divine Object rejected by sin and practically annihilated as a spiritual conception, needs to be imported into sense. Then, when God appears in His beauty, loving and lovely, the good, the glory, the sunlight of soul, the affections, previously dead, wake into life and joyful play, and what before was only a self-lifting and slavish effort becomes an exulting spirit of liberty. The body of sin and death that lay upon the soul is heaved off, and the law of the spirit of life in Christ Jesus—the Eternal Life manifested in him, and received by faith into a vital union—quickens it in good, and makes it free.

But there is yet another difficulty, over and above the deadness and the moral estrangement of the affections; I speak of the fearful and self-accusing spirit of sin. Reason as we may about human depravity, apologize for men, or justify them as we may, they certainly do not justify themselves. Even in the deepest mental darkness concerning God, stifled, we may almost say, as regards their proper humanity, under the sottish and debasing effects of idolatry, still we see the conscience struggling with guilty fears, unable to find rest. An indescribable dread of evil still over-hangs the human spirit. The being is haunted by shadows of wrath and tries all painful methods of self pacification. Vigils, pilgrimages, sacrifices, tortures, nothing is too painful or wearisome that promises to ease the guilt of the mind. Without any speculations about justification, mankind refuse to justify themselves. A kind of despair fills the heart of the race. They have no courage. Whether they know God or not, they know them-selves, and they sentence themselves to death. If they have only some obscure notions of a divine Being, then they dread the full discovery of Him. If He lurks in their gods, they fear lest their gods should visit them in vengeance, or plague them by some kind of mischief. The sky is full of wrathful powers, and the deep ground also is full. Their guilty soul peoples the world with vengeful images of its own creation.

And here, now, if we desire to find it, is the true idea of Christian justification. We discover what it is by the want of it. Justification is that which will give confidence, again, to guilty minds; that which will assure the base and humiliated soul of the world, chase away the demons of wrath and despair it has evoked, and help it to return to God in courage, whispering still to itself—soul be of good cheer, thy sins are forgiven thee.

And this result is beautifully prepared by the advent of Christ, as well as by the crowning act of his death. God thus enters humanity as the Word made flesh, and unites himself to it, declaring by that sign, that he is ready to unite it unto himself. We perceive also and hear that he has come, not to condemn the world, but to save it. No storm wraps him about when he comes. The hymn that proclaims him, publishes—"peace on earth." He appears in a form to indicate the gentlest errand and the closest approach to our human lot; one, too, that never appalls the guiltiest—the form of a child. In his ministry he sometimes utters piercing words, still he is a friend, even a brother to the guilty. He calls the heavy-laden to come unto him, and promises rest. In short, he lives confidence into the world. Apart from all theologic theories, we know, we see with our eyes, that God will justify us and give us still his peace. And then, when we truly come unto him, believing that Christ the Word is He, when, forsaking all things for him, we embrace him as our life, then are we practically justified. It is impossible for us to fear. No guilt of the past can disturb us; a peace that passeth understanding fills our nature. Being justified by faith, we have peace with God through our Lord Jesus Christ.

Or, if we advert, in this connection, to the sufferings and death of Christ, we shall see how these, without the imputation of any penal quality or frown of God upon his person, have a special efficacy in fortify-ing our assurance or hope of justification with God. Dismiss all speculation about the mode, possibility, interior reality of this suffering; understand that God, having proposed, in this manner, to express His love, all logical, theological, ontological, physiological questions are, by the supposition, out of place. Come, then, to the spectacle of Christ's suffering life and death, as to a mystery wholly transcendent, save in what it expresses of

Divine feeling. Call what of this feeling you receive the reality—all else the *machina Dei* for the expression of this. With deepest reverence of soul, approach that most mysterious sacrament of love, the agony of Jesus; note the patience of his trial, the meekness of his submission to injustice, and the malignant passions of his enemies; behold the creation itself darkening and shuddering with a horror of sensibility at the scene transpiring in his death; hear the cry of the crucified—"Father, forgive them, for they know not what they do"; then regard the life that was manifested, dropping into cessation, and thereby signifying the deposit of itself in the bosom of that malign world, to whose enmity it is yielded—who, what man of our race beholding this strange history of the Word, will not feel a new courage enter into his soul? Visibly, God is not the implacable avenger his guilty fears had painted. But he is a friend, he is love. And so great is this change, apart from all theology, that I seem even to see another character produced by it, in the Christian nations. They dare to hope. God is closer to them and in a way to inspire courage. They are not withered, humiliated even to baseness, under those guilty and abject fears that take away at last the spirit of other nations. It is not that they have all a theory of justification by faith, but that their current conceptions of God are such as the history of Jesus, the suffering redeemer, has imparted. They have a feeling of something like justification, even if they never heard of it—a feeling, which, if it were to vent itself in language, would say—Therefore we are freely justified by grace. It is not that the suffering appeases God, but that it expresses God—displays, in open history, the unconquerable love of God's Heart.

**33**

**Hugo Grotius**

*Moral Government Theory*

# The Catholic View
# of the Satisfaction
# of Christ

To sum up what has been already said: since the scripture says that Christ was chastised by God, i.e., punished; that Christ bore our sins, i.e. the punishment of sins; was made sin, i.e. was subjected to the penalty of sins; was made a curse with God, or was exposed to the curse, that is, the penalty of the law; since, moreover, the very suffering of Christ, full of tortures, bloody, ignominious, is most appropriate matter of punishment; since, again, the scripture says that these were inflicted on him by God on account of our sins, i.e. our sins so deserving; since death itself is said to be the wages, i.e. the punishment of sin; certainly it can by no means be doubted that with reference to God the suffering and death of Christ had the character of a punishment. Nor can we listen to the interpretations of Socinus, which depart from the perpetual use of the words without authority, especially when no reason prevents us from retaining the received meaning of the words, as will be made plain below. There is, therefore, a punishment, in God actively, in Christ passively. Yet in the passion of Christ there is also a certain action, viz. the voluntary endurance of penal suffering.

From *A Defense of the Catholic Faith Concerning the Satisfaction of Christ, Against Faustus Socinus*, trans. Frank Hugh Foster (Andover: Warren F. Draper, 1889), pp. 253-61.

The end of the transaction of which we treat, in the intention of God and Christ, which, proposed in the act, may also be said to have been effected, is two-fold; namely, the exhibition of the divine justice, and the remission of sins with respect to us, i.e. our exemption from punishment. For if you take the exaction of punishment impersonally, its end is the exhibition of the divine justice; but if personally, i.e. why was Christ punished, the end is that we might be freed from punishment.

*The former end* is indicated by Paul when he says of Christ, "Whom God hath set forth to be a propitiation in his blood to declare his righteousness for the remission of sins that are past, through the forbearance of God." Then he adds, repeating almost the same words: "To declare, I say, at this time his righteousness, that he might be just and the justifier of him that believeth in Jesus." Here, in close connection with the blood, i.e. the bloody death, stands the end, "to declare his righteousness."

By the expression "righteousness of God" is not to be understood that righteousness which God works in us, or which he imputes to us, but that which is in God. For he proceeds: "That he might be just," i.e. appear to be just. This justice of God, i.e. rectitude, for different objects has different effects. With reference to the good or evil deeds of a creature its effect, among other things, is retribution, with reference to which Paul said; "It is a righteous thing with God to recompense tribulation to them that trouble you." In another place: "Every transgression and disobedience received a just recompense of reward." And the following: "Whose damnation is just." The Syriac has it: "Whose condemnation is reserved for justice." So also, "day of wrath," and "day of just judgment" are the same. It is said that the final judgment will be "in equity." Elsewhere, "to judge in equity" is to take severe vengeance, which is shown by the additional words "make war," and much more by those that follow a little after: "And out of his mouth goeth a sharp sword, that with it he should smite the nations; and he shall rule them with a rod of iron; and he treadeth the wine-press of the fierceness and wrath of Almighty God." So both God is said to be just, and his punishments to be just, because he severely punishes sin. Vengeance is accordingly the name given now to the punitive justice of God, and now to the punishment inflicted by it. The judgment of God is explained by Paul to be this: that they who commit, or approve evil things, are worthy of death. Conjugate to these are "revenger" and "vengeance," the force of which is explained by the word "repay."

It is true that by the word *justice* is frequently meant *veracity*, frequently also *equity*. But since by this word, as has already been shown by many examples, that attribute of God is indicated which moves him to punish sin, and which is exhibited in this punishment of sin, we say that this is the proper signification of our passage. Different ages are set in opposition; e.g. the ages before Christ and that of Christ. To the former is attributed the passing over of sins, which is also explained by the word "forbearance." πάρεσις does not mean *remission*, but *passing over*, to which ἀνοχή, *forbearance*, is rightly added. By this word the Greeks designate a truce, because by it war was for a time kept in check. To this passing over and checking is opposed such a demonstration of justice that by it God may be, i.e. may appear, just. Once, when God passed over very many sins unpunished, his retributive justice did not sufficiently appear. At length, therefore, he showed how he was a just retributor when he determined that his own Son for this cause should shed his blood to become a propitiation for the human race, and to redeem all those who had ever believed, or should ever believe, in God. So the apostle has put the open demonstration in close connection with the grace, i.e. the divine goodness which is bestowed upon creatures, and with the justice of him who is the guardian of right order and also of retribution. Certainly the very word *blood,* the word *propitiation,* and even *redemption,* show that he is not engaged here with the simple testimony to goodness. He has also connected impetration with application. The impetration is through the blood; the application through faith. Rightly is that justice, of which we are treating, said to be made manifest through faith; that faith, namely, by which the blood of Christ is believed to have been shed to propitiate God; which faith entirely excludes all glory in works, all trust in the law.

This end, viz. the exhibition of the divine justice, is also rightly inferred from the form of the transaction of which we treat. For the end of punishment is the exhibition of retributive justice concerning sins, also upon antecedent cause, which we have above shown to be meritorious. But the impelling cause of an action cannot be meritorious except also the end be to make retribution.

. . . exemption from the punishment of our sins is the [second] end of the death of Christ, and the effect of that death. . . .

Having examined the part which God performs in this matter, we shall easily find a name for the act itself. And, first, since God, as we have proved, is to be considered here as a ruler, it follows that his act is an act of the administration of justice, generally so called. From this it follows that we are not treating here of acceptilation, as Socinus thinks, for that is not an act of the administration of justice. To designate the class of this act more particularly it may be considered either in relation to the divine sanction (or, as more recent jurists say, the penal law), or without regard to that relation. We add this specification because, even if the law had made no reference to punishment, yet, in the nature of things, man's act, either as having an intrinsic depravity from the immutable nature of the case, or also an extrinsic depravity on account of the contrary precept of God, deserved, on that very account, some punishment, and that, too, a grave one. That is, it was equitable to punish man as a sinner. If we take our stand here, the act of God of which we treat will be the punishment of one to obtain the impunity of another. Of the justice of this we shall soon treat. But if further we have regard to the sanction, or penal law, the act will be a method of relaxing or moderating the same law, which relaxation we call, in these days, dispensation. It may be defined: The act of a superior by which the obligation of an unabrogated law upon certain persons or things is removed. This is the sanction: the man that eateth of the forbidden tree shall surely die. In this passage by one species of sin every class of sin is indicated, as is expressed by the same law more clearly brought out, "Cursed is every one that continueth not in all the precepts of the law." By the words *death* and *curse*, in these passages, we understand especially eternal death. For this reason it is as if the law had been expressed in this manner: Every man that sinneth shall bear the punishment of eternal death.

There is, therefore, here no *execution* of that law; for if God always executed the law no sinner could be saved from the penalty of eternal death. But now we know that for believers there is no condemnation, because they are liberated from death and redeemed from the curse.

Again, this act is not an *abrogation* of the law; for abrogated law has no binding force. But unbelievers are still exposed to the penalty of the same law. Thus we find written that the wrath of God abideth upon them that believe not, and that the wrath of God is come upon them to the uttermost.

Again, it is not an *interpretation of the law according to equity;* for that interpretation shows that some person or act never was comprehended under the obligation of the law. Works of religion and mercy, for example, were never comprehended under the interdiction of working upon the Sabbath. But indeed all men (assuredly concluded under sin), even those who are liberated, are, by nature or by act, children of wrath, that is, bound by the sanction of the law. It is therefore not declared that there is no obligation; but this is done that what was may be removed; that is, that a relaxation or dispensation of the law may be made.

It may be asked here whether the penal law is relaxable? There are certain irrelaxable laws, either absolutely or by hypothesis. Those are absolutely irrelaxable whose opposite involves, from the nature of the case, immutable wickedness; as, for example, the law which forbids perjury, or bearing false witness against one's neighbor. For, as we say that God cannot lie, or deny himself, so, no less rightly, do we say that God cannot perform actions in themselves wicked, or approve them, or grant the right to do them.

Those laws are irrelaxable of hypothesis which arise from a definite decree; such as the law of condemning those who will not believe in Jesus Christ.

But all positive laws are absolutely relaxable; and we are not compelled to resort to hypothetical necessity, of a definite decree, where no mark of such decree exists.

It is a great error to be afraid, as some are, lest in making such a concession we do injury to God, as if we made him mutable. The law is not something internal within God, or the will of God itself, but only an effect of that will. It is perfectly certain that the effects of the divine will are mutable. By promulgating a positive law which at some time he may wish to relax God does not signify that he wills anything but what he really does will. God shows that he seriously wills that the law should be valid and obligatory, yet with the reserved right of relaxing it. This inheres in positive law, of its own nature, nor by any sign can it be understood to have been abdicated by God. More than that, God does not deprive himself of the right even of abrogating the law, as appears from the example of the ceremonial law. To be sure it is a different thing, if with the positive law be connected an oath, or a promise; for an oath is a sign of the immutability of that with which it is joined. Moreover, a promise gives a right to the party which cannot be taken away from it without injury. Wherefore, although it is optional to promise, yet to break promises is not optional. This is one of the cases, therefore, in which is involved immutable wickedness. God cannot break his promises, who is called faithful especially because he keeps them.

Let us therefore inquire whether there is anything in the said penal law when promulgated which plainly repudiates relaxation.

First, it may be objected that it is just, in the nature of things, that the wicked should themselves be punished with such a punishment as shall correspond to their crime, and that this is, consequently, not subject to free-will and so not relaxable.

To answer this objection we must know that injustice does not result from every negation of justice, even under the same circumstances. For as it does not follow that if a king ought to be called liberal because he has given a thousand talents to a certain man, he would therefore be illiberal if he should not do so, so it is not a general rule that what may be done justly cannot be omitted without injustice. Anything may be called natural in morals as well as in physics, properly or less properly. That is properly natural in physics which necessarily coheres in the essence of anything, as feeling in a living object; but less properly that which is convenient to the nature of anything, and, as it were, accommodated to it, as for a man to use his right arm. So in morals there are certain things properly natural which necessarily follow from the relation of things to rational natures, as that perjury is unlawful; and certain things improperly natural, as that a son should succeed a father. According to this, that he who has committed a crime, deserves punishment, and is on that account liable to punishment, necessarily follows, from the very relation of sin and the sinner to the superior, and is properly natural. But that all sinners should be punished with a punishment corresponding to the crime is not simply and universally necessary, nor properly natural, but only harmonious with nature. Hence it follows that nothing prevents the law which demands this from being relaxable.

The mark of definite decree, or of irrevocability, does not appear in the law of which we are treating. Neither is the law a promise. Therefore nothing prevents the relaxation of these things. For we should not admit that a threat is equivalent to a promise. For from a promise a certain right is gained by him to whom the promise is made; but by a threat there is merely a more open declaration made of the desert of punishment in the sinner and the right of punishing in the threatener. Nor should we fear lest the veracity of God is impaired in any respect if he does not fulfill all his threats. For all threats which have not the sign of irrevocability must be understood, from their own nature, to diminish in no degree the right of the threatener to relax, as has been explained above. The example of the divine clemency towards the Ninevites proves this.

We must not omit here to show that the ancient philosophers judged by the light of nature that there was nothing more relaxable than a penal law. Aristotle says that the just man is inclined to forgive. Sopater, in his Epistle to Demetrius, says: "The right which is called equity, modifying the stern voice of the law, seems to me to be an irreprehensible class of genuine and liberal favors. That part of justice which reduces contracts to equity, entirely rejects every kind of favors. But that part which is engaged upon crimes does not disdain the mild and humane countenance of grace."

From what has already been said it appears that the positive and penal law of God was dispensable. But this does not prove that there were no reasons which (to stammer, as man must) might oppose their relaxation. These may be sought either in the nature of universal laws, or in the peculiar matter of the law. It is common to all laws that in relaxing, the authority of the law seems to be diminished in some respects. It is peculiar to this law that, although, as we have said, it is not of inflexible rectitude, yet it is entirely in harmony with the nature and order of things. Hence it follows, not that the law could not be relaxed at all, but that it could not be relaxed easily, or upon slight cause. And this has been followed by that sole all-wise Lawgiver. For he had a most weighty reason, when the whole human race had fallen into sin, for relaxing the law. If all sinners had been delivered over to eternal death, from the nature of the case, two most beautiful things would have entirely perished: on the part of men religion toward God, and on the part of God the declaration of especial favor toward men. God has not only followed reasons, and those most weighty, in relaxing the law, but he has also made use of a singular method of relaxation. For speaking of this a more suitable place will be found below. . . .


It will not be difficult to assign from the scriptures a sufficient cause, and, indeed, a most weighty cause, whether we inquire why God chose to remit to us eternal punishment, or why he did not choose to remit the same otherwise than by the punishment of Christ. The former has its cause in benevolence, which is, of all the attributes of God, most truly peculiar to him. For everywhere God describes himself chiefly by this attribute, that he is benignant and clement. Therefore, God is inclined to aid and bless men, but he cannot do this while that dreadful and eternal punishment remains. Besides, if eternal death should fall upon all, religion had totally perished through despair of felicity. There were, therefore, great reasons for sparing man.

On the other hand, those passages of scripture already adduced by us, which declare that Christ was delivered, suffered, died for our sins, show the reason why God imposed punishment upon Christ. This manner of speaking, as we have shown, points to the impulsive cause. It may be seen from what we have said of the end not only that there was a cause, but what it was, viz. that God was unwilling to pass over so many sins, and so great sins, without a distinguished example. This is so because every sin is seriously displeasing to God, and the more displeasing the more grave it is. Since God is active, and has created rational creatures in order to give more abundant testimony to his attributes, it is proper for him also to testify by some act how greatly he is displeased with sin. The act most suitable for this is punishment. Hence, arises that in God which the Sacred Writings, because there is no other more significant word, call wrath. God declares he is prevented by this wrath from blessing men.

Again, all neglect to punish sin leads *per se* to a lower estimation of sin, as, on the other hand, the most ready means of preventing sin is the fear of punishment. Hence, the well-known saying: "By bearing an old injury you invite a new." Therefore prudence also, on this account, invites the ruler to inflict punishment.

Moreover, the reasons for punishing are increased when a law has been published threatening punishment, for then the omission of punishment almost always detracts from the authority of the law among the subjects. Hence, the precept of politics: "Guard the established laws with the greatest care."

God has, therefore, most weighty reasons for punishing, especially if we are permitted to estimate the magnitude and multitude of sins. But because among all his attributes love of the human race is pre-eminent, God was willing, though he could have justly punished the sins of all men with deserved and legitimate punishment, that is, with eternal death, and had reasons for so doing, to spare those who believe in Christ. But since we must be spared either by setting forth, or not setting forth, some example against so many great sins, in his most perfect wisdom he chose that way by which he could manifest more of his attributes at once, viz. both clemency and severity, or his hate of sin and care for the preservation of his law.

So Aelianus, in commending the deed of Zaleucus, mentions two reasons for it, that the youth might not be made entirely blind, and that what had been once established should not become invalid. Of these reasons, the former operated to bring about some change in the law through clemency, the latter prevented too great a change. Those who have written on the relaxation of laws, observe that those are the best relaxations, which are accompanied by a commutation, or compensation. In this way the least injury is done to the law, and the particular precept is executed in some accordance with the reason upon which the law was founded. It is as if a man held to deliver a certain article should be excused upon paying the price. For the same thing and the same value are very nearly related.

Such commutation is admissable not only among things, but sometimes also among persons, provided that it can be done without injury to another. Thus sons are permitted to go into prison in place of their fathers, as Cimon for Miltiades. And not to go beyond penal judgments, and that too the divine, there exist in the Sacred Scriptures traces of a similar fact.

To David, the homicide and adulterer, is pronounced at the command of God by Nathan: "The Lord hath put away thy sin (that is, the punishment of thy sin); thou shalt not die (which otherwise the law demanded); Howbeit because by this deed thou hast given great occasion to the enemies of the Lord to blaspheme, the child also that is born to thee (evidently since it is very closely connected with thee, and the substitute in thy punishment) shall surely die." Ahab had defiled himself with both murder and rapine. God announces to him through Elijah that the dogs will lick his blood. Yet immediately when his fear, and a certain reverence for the divine majesty was manifest, the same God said: "I will not bring the evil (viz. what both he had merited, and I threatened) in his days; but in his son's days (who shall bear not only his own, but also his father's punishment) will I bring the evil upon his house." In both cases God relaxes the law, or the threat of punishment, but not without some compensation, by transferring the punishment upon another. Thus at the same time he exhibits both his clemency and severity or hatred of sin. So, therefore, God, wishing to spare those who should believe in Christ, had sufficient, just, and great reasons for exacting of the willing Christ the punishment of our sins, viz. to use the words of Aelianus, "that what had been once established should not become invalid"; and that sin should not be thought of less importance, if so many great sins should be remitted without an example.

Further, God not only testified his own hatred of sin by this act, and so deterred us from sin (for it is an easy inference that if God would not remit the sins even of those who repented except Christ took their punishment, much less will he permit the contumacious to go unvisited); but more than that, he also declared in a marked way his great love for us in that we were spared by one to whom it was not a matter of indifference to punish sins, but who regarded it of so much importance that rather than dismiss them altogether unpunished, he delivered his only-begotten son to punishment for them! The ancients said of forgiveness that it was neither *according to* law, nor *against* law, but *above* law, and *for* law. So may we say with emphasis of this divine grace. It is *above* law, because we are not punished; *for* law, because punishment is not omitted; and remission is granted that we may live hereafter *to* the divine law.

# 34

Socinian theory
(example theory)

# The Racovian Catechism

## The Person and Death
## of Christ

### The Person of Christ

As you have stated that there are some things relating to the Will of
God, which were first revealed by Jesus Christ, and also asserted, at the
commencement, that the way of salvation consisted in the knowledge of
him,—I now wish you to specify what those particulars are, concerning
Jesus Christ, which I ought to know?

Certainly: You must be informed, then, that there are some things
relating to the *Person,* or nature, of Jesus Christ, and some, to his *Office,*
with which you ought to be acquainted.

What are the things relating to his Person, which I ought to know?

This one particular alone,—that by nature he was truly a man; a mortal
man while he lived on earth, but now immortal. That he was a real man
the scriptures testify in several places: Thus I Timothy 2:5, "There is one
God, and one mediator between God and men, the *man* Christ Jesus."
I Corinthians 15:21, 22, "Since by *man* came death, by *man* came also the
resurrection of the dead. For as in *Adam* all die, even so in *Christ* shall all
be made alive." Romans 5:15, "If through the offence of one, many be

---

From *The Racovian Catechism*, trans. Thomas Rees (London: Longman,
Horst, Rees, Orme, and Brown, 1818), sections 4-5.

dead, much more the grace of God, and the gift by grace, which is by one *man,* Jesus Christ, hath abounded unto many." John 8:40, "But now ye seek to kill me, *a man* that hath told you the truth." See also Hebrews 5:1, &c. Such, besides, was the person whom God promised of old by the prophets; and such also does the Creed called the Apostles', which all Christians, in common with ourselves, embrace, declare him to be.

Was, then, the Lord Jesus a mere or common man?

By no means: because, first, though by nature he was a man, he was nevertheless, at the same time, and even from his earliest origin, the only begotten Son of God. For being conceived of the Holy Spirit, and born of a virgin, without the intervention of any human being, he had properly no father besides God: though considered in another light, simply according to the flesh, without respect to the Holy Spirit, of which he was conceived, and with which he was anointed, he had David for his father, and was therefore his son. Concerning his supernatural conception, the angel thus speaks to Mary, Luke 1:35, "The Holy Ghost shall come upon thee, and the Power of the Highest shall overshadow thee; therefore also that holy thing which shall be born of thee shall be called the Son of God." Secondly, because, as Christ testifies of himself, he was sanctified and sent into the world by the Father; that is, being in a most remarkable manner separated from all other men, and, besides being distinguished by the perfect holiness of his life, endued with divine wisdom and power, was sent by the Father, with supreme authority, on an embassy to mankind. Thirdly, because, as the apostle Paul testifies, both in the Acts of the Apostles, and in his Epistle to the Romans, he was raised from the dead by God, and thus as it were begotten a second time;—particularly as by this event he became like God immortal. Fourthly, because by his dominion and supreme authority over all things, he is made to resemble, or, indeed, to equal God: on which account, "a king anointed by God," and "Son of God," are used in several passages of scripture as phrases of the same import. And the sacred author of the Epistle to the Hebrews (chap. 1 ver. 5) shows from the words of the Psalmist (Psalm 2:7), "Thou art my Son, this day have I begotten thee," that Christ was glorified by God, in order that he might be made a Priest, that is, the chief director of our religion and salvation,—in which office are comprised his supreme authority and dominion. He was, however, not merely the only begotten Son of God, but also *a God,* on account of the divine power and authority which he displayed even while he was yet mortal: much more may he be so denominated now that he has received all power in heaven and earth, and that all things, God himself alone excepted, have been put under his feet.—But of this you shall hear in its proper place.

But do you not acknowledge in Christ a divine, as well as a human nature or substance?

If by the terms divine nature or substance I am to understand the very essence of God, I do not acknowledge such a divine nature in Christ; for this were repugnant both to right reason and to the Holy Scriptures. But if, on the other hand, you intend by a divine nature the Holy Spirit which dwelt in Christ, united, by an indissoluble bond, to his human nature, and displayed in him the wonderful effects of its extraordinary presence; or if you understand the words in the sense in which Peter employs them (II Peter 1:4), when he asserts that "we are partakers of a divine nature," that is, endued by the favour of God with divinity, or divine properties,—I certainly do so far acknowledge such a nature in Christ as to believe that next after God it belonged to no one in a higher degree.

Show me how the first mentioned opinion is repugnant to right reason?

First, on this account, That two substances endued with opposite and discordant properties, such as are God and man, cannot be ascribed to one and the same individual, much less be predicated the one of the other. For you cannot call one and the same thing first fire, and then water, and afterwards say that the fire is water, and the water fire. And such is the way in which it is usually affirmed;—first, that Christ is God, and afterwards that he is a man; and then that God is man, and that man is God.

But what ought to be replied, when it is alleged that Christ is constituted of a divine and human nature, in the same way as man is composed of a soul and body?

The cases are essentially different:—for it is stated that the two natures are so united in Christ, that he is both God and man: whereas the union between the soul and body is of such a kind that the man is neither the soul nor the body. Again, neither the soul nor the body, separately, constitutes a person: but as the divine nature, by itself, constitutes a person, so also must the human nature, by itself, constitute a person; since it is a primary or single intelligent substance. . . .

I perceive that Christ has not the divine nature which is claimed for him; but that he is a real man:—inform me now in what way the knowledge of this eminently conduces to salvation?

This you may perceive from hence: first, because the contrary opinion greatly tarnishes the glory of God; secondly, because it materially weakens and nearly destroys the certainty of our hope; and thirdly, because it makes one thing of Christ, and another of the Son of God; so that divine honour being transferred to the latter, the divine honour of him who is actually the Christ and the Son of God, is either taken away, or essentially impaired.

How does the opinion of our adversaries tarnish the glory of God?

Not only because the glory of the one God, which pertains to the Father alone, is transferred to another, concerning which I have already treated; but also because God is deprived of that glory which he seeks in the exaltation of Jesus Christ. For if Christ were the most high God, he could not be exalted; or if he could, his exaltation could refer to nothing but the reception of his divine nature entire. Paul, however, says (Eph. 1:17-21) that "the God of our Lord Jesus Christ, the Father of Glory,— wrought his mighty power in Christ, when he raised him from the dead, and set him at his own right hand in the heavenly places, far above all principality," &c. and also (Phil. 2:9, 10), that "God had highly exalted Christ, and given him a name which is above every name, that in the name of Jesus every knee should bow, and every tongue should confess that Jesus Christ is Lord to the glory of God the Father": *"To the glory,"* the apostle writes, *"of God the Father,"* who *gave* him such a name, and such glory.

How, secondly, does the opinion of our adversaries destroy or weaken our hope?

Because the greatest force which pertains to the resurrection of Christ, as a proof of our resurrection, is taken away by attributing this divine nature to him. For it would hence follow that Christ rose from the dead by virtue of his divine nature, as indeed is commonly maintained, and that, on this account, he could by no means be detained by death. But we have nothing in us by nature, which, after we are dead, can recall us to life, or which can in any way prevent our remaining dead perpetually. How then can the certainty of our resurrection be demonstrated from the example of Christ's resurrection, as the apostle Paul has done (I Cor. 15), when there exists such a disparity between Christ and us? And, indeed, if this opinion be admitted, Christ, in reality, could not die, and rise from the dead; since it would follow from it, that Christ was not a person, or, as they say, *suppositum humanum*, that is, a man subsisting of himself. But to die and to rise from the dead can comport with no other than a subject, [*suppositum*] or thing subsisting of itself. A divine person could not die. If therefore Christ was destitute of a human person, capable of dying and rising from the dead, how could he die, or rise from the dead? The same reason shows that Christ was not truly a man, since every one who is a real man is a human person. But that opinion which acknowledges Christ as subsisting of himself, and therefore truly a man, who was obedient to his Father unto death; and asserts and clearly determines that he died, was raised from the dead by God, and endowed with immortality; does in a wonderful manner sustain our hope of eternal salvation; placing before us the very image of the thing, and assuring us that we also, though we be mortal and die, shall nevertheless, if we follow his footsteps, be in due time raised from the dead, and be brought to a participation of the immortality which he now enjoys.

How, thirdly, does the opinion of our adversaries make one thing of Christ, and another of the Son of God?

Because it makes of Christ, the one God himself, and calls him the Son of God, who actually existed before the conception of the man Jesus by the Holy Spirit, and his birth of the Virgin, and indeed before all ages, and directs to the worship of him, our honour and faith:—while in the meantime, either he who is truly Christ and the Son of God, is to them an idol, if they worship him; or else it does not appear how he is at once the one God, and a man, and can be worshipped both as God, and as a man whom God has exalted. . . .

### The Death of Christ

But did not Christ die also, in order, properly speaking, to purchase our salvation, and literally to pay the debt of our sins?

Although Christians at this time commonly so believe, yet this notion is false, erroneous, and exceedingly pernicious; since they conceive that Christ suffered an equivalent punishment for our sins, and by the price of his obedience exactly compensated our disobedience. There is no doubt, however, but that Christ so satisfied God by his obedience, as that he completely fulfilled the whole of his will, and by his obedience obtained, through the grace of God, for all of us who believe in him, the remission of our sins, and eternal salvation.

How do you make it appear that the common notion is false and erroneous?

Not only because the scriptures are silent concerning it, but also because it is repugnant to the scriptures and to right reason.

Prove this, in order.

That nothing concerning it is to be found in the scriptures appears from hence; that they who maintain this opinion never adduce explicit texts of scripture in proof of it, but string together certain inferences by which they endeavour to maintain their assertions. But, besides that a matter of this kind, whereon they themselves conceive the whole business of salvation to turn, ought certainly to be demonstrated not by inferences alone but by clear testimonies of scripture, it might easily be shown that these inferences have no force whatever: otherwise, inferences which necessarily spring from the scriptures, I readily admit.

How is this opinion repugnant to the scriptures?

Because the scriptures everywhere testify that God forgives men their sins freely, and especially under the New Covenant (II Cor. 5:19; Rom. 3:24, 25; Matt. 18:23; &c.). But to a free forgiveness nothing is more opposite than such a satisfaction as they contend for, and the payment of an equivalent price. For where a creditor is satisfied, either by the debtor himself, or by another person on the debtor's behalf, it cannot with truth be said of him that he freely forgives the debt.

How is this repugnant to reason?

This is evident from hence; that it would follow that Christ, if he has satisfied God for our sins, has submitted to eternal death; since it appears that the penalty which men had incurred by their offences was eternal death; not to say that one death, though it were eternal in duration,— much less one so short,—could not of itself be equal to innumerable eternal deaths. For if you say that the death of Christ, because he was a God infinite in nature, was equal to the infinite deaths of the infinite race of men,—besides that I have already refuted this opinion concerning the nature of Christ,—it would follow that God's infinite nature itself suffered death. But as death cannot any way belong to the infinity of the divine nature, so neither, literally speaking (as must necessarily be done here where we are treating of a real compensation and payment), can the infinity of the divine nature any way belong to death. In the next place, it would follow that there was no necessity that Christ should endure such sufferings, and so dreadful a death; and that God—be it spoken without offence,—was unjust, who, when he might well have been contented with one drop (as they say) of the blood of Christ, would have him so severely tormented. Lastly, it would follow that we were more obliged to Christ than to God, and owed him more, indeed owed him every thing; since he, by this satisfaction, showed us much kindness; whereas God, by exacting his debt, showed us no kindness at all.

State in what manner this opinion is pernicious?

Because it opens a door to licentiousness, or, at least, invites men to indolence in the practice of piety, in what way soever they urge the piety of their patron. For if full payment have been made to God by Christ for all our sins, even those which are future, we are absolutely freed from all liability to punishment, and therefore no further condition can by right be exacted from us to deliver us from the penalties of sin. What necessity then would there be for living religiously? But the scripture testifies (Titus 2:14; Gal. 1:4; I Peter 1:18; Heb. 9:14; II Cor. 5:15; Eph. 5:26) that Christ died for this end, among others, that he might "redeem us from all iniquity, and purify us unto himself a peculiar people zealous of good works"; "that he might deliver us from the present evil world"; "might redeem us from our vain conversation, received by tradition from our fathers," in order that being "dead to sin" we might "live unto righteousness," that our consciences might be "purged from dead works to serve the living God."

But how do they maintain their opinion?

They endeavour to do this first by a certain reason, and then by the authority of scripture.

What is this reason?

They say that there are in God, by nature, justice and mercy: that as it is the property of mercy to forgive sins, so is it, they state, the property of justice to punish every sin whatever. But since God willed that both his mercy and justice should be satisfied together, he devised this plan, that Christ should suffer death in our stead, and thus satisfy God's justice in the human nature, by which he had been offended; and that his mercy should at the same time be displayed in forgiving sin.

What reply do you make to this reason?

This reason bears the appearance of plausibility, but in reality has in it nothing of truth or solidity; and indeed involves a self-contradiction. For although we confess, and hence exceedingly rejoice, that our God is wonderfully merciful and just, nevertheless we deny that there are in him the mercy and justice which our adversaries imagine, since the one would wholly annihilate the other. For, according to them, the one requires that God should punish no sin; the other, that he should leave no sin unpunished. If then it were naturally a property of God to punish no sin, he could not act against his nature in order that he might punish sin: in like manner also, if it were naturally a property of God to leave no sin unpunished, he could not, any more, contrary to his nature, refrain from punishing every sin. For God can never do any thing repugnant to those properties which pertain to him by nature. For instance, since wisdom belongs naturally to God, he can never do any thing contrary to it, but whatever he does he does wisely. But as it is evident that God forgives and punishes sins whenever he deems fit, it appears that the mercy which commands to spare, and the justice which commands to destroy, do so exist in him as that both are tempered by his will, and by the wisdom, the benignity, and holiness of his nature. Besides, the scriptures are not wont to designate the justice, which is opposed to mercy, and is discernible in punishments inflic d in wrath, by this term, but style it the *severity,* the *anger,* and *wrath* of God:—indeed, it is attributed to the justice of God in the scriptures that he forgives sins: I John 4:9; Rom. 3:25, 26; and frequently in the Psalms.

What then is your opinion concerning this matter?

It is this;—that since I have shown that the mercy and justice which our adversaries conceive to pertain to God by nature, certainly do not belong to him, there was no need of that plan whereby he might satisfy such mercy and justice, and by which they might, as it were by a certain tempering, be reconciled to each other: which tempering nevertheless is such that it satisfies neither, and indeed destroys both;—For what is that justice, and what too that mercy, which punishes the innocent, and absolves the guilty? I do not, indeed, deny that there is a natural justice in God, which is called rectitude, and is opposed to wickedness: this shines in all his works, and hence they all appear just and right and perfect; and that, no less when he forgives than when he punishes our transgressions. . . .

But what do you conceive to be the meaning of the declaration,—that Christ has redeemed us and given himself a ransom for us?

The term *redemption,* in most passages of scripture, means simply *liberation;* but by a more extended figure, it is put for that liberation for effecting which a certain price is paid. And it is said of the death of Christ that he has liberated us by it, because by means of it we have obtained our freedom both from our sins themselves, that we no longer serve them; and also from the punishment of them, that being snatched from the jaws of eternal death we may live for ever.

But why is this deliverance expressed by the term redemption?

Because there is a very great similarity between our deliverance and a redemption properly so called. For as in a proper redemption there must be a captive, the person who detains the captive, the redeemer, and lastly, the ransom, or price of the redemption; so also in our deliverance, if we speak of our sins themselves, man is the captive—they who detain him are sin, the world, the devil, and death: the redeemer of the captive are God and Christ; and the ransom, or price of the redemption, is Christ, or his soul paid by God and by Christ himself. The only difference lies here, that in this deliverance of us from our sins themselves, no one receives any thing under the name of ransom, which must always happen in a redemption properly so called. But if we speak of our deliverance from the punishment of our sins, we owe this to God, Christ having delivered us from it when, in compliance with the will of God, he gave himself up to death for us, and through his own blood entered into the heavenly place:

which obedience of his son unto death, and the death of the cross, God accepted as an offering of all the most agreeable to him. But this is not to be understood nevertheless as importing that God, literally speaking, had received the full payment of our debts; since Christ was a victim of his own, provided by himself, as was also the case in the yearly sacrifice (the type of the sacrifice of Christ): and owed every thing to God through himself, and in his own name; and although his obedience was the highest and most perfect of any, yet he received an incomparably greater reward for it. Wherefore this ought to be ascribed to the unbounded grace and bounty of God; because he not only did not receive any part of what we owed to him, and because he not only forgave us all our debts; but also because he gave a victim of his own, and that his only-begotten and best-beloved son, that lamb without blemish, for us and our sins, not that he might pay himself any thing for us (for this would be a fictitious not a real payment), but might create for us so much greater and more certain a right to pardon and eternal life, and might bind himself by such a pledge to confer this upon us; and might also convert us to himself, and bless us with the other signal benefits of which we stood in need.

## 35

## Anselm

# Cur Deus Homo

*Anselm.* We must needs inquire ... in what manner God puts away men's sins; and, in order to do this more plainly, let us first consider what it is to sin, and what it is to make satisfaction for sin.

*Boso.* It is yours to explain and mine to listen.

*Anselm.* If man or angel always rendered to God his due, he would never sin.

*Boso.* I cannot deny that.

*Anselm.* Therefore to sin is nothing else than not to render to God his due.

*Boso.* What is the debt which we owe to God?

*Anselm.* Every wish of a rational creature should be subject to the will of God.

*Boso.* Nothing is more true.

*Anselm.* This is the debt which man and angel owe to God, and no one who pays this debt commits sin; but every one who does not pay it sins. This is justice, or uprightness of will, which makes a being just or upright in heart, that is, in will; and this is the sole and complete debt of honor

From *Cur Deus Homo*, book 1 (chaps. 11-16, 19-25) and book 2 (chaps. 6-7). In *Basic Writings* (LaSalle, Ill.: Open Court, 1962).

which we owe to God, and which God requires of us. For it is such a will only, when it can be exercised, that does works pleasing to God; and when this will cannot be exercised, it is pleasing of itself alone, since without it no work is acceptable. He who does not render this honor which is due to God, robs God of his own and dishonors him; and this is sin. Moreover, so long as he does not restore what he has taken away, he remains in fault; and it will not suffice merely to restore what has been taken away, but, considering the contempt offered, he ought to restore more than he took away. For as one who imperils another's safety does not enough by merely restoring his safety, without making some compensation for the anguish incurred; so he who violates another's honor does not enough by merely rendering honor again, but must, according to the extent of the injury done, make restoration in some way satisfactory to the person whom he has dishonored. We must also observe that when any one pays what he has unjustly taken away, he ought to give something which could not have been demanded of him, had he not stolen what belonged to another. So then, every one who sins ought to pay back the honor of which he has robbed God; and this is the satisfaction which every sinner owes to God.

*Boso.* Since we have determined to follow reason in all these things, I am unable to bring any objection against them, although you somewhat startle me.

*Anselm.* Let us return and consider whether it were proper for God to put away sins by compassion alone, without any payment of the honor taken from him.

*Boso.* I do not see why it is not proper.

*Anselm.* To remit sin in this manner is nothing else than not to punish; and since it is not right to cancel sin without compensation or punishment; if it be not punished, then is it passed by undischarged.

*Boso.* What you say is reasonable.

*Anselm.* It is not fitting for God to pass over anything in his kingdom undischarged.

*Boso.* If I wish to oppose this, I fear to sin.

*Anselm.* It is, therefore, not proper for God thus to pass over sin unpunished.

*Boso.* Thus it follows.

*Anselm.* There is also another thing which follows if sin be passed by unpunished, viz., that with God there will be no difference between the guilty and the not guilty; and this is unbecoming to God.

*Boso.* I cannot deny it.

*Anselm.* Observe this also. Every one knows that justice to man is regulated by law, so that, according to the requirements of law, the measure of award is bestowed by God.

*Boso.* This is our belief.

*Anselm.* But if sin is neither paid for nor punished, it is subject to no law.

*Boso.* I cannot conceive it to be otherwise.

*Anselm.* Injustice, therefore, if it is cancelled by compassion alone, is more free than justice, which seems very inconsistent. And to these is also added a further incongruity, viz., that it makes injustice like God. For as God is subject to no law, so neither is injustice.

*Boso.* I cannot withstand your reasoning. But when God commands us in every case to forgive those who trespass against us, it seems inconsistent to enjoin a thing upon us which it is not proper for him to do himself.

*Anselm.* There is no inconsistency in God's commanding us not to take upon ourselves what belongs to Him alone. For to execute vengeance belongs to none but Him who is Lord of all; for when the powers of the world rightly accomplish this end, God himself does it who appointed them for the purpose.

*Boso.* You have obviated the difficulty which I thought to exist; but there is another to which I would like to have your answer. For since God is so free as to be subject to no law, and to the judgment of no one, and is so merciful as that nothing more merciful can be conceived; and nothing is right or fit save as he wills; it seems a strange thing for us to say that he is wholly unwilling or unable to put away an injury done to himself, when we are wont to apply to him for indulgence with regard to those offences which we commit against others.

*Anselm.* What you say of God's liberty and choice and compassion is true; but we ought so to interpret these things as that they may not seem to interfere with His dignity. For there is no liberty except as regards what is best or fitting; nor should that be called mercy which does anything improper for the Divine character. Moreover, when it is said that what God wishes is just, and that what He does not wish is unjust, we must not understand that if God wished anything improper it would be just, simply because he wished it. For if God wishes to lie, we must not conclude that it is right to lie, but rather that he is not God. For no will can ever wish to lie, unless truth in it is impaired, nay, unless the will itself be impaired by forsaking truth. When, then, it is said: "If God wishes to lie," the meaning is simply this: "If the nature of God is such as that he wishes to lie"; and, therefore, it does not follow that falsehood is right, except it be understood in the same manner as when we speak of two impossible things: "If this be true, then that follows; because neither *this* nor *that* is true"; as if a man should say: "Supposing water to be dry, and fire to be moist"; for neither is the case. Therefore, with regard to these things, to speak the whole truth: If God desires a thing, it is right that he should desire that which involves no unfitness. For if God chooses that it should rain, it is right that it should rain; and if he desires that any man should die, then is it right that he should die. Wherefore, if it be not fitting for God to do anything unjustly, or out of course, it does not belong to his liberty or compassion or will to let the sinner go unpunished, who makes no return to God of what the sinner has defrauded him.

*Boso.* You remove from me every possible objection which I had thought of bringing against you.

*Anselm.* Yet observe why it is not fitting for God to do this.

*Boso.* I listen readily to whatever you say.

*Anselm.* In the order of things, there is nothing less to be endured than that the creature should take away the honor due the Creator, and not restore what he has taken away.

*Boso.* Nothing is more plain than this.

*Anselm.* But there is no greater injustice suffered than that by which so great an evil must be endured.

*Boso.* This, also, is plain.

*Anselm.* I think, therefore, that you will not say that God ought to endure a thing than which no greater injustice is suffered, viz., that the creature should not restore to God what he has taken away.

*Boso.* No; I think it should be wholly denied.

*Anselm.* Again, if there is nothing greater or better than God, there is nothing more just than supreme justice, which maintains God's honor in the arrangement of things, and which is nothing else but God himself.

*Boso.* There is nothing clearer than this.

*Anselm.* Therefore God maintains nothing with more justice than the honor of his own dignity.

*Boso.* I must agree with you.

*Anselm.* Does it seem to you that he wholly preserves it, if he allows himself to be so defrauded of it as that he should neither receive satisfaction nor punish the one defrauding him?

*Boso.* I dare not say so.

*Anselm.* Therefore the honor taken away must be repaid, or punishment must follow; otherwise, either God will not be just to himself, or he will be weak in respect to both parties; and this it is impious even to think of.

*Boso.* I think that nothing more reasonable can be said.

*Boso.* But I wish to hear from you whether the punishment of the sinner is an honor to God, or how it is an honor. For if the punishment of the sinner is not for God's honor when the sinner does not pay what he took away, but is punished, God loses his honor so that he cannot recover it. And this seems in contradiction to the things which have been said.

*Anselm.* It is impossible for God to lose his honor; for either the sinner pays his debt of his own accord, or, if he refuse, God takes it from him. For either man renders due submission to God of his own will, by avoiding sin or making payment, or else God subjects him to himself by torments, even against man's will, and thus shows that he is the Lord of man, though man refuses to acknowledge it of his own accord. And here we must observe that as man in sinning takes away what belongs to God, so God in punishing gets in return what pertains to man. For not only does that belong to a man which he has in present possession, but also that which it is in his power to have. Therefore, since man was so made as to be able to attain happiness by avoiding sin; if, on account of his sin, he is deprived of happiness and every good, he repays from his own inheritance what he has stolen, though he repay it against his will. For although God does not apply what he takes away to any object of his own, as man transfers the money which he has taken from another to his own use; yet what he takes away serves the purpose of his own honor, for this very reason, that it is taken away. For by this act he shows that the sinner and all that pertains to him are under his subjection.

*Boso.* What you say satisfies me. But there is still another point which I should like to have you answer. For if, as you make out, God ought to sustain his own honor, why does he allow it to be violated even in the least degree? For what is in any way made liable to injury is not entirely and perfectly preserved.

*Anselm.* Nothing can be added to or taken from the honor of God. For this honor which belongs to him is in no way subject to injury or change. But as the individual creature preserves, naturally or by reason, the condition belonging, and, as it were, allotted to him, he is said to obey and honor God; and to this, rational nature, which possesses intelligence, is especially bound. And when the being chooses what he ought, he honors God; not by bestowing anything upon him, but because he brings himself freely under God's will and disposal, and maintains his own condition in the universe, and the beauty of the universe itself, as far as in him lies. But when he does not choose what he ought, he dishonors God, as far as the being himself is concerned, because he does not submit himself freely to God's disposal. And he disturbs the order and beauty of the universe, as relates to himself, although he cannot injure nor tarnish the power and majesty of God. For if those things which are held together in the circuit of the heavens desire to be elsewhere than under the heavens, or to be further removed from the heavens, there is no place where they can be but under the heavens, nor can they fly from the heavens without also approaching them. For both whence and whither and in what way they go, they are still under the heavens; and if they are at a greater distance from one part of them, they are only so much nearer to the opposite part. And so, though man or evil angel refuse to submit to the Divine will and appointment, yet he cannot escape it; for if he wishes to fly from a will that commands, he falls into the power of a will that punishes. And if you ask whither he goes, it is only under the permission of that will; and even this wayward choice or action of his becomes subservient, under infinite wisdom, to the order and beauty of the universe before spoken of. For when it is understood that God brings good out of many forms of evil, then the satisfaction for sin freely given, or if this be not given, the exaction of punishment, hold their own place and orderly beauty in the same universe. For if Divine wisdom were not to insist upon these things, when wickedness tries to disturb the right appointment, there would be, in the very universe which God ought to control, an unseemliness springing from the violation of the beauty of arrangement, and God would appear to be deficient in his management. And these two things are not only unfitting, but consequently impossible; so that satisfaction or punishment must needs follow every sin.

*Boso.* You have relieved my objection.

372     *The Work of Christ*

*Anselm.* It is then plain that no one can honor or dishonor God, as he is in himself; but the creature, as far as he is concerned, appears to do this when he submits or opposes his will to the will of God.

*Boso.* I know of nothing which can be said against this.

*Anselm.* Let me add something to it.

*Boso.* Go on, until I am weary of listening.

*Anselm.* It was proper that God should design to make up for the number of angels that fell, from human nature which he created without sin.

*Boso.* This is a part of our belief, but still I should like to have some reason for it.

*Anselm.* You mistake me, for we intended to discuss only the incarnation of the Deity, and here you are bringing in other questions.

*Boso.* Be not angry with me; "for the Lord loveth a cheerful giver"; and no one shows better how cheerfully he gives what he promises, than he who gives more than he promises; therefore, tell me freely what I ask.

*Anselm.* There is no question that intelligent nature, which finds its happiness, both now and forever, in the contemplation of God, was foreseen by him in a certain reasonable and complete number, so that there would be an unfitness in its being either less or greater. For either God did not know in what number it was best to create rational beings, which is false; or, if he did know, then he appointed such a number as he perceived was most fitting. Wherefore, either the angels who fell were made so as to be within that number; or, since they were out of that number, they could not continue to exist, and so fell of necessity. But this last is an absurd idea.

*Boso.* The truth which you set forth is plain.

*Anselm.* Therefore, since they ought to be of that number, either their number should of necessity be made up, or else rational nature, which was foreseen as perfect in number, will remain incomplete. But this cannot be.

*Boso.* Doubtless, then, the number must be restored.

*Anselm.* But this restoration can only be made from human beings, since there is no other source. . . .

*Anselm.* It was fitting for God to fill the places of the fallen angels from among men.

*Boso.* That is certain.

*Anselm.* Therefore there ought to be in the heavenly empire as many men taken as substitutes for the angels as would correspond with the number whose place they shall take, that is, as many as there are good angels now; otherwise they who fell will not be restored, and it will follow that God either could not accomplish the good which he begun, or he will repent of having undertaken it; either of which is absurd.

*Boso.* Truly it is fitting that men should be equal with good angels.

*Anselm.* Have good angels ever sinned?

*Boso.* No.

*Anselm.* Can you think that man, who has sinned, and never made satisfaction to God for his sin, but only been suffered to go unpunished, may become the equal of an angel who has never sinned?

*Boso.* These words I can both think of and utter, but can no more perceive their meaning than I can make truth out of falsehood.

*Anselm.* Therefore it is not fitting that God should take sinful man without an atonement, in substitution for lost angels; for truth will not suffer man thus to be raised to an equality with holy beings.

*Boso.* Reason shows this.

*Anselm.* Consider, also, leaving out the question of equality with the angels, whether God ought, under such circumstances, to raise man to the same or a similar kind of happiness as that which he had before he sinned.

*Boso.* Tell your opinion, and I will attend to it as well as I can.

*Anselm.* Suppose a rich man possessed a choice pearl which had never been defiled, and which could not be taken from his hands without his permission; and that he determined to commit it to the treasury of his dearest and most valuable possessions.

*Boso.* I accept your supposition.

*Anselm.* What if he should allow it to be struck from his hand and cast in the mire, though he might have prevented it; and afterwards taking it all soiled by the mire and unwashed, should commit it again to his beautiful and loved casket; will you consider him a wise man?

*Boso.* How can I? for would it not be far better to keep and preserve his pearl pure, than to have it polluted?

*Anselm.* Would not God be acting like this, who held man in paradise, as it were in his own hand, without sin, and destined to the society of angels, and allowed the devil, inflamed with envy, to cast him into the mire of sin, though truly with man's consent? For, had God chosen to restrain the devil, the devil could not have tempted man. Now I say, would not God be acting like this, should he restore man, stained with the defilement of sin, unwashed, that is, without any satisfaction, and always to remain so; should He restore him at once to paradise, from which he had been thrust out?

*Boso.* I dare not deny the aptness of your comparison, were God to do this, and therefore do not admit that he can do this. For it should seem either that he could not accomplish what he designed, or else that he repented of his good intent, neither of which things is possible with God.

*Anselm.* Therefore, consider it settled that, without satisfaction, that is, without voluntary payment of the debt, God can neither pass by the sin unpunished, nor can the sinner attain that happiness, or happiness like that, which he had before he sinned; for man cannot in this way be restored, or become such as he was before he sinned.

*Boso.* I am wholly unable to refute your reasoning. But what say you to this: that we pray God, "put away our sins from us," and every nation prays the God of its faith to put away its sins. For, if we pay our debt, why do we pray God to put it away? Is not God unjust to demand what has already been paid? But if we do not make payment, why do we

374    The Work of Christ

supplicate in vain that he will do what he cannot do, because it is unbecoming?

*Anselm.* He who does not pay says in vain: "Pardon"; but he who pays
makes supplication, because prayer is properly connected with the payment; for God owes no man anything, but every creature owes God; and,
therefore, it does not become man to treat with God as with an equal. But
of this it is not now needful for me to answer you. For when you think
why Christ died, I think you will see yourself the answer to your question.

*Boso.* Your reply with regard to this matter suffices me for the present.
And, moreover, you have so clearly shown that no man can attain happiness in sin, or be freed from sin without satisfaction for the trespass, that,
even were I so disposed, I could not doubt it.

*Anselm.* Neither, I think, will you doubt this, that satisfaction should
be proportionate to guilt.

*Boso.* Otherwise sin would remain in a manner exempt from control
(*inordinatum*), which cannot be, for God leaves nothing uncontrolled in
his kingdom. But this is determined, that even the smallest unfitness is
impossible with God.

*Anselm.* Tell me, then, what payment you make God for your sin?

*Boso.* Repentance, a broken and contrite heart, self-denial, various
bodily sufferings, pity in giving and forgiving, and obedience.

*Anselm.* What do you give to God in all these?

*Boso.* Do I not honor God, when, for his love and fear, in heartfelt
contrition I give up worldly joy, and despise, amid abstinence and toils,
the delights and ease of this life, and submit obediently to him, freely
bestowing my possessions in giving to and releasing others?

*Anselm.* When you render anything to God which you owe him, irrespective of your past sin, you should not reckon this as the debt which
you owe for sin. But you owe God every one of those things which you
have mentioned. For, in this mortal state, there should be such love and
such desire of attaining the true end of your being, which is the meaning
of prayer, and such grief that you have not yet reached this object, and
such fear lest you fail of it, that you should find joy in nothing which does
not help you or give encouragement of your success. For you do not
deserve to have a thing which you do not love and desire for its own sake,
and the want of which at present, together with the great danger of never
getting it, causes you no grief. This also requires one to avoid ease and
worldly pleasures such as seduce the mind from real rest and pleasure,
except so far as you think suffices for the accomplishment of that object.
But you ought to view the gifts which you bestow as a part of your debt,
since you know that what you give comes not from yourself, but from him
whose servant both you are and he also to whom you give. And nature
herself teaches you to do to your fellow servant, man to man, as you
would be done by; and that he who will not bestow what he has ought not
to receive what he has not. Of forgiveness, indeed, I speak briefly, for, as
we said above, vengeance in no sense belongs to you, since you are not

your own, nor is he who injures you yours or his, but you are both the servants of one Lord, made by him out of nothing. And if you avenge yourself upon your fellow servant, you proudly assume judgment over him when it is the peculiar right of God, the judge of all. But what do you give to God by your obedience, which is not owed him already, since he demands from you all that you are and have and can become?

*Boso.* Truly I dare not say that in all these things I pay any portion of my debt to God.

*Anselm.* How then do you pay God for your transgression?

*Boso.* If in justice I owe God myself and all my powers, even when I do not sin, I have nothing left to render to him for my sin.

*Anselm.* What will become of you then? How will you be saved?

*Boso.* Merely looking at your arguments, I see no way of escape. But, turning to my belief, I hope through Christian faith, "which works by love," that I may be saved, and the more, since we read that if the sinner turns from his iniquity and does what is right, all his transgressions shall be forgotten.

*Anselm.* This is only said of those who either looked for Christ before his coming, or who believe in him since he has appeared. But we set aside Christ and his religion as if they did not exist, when we proposed to inquire whether his coming were necessary to man's salvation.

*Boso.* We did so.

*Anselm.* Let us then proceed by reason simply.

*Boso.* Though you bring me into straits, yet I very much wish you to proceed as you have begun.

*Anselm.* Suppose that you did not owe any of those things which you have brought up as possible payment for your sin, let us inquire whether they can satisfy for a sin so small as one *look* contrary to the will of God.

*Boso.* Did I not hear you question the thing, I should suppose that a single repentant feeling on my part would blot out this sin.

*Anselm.* You have not as yet estimated the great burden of sin.

*Boso.* Show it me then.

*Anselm.* If you should find yourself in the sight of God, and one said to you: "Look thither"; and God, on the other hand, should say: "It is not my will that you should look"; ask your own heart what there is in all existing things which would make it right for you to give that *look* contrary to the will of God.

*Boso.* I can find no motive which would make it right; unless, indeed I am so situated as to make it necessary for me either to do this, or some greater sin.

*Anselm.* Put away all such necessity, and ask with regard to this sin only whether you can do it even for your own salvation.

*Boso.* I see plainly that I cannot.

*Anselm.* Not to detain you too long; what if it were necessary either that the whole universe, except God himself, should perish and fall back into nothing, or else that you should do so small a thing against the will of God?

*Boso.* When I consider the action itself, it appears very slight; but when I view it as contrary to the will of God, I know of nothing so grievous, and of no loss that will compare with it; but sometimes we oppose another's will without blame in order to preserve his property, so that afterwards he is glad that we opposed him.

*Anselm.* This is in the case of man, who often does not know what is useful for him, or cannot make up his loss; but God is in want of nothing, and, should all things perish, can restore them as easily as he created them.

*Boso.* I must confess that I ought not to oppose the will of God even to preserve the whole creation.

*Anselm.* What if there were more worlds as full of beings as this?

*Boso.* Were they increased to an infinite extent, and held before me in like manner, my reply would be the same.

*Anselm.* You cannot answer more correctly, but consider, also, should it happen that you gave the look contrary to God's will, what payment you can make for this sin?

*Boso.* I can only repeat what I said before.

*Anselm.* So heinous is our sin whenever we knowingly oppose the will of God even in the slightest thing; since we are always in his sight, and he always enjoins it upon us not to sin.

*Boso.* I cannot deny it.

*Anselm.* Therefore you make no satisfaction unless you restore something greater than the amount of that obligation, which should restrain you from committing the sin.

*Boso.* Reason seems to demand this, and to make the contrary wholly impossible.

*Anselm.* Even God cannot raise to happiness any being bound at all by the debt of sin, because He ought not to.

*Boso.* This decision is most weighty.

*Anselm.* Listen to an additional reason which makes it no less difficult for man to be reconciled to God.

*Boso.* This alone would drive me to despair, were it not for the consolation of faith.

*Anselm.* But listen.

*Boso.* Say on.

*Anselm.* Man being made holy was placed in paradise, as it were in the place of God, between God and the devil, to conquer the devil by not yielding to his temptation, and so to vindicate the honor of God and put the devil to shame, because that man, though weaker and dwelling upon earth, should not sin though tempted by the devil, while the devil, though stronger and in heaven, sinned without any to tempt him. And when man could have easily effected this, he, without compulsion and of his own accord, allowed himself to be brought over to the will of the devil, contrary to the will and honor of God.

*Boso.* To what would you bring me?

*Anselm.* Decide for yourself if it be not contrary to the honor of God for man to be reconciled to Him, with this calumnious reproach still heaped upon God; unless man first shall have honored God by overcoming the devil, as he dishonored him in yielding to the devil. Now the victory ought to be of this kind, that, as in strength and immortal vigor, he freely yielded to the devil to sin, and on this account justly incurred the penalty of death; so, in his weakness and mortality, which he had brought upon himself, he should conquer the devil by the pain of death, while wholly avoiding sin. But this cannot be done, so long as from the deadly effect of the first transgression, man is conceived and born in sin.

*Boso.* Again I say that the thing is impossible, and reason approves what you say.

*Anselm.* Let me mention one thing more, without which man's reconciliation cannot be justly effected, and the impossibility is the same.

*Boso.* You have already presented so many obligations which we ought to fulfil, that nothing which you can add will alarm me more.

*Anselm.* Yet listen.

*Boso.* I will.

*Anselm.* What did man take from God, when he allowed himself to be overcome by the devil?

*Boso.* Go on to mention, as you have begun, the evil things which can be added to those already shown for I am ignorant of them.

*Anselm.* Did not man take from God whatever He had purposed to do for human nature?

*Boso.* There is no denying that.

*Anselm.* Listen to the voice of strict justice; and judge according to that whether man makes to God a real satisfaction for his sin, unless, by overcoming the devil, man restore to God what he took from God in allowing himself to be conquered by the devil; so that, as by this conquest over man the devil took what belonged to God, and God was the loser, so in man's victory the devil may be despoiled, and God recover his right.

*Boso.* Surely nothing can be more exactly or justly conceived.

*Anselm.* Think you that supreme justice can violate *this* justice?

*Boso.* I dare not think it.

*Anselm.* Therefore man cannot and ought not by any means to receive from God what God designed to give him, unless he return to God everything which he took from him; so that, as by man God suffered loss, by man, also, He might recover His loss. But this cannot be effected except in this way: that, as in the fall of man all human nature was corrupted, and, as it were, tainted with sin, and God will not choose one of such a race to fill up the number in his heavenly kingdom; so, by man's victory, as many men may be justified from sin as are needed to complete the number which man was made to fill. But a sinful man can by no means do this, for a sinner cannot justify a sinner.

*Boso.* There is nothing more just or necessary; but, from all these things, the compassion of God and the hope of man seems to fail, as far as regards that happiness for which man was made.

*Anselm.* Yet wait a little.

*Boso.* Have you anything further?

*Anselm.* If a man is called unjust who does not pay his fellow-man a debt, much more is he unjust who does not restore what he owes God.

*Boso.* If he can pay and yet does not, he is certainly unjust. But if he be not able, wherein is he unjust?

*Anselm.* Indeed, if the origin of his inability were not in himself, there might be some excuse for him. But if in this very impotence lies the fault, as it does not lessen the sin, neither does it excuse him from paying what is due. Suppose one should assign his slave a certain piece of work, and should command him not to throw himself into a ditch, which he points out to him and from which he could not extricate himself; and suppose that the slave, despising his master's command and warning, throws himself into the ditch before pointed out, so as to be utterly unable to accomplish the work assigned; think you that his inability will at all excuse him for not doing his appointed work?

*Boso.* By no means, but will rather increase his crime, since he brought his inability upon himself. For doubly hath he sinned, in not doing what he was commanded to do and in doing what he was forewarned not to do.

*Anselm.* Just so inexcusable is man, who has voluntarily brought upon himself a debt which he cannot pay, and by his own fault disabled himself, so that he can neither escape his previous obligation not to sin, nor pay the debt which he has incurred by sin. For his very inability is guilt, because he ought not to have it; nay, he ought to be free from it; for as it is a crime not to have what he ought, it is also a crime to have what he ought not. Therefore, as it is a crime in man not to have that power which he received to avoid sin, it is also a crime to have that inability by which he can neither do right and avoid sin, nor restore the debt which he owes on account of his sin. For it is by his own free action that he loses that power, and falls into this inability. For not to have the power which one ought to have, is the same thing as to have the inability which one ought not to have. Therefore man's inability to restore what he owes to God, an inability brought upon himself for that very purpose, does not excuse man from paying; for the result of sin cannot excuse the sin itself.

*Boso.* This argument is exceedingly weighty, and must be true.

*Anselm.* Man, then, is unjust in not paying what he owes to God.

*Boso.* This is very true; for he is unjust, both in not paying, and in not being able to pay.

*Anselm.* But no unjust person shall be admitted to happiness; for as that happiness is complete in which there is nothing wanting, so it can belong to no one who is not so pure as to have no injustice found in him.

*Boso.* I dare not think otherwise.

*Anselm.* He, then, who does not pay God what he owes can never be happy.

*Boso.* I cannot deny that this is so.

*Anselm.* But if you choose to say that a merciful God remits to the suppliant his debt, because he cannot pay; God must be said to dispense with one of two things, viz., either this which man ought voluntarily to render but cannot, that is, an equivalent for his sin, a thing which ought not to be given up even to save the whole universe besides God; or else this, which, as I have before said, God was about to take away from man by punishment, even against man's will, viz., happiness. But if God gives up what man ought freely to render, for the reason that man cannot repay it, what is this but saying that God gives up what he is unable to obtain? But it is mockery to ascribe such compassion to God. But if God gives up what he was about to take from unwilling man, because man is unable to restore what he ought to restore freely, He abates the punishment and makes man happy on account of his sin, because he has what he ought not to have. For he ought not to have this inability, and therefore as long as he has it without atonement it is his sin. And truly such compassion on the part of God is wholly contrary to the Divine justice, which allows nothing but punishment as the recompense of sin. Therefore, as God cannot be inconsistent with himself, his compassion cannot be of this nature.

*Boso.* I think, then, we must look for another mercy than this.

*Anselm.* But suppose it were true that God pardons the man who does not pay his debt because he cannot.

*Boso.* I could wish it were so.

*Anselm.* But while man does not make payment, he either wishes to restore, or else he does not wish to. Now, if he wishes to do what he cannot, he will be needy, and if he does not wish to, he will be unjust.

*Boso.* Nothing can be plainer.

*Anselm.* But whether needy or unjust, he will not be happy.

*Boso.* This also is plain.

*Anselm.* So long, then, as he does not restore, he will not be happy.

*Boso.* If God follows the method of justice, there is no escape for the miserable wretch, and God's compassion seems to fail.

*Anselm.* You have demanded an explanation; now hear it. I do not deny that God is merciful, who preserveth man and beast, according to the multitude of his mercies. But we are speaking of that exceeding pity by which he makes man happy after this life. And I think that I have amply proved, by the reasons given above, that happiness ought not to be bestowed upon any one whose sins have not been wholly put away; and that this remission ought not to take place, save by the payment of the debt incurred by sin, according to the extent of sin. And if you think that any objections can be brought against these proofs, you ought to mention them.

*Boso.* I see not how your reasons can be at all invalidated.

*Anselm.* Nor do I, if rightly understood. But even if one of the whole number be confirmed by impregnable truth, that should be sufficient. For truth is equally secured against all doubt, if it be demonstrably proved by one argument as by many.

*Boso.* Surely this is so. But how, then, shall man be saved, if he neither pays what he owes, and ought not to be saved without paying? Or, with what face shall we declare that God, who is rich in mercy above human conception, cannot exercise this compassion?

*Anselm.* This is the question which you ought to ask of those in whose behalf you are speaking, who have no faith in the need of Christ for man's salvation, and you should also request them to tell how man can be saved without Christ. But, if they are utterly unable to do it, let them cease from mocking us, and let them hasten to unite themselves with us, who do not doubt that man can be saved through Christ; else let them despair of being saved at all. And if this terrifies them, let them believe in Christ as we do, that they may be saved.

*Boso.* Let me ask you, as I have begun, to show me how a man is saved by Christ.

*Anselm.* Is it not sufficiently proved that man can be saved by Christ, when even infidels do not deny that man can be happy somehow, and it has been sufficiently shown that, leaving Christ out of view, no salvation can be found for man? For, either by Christ or by some one else can man be saved, or else not at all. If, then, it is false that man cannot be saved at all, or that he can be saved in any other way, his salvation must necessarily be by Christ.

*Boso.* But what reply will you make to a person who perceives that man cannot be saved in any other way, and yet, not understanding how he can be saved by Christ, sees fit to declare that there cannot be any salvation either by Christ or in any other way?

*Anselm.* What reply ought to be made to one who ascribes impossibility to a necessary truth, because he does not understand how it can be?

*Boso.* That he is a fool.

*Anselm.* Then what he says must be despised.

*Boso.* Very true; but we ought to show him in what way the thing is true which he holds to be impossible.

*Anselm.* Do you not perceive, from what we have said above, that it is necessary for some men to attain to felicity? For, if it is unfitting for God to elevate man with any stain upon him, to that for which he made him free from all stain, lest it should seem that God had repented of his good intent, or was unable to accomplish his designs; far more is it impossible, on account of the same unfitness, that no man should be exalted to that state for which he was made. Therefore, a satisfaction such as we have above proved necessary for sin, must be found apart from the Christian faith, which no reason can show; or else we must accept the Christian doctrine. For what is clearly made out by absolute reasoning ought by no means to be questioned, even though the method of it be not understood.

*Boso.* What you say is true.

*Anselm.* Why, then, do you question further?

*Boso.* I come not for this purpose, to have you remove doubts from my faith, but to have you show me the reason for my confidence. Therefore, as you have brought me thus far by your reasoning, so that I perceive that man as a sinner owes God for his sin what he is unable to pay, and cannot be saved without paying; I wish you would go further with me, and enable me to understand, by force of reasoning, the fitness of all those things which the Catholic faith enjoins upon us with regard to Christ, if we hope to be saved; and how they avail for the salvation of man, and how God saves man by compassion; when he never remits his sin, unless man shall have rendered what was due on account of his sin. And, to make your reasoning the clearer, begin at the beginning, so as to rest it upon a strong foundation.

*Anselm.* Now God help me, for you do not spare me in the least, nor consider the weakness of my skill, when you enjoin so great a work upon me. Yet I will attempt it, as I have begun, not trusting in myself but in God, and will do what I can with his help. But let us separate the things which remain to be said from those which have been said, by a new introduction, lest by their unbroken length, these things become tedious to one who wishes to read them. . . .

*Anselm.* But this [atonement] cannot be effected, except the price paid to God for the sin of man be something greater than all the universe besides God.

*Boso.* So it appears.

*Anselm.* Moreover, it is necessary that he who can give God anything of his own which is more valuable than all things in the possession of God, must be greater than all else but God himself.

*Boso.* I cannot deny it.

*Anselm.* Therefore none but God can make this satisfaction.

*Boso.* So it appears.

*Anselm.* But none but a man ought to do this, other wise man does not make the satisfaction.

*Boso.* Nothing seems more just.

*Anselm.* If it be necessary, therefore, as it appears, that the heavenly kingdom be made up of men, and this cannot be effected unless the aforesaid satisfaction be made, which none but God can make and none but man ought to make, it is necessary for the God-man to make it.

*Boso.* Now blessed be God! we have made a great discovery with regard to our question. Go on, therefore, as you have begun. For I hope that God will assist you.

*Anselm.* Now must we inquire how God can become man.

*Anselm.* The Divine and human natures cannot alternate, so that the Divine should become human or the human Divine; nor can they be so commingled as that a third should be produced from the two which is neither wholly Divine nor wholly human. For, granting that it were possible for either to be changed into the other, it would in that case be only God and not man, or man only and not God. Or, if they were so commingled that a third nature sprung from the combination of the two (as from two animals, a male and a female of different species, a third is produced, which does not preserve entire the species of either parent, but has a mixed nature derived from both), it would neither be God nor man. Therefore the God-man, whom we require to be of a nature both human and Divine, cannot be produced by a change from one into the other, nor by an imperfect commingling of both in a third; since these things cannot be, or, if they could be, would avail nothing to our purpose. Moreover, if these two complete natures are said to be joined somehow, in such a way that one may be Divine while the other is human, and yet that which is God not be the same with that which is man, it is impossible for both to do the work necessary to be accomplished. For God will not do it, because he has no debt to pay; and man will not do it, because he cannot. Therefore, in order that the God-man may perform this, it is necessary that the same being should be perfect God and perfect man, in order to make this atonement. For he cannot and ought not to do it, unless he be very God and very man. Since, then, it is necessary that the God-man preserve the completeness of each nature, it is no less necessary that these two natures be united entire in one person, just as a body and a reasonable soul exist together in every human being; for otherwise it is impossible that the same being should be very God and very man.

*Boso.* All that you say is satisfactory to me.